Women in Purple

By the same author

THE FORMATION OF CHRISTENDOM
MEDIEVAL MISCELLANY

Women in Purple

RULERS OF MEDIEVAL BYZANTIUM

Judith Herrin

Princeton University Press
Princeton and Oxford

Published in the United States and the Philippine
Islands by Princeton University Press, 41 William
Street, Princeton, New Jersey 08540

First published by Weidenfeld & Nicolson, London

Library of Congress Control Number 2001093788

ISBN 0-691-09500-0

This book has been composed in Plantin Light

www.pup.princeton.edu

Printed in Great Britain by
Butler & Tanner Ltd,
Frome and London

1 3 5 7 9 10 8 6 4 2

For Eleanor,
best of mothers

Contents

Illustrations

1 Coins of Irene and Theodora
2 Mosaic of Theodora, wife of Justinian, and her court
3 Mosaic with monogram of Irene
4 The Fieschi-Morgan reliquary
5 Charioteer silk
6 Icon of the Virgin and Child
7 The daughters of Theophilos and Theodora, from the *Chronicle* of Skylitzes
8 Eagle silk from Brixen Cathedral
9 The Triumph of Orthodoxy icon

The author and publishers would like to thank the following for their permission to reproduce pictures: The Barber Institute of Fine Arts, University of Birmingham, 1; The Art Archive/Dagli Orti, 2; The Ephoreia of Byzantine Antiquities, Thessaloniki, 3; The Metropolitan Museum of Art, Gift of J. Pierpont Morgan, 1917, photograph © 1996 The Metropolitan Museum of Art, 4; Musée de Cluny, Paris © Réunion des musées nationaux, 5; The Museum of Western and Oriental Arts, Kiev, 6; The Biblioteca Nacional, Madrid, 7; Brixen Cathedral Treasury, 8; The Trustees of the British Museum, 9.

Acknowledgements

I want to start by thanking those who have supported me the longest in the writing of *Women in Purple*: Portia, Tamara and Anthony, and Eleanor, whose passionate interest in history inspired my own. To them I express a deep appreciation for years of many forms of assistance, as well as their subversive distraction and not least their tolerance.

My colleagues at King's College London provided substantial help in the form of a semester of sabbatical leave, which was extended by an award from the Arts and Humanities Research Board of the British Academy, making a total of seven months. This material assistance was further enhanced by the Program of Hellenic Studies and the Department of History at Princeton University, who invited me to spend six weeks there in the Spring of 1999. The stimulus of that exciting environment and the resources of Firestone Library made a significant difference to the shape of the first half of the book. And for help on numerous occasions I would particularly like to thank Dimitri Gondicas, Phil Nord, Claire Myonas and Judith Hansen.

At King's my colleagues also encouraged me with critical comments and useful references. Different versions of the chapter on Irene and many other ideas were floated at presentations in the subsequent months before a variety of audiences. In several instances, questions and doubts raised by persons unknown forced me to rethink what I had prepared. To all of them I am most grateful, since disagreement at this stage undoubtedly saved me some errors and avoided a few forced interpretations of ambiguous passages in the sources.

I am therefore very glad of the opportunity to thank the following friends and colleagues who invited me to speak, often in the most beautiful surroundings, and with their generous hospitality helped to improve this book in many ways: Costas Constantinides at the University of Ioannina; Dionysia Missiou, Thessaloniki; David Blackman, Director of the British School at Athens; Kari Børressen and the Norwegian Research Council, for sessions of the project 'Gender Models in Formative Christianity and Islam' held in Oslo, Rome and Florence; John Matthews and the Classics Department, Yale University; Claudia Rapp and the History Department at the University of California, Los Angeles, and the Byzantine and Modern Greek seminar at King's College London.

Towards the final stages, two invitations allowed me to visit Paris and Munich, where I had studied in the 1970s. Returning to the Collège de France and the Institut für Byzantinistik und Neugriechische Philologie was not without anxiety, but also provoked vivid memories of seminars directed by Professors Paul Lemerle and Hans-Georg Beck. It is a special pleasure to acknowledge the debt I owe to these outstanding centres of Byzantine research run by such great teachers, and I am all the more grateful to their successors. In July 1999 Professor Armin Hohlweg made possible the journey to Munich and I would also like to thank Franz Tinnefeld for his help in arranging this, as well as a delightful evening in Pasing. In November 2000 Professor Gilbert Dagron arranged a particularly agreeable week in Paris, where the facilities of the Collège de France and his most generous hospitality made this a memorable trip.

In addition, many anonymous critics, students and colleagues at Princeton and London have discussed awkward matters with me in a most productive and helpful fashion. It is a privilege to have worked on *Women in Purple* in their company, often provoked by their questioning. Without the computer skills of the KCL experts Wendy Pank and Harold Short, the manuscript would have been lost more than once. I have also been assisted by many librarians and staff in the British Library, and the library of the Warburg Institute, University of London, whose kindness is rightly judged proverbial. Colleagues on the editorial board of *Past and Present* had a decisive influence on my article 'The Imperial Feminine in Byzantium' and I thank them for permission to reproduce some of its arguments.

When publications were not available in the UK, colleagues abroad filled the gaps: Ralph-Johannes Lilie kindly provided proof copy in advance of publication from forthcoming volumes of the *Prosopographie der mittelbyzantinischen Zeit*; Christine Angelidi, Jeffrey-Michael Featherstone, Thalia Gouma-Peterson, Manuela Marín, Cécile Morrisson, Jinty Nelson, Charlotte Roueché and Maria Vassilaki shared their research with me. For bibliographic references and practical help in the final stages of writing, I would like to thank Celia Chazelle, Scarlett Freund, Anna Kartsonis, Claudia Rapp, Teo Ruiz, Margaret Trenchard-Smith and Mona Zaki. For assistance with the illustrations I am most grateful to Charalambos Bakirtis, Christ Entwhistle, Helen Evans; Eurydice Georgantelli and Andrew Burnett.

Friends performed an even more valuable service by reading the entire manuscript, and the comments of Anthony Barnett, Tamara Barnett-Herrin, Hugh Brody and Eleanor Herrin guided many revisions of its numerous drafts. Over many years Anthony's provocative questions have forced me to examine the broader implications of specific arguments and I thank him most particularly for his persistence and his generosity. All the errors remaining in the text are mine. Throughout the writing my agent, Georgina Capel, and my publisher, Anthony Cheetham, gave unstinting encouragement and support. I also want to thank my editor at Weidenfeld & Nicolson, Benjamin Buchan, and Jane Birkett for her expert copy-editing.

Judith Herrin, March 2001

Family tree of the three women in purple

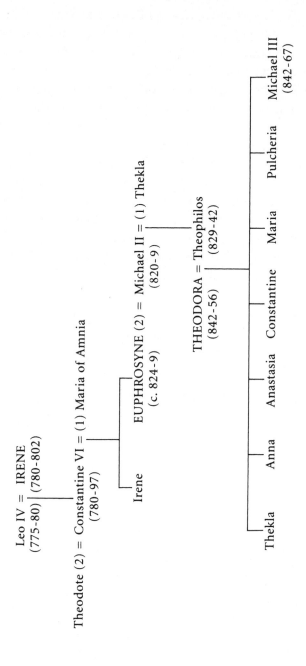

Leo IV = IRENE
(775-80) (780-802)

Theodote (2) = Constantine VI = (1) Maria of Amnia
(780-97)

Irene

EUPHROSYNE (2) = Michael II = (1) Thekla
(c. 824-9)   (820-9)

THEODORA = Theophilos
(842-56)   (829-42)

Thekla   Anna   Anastasia   Constantine   Maria   Pulcheria   Michael III
(842-67)

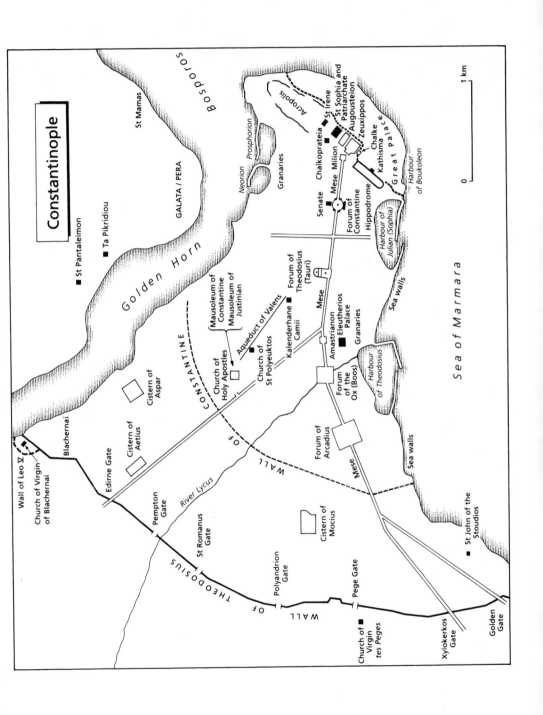

Constantinople

St Pantaleimon

Ta Pikridiou

St Mamas

GALATA / PERA

Bosporos

Neorion Prosphorion

Golden Horn

Granaries

Acropolis

St Irene

St Sophia and Patriarchate
Augousteion
Chalkoprateia
Mese Milion
Zeuxippos
Senate
Chalke
Kathisma
Mese

Great Palace

Harbour of Boukoleon

Senate

Forum of Constantine

Hippodrome

Harbour of Julian (Sophia)

Sea walls

Sea of Marmara

Mausoleum of Constantine
Mausoleum of Justinian

Aqueduct of Valens

Church of Holy Apostles

Church of St Polyeuktos

Kalenderhane Camii

Forum of Theodosius (Tauri)

Mese

Amastrianon
Eleutherios Palace
Granaries

Harbour of Theodosius

CONSTANTINE

Cistern of Aspar

Cistern of Aetius

Forum of the Ox (Boos)

WALL OF

Forum of Arcadius

Mese

Sea walls

Blachernai

Wall of Leo V

Church of Virgin of Blachernai

Edirne Gate

River Lycus

Pempton Gate

St Romanus Gate

Cistern of Mocius

WALL OF THEODOSIUS

Polyandrion Gate

Pege Gate

Church of Virgin tes Peges

Xylokerkos Gate

Golden Gate

St John of the Stoudios

0   1 km

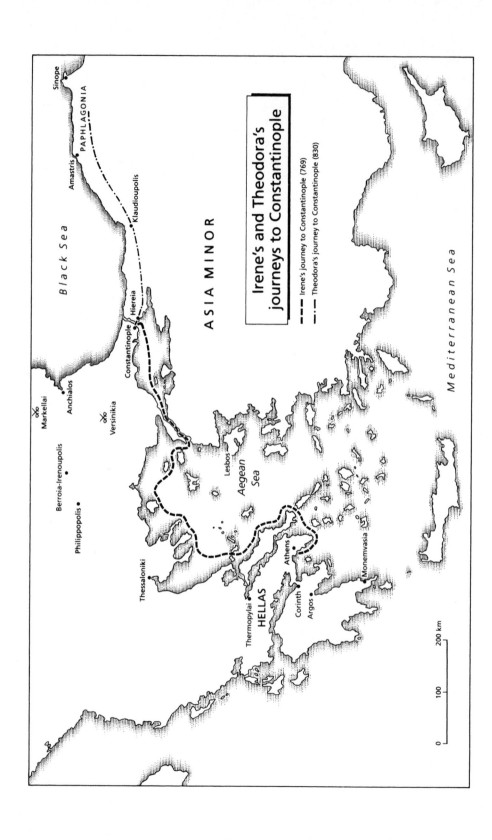

Irene's and Theodora's journeys to Constantinople

Irene's journey to Constantinople (769)
Theodora's journey to Constantinople (830)

Black Sea

Mediterranean Sea

Aegean Sea

ASIA MINOR

PAPHLAGONIA

Sinope
Amastris
Klaudioupolis
Hiereia
Constantinople
Anchialos
Markellai
Versinikia
Berroia-Irenoupolis
Philippopolis
Thessaloniki
Lesbos
Thermopylai
HELLAS
Corinth
Argos
Athens
Monemvasia

0   100   200 km

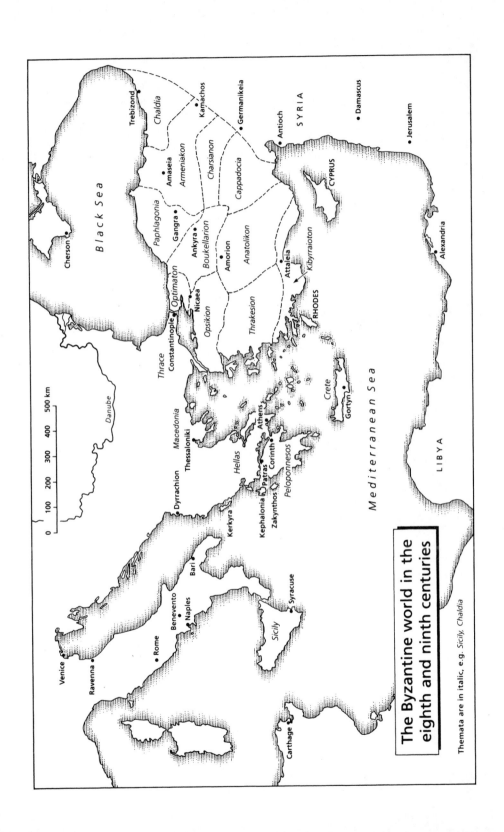

The Byzantine world in the eighth and ninth centuries

Themata are in italic, e.g. *Sicily, Chaldia*

Black Sea

Cherson

Trebizond
Chaldia
Kamachos
Germanikeia
SYRIA
Damascus
Jerusalem

Amaseia
Armeniakon
Charsianon
Antioch
CYPRUS
Alexandria

Paphlagonia
Gangra
Cappadocia
Cappadocia

Ankyra
Boukellarion
Amorion
Anatolikon
Attaleia
Kibyrraioton

Constantinople
Optimaton
Nicaea
RHODES

Opsikion
Thrakesion

Thrace

Crete
Gortyn

Mediterranean Sea

Thessaloniki
Athens
Macedonia
Hellas
Patras
Corinth
Peloponnesos

Dyrrachion
Kerkyra
Kephalonia
Zakynthos

LIBYA

Venice
Ravenna
Rome
Benevento
Naples
Bari

Sicily
Syracuse

Carthage

Danube

500 km
0 100 200 300 400 500 km

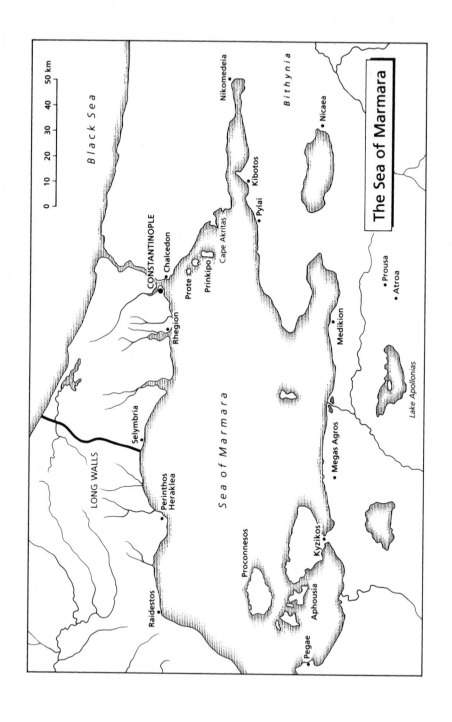

The Sea of Marmara

Introduction

Towards the close of the eighth century, in AD 787, representatives of the entire Christian world were summoned to the walled city of Nicaea, now called Iznik in north-west Turkey. Their aim was to put an end to iconoclasm, the destruction of icons, by restoring the holy images to their rightful place of reverence in the church. Altogether 365 bishops, including two papal legates and representatives of the other great patriarchates of Alexandria, Antioch and Jerusalem, and 132 monks attended this Seventh Ecumenical Council. After seven sessions, all the participants were transported fifty miles by land and across the Bosphoros to Constantinople, so that the Byzantine emperors could witness the council's triumphant conclusion. The assembly convened in the imperial palace called the Magnaura on 14 November 787. According to the acts of the council:

> The Patriarch took the Definition of Faith and together with the
> entire council he begged the emperors to seal it with their holy
> signatures. Taking it, the truly resplendent and most pious empress
> signed it, and giving it to her son and co-emperor he signed it . . .

The empress was Irene who had been ruling in her son's name for seven years, while he was a minor.

> And in unison all the bishops acclaimed the emperors in this
> way: 'Many years to the emperors Constantine and Irene, his
> mother; many years to the orthodox emperors, many years to the
> victorious emperors, many years to the peace-making emperors.
> To the new Constantine and new Helena, may their memory be

1

eternal! O Lord, guard their empire! Grant them a peaceful life! Sustain their rule! O Heavenly Lord, guard those (who rule) on earth.' Then the emperors ordered that the texts of the Fathers which had been read and signed at the fourth session at Nicaea should be read out ... Thus the council concluded its work.

These acclamations compare the widowed empress and her sixteen-year-old son to Constantine I, the first Roman emperor to embrace Christianity and his mother Helena who discovered the True Cross (the actual wood on which Jesus was crucified in the early fourth century). The new Constantine and new Helena of the eighth century are likened to saints of the Orthodox Church, whose feast-day is celebrated annually on 18 August. Just as Constantine I had presided over the First Ecumenical Council in 325, also held in Nicaea, Irene took charge of this final session to emphasise her leading role in the restoration of icons. Yet she was a woman. Married into the imperial family, she had adopted the role of a male ruler during her son's minority, and would later assert sole control over the empire, after he gained his majority and tried to rule on his own.

After twenty-eight years, Irene's effort to restore iconphile worship was to fail. But her granddaughter, Euphrosyne was to play a key role when her stepson Theophilos was due to be married at the age of about sixteen. She performed the maternal role of helping him to choose his bride. Of the seven possible candidates, Theophilos selected Theodora, and 'in full view of the senate, gave her a golden ring to mark the imperial betrothal. Immediately after this, the ladies-in-waiting of the Empress Euphrosyne ... took her and attended her with decency, decorum and with the respect that was due. Twenty-two days later, the aforementioned Theodora was crowned along with the Emperor Theophilos ... in the all-holy and venerable church of St Stephen the Protomartyr in Daphne.'

Twelve years later, Theophilos died in 842 aged twenty-nine, leaving Theodora with their two-year-old son Michael. She decided to protect his claims to his father's throne. When criticised by an ascetic holy man, Symeon, who had been persecuted by Theophilos, she said: 'Since you have reached this conclusion, depart from me. For as I received and learned from my spouse and husband, I will rule with a firm hand. You will see.' Within a year she had restored the veneration of icons. Theodora is celebrated as a saint for this act, which is still commemorated as the Triumph of Orthodoxy. In this way, the daughter-in-law of Irene's granddaughter repeated a process of setting the religious images of Byzantium in a commanding position. She also maintained her hold on imperial power for the following twelve years, until her son Michael came of age and began to rule in his own name.

These three widowed women exercised imperial power and changed the course of the empire's history in a purposive, deliberate and connected fashion. Irene, Euphrosyne and Theodora held authority and influence in Byzantium in the last quarter of the eighth century and the first half of the ninth as wives of emperors: Leo IV (775–80), Michael II (820–29) and Theophilos (829–42) respectively. It is not only that they personally supported the cult of icons. First Irene and then, definitively, Theodora restored the veneration of icons after two periods of their official destruction. Euphrosyne also played a critical role, linking the other two women. Her contribution is particularly significant in transmitting an awareness of the duties of imperial office, and of sustaining dynastic responsibilities in adverse conditions. As the granddaughter of one highly successful empress, and the effective mother-in-law of another, Euphrosyne connected an unprecedented repetition of feminine prominence. Her role in between the two well-known iconophile female rulers is the more significant for being almost hidden from us. Contemporary sources did not recognise her importance and she has rarely received attention in historical analysis.

Marrying into the ruling dynasty gave these women a special relationship with the all-pervasive authority of the Byzantine ruler, at first through their husbands and later through their sons. As widows, they continued to wear the imperial purple and found additional ways to influence the course of events. They were not alone in their efforts and they received the help of men. Indeed, they restored a profoundly patriarchal order and proved themselves its true preservers. Their combined achievement, however, saw the shrewd use of imperial resources, political skills and a firmness of commitment that was to preserve the role of Christian icons. There seems to be no equivalent example of three generations of women placing themselves at the head of what became a clearly identified movement and succeeding against all the odds.

Byzantium is famous for its empresses. The classical world revealed few to equal them, apart from Cleopatra and Agrippina; the Islamic world, none. Under Camilla and Boudicca, the Volsci and the ancient Britons triumphed over Roman forces, making a colourful impression but leaving no tangible results. Later on, powerful queens are found dotted through medieval history, often represented in a manner inspired by what they knew of the Byzantines. In the early modern period individuals such as Elizabeth I were exceptional. But in medieval Byzantium, from Helena in the fourth century, to Zoe, who raised four men to the position of emperor in the eleventh, via the circus entertainer who seduced the Emperor Justinian in the sixth century, imperial history is studded with empresses who glitter from its pages. And in stories associated with those of Late Antiquity, the three empresses of the eighth and ninth centuries found a model.

The best known of all these stories was probably one involving the first Theodora, who became the wife of Justinian: it concerns her role in preventing the emperor from abandoning the imperial capital, Constantinople, during the riots of 532. While the assembled rebel forces chanted their 'Victory' slogan in the Hippodrome (*Nika! Nika!*), the council of war inside the palace debated how to react within earshot of the threat to the emperor's authority. The empress stepped forward and denounced the idea of flight: 'May I never be separated from this purple, and may I not live that day on which those who meet me shall not address me as Mistress (*despoina*) ... If, now, it is your wish to save yourself, O Emperor, there is no difficulty. For we have much money, and there is the sea, here the boats ... As for myself, I approve a certain ancient saying that royalty is a good burial shroud.' After this declaration, Justinian decided to stay and ordered his generals to put down the revolt with extreme severity. This Theodora was also known as a determined supporter of particular policies, a woman of conviction who used the resources of the office of empress for her own purposes, a powerful personality who did not flinch from imposing her own views. It is clear that she had no imperial credentials: before Justinian changed the law in order to marry her, she had earned her living as a mime and entertainer, doing the most popular variety acts in the circus. Indeed, she is condemned by certain sixth-century writers as a prostitute of the most common sort.

None the less, her imperial image is one of the most celebrated Byzantine mosaics. In the church of San Vitale at Ravenna, completed in 547, she is shown wearing the official robes of office, holding a chalice which she will present to the church, its bishop and patron saint, accompanied by ladies of her court wearing their exquisite silk gowns and elegant slippers. Their costume covers their heads in the typically modest style required at the time, but they are not, strictly speaking, veiled. The

Theodora panel faces a parallel image of Justinian and his courtiers and soldiers, together with the bishop responsible for putting up these imperial portraits. Not only are they a brilliant picture of the ruling couple, who never went to Ravenna; they also show us the power of the emperor and empress of distant Constantinople as it was felt in northern Italy. Whether these were officially sanctioned portraits or merely stereotypical ideas of how the imperial couple should look, the combination of purple, gold and jewellery invokes the grandeur of official costume as it was understood in the sixth century (see plate 2).

From this, and other more formal images of empresses, we know that in the eighth and ninth centuries they still wore the same official regalia, including spectacular crowns with pendants of large pearls, and carried the orb and sceptre of office. The costumes of high office included many layers of silken clothing embroidered in gold and silver thread and adorned with numerous precious stones. The colour purple predominated and in Theodora's case the hem of her purple cloak has woven into it the image of the three Magi arriving with their gifts at Christ's Nativity. As the wife of an emperor, the empress was 'clothed in the purple', a colour traditionally associated with high status. Because the purple dye was created only by intensive labour, being derived from a tiny shellfish, it was very expensive to produce. More common dyes made from indigo and madder were also employed to make imitations, but purple remained associated exclusively with the imperial family. Silks coloured by murex purple were made into the official costumes they wore on ceremonial occasions. Porphyry, the equivalent coloured stone, was similarly employed for imperial busts and sarcophagi. For centuries Roman emperors had used such methods to elevate the dignity of the ruler and his consort, to associate the ruler with the sun. In Byzantium such exclusive costumes, including red boots, another privilege of the imperial couple, were designed to add to that radiance, which was often commented on by visitors to the imperial court. On such official occasions, where particular colours, enhanced by the use of gold, silver and precious gems, marked the status of every courtier, the empress might even outshine her partner.

Despite this visual claim, it is often difficult to evaluate the specific contribution of Irene, Euphrosyne and Theodora to the political process of the time. The intervention of Justinian's wife during the Nika riots remains a unique example. In the case of female rulers, the question of agency is particularly acute. Under the imperial system of government inherited from the Romans, anonymous administrators were responsible for maintaining the basic system of government: collecting taxes, paying the army and covering court expenditure, which was exceptionally high. A vast hierarchy of civil servants, recruited according to contemporary educational standards, kept records in triplicate noting any shortfalls and anomalies. Within separate ministries, devoted to foreign policy, domestic affairs, military and naval matters and so on, a considerable bureaucracy maintained the mechanism of government regardless of the individual who was actually in power. Many of the officials worked either within the imperial palace or in offices close by, concentrated in the heart of the capital. Those who were sent out to the provinces to ensure the proper functioning of government were rotated regularly from one area to another, to prevent them establishing a regional power base. Under such a developed system of administration, what impact did an individual ruler, male or female, have?

Byzantine emperors were expected to take charge of two particular aspects of government: they had to lead their troops in battle and they had to perform particular roles as the head of the church. But there had always been armchair rulers, such as Justinian, who employed skilled generals like Belisarios and Narses to perform the military tasks. So female rulers were not at a total disadvantage in this respect; they too could use army generals to lead their troops into battle. But in the case of the church, a female ruler was generally considered incapacitated by her sex: women could not be priests, nor were they allowed into the sanctuary area of the church, around the altar. In this respect, female rulers had to devise novel methods of co-operation with the patriarch who, as the ecclesiastical leader of the church, could be more or less accommodating.

Who gave the orders, for example, for a new military initiative? Of course such issues were debated in the imperial court, occasionally by the full Senate, and decisions were made on the advice of the most experienced advisers. The most relevant information, collected by a developed system of espionage, was taken into account. For much of the period under discussion, Byzantine warfare was more reactive than offensive. Invading Arab forces frequently determined imperial military activity. So the reliance of a female leader on experienced generals may not have made much difference.

In other spheres, such as diplomacy, administrative reform and ecclesiastical policy, Byzantine chronicles record imperial decisions in the most neutral terms: 'the emperor sent an embassy to the Arabs', for instance. But behind these bland statements the process by which such decisions were made can be reconstructed. The ruler in council seeks advice about the best way of handling a negotiation with the caliph; ambassadors have to be chosen (both lay and ecclesiastical figures are employed), suitable gifts selected, a military escort set up, sufficient funds raised for any possible misadventures that might occur along the way. At many of these stages, the individual ruler may have an input – securing the service of a trusted adviser as the chief negotiator, insisting on a length of silk rather than a manuscript as the central gift, and so on. Usually such details are not recorded; the historical sources seem to imply that everything is looked after by ministers and their underlings. But clearly, some rulers are much more skilled at this aspect of government than others.

According to the male historians who write about them, empresses are much less well equipped to rule than emperors. As women, they suffer from inherent weakness, both physical and moral; they lack experience and knowledge of politics, so they are not considered capable of having a positive impact on such matters. Normally it is assumed that they rely even more than male rulers on the advice of trusted servants and experienced administrators. In particular, they are said to be highly dependent on their eunuchs, court officials who had immediate access to the women's quarters of the palace. When things turn out badly, however, women may be saddled with more than their fare share of the blame. While some male rulers are equally dependent on their eunuchs, women are more often the victims of such a process of historical misinterpretation. The sources grant men much greater influence in the process of government than females. Gender stereotypes flourished in Byzantium and are evident in the historical canon.

Indeed, in matters of religion and the definition of correct belief, male rulers are both praised for imposing orthodoxy and can be held responsible for insisting on incorrect practice and heretical beliefs. This is related to their presumed capacity to understand or misunderstand theology. In contrast, it is assumed that women are incapable of following complicated theological arguments and have a blind faith in visual aids to worship, such as icons. In this area as well as others, the prejudices of male commentators and record-keepers shine out quite clearly. As an example, this is how Ignatios the deacon recalls the role of the empress in the council of 787: 'Irene was a mere woman, but she possessed both

7

the love of God and firmness of understanding, if it is right to give the name of woman to one who surpassed even men in the piety of her understanding; for she was God's instrument in His love and pity for mankind.' While intended as a compliment, the assumptions behind the high praise are anything but complimentary to women.

It is precisely in the field of religious practice that the three empresses studied in this book clearly initiated new policies. They insisted on the rejection of what they saw as an innovation – the ban on holy images instituted by their male relatives. By securing the reversal of official iconoclasm and restoring icons to their place of veneration in the eastern church, Irene, Euphrosyne and Theodora profoundly altered the course of history. The art, and not just the art, of Byzantium, of Islam and of the West would have been different, perhaps very different, without them. The methods they used to manipulate court factions, to get round iconoclast advisers and theologians, and their insistence, all seem to reflect a determination to act as agents, to take the initiative and then impose their decision with all the force at their disposal as very powerful rulers. But first, the story of how they did this needs to be set within the context of Byzantium in the eighth century.

CHAPTER 1

Constantinople and the World of Byzantium

During the fourth century AD the East Mediterranean world which had long formed part of the Roman Empire was dramatically altered by the establishment of a new capital city. On the site of the ancient Greek colony of Byzantium (*Byzantion*), overlooking the Bosphoros which separates Europe from Asia, Constantine I inaugurated the city named after himself in 330. Constantinople was also known from the beginning as New Rome to indicate its role as an eastern capital equivalent to Old Rome on the Tiber. It was to outlive its predecessor as a centre to which all Roman roads and all shipping lanes led, as well as the seat of imperial government for over a millennium, until 1453. It persistently identified itself as the capital of the Roman Empire, whose citizens were Romans (*Romaioi* in Greek). The inhabitants of the capital also took pride in the name Byzantine (derived from the ancient colony), which they reserved to themselves. During the Christian Middle Ages the city of Constantine was the largest, finest and wealthiest metropolis of the known world.

Such an outcome was far from inevitable. Constantinople remained little more than a vast construction site during its founder's lifetime. Constantine I's sons and more distant relatives who governed the eastern half of the empire might well have preferred the established centres of imperial rule: Nikomedeia, grandly rebuilt and beautified by Diocletian in the late third century, or Antioch, favoured by Julian. But several factors ensured that by the second quarter of the fifth century Constantinople had assumed a dominant position and was already referred to as the 'Queen City' or 'imperial city'.

The first of these lay in its geographical situation. When they had selected this triangular peninsula of land, the ancient Greeks from Megara picked a spectacular bluff controlling the naval passage between the Black Sea and the Aegean. It was easily defended and included a deep-water harbour on an inlet called the Golden Horn, which could be protected by an iron chain suspended between the city and the area to the north, later called Galata or Pera, 'over there'. This permitted sailing vessels to moor and unload safely on the northern edge of the city, encouraging the development of both long-distance trade and naval repairs. Within a few generations of the foundation of Constantinople, emperors had taken advantage of this strategic spot to exact taxes on all cargoes carried by sea past the city. Naval expertise on the Bosphoros, with its dangerous deep and upper currents, guaranteed the city's control of the narrow strip of water, and helped to turn Constantinople into an international entrepôt.

The confluence of land and sea routes similarly brought a vast range of goods to the city's markets. Spices, pepper, ivory, precious stones and incense came from the east via the Red Sea and Egypt; furs, amber, gold and garnets from the north; silks, jewels and porcelain were carried overland from China, which sustained contacts with Byzantium into the seventh century, and fish paste, wine, fine pottery and lamps from the western Mediterranean. All this economic activity was encouraged by Constantine's decision to divert grain supplies from Egypt to feed the population of his new capital, based on the model employed for Old Rome. Selected residents of the city received distributions of free bread made from the high-quality wheat grown in the Nile valley. Once the construction of the Hippodrome, the chief place of public entertainment, was completed, and chariot- and horse-racing were instituted, the Roman tradition of free bread and circuses in turn rapidly attracted a growing population.

A second factor reinforced the city's imperial momentum: the lavish endowment and decoration of the grandest public buildings, designed in a manner typical of capital cities but adapted to take account of the hills of ancient Byzantium, which commanded magnificent views over the Sea of Marmara to the south and the Bosphoros to the north. Constantinople was laid out in traditional style with a notable palace adjoining the Hippodrome, (already partly constructed by Septimius Severus), grand colonnaded avenues linking the public buildings and commemorative monuments. In a competitive spirit, successive emperors left their mark on the growing capital, setting up honorary columns topped by imperial statues, building triumphal arches and more lavish baths, markets, forums and hostels for public use. Nor did they neglect

the traditional decoration of ancient cities with acclaimed works of classical art: a huge bronze Athena was brought from Athens, and four
gilded bronze horses allegedly taken from Chios were erected above the
entrance to the Hippodrome. (After 1204 they were to be looted by the
Venetians, who put them on the façade of the church of San Marco.)
Inside the racing area, on the central *spina* which divided the tracks, a
reclining Herakles by Lysippos, the twisted serpent column from Delphi
and an obelisk from Egypt, recording a military victory in hieroglyphs,
joined other famous monuments.

Many public spaces in the new capital were named after the notable
imperial statues which decorated them: the Forum of Constantine by a
monumental statue of the founder on top of a porphyry column. Because
the statue had a radiate crown, people said it was originally of Apollo,
and had been reused by the Emperor Constantine to confirm his personal
dedication to the sun god. In the same way, the Augousteion was identified by a statue of the famous *augousta* Helena, Constantine's mother,
and several other emperors and empresses. In addition, many ancient
statues of gods and goddesses adorned the city centre: Zeus, Hera and
Aphrodite, the sun and moon represented by Apollo and Artemis. On
the Acropolis of ancient Byzantium, temples dedicated to Rhea, mother
of the gods, and Fortuna remained with their familiar representations of
these important deities. Statues of the Muses and many other less familiar
local gods decorated the street crossings and public spaces. In the mid-
sixth century, when the emperor decided to distribute them to other
districts, over four hundred works of classical art were removed from the
central area alone.

Yet from its inception Constantinople was also a Christian foundation,
marked by Constantine's construction of a church dedicated to the Holy
Apostles, in which he deposited relics of Saints Andrew and Luke.
This new character, and the third factor in the growth of the city, was
emphasised by the establishment of an imperial mausoleum attached to
the same church, in which the emperor chose to be buried. In adopting
the Christian form of burial in a sarcophagus, rather than the Roman
tradition of cremation, the city's founder set an important precedent. It
appealed to all his descendants and many later rulers, who also sought a
burial spot in the same rotunda. They, too, continued to patronise the
building of Christian churches, each trying to outdo the last in grandeur
and extravagant decoration. The growth in Christian monuments was
phenomenal. Over the centuries emperors as well as private patrons

devoted their wealth to the collection of the most notable Christian relics, which they placed in their new foundations. They built institutions of Christian charity which were often dedicated to a particular social function: monasteries, almshouses, hostels, orphanages, homes for the elderly or burial grounds for foreigners. Gradually the Christian buildings came to dominate as they jostled with classical monuments such as the Senate House, the Mint and the Hippodrome, all decorated with ancient statuary. What we now see as sacred and profane mingled in glorious abundance.

Soon Constantinople outgrew the boundary drawn by Constantine I. Its rapid development meant that under Theodosius II (408–50), a vast area extending beyond the original wall was enclosed, almost doubling the city's size. The new triple line of defensive walls constructed under the city prefect (mayor) is still the first sight of ancient Constantinople appreciated by a visitor arriving by land. It signals the achievement of fifth-century builders, whose massive protective ring withstood numerous sieges and kept all enemies at bay until 1204. Along the coast of Marmara and the Golden Horn, defensive structures linked with the land walls to encircle the new city area. These remained unchanged, apart from stronger protection to the fortifications around the church of Blachernai in the north-east, and to the sea walls. Within this enclosure granaries and cisterns, some vaulted, others open to the sky, were constructed to secure adequate grain and water for the growing population. Valens (364–78) had already linked the city with the forests to the northwest by a long aqueduct, which brought water supplies to service the bathing, cooking and horticultural needs of its growing population. Additional harbours were created for the unloading of cattle and foodstuffs. Constantinople became famous both for its magnificent defences and for its ability to maintain life under siege within its ring of fortifications.

Inside the city the building which still dominates the skyline is the church of Holy Wisdom, Hagia Sophia. It was built on the orders of Emperor Justinian after the Nika rioters set fire to the city centre in 532. Five years later, at its dedication, it was the largest church in the known world, lit by numerous windows in the vast dome (31 metres in diameter), which rises to a height of 55 metres. Until 1547, when Brabante and Michelangelo raised the dome of St Peter's in Rome, this roof was unique. For centuries it elicited the awe and admiration of visitors. Even today, its colossal size and sheer bulk impresses by its power. In this respect it reflects the founder's desire to outdo Solomon, to construct a monument larger and more grandiose than any other. Justinian's ambition was matched by the technical skill of two mathematicians, Anthemios of Tralles and Isidoros of Miletos, who designed the building. Their plans for the dome did not prevent its collapse on more than one occasion, but it has always been patched up. Re-buttressed, the building has survived earthquakes and invasions. Its style established a model for the great mosques of Istanbul which now echo its grandeur.

By the sixth century the city's character was assured: it was a cosmopolitan metropolis, a megalopolis in comparison with all other cities, and the seat of Roman imperial government which held sway throughout the East Mediterranean. It was secured by its walls and symbolised by Hagia Sophia; it was governed from the palace, which covered a large area between the seashore and the Hippodrome. This 'Great Palace' had grown in stages from Constantine I's original constructions (the Daphne Palace, the Augousteos hall, the basilica church and related buildings for guards), which were all laid out following the model of Old Rome. They were linked to the Hippodrome in the same way as the Palatine was connected to the Circus Maximus in Rome. Nearly all emperors added their own buildings. In the late seventh century, Justinian II enclosed the entire area of the Great Palace behind walls and fulfilled his ambitious plans for a new palace, the Chrysotriklinos, which ensured the imperial family even grander living quarters. Constantine V (741–75) affirmed the centrality of the Chrysotriklinos by adding a new church nearby, one dedicated to the Mother of God at the Pharos (the lighthouse which guided ships into the palace harbour). By the middle of the eighth century, this vast area encompassed a series of buildings: residences, reception and banqueting halls, churches, government offices, barracks, archives, all linked by gardens, terraces, porticoes, corridors and passageways, some more secret than others, elegantly laid out to take advantage of the natural incline.

At the top of the slope lay the Hippodrome, the hub of the city, where horse- and chariot-racing, athletic contests and theatrical performances took place. Chariot racing was the passion not only of the people of Constantinople, but also of their rulers who occasionally took part. It created sporting heroes whose triumphs were celebrated by carved monuments erected within the racing area. In the sixth century, Porphyrios was so honoured with a sculpture showing him winning a race with his quadriga of four horses. This public entertainment was organised by the Blues and the Greens, two groups of officials identified by the colours they wore. They arranged not only the races but also gymnastic displays, wrestling matches and the very popular performances of mimes, who acted out familiar stories to musical accompaniment, often with displays of dancing. By the time of Constantine, the combat of gladiators and of wild beasts against poorly armed slaves, prisoners and persecuted Christians, had been banned as an inappropriate form of entertainment.

As in ancient Rome, the Hippodrome was also used for victory parades and other imperial ceremonies. From the imperial box (*kathisma*), a large balcony which was accessible from within the palace, the emperor could address the assembled population: the senators seated on marble seats and the rest on tiers of benches above. To facilitate easy access the box was connected to the palace by an internal stairway. Justinian II provided a direct link between the Chrysotriklinos complex and the Hippodrome by means of a long covered way. These connections were vital because the circus served as such an important venue in the city. In less regulated moments, it was also the central place where crowds might gather to protest, to demand change, to riot and even to attack their rulers. But its normal use brought emperors and their courtiers to preside at the games from the imperial box overlooking the finishing line of the races. From this vantage point they would cheer the triumphs of the charioteers, retire within the palace during the intervals between races, and reappear in different costume to award wreaths to the victors.

The emperor was shielded from the surrounding city by a similarly private route which permitted him to visit Hagia Sophia without leaving the palace. Through a long, raised walkway that followed the line of the Augousteion and part of the church connected with the patriarchate, rulers had access to the gallery in the south-west corner which was reserved for them. The same route provided a secure link with the patriarch (archbishop, metropolitan) of the city whose palace adjoined the cathedral church at this point. He might also use this walkway to make a private visit to the imperial palace. In this way, the central government of the empire, largely housed inside the Great Palace, the imperial court, the ecclesiastical centre, the main focus of worship and one of the chief public assembly points for the inhabitants of Constantinople were all linked. The rest of the city stretched to the walls in the west, divided into thirteen regions and identified by seven hills, on the model of ancient Rome. Different areas were linked by broad main streets, lined by porticoes with shops and punctuated by triumphal arches, spacious forums with public buildings, water fountains, markets and gardens – in short, all the features of a classical city. And at the hub of this newly constructed capital, deep within the palace, was the imperial court.

COURT CEREMONIAL

The court of Constantinople combined three distinct elements: a traditional Roman hierarchy of ranks of attendants, some with specific tasks, others with honorary functions; Persian-style rituals, ceremonial costume and the employment of eunuchs, extended by Diocletian at the turn of the third century; and ever-increasing Christian influence, which adapted the physical setting of the court to resemble the court of heaven. According to the analysis initiated by Bishop Eusebios during Constantine's lifetime, the emperor represented God and served as His regent on earth; he was divinely ordained to rule over the empire and did so only with God's help. The imperial rituals of reception, audience and judgement developed according to this model, constantly enhancing the authority of the God-like ruler, creating greater distance between him and persons admitted to the imperial presence. The emperor was seated on a raised throne while visitors made *proskynesis* (putting the forehead to the ground) before him. In this imagined reflection of the court of the Last Judgement, the empress espoused the role of the Virgin Mary. As Theotokos, Mother of God, Mary was designated the most powerful intercessor in the court of heaven, a role which many imperial consorts effectively emulated in the court of Byzantium.

There was also a very practical side to court life; it filled multiple functions which revolved around the imperial couple. The court provided the machinery of government and the locus of most important decisions. When the emperor needed advice, he summoned the Senate, which met at his request and was no longer an independent body; the appointment, reception and debriefing of ambassadors took place within the court; all the grandest distributions of rewards and feasts were held there; most government business was conducted in offices attached to the court, and the imperial family including their children and all their servants resided within the walls. Over the centuries, a further aspect of court life evolved: this was an annual calendar of ceremonies performed by the emperor and members of the court to mark the commemoration of important dates (birthdays, anniversaries, most importantly of the foundation of the city), the liturgical celebrations of the church, and traditional activities associated with imperial philanthropy – the distribution of free food, clothing, coin, and other donations. Many of these functions took place within the Great Palace and concerned only members of the imperial family and court officials. But other events, for instance when he inspected the granaries, took the emperor outside the walls of the palace.

The language spoken at court was generally Greek. Although Byzantium had always been a Greek city, in his new capital Constantine I only used the Latin he had learned in Illyricum and the West. By the middle of the sixth century, Greek had become the official language of government, a development symbolised by the linguistic history of Justinian's *Code* of civil law. While this was drawn up in Latin, the traditional language of Roman law, it was translated into Greek immediately after its publication in 534. Subsequent new laws were issued in Greek. Although law schools and certain court poets still used Latin, and military orders as well as some ceremonial acclamations continued to be given in this traditional form, Greek predominated in most activities. And spoken Greek was the lively vernacular tongue used on the streets of Constantinople and in the liturgy of the church, understood by all. Writers often employed a much more learned and arcane literary Greek, modelled on the Attic spoken in Athens of the fifth century BC, seeking to emphasise their knowledge of the past. In contrast, the common tongue (*koine*) allowed all members of the imperial court to participate in the language of government, of Christian belief and daily conversation.

This made a sharp contrast with the predominance of Latin in the West. There, Latin remained a learned classical language, while the Romance dialects developed into medieval versions of French, Spanish and Italian. To be educated meant to learn Latin, a skill which became increasingly confined to clerics, monks and members of the social élite. Latin dominated the life of the church, which meant that the liturgy gradually became less comprehensible to those who spoke Anglo-Saxon, Old High German, Provençal or Catalan. And because the western church subscribed to the view that there were only three Sacred Languages – Hebrew, Greek and Latin – it denounced the use of vernaculars in Christian practice. Prayers had to be said in one of the three ancient languages to be effective. This restriction eventually excluded the vast majority of inhabitants from the life of the church, while it also elevated the role of clerics and monks who did master Latin. It established a gulf between the educated and the laity. In the East, however, this was prevented. Once vernacular Greek became the *lingua franca* of the Byzantine court as well as of the empire as a whole, the uneducated, including women, had access to the medium of both church and state.

THE THIRD SEX

Within the palace, a hierarchy of 'beardless men', or eunuchs, ran the ceremonial life of the court under the direction of the *praipositos* (literally, the one set in place). These mutilated males were considered particularly reliable because their condition forced them to remain free of the vested interests of close family relations and offspring. The court of Constantinople reserved a distinct number of positions for eunuchs, thus creating a cohort of beardless men in contrast to all the others, officials with beards. In a society where becoming an adult male was marked by growing a beard, body hair was only one of the many features that separated normal men from the castrated. Depending on the age at which the operation was performed, some eunuchs retained their high voices, blond hair and the skin texture of childhood, though they often developed very long limbs. Those castrated as adults retained their male characteristics. But both were employed in the personal service of the rulers and were entrusted with particular responsibility for the emperor's wardrobe and bedroom, and the women's quarters within the palace. Since castration was illegal within the empire, the source of eunuchs lay among enslaved males, who were often operated on beyond the imperial borders. Young, educated eunuch slaves were particularly expensive, because they offered the combination of loyalty to their owners and training in specific skills.

The dominance of eunuchs at the Byzantine court established a third sex, a neutered as well as neutral sector between men and women. Because of their procreative incapacity these beardless men were entrusted with the protection of female members of the imperial family. In turn, imperial women were permitted much greater intimacy with their eunuch servants than would have been permitted with normal men. The particular prominence of members of the third sex in the women's quarters was also related to the fact that trained eunuchs were frequently given responsibility for the education of the imperial children. Classes in the basic cycle of elementary education might also include children of palace officials. Under their eunuch tutors, princes and princesses would master the essential features of classical education: grammar, rhetoric and logic. Such learning was expected of daughters as well as sons, for children of both sexes might be married to foreign rulers as part of imperial diplomatic alliance-building, and they were expected to represent Byzantine culture abroad. It is thus very likely that princesses and princes were not merely literate but also had an extensive education. If they went on to the higher sciences of mathematics: arithmetic, geometry, astronomy and music, more expert teachers might need to be employed. There is evidence that the sons of many relatively uneducated emperors mastered the secondary stage of a classical education within the Great Palace (Constantine V or Theophilos, for instance). This pedagogic role meant that the eunuch hierarchy had to maintain high standards and trained its own members as well as recruiting well-educated newcomers whenever possible.

Another major function of the beardless *corps de chambre* was to maintain the rituals appropriate for each date in the imperial calendar. When this involved the court within the palace, eunuch officials had to make sure that all participants knew what to do and could perform the ceremony correctly. Their close connection with the imperial wardrobe, coupled with the fact that dress formed such a conspicuous part of the ceremonial agenda, brought their expertise to the centre of court activity. In addition to the correct costume and insignia of office, it was vital that all members of the imperial family knew what each ceremony entailed. Here eunuchs had important responsibilities for training both the imperial family and non-imperial spouses. Since sons and daughters were expected to be present from earliest childhood, as well as all the in-laws, they had to learn their roles in order to perform them accurately. They were instructed how to observe and imitate what the ruling couple did on particular occasions, in preparation for the time when they might have to perform the same ceremonies. In medieval times most practical knowledge of this sort was transmitted by oral tradition from one generation to the next. The eunuch hierarchy thus represented continuity within imperial traditions in a way that no single family could.

THE BOOK OF CEREMONIES

The experience of eunuchs was particularly important for the lengthier and more complex rituals, such as imperial coronations, some of which had been committed to writing from the fifth century onwards. The original reason for the record had been to document the novel role of the patriarch in crowning a new emperor in church. Over time, the process encouraged the recording in written form of even the most ancient and pagan rites. Because of their organising function and pedagogic role, eunuchs thus became associated with the collection and copying of the texts of these rituals. The *Book of Ceremonies*, which survives in a tenth-century edition, highlights the crucial rule of the *praipositos*, the major-domo of the palace and head of the eunuch corps. In numerous accounts, he directs the ceremony, marking the different stages with the command: 'If you please . . .' It is only when he gives this signal that the participants move on from one stage to the next. And since there are often very large groups of people, sumptuously dressed and very anxious to attract imperial attention, the *praipositos* masterminds what is a complex performance, a true re-enactment of ceremony whose symbolism may be overshadowed by repeated bowing and scraping.

Within an imperial court imagined as a reflection of 'the heavenly one', eunuchs took on the role of angels, another category of sexless persons, and the ultimate go-betweens. They carried messages from the court to the wider society, between the women's quarters and the outside world. Female members of the imperial family employed their personal eunuch servants as diplomats, appointing them to positions of political responsibility. Their example was followed in all aristocratic households, where the employment of at least one eunuch servant was considered essential. And in this context also, they served similar purposes, carrying messages, undertaking sensitive negotiations and teaching the younger generation. These jobs were by no means new for eunuchs. In the past particular officials had wielded immense power, almost to the extent of running the entire government in the emperor's name (as Chrysaphios did at the end of the fourth century). Empresses learned to exploit the circumstances which brought them into close physical contact with these representatives of the third sex.

PUBLIC RITUALS IN CONSTANTINOPLE

Beyond the walls of the Great Palace, the eunuch corps did not have such a defined presence although some beardless officials always attended the imperial couple. Whenever the emperor or his consort made a public appearance outside the palace, they were accompanied by palace guards, and by members of the Greens and the Blues, whose primary duty was to acclaim the rulers as they progressed through the city. City officials were often on duty as well as soldiers, senators and members of the public who tagged along to view the spectacle. For such events were indeed spectacular. Often the emperor would spend all day visiting churches to light candles at shrines, pray for his ancestors, distribute money to the crowds, stopping at numerous staging posts, where he rested, changed clothes, mounted a chariot rather than riding a horse, or walked in humility to commemorate a particular event. The Blues and the Greens participated with musical accompaniment which advertised these noisy and exciting processions, dominated by colourful banners and military uniforms, mounted guards, chants and the sound of portable organs.

Such a pattern of regular imperial appearances on the streets of the capital meant that members of the court became more familiar to the ordinary inhabitants of Constantinople, who frequently tried to use the occasion to make their views known. Whether they were bringing injustices to the attention of the rulers, or simply shouting their disapproval of corrupt ministers, their hope of gaining a hearing stemmed from the regularity of ceremonial court activity. Under the direction of the Greens and the Blues, the Hippodrome remained the stage for the most intense dialogue between ruler and ruled. Whenever the emperor presided from the imperial box, these circus officials led the formal acclamations, which could be altered to take account of particular popular demands. The Blues and Greens thus presented themselves as the voice of the people. But on the many occasions when the ruler made a ceremonial procession outside the palace, the whole city of Constantinople became an arena for popular confrontation with the emperor.

New ceremonies were also developed to mark the lifetime of all members of the imperial family, from baptism to burial. Every *rite de passage* was observed in a special ritual which often took the imperial family to the cathedral church of Holy Wisdom; to the church of the Holy Apostles, where so many emperors were buried; and to other shrines which housed the relics of particular saints. Other ceremonies developed from ancient traditions, for example, the blessing of the grape harvest on the Asian side of the Bosphoros. Although it marked the inclusion of a seasonal festivity as a medieval Christian ritual, its previous character remained evident and caused church leaders no little concern. On this occasion, practically the entire hierarchy of court officials would accompany the imperial couple on barges from the palace harbour to the site nearest the vineyards, where the patriarch and his clergy would be waiting to perform the blessing. In this way ancient secular traditions and pagan rites associated with Bacchus, the patron of wine, were gradually incorporated into the Christian cycle of ceremonial events. Instead of invoking the god's name as the first grapes were picked and pressed, church officials now blessed the crop and assisted in the autumnal feast which followed, a type of grand al fresco picnic. In ceremonial terms, however, this development meant that the imperial court celebrated a long-established pagan feast in its new Christian guise. The stage-managing of such complicated movements of large numbers of important people, significant objects and the provisions necessary for the celebration, was entrusted to members of the court.

CHRISTIAN PATRONAGE

While empresses did not always attend the races and perform as many journeys outside the walls of the Great Palace as their husbands, they had similar resources to be used for philanthropic purposes and took part in many charitable events. This public role may have developed following the example of Constantine I's mother, Helena, who had undertaken a very significant diplomatic journey to Jerusalem in 330s. She may have been sent principally to calm military unrest in the garrisons but she also lavished a great deal of imperial gold on the construction and decoration of churches, hostels and other facilities for pilgrims to the Holy City. Her role as Christian benefactor also supported the notion of a Christian dynasty established by Constantine. And the fact that she was later acclaimed as a saint by the Orthodox Church, and identified as the discoverer of the True Cross, undoubtedly contributed to her prominence in the popular memory.

This combination of imperial women with money to invest in Christian monuments provided a major impetus to the cult of the Virgin, who gradually became a new protector of the city of Constantinople and its spiritual defender. In the first half of the fifth century Pulcheria, the eldest child of the Emperor Arcadius, built a number of churches dedicated to the Virgin Mary, and personally directed rituals which linked and enhanced what was then a relatively new cult. Through processions between these churches and all-night vigils at the Blachernai shrine, Pulcheria led the movement to proclaim Mary as Theotokos, Mother of

God. This exalted title, agreed at the Council of Ephesos in 431, contributed to the process by which the Ever-Virgin gradually became a powerful intercessor. The development was strengthened by the discovery of two precious relics, the Virgin's veil and girdle, which were solemnly installed in special shrines attached to her churches. Similar patronage by the wealthy senatorial lady Juliana Anicia, a century later, established a magnificent church of St Polyeuktos close to the major aqueduct of the city and recently excavated. Although nothing survives of the structure above ground level, the foundations and fallen masonry reveal a monumental building adorned with exquisite carvings, which include a long verse dedication. This epigram is also preserved in a literary collection of such inscriptions and made possible the identification of the building, the name of its patron and the saint to whom Juliana dedicated her church.

Sixth-century *lithomania*, literally stone-mania, was shared by bishops, provincial governors and rulers alike, in a competitive spirit which culminated in Justinian and Theodora's extraordinary investments in buildings of all types. The empress was personally held responsible for many philanthropic institutions devoted to the relief of poverty, for which the citizens of the capital erected a statue of her to express their gratitude. This monument, mounted on an honorary column outside the city in the 'pleasure gardens' of Arcadianai, was carved in porphyry, the purple stone reserved for imperial sarcophagi, and was said to be nearly as beautiful as Theodora herself. The public role of imperial women as benefactors and patrons of Christian churches permitted them to participate in the expansion of Constantinople and its further glorification. They thus took responsibility for a very significant sector of construction work which gave the inhabitants of New Rome a growing sense of their city's beauty and standing in the world.

Although this Theodora is known to have shared in much of Justinian's enormous building programme, later empresses sometimes realised a comparable role only after the death of their husbands. As widows, they had first to oversee the burial of the deceased ruler, sometimes in a new shrine, and to ensure the commemoration of his date of death. New anniversaries were therefore constantly added to the calendar of obligations and new ceremonies had to be devised to ensure their correct observation. In addition, empresses regularly established new charitable institutions which perpetuated their own names. In several cases shrines were constructed for their own families who were gathered into one final resting place where prayers could be said for their souls. All this activity drew attention to imperial women as the guardians of dynasty.

HEREDITARY RULE IN BYZANTIUM

Central to the Byzantine concept of imperial rule was a dynastic principle, to which women inevitably made an essential contribution. Female members of the ruling family played a critical role in the legitimate transmission of imperial power, authority and property between generations. The inheritance of power was particularly emphasised from the reign of Theodosius I (379–95), whose two young sons were established as rulers in the western and eastern halves of the Roman Empire while still minors. By the middle of the fifth century, this commitment to the dynastic principle ensured that sisters, daughters and widows of emperors might all play a significant part in the transition between rulers. The role was demonstrated by Ariadne, daughter of the emperor Leo (457–74), who was first married to a general with a totally barbarian name; through her the 'Isaurian', Tarasicodissa, became the Emperor Zeno. On his death in 491, the Senate officially requested Ariadne the empress to choose another candidate to rule, and she selected Anastasios, a court official with financial expertise, as her second husband. Through her first marriage arranged by her father, the defence of the empire was ensured, and through her second, which may have represented her own choice, its secure management. In the late fifth century Ariadne personified a truly imperial inheritance as no one else could.

During the sixth and seventh centuries the hereditary principle was subject to intense pressures as the empire was attacked by new enemies, and regularly gave way beneath the challenge of military *coups d'état*. Normally a newly established emperor would try to impose a successor of his choice. If he had no sons, a son-in-law or an adopted colleague might fulfil the necessary role in an imperial dynasty, a process in which empresses were frequently called upon to play a significant part. Whether as widows or as mothers, their support for a particular successor could make a difference. In particular, their legal position as guardians of minor children enabled them to take a part in any Regency, if one had to be established to govern in the name of an heir too young to rule alone. And in circumstances where there was no legitimate or designated heir, a widowed empress could raise an emperor to the throne by remarriage.

Many imperial women exercised considerable indirect power in these ways.

In the middle of the seventh century, the hereditary principle was severely tested and the events of 641–2 provide an illuminating example of the powers and weaknesses of imperial women. When the Emperor Herakleios realised he was about to die, he arranged for two of his sons to inherit his authority: the older one, Herakleios-Constantine, the son of his first wife Fabia-Eudokia, and Heraklonas, a son by his second marriage to Martina. The eldest was then twenty-eight and the younger only fifteen. Herakleois also instructed that the two half-brothers were to revere Martina as their mother and empress, indicating that she would play an important role in imperial government. But the Senate overruled the emperor's will and insisted on the superior claim of the descendants of his first marriage. They accused the widowed empress of trying to poison her stepson, who died in confused circumstances only a few months after his accession. Martina and her own son were mutilated and exiled from the court. The Senate then proclaimed Constans, the young son of Herakleios-Constantine and grandson of Herakleios, as the legal emperor, although he was only eleven years old. By upholding the hereditary principle in this way, the ruling élite may have avoided the indirect rule of a strong-willed empress, but the accession of a minor meant that a Council of Regency was required to rule until Constans attained his majority.

The Byzantine concept of dynasty thus revealed its weaknesses as well as its strengths: in the interests of the legitimate descendants of Herakleios, the empire had to be ruled for several years by committee. Unfortunately this period is almost totally undocumented, so how the Regency Council was constituted is unknown. But it is probably safe to conclude that Constans' widowed mother, Empress Gregoria, would have taken her place on it while he was under her guardianship. As she was herself closely related to the imperial family, being a niece of Herakleios, Gregoria was familiar with matters of government. As the prince's mother, she was considered the one person who would most naturally protect his right to inherit until he came of age. The patriarch would also have sat on any Regency Council along with leading members of the Senate, the court, the civil service and the military. Once constituted, it ruled in the name of the young emperor until he was old enough to assert his own authority. The apparently undisputed transition suggests that the Council served its purpose and returned power to Constans as soon as he attained his majority shortly before 650.

THE WIDER WORLD

At this point it is necessary to look beyond the capital to the provinces of the East Roman Empire, which provided for the main needs of Constantinople through taxation, manpower and agricultural produce. At the time of the foundation of Constantinople the eastern half of the Roman world embraced a large number of provinces, forming a populous and prosperous area which extended as far east as the Tigris, where the buried city of Dura Europos reveals a typical Roman border garrison; and as far south as the great Egyptian temples at Luxor. The entire East Mediterranean hinterland had been firmly Hellenised, though local languages were also spoken, and had lived under Roman rule for centuries. The establishment of a new capital offered a closer centre of government than Old Rome, where judicial appeals were heard, provincial delegations could negotiate with the emperor, and ambitious men could seek employment. The construction and lavish decoration of Constantine's city, as well as the distribution of free bread to selected residents, exploited the wealth of this vast region.

Despite continual rivalry with the Persian empire, the other 'eye' of the ancient Near East, this part of the Roman world survived more or less intact until the middle of the sixth century. Once Justinian had secured a peace treaty with the Persians in 532, he directed his generals Belisarios and later Narses to undertake the reconquest of areas of the western half of the empire which had been taken over by non-Roman forces. In this way, the Vandal kingdom centred on Carthage in North Africa was conquered, and gradually the Ostrogoths were removed from Italy. Their capital at Ravenna was returned to Roman control, an event symbolised by the decoration of the church of San Vitale with the famous mosaics of Justinian and Theodora, and Old Rome finally came under imperial authority. Even parts of southern Spain were won back from the Visigoths, but this was to prove the most ephemeral of the conquests. The rest of the Roman Empire in the West had effectively passed out of imperial control and would never be regained.

CONSEQUENCES OF THE SLAVIC AND ARAB CONQUESTS

Whether these ambitious campaigns weakened imperial defences in the Balkans, or merely diverted resources further west, it was on the Danube frontier that Justinian's troops first experienced a new enemy: Slavonic tribes. From about 558 onwards these disorganised military forces took advantage of garrison failures to breach the frontier and advance into more developed agricultural regions south of the Danube. They appear to have lacked a developed social structure but could successfully besiege a fortified city if necessary. Accompanied by their women and children, they sought more fertile lands to cultivate and gradually took over certain areas of the northern Balkans. Their advance was less of an invasion than an infiltration of imperial territory: local inhabitants were attacked and driven off, so that the newcomers could take over. Such unusual and unexpected campaigning was not countered by serious military reaction from Constantinople for many years. And by the early seventh century, when imperial troops were repeatedly sent to fight on the Danube frontier, Slavonic forces were already well established. It was on one such occasion during a winter campaign in 602 that the troops rebelled, raised their own commander on a shield as a way of proclaiming him emperor and marched on Constantinople. This paved the way for a period of instability during which Slavonic tribes extended their occupation of imperial territory in the Balkans.

While this slow but steady loss of control occurred in western regions of the empire, the Persians mounted another onslaught from the east which challenged the authority of Herakleios (610–41). This prolonged invasion extended so far that it terrified the population not only of the eastern provinces but also of the capital. For, in 626, during the emperor's absence in the east, troops of the 'King of Kings' appeared on the Asiatic shore of the Bosphoros, opposite Constantinople. They had co-ordinated their attack with the Avars and Slavs who appeared simultaneously in the west. On this occasion Patriarch Sergios, a member of the ruling Council left in control of Constantinople, devised a new form of protection by parading the city's most important icons of the Virgin and Christ round the city walls, accompanied by the entire population who sang the famous hymn to the Invincible (another epithet of the Theotokos). This composition by Romanos, a hymn writer from Syria, which had become a much-loved chant, was now invoked to secure the spiritual aid of the Theotokos against the fire-worshipping Zoroastrians.

At the same time General Bonos organised military manoeuvres which also involved the use of Greek fire to attack the Slavonic naval forces attempting to ferry the Persians across the Bosphoros. To the Byzantines' relief, the enemy withdrew. And two years later, in 628, when Herakleios sent word of his complete victory over the Persian empire, the inhabitants of Constantinople celebrated, confident in the protection of their spiritual defender, the Virgin.

This great triumph, however, was rapidly followed by a more serious threat to the stability of the Roman world, now restricted to the East Mediterranean. Few written sources record the development of the desert tribes who occupied the Arabian peninsula prior to their encounter with the Roman world. For many years they had lived in relatively peaceful coexistence with imperial forces on the frontiers of Syria, Palestine and Egypt. But in the decade following Herakleios' conquest of Persia, increasingly aggressive activity took place, leading to serious hostilities in the 630s. Despite, or perhaps because of his military successes, Herakleios was unable to find a means of repulsing the advances of Arabic tribes, familiar with the desert terrain, fighting on camel- and horse-back with techniques completely different to those of established Roman or Persian armies. In addition, the Arabs were inspired by the new religious revelation of Allah to the Prophet Muhammad. In a brief period, Damascus, the capital of Syria, and then Jerusalem, the holiest of Christian holy cities, fell to the enemy. By 638 Herakleios witnessed a total rout of his forces and retreated to a safe position behind the Taurus Mountains. In this way, although it may have seemed only a temporary strategic withdrawal, he set a new eastern border for the Roman Empire in the extreme east of Asia Minor. This effectively abandoned to the Arabs a vast area previously under Roman administration: the provinces of Syria, Palestine, Egypt and North Africa, as well as the rich agricultural hinterland which had supported the capital in food, manpower and taxes for centuries.

By 647 the Arab conquests of the Near East had created a vast zone loyal to the new religious observance of Islam, which stretched from Basra on the Persian Gulf and Nineveh on the Tigris in the east, to Libya in North Africa in the west. Antioch, Alexandria and Jerusalem, the three most ancient centres of Christian authority, had passed under Islamic control. While the Byzantines knew of the existence of Bedouin tribes whom they called Arabs, Saracens, Ishmaelites or Hagarenes, they never imagined that these desert warriors could win such military triumphs, inspired by the revelations granted to the Prophet Muhammad. They condemned this new religion as a heresy. It is particularly regrettable that so few sources for the reign of Constans II (642–68) have survived, since the central span of the seventh century was to prove one of the most momentous periods in the history of Byzantium. While some reforms of military defence were realised in new administrative units called *themata*, during his reign the Arabs consolidated their extraordinarily rapid conquest. They also established a definite naval superiority, raiding the islands of Cyprus, Crete and Cos in an uncheckable advance into the Aegean. By 669 Constantinople itself was besieged.

Nor was the new eastern border of the empire, which followed the line of the Taurus Mountains in south-eastern Asia Minor, a firm and fixed one. Despite its natural defensive advantages, Byzantine garrisons stationed in their mountain forts regularly failed to check Arab raids on to imperial territory. By the middle of the seventh century there was no doubt about the damage inflicted on Byzantium by the new Islamic power, whose leaders (Caliphs) established themselves in Damascus. The catastrophic reduction of provinces under Roman control provoked a decline in imperial power, which was of course accompanied by much self-questioning by those who had considered themselves the heirs of eternal Rome.

Indeed, as the Arabs mounted ever more destructive attacks on Constantinople during the seventh century, it became clear that their aim was to destroy the Roman Empire. In its place they intended to establish an Islamic empire, making the old and admired capital on the Bosphoros their centre. To counter this threat to the empire's survival, serious reforms of administration, military organisation and even religious culture were needed. It is quite possible that, had such changes not been implemented by the iconoclast rulers of the eighth century, Constantinople would have fallen to the Arabs seven centuries before 1453, thus foreclosing on Byzantine history before it had really begun. Back in the mid-seventh century, while few were aware of such potential dangers, the anxiety caused by the revelation of Islam was quite severe enough to provoke dramatic developments.

Constans II reacted to the initial expansion of Islam by moving to Syracuse in Sicily, a city which still maintained the traditions of classical life. But when he demanded that his family join him there, the officials in charge of the imperial court in Constantinople refused his request. His wife, Fausta, and three sons remained in the east. In 668 Constans was murdered in mysterious circumstances and a usurper laid claim to imperial authority from Sicily. As soon as the news reached Constantinople, however, the eldest son of Constans was acclaimed emperor and the usurper denounced. The great majority of courtiers and state officials were clearly committed to the eastern capital and had no intention of abandoning it. In due course the new emperor, Constantine IV, resumed the military struggle against the Arabs and realised the full potential of a new defensive system of *themata* (military provinces).

His success in stabilising the eastern frontier was balanced, however, by a neglect of the north-western frontier in the Balkans, which disappeared under the impact of Slavic tribes. Although the Slavs' occupation of large parts of the western provinces was much less violent, the settlements they established (*Sklaviniai*) removed large areas from imperial rule. The Slavs rapidly became curious about aspects of Roman administration, such as a stable coinage, a legal system and Christian religion. Eventually, Byzantium would supply them with a written form of their own language, which led to a far more positive symbiosis than anything that might be envisaged with the Arabs.

GREECE DURING THE EARLY MIDDLE AGES

Under the impact of these changes, the classical traditions of urban centres gave way to new medieval forms. The history of Athens is typical. During the early Christian centuries, it continued as one of the centres of classical learning but in 529 Justinian closed the Platonic Academy of Athens and the city lost its main attraction. It had already suffered attack by non-Greek tribes, first the Heruli, then Alaric and the Goths, and shrank to a shadow of its former size within new defensive walls. The Acropolis became its fortress and centre and the Parthenon was converted into a church dedicated to the Virgin Mary, Mother of God (Theotokos). Armed challenges in the Balkans were renewed in the 580s when many Slav tribes crossed the Danube and pressed south in search of productive farming land. Neither the fortifications at Thermopylai or at the Gulf of Corinth deterred their advance. They settled in rural parts deep in the south of Peloponnesos and caused the local population to flee to mountains, islands and new defensible forts such as Monemvasia (founded in 586). Even Thessaloniki, the second city of the empire, was frequently besieged though always saved. This outcome was attributed to its patron saint, Demetrios, who was sometimes seen fighting among the defenders. Entire communities abandoned their homes and took refuge in more protected sites: the population of Argos, for instance, removed to the island of Orove in the Saronic Gulf, while the Bishop of Patras led some of his Christian flock overseas to Sicily.

Other ancient sites declined similarly, not only as a result of military threats but also due to social changes in the status of senators who had formed the city councils. It became harder and harder for urban communities to sustain their traditional lifestyle. Theatres fell into disrepair and were then looted for building materials. Baths ceased to function as the water supplies failed. Across the entire empire, ruralisation accompanied the destruction of many features of classical urban city life. It also provoked considerable anxiety, evident from the circulation of apocalyptic texts about the end of the world. Though the *Sklaviniai* did not pose an immediate challenge to the remaining inhabitants of Greece, they forced many to flee from their homes and constituted a non-Byzantine intrusion which was not subordinate to the emperor. For many decades the government in Constantinople had devoted much greater attention to the eastern regions of the empire, leaving the local inhabitants of the Balkans to fend for themselves. One major consequence was that the Slavic infiltration destroyed the Via Egnatia, which linked Constantinople with Rome. This major road ran overland via Thessaloniki and the mountains of northern Greece to Dyrrachion, on the eastern coast of the Adriatic (in present-day Albania), where the route continued by boat to Bari in southern Italy and on to Rome. For centuries it had facilitated contacts between Old and New Rome as well as stimulating trade. Thessaloniki, the most important centre of Byzantine authority in the European half of the empire, was the linchpin of the route and its survival was essential to imperial control. During the early part of the seventh century its strong fortifications, coupled with the determination of its bishops and inhabitants, especially its spiritual patron, saved Thessaloniki from the Slavs. But in the 690s Justinian II had to fight his way through Slavic settlements to re-establish imperial contact with the city. Further to the west of the city there was no possibility of restoring the emperor's authority. Large tracts of the Balkans and Greece thus came under the domination of Slavic settlements, causing a further reduction in imperial income in tax and produce.

During his first reign (685–95) Justinian II took two important steps to bring some *Sklaviniai* under imperial control. The first involved the resettlement in Asia Minor of Slav prisoners of war captured during his campaigns of the 680s. This method of bringing unruly elements under closer official surveillance was an established one; the transplantation of particular populations from one region to another had been practised for many centuries. In this case it brought some Slavic peoples into closer contact with imperial government, Christian traditions, and other aspects of Byzantine rule which their loosely organised tribes appear to have lacked.

PROVINCIAL ORGANISATION IN CENTRAL GREECE

The second step taken by Justinian turned on the establishment of some form of imperial control over specific areas of Greece. A new military-style administration was adapted from the system developed to secure the eastern border of the empire against the Arabs. This involved a type of provincial government which is identified by the term *thema*. It is documented initially in Asia Minor and Thrace, and later expanded to parts of Greece, the Balkans and some of the Aegean islands. The first hint that it is being introduced into a particular region is usually a record of the appointment of a military leader to head the new provincial administration, with the title *strategos* (general). In central Greece, such a development is documented in 695 when Leontios was nominated *strategos* of Hellas, although he refused to take the job. Instead, he led a revolt against Justinian II and imposed himself as emperor: he exiled Justinian and ruled for three years. But some contact with the capital must have been established. A gold coin of Justinian II dating from 692–5 was recently found in Athens during excavations for the new metro system. This is a first, since coin finds at excavated sites are completely lacking between issues of the mid-seventh century and the mid-ninth, when coins of Theophilos are found. The new discovery confirms that someone in central Greece was once in possession of a coin minted in the capital under Justinian II.

Setting up an administration responsive to the needs of the capital would also involve financial officials to record the resources of the area. Their survey of even a small region would establish the possibility of recruiting men for military service and extracting taxation on a regular basis, which was the fundamental task of the new administrative machinery associated with the *thema* system. Gradually it became possible for the provincial administration to draw up military catalogues: lists of families required to provide a soldier mounted and fully equipped for military service. These also recorded what landed property was held at a reduced tax to sustain the family while the soldier was away on duty. Families who did not feature in the military catalogues were recorded on separate tax registers which stipulated what taxes they paid on the land they owned.

As a result of the intimate link between military and tax matters, officials responsible for these registers were required to measure and assess all the land under cultivation by people who identified themselves as loyal subjects of the emperor in Constantinople. In order to establish a fair system, poor quality land was not rated as highly as fertile, well-watered land, and families owning a pair of oxen had to pay more tax than those with only one ox, packhorse or donkey, or no livestock at all. Eventually the calculation of taxes took account of all the animals, fruit trees, buildings, and farming equipment owned by each family and complex methods of assessment were set up. In the absence of surviving records for the seventh and eighth centuries, it is difficult to recreate the earliest workings of this system. But references to military catalogues and the tax officials who maintained them suggest the active overseeing of provincial life. While its primary aim was to secure armed forces for military service in more distant areas, other measures were designed to support local defence, to maintain castles, bridges, roads and for-tifications. Under the authority of the *strategos*, the presence of civilian officials stimulated the building of official residences and new churches, and created greater awareness of the central government in the far-flung provinces.

There is no surviving evidence that Leontios pursued an interest in central Greece as emperor (695–8), yet some activity associated with a *thema* of Hellas must have taken place because a generation later, in the 720s, Agallianos, the *tourmarches* (a junior military official) led an unsuccessful political rebellion. The title derives from the word *tourma*, usually a small military subdivision of a *thema*. It is recorded when the *Helladikoi* (inhabitants of Hellas), under Agallianos, set sail from Greece and were wrecked in a storm. So undoubtedly some administrative structures had been established; their naval character corresponds to Constantinople's interest in controlling the coastline and harbours of Greece. How far inland such control extended is impossible to guess. Seals of officials attached to the *thema Hellados* (province of Hellas, central Greece) appear during the course of the eighth century. While they are notoriously difficult to date, the fact that quite a number have survived, often found by chance on excavated sites, implies a growing body of provincial administrators appointed by the capital.

ECCLESIASTICAL ORGANISATION IN GREECE

One additional aspect of imperial control in Greece survived the long period of adaptation as the Slavs extended their settlements and occupied areas: the hierarchy of Christian bishops. This second structure of the Byzantine imperial command placed high-ranking clerics in charge of the two metropolitan churches, Thessaloniki in the north and Corinth at the Isthmus. Despite some disruption, archbishops of these two leading ecclesiastical sees, both established in early Christian times, maintained a constant Christian presence in the areas under their sway. To assist in this task they appointed bishops, who may often have been drawn from the local clergy. These were the men who had to organise defence when danger threatened the existence of entire communities. Some of them clearly ensured the survival of cities by moving to more secure settlements on mountain peaks and islands. Episcopal lists (known as *Notitiae episcopatuum*) preserve a basic skeleton of the hierarchy, while local records such as the series of graffiti on the columns of the Parthenon, indicate that whenever a prelate died he was usually replaced. But even in these major bishoprics it is hard to judge what Christian control meant or how far Christian influence extended beyond the walls of the episcopal city.

None the less, these church officials had direct contact with the capital whenever a church council was summoned. Several bishops from Greece who participated in the Sixth Ecumenical Council and its follow-up, the Quini-sext or Council *in Trullo* in 692, had occasion to travel to Constantinople twice in twelve years. These links between the regions of the empire and the centre were extremely important as a means of strengthening imperial control: they exposed local bishops to the intellectual climate of the Queen City and the culture of its patriarch. They permitted clerics to travel at governmental expense to a gathering where theological problems and matters of ecclesiastical discipline would be debated. In addition, such visits spread knowledge of metropolitan styles of church building and decoration, icon painting, liturgical practice and a host of other features of religious life. By this means stories of miraculous cures effected by particular relics, for example those of St Artemios housed in the capital, of important new icons installed in particular churches, or of new hymns written to commemorate particular saints, might become more widely known. A similar form of dissemination operated from Rome in the early medieval West: methods of chanting, or of constructing more beautiful churches, were spread to remote areas by pilgrims and visitors to the see of St Peter.

By the seventh century it is evident that the two most important centres of Christian authority, which had survived the Arab conquest of the Near East, were encouraging different ecclesiastical traditions within their spheres of interest. Rome was developing its own spiritual resources based on a Latin inheritance, increasingly unfamiliar with Greek. And Constantinople was insisting on its Greek heritage as well as the God-given authority of its rulers in the process of adapting to its much smaller world. Challenged by the Arabs and the Slavs, who represented an entirely new religious revelation and a vibrant pagan tradition respectively, it was forced into a narrower mould. The reality of its position as one power among many had the effect of transforming its culture while limiting its scope. Combined pressures generated a new emphasis on the Hellenic and Christian character of Byzantium, which is represented by the epic poetry of George of Pisidia. As one of the guardians of Byzantine culture, this court scholar-poet endowed the emperor with a new epithet, 'faithful in Christ', *pistos en Christo basileus.* While using the most sophisticated ancient Greek of his day, George also recognised popular influence which acclaimed the ruler as *basileus ton Romaion,* emperor of the Romans. This titulature signalled the final disappearance of Latin, and Greek became the language of the law courts as well as all departments of government. At the same time, official definitions of orthodox belief and practice took less account of Rome's views, thus further alienating the Latin West from imperial control.

THE COUNCIL *IN TRULLO*

Some of the major concerns of the Byzantines are indirectly illustrated by the decisions of the Council *in Trullo,* a gathering of bishops held in the Queen City in 692 on the order of Justinian II to update church laws. These ecclesiastical rulings represent an effort to consolidate Christian unity faced by the loss to Islam of three leading patriarchal sees, Jerusalem, Antioch and Alexandria. When Justinian II summoned this universal council, Pope Sergius I did not participate in person but appointed Basil, Bishop of Gortyna in Crete, as his representative, selecting a leading cleric from the ecclesiastical diocese of East Illyricum, which was subject to his control. This was a vast area including the Balkan peninsula, Greece, Crete, Sicily and southern Italy, which originated in the political division of the Roman Empire under Diocletian. Illyricum had then been assigned to the West. The ecclesiastical diocese of East Illyricum represented an overlapping authority, not corresponding to political or linguistic divisions. By the late seventh century, this extension of papal authority into the eastern half of the empire, which was largely Greek-speaking, was an anomaly. Given that Rome was increasingly limited to the use of Latin in both its secular and spiritual records, there was probably little 'western' influence in Illyricum. Basil none the less took precedence over all the other bishops as the representative of the see of St Peter.

The decisions taken in 692 provide three types of evidence: about the regions under imperial control at that date; about the relationship of the Bishop of Rome to Byzantium; and about the preoccupations of bishops in the now shrunken empire.

First, the bishoprics represented at the council, reveal that by the end of the seventh century the Byzantine Empire covered only a fraction of its former extent. The assembled clerics came from a large number of cities, 211, in contrast with the 338 Fathers of the First Ecumenical Council held at Nicaea in 325, but from a greatly restricted area: the majority from Asia Minor, the heartland of the Christian empire, the islands of the Aegean and southern Italy.

Second, in 451 Constantinople had succeeded in establishing its status as equivalent to that of Old Rome. But the successors of St Peter still claimed higher authority based on the New Testament saying of Jesus: 'Thou art Peter and on this rock (*petra*) I will build my church' (Matthew 16:18). In disciplinary matters, bishops of Rome had long served as the highest court for churches of the West. But the papal decrees (also called decretals from the Latin *decretum*) had made no impact in the East and were ignored by the council. Additional matters also provoked divisions: celibacy, fasting, the use of unleavened bread in the Eucharist, and above all the wording of the creed, where the additional Latin clause *Filioque* (and from the Son) in the declaration about the procession of the Holy Ghost, was accepted only in the West.

Old Rome and New Rome were also divided by customs which reflected their different inheritance. The East's concern with the survival of specific pagan traditions appeared obscure to the Roman authorities, who had no direct experience of the type of urban festivities condemned in 692. While there were probably seers who foretold the future by interpreting cloud formations, and entertainers who brought dancing bears on to the streets, Rome had lost all knowledge of the festivals celebrated by women and men cross-dressing, dancing in public, or wearing the masks associated with ancient Greek drama. Even in the time of Pope Gregory I (590–604), the activity of law students celebrating in a generally inappropriate, i.e. pagan, fashion had become unfamiliar. Christians in the West were not so concerned with Jewish customs as in the East, and even less familiar with Armenians, whose distinctive Christian customs worried the council. The canons against fraternising with Jews – visiting their homes, going to the public bath with them, attending their festivals, consulting them for medical purposes – or following Armenian traditions, such as bringing meat offerings to church, therefore meant little. East and West also had different traditions of fasting and Roman practice was deeply resented by the council.

Anxieties about Christians in the three eastern patriarchates, now living under Islam, formed the third set of preoccupations. Extremely reduced representation at the council from the areas conquered by the Arabs reflected the endangered state of Christianity in the land of its birth. Those bishops who had fled from the Muslim-occupied regions and were living as refugees either in neighbouring territory or in Constantinople were encouraged to return as soon as possible to look after their Christian communities. Those still resident were to uphold the traditional customs of the church. But the council recognised that Arab control posed serious problems. The rapid spread of Islam, which the Byzantines considered a new heresy, made them all the more sensitive to the question of defining their own orthodoxy.

An additional aspect of this concern may be found in the council's regulations on the role of art in Christian churches. For the first time ever a universal council legislated against the sort of art that might provoke impure feelings. Instead, it praised depictions of Christ in His human form, in order to commemorate His incarnation and life on earth. Its attention to the didactic role of Christian art encouraged a major initiative in imperial art. While the symbol of the cross had been used for centuries, Christ was now given the emperor's place on the obverse (front) of a coin. In another, possibly related development icon painters in the East began to paint the Crucifixion with images of the suffering

Christ flanked by the grieving Virgin Mary and St John. The use of art as imperial propaganda against the Muslim ban on human representation was particularly developed in monasteries existing under Islamic authority, such as Mar Sabas, and other Palestinian monasteries near Jerusalem and Bethlehem, as well as the famous community on Mount Sinai patronised by Justinian I.

The council of 692 thus illustrates the new, beleaguered situation in which Christians of Egypt, Palestine and Syria found themselves; its rulings also addressed many issues that stemmed from the increasing isolation of the empire and its East Christian inhabitants. This in turn drew attention to its Greek, rather than Latin character, and its preoccupations with the Islamic heresy. While Basil and his Cretan bishops knew all too well what havoc was created by Arab attacks, it is not clear that Pope Sergius was yet aware of them. And although the Bishop of Rome appreciated the dangers of pagan practices for Christians, many of the instances cited at Constantinople had long been forgotten in the West. So the canons issued by the assembled bishops reflected not only the specific difficulties of the churches of the East, but also the development of distinct practices there. When the acts of the Council were brought to Rome Pope Sergius refused to accept them, and they were not acknowledged in the West until 711. Even then, the Trullan regulations never attained the widespread circulation or observation of earlier canonical collections.

In the East, however, the canons reinforced the narrower base of Christian faith while they marked the beginning of a more fundamental, underlying separation of western from eastern churches. Forty years later (c.733) Emperor Leo III claimed the whole diocese of East Illyricum back from Rome. The bishops of Sicily, southern Italy, Crete, mainland Greece, the Balkans and the Aegean passed into the control of the patriarchate of Constantinople. By gathering in these outlying Greek-speaking parts of the church in the West, he thus compensated a little for the losses sustained in the eastern regions conquered by the Arabs. In depriving Rome of its base in the Balkan region, the emperor also wished to punish the pope for his lack of co-operation over a new census of land and property, designed to increase imperial taxation in the West. Rome protested in vain against the loss of East Illyricum. The arbitrary decision was never reversed and it increased western resentment at eighth-century emperors. In its precarious situation, when central Italy was regularly under threat from Lombard attacks, the dispute over property and taxes deepened cultural differences between Old Rome and New Rome.

In both canon and civil law, East and West thus began to diverge quite markedly. Byzantium maintained its commitment to Roman law albeit in Greek translation, while the separate kingdoms of the West adapted their own traditions to fit medieval circumstances. Although the western model enhanced Rome's universal claims to discipline all the Christians of the West, civil law codes continued to develop independently within very different regional practices. In the East, on the other hand, an ideal of universal Roman civil law was matched by an overarching system of church law, the two systems mutually reinforcing each other. The canons issued in 692, for instance, were immediately recognised as regulations to be enforced by imperial power. Reciprocal influence between the two systems brought church and state in Byzantium into very close co-operation and meant that ecclesiastical offences could be prosecuted by the full force of secular authority. In this respect a significant contrast was developing between the eastern half of the old Roman world and the western half, where political fragmentation and the parcellisation of sovereignty prevented any similar overall alliance between the powers civil and ecclesiastical.

LEO III AND IMPERIAL REFORM

These divisions between East and West crystallised differences between the Greek and Latin halves of the Christian world. In political, economic and theological terms the two had grown so far apart that the next major dispute took the most extreme form. It was a clash over the role of icons which was to dominate the next 150 years and is central to the concerns of this book. Its origins must be sought in the context of the early-eighth-century victories of the Arab heretics over Byzantium. From at least the late seventh century, if not earlier, the Caliphate of Damascus was intent on conquering Constantinople, in order to make it the Islamic capital of the East Mediterranean. So grave was the threat that during the brief reign of Anastasios III (713–15), all inhabitants of the Byzantine capital were ordered to leave the city unless they could show that they had a year's food supplies and were prepared to fight. The emperor also repaired weak points in the defences since the Arabs were planning a three-pronged attack by land and sea. His successor Theodosios III (715–17) resigned when this campaign took physical shape, leaving the general of the Anatolikon province to assume responsibility for the city's protection. In this way, a career soldier named Konon, born on the Syrian frontier, was transformed into the emperor of Byzantium and acclaimed as Leo III. He founded what became known as the Syrian dynasty (frequently but misleadingly identified as 'Isaurian'), which was to rule on and off for the next eighty years. He immediately set about organising the defence of the Queen City against the Arabs, whose military tactics he knew well from past experience. He also initiated diplomatic moves to involve the Bulgars and to bribe the Khazars into attacking the besiegers from their rear.

After a siege that lasted over a year, the Arabs received orders from Damascus to return to Syria and on 15 August 718 prepared to withdraw. On this important date, the Feast of the Assumption (called the Dormition of the Virgin in the East), the Byzantines celebrated a great victory. Many attributed it to the power of the Mother of God, the divine patron of the city. Leo, however, took some credit for the skilful use of Greek fire, an inflammable naphtha which burned on contact with water, and for his negotiations which had brought help from the Bulgars and the Khazars. He also benefited from a violent storm in the Aegean which destroyed the Arab fleet as it sailed home. This triumph over the forces of Islam was marked by annual commemorative services from 719 onwards and should have put an end to Arab hopes of capturing the capital.

Yet throughout the 720s and 30s, the Saracens continued their assaults, advancing every summer into Byzantine territory to drive off herds, burn crops and terrorise the inhabitants of every castle or city they managed to capture. The troops attached to the main provinces remained shut up in their garrisons rather than risking a military clash. Leo's strategic experience did not produce a clear victory in the conflict for over two decades, until he defeated a major Arab force at Akroinon in 740. But unlike the previous six emperors, who had ruled for a maximum of five to six years and often for less than three, Leo had governed for twenty-four years and had reformed the empire through a series of measures designed to bring greater stability. His attention to the legal system, imperial coinage, military reform, dynastic continuity and ecclesiastical change strengthened the administration in ways that were to prove essential to the survival of Byzantium. Of these measures, his religious reform was possibly the least important in the long term, although it was to brand the emperor as a heretic and persecutor.

ICONOCLASM

According to the surviving Byzantine sources, which take a critical view of him, in 730 Leo III issued an arbitrary edict imposing iconoclasm. This policy enshrined the necessity of destroying all icons ('idols'), figurative images of the holy family, Christian saints, martyrs, bishops, Old Testament characters as well as of living holy men. The chief justification for such acts was that the worship of graven images is specifically condemned in the Second Commandment, and icons could easily become idols. This view of idolatry was held by the Arabs who had taken it directly from the law of Moses. But for centuries Christians, whose political authority was visualised very much in the ancient pagan style, had made pictures of their holy figures and used them as aids in their worship. Following St Basil of Caesarea, they believed that the honour given to the icon passed on to its prototype, the figure represented. True worship was of course reserved to God who could never be depicted, being invisible and unknowable.

The two major chronicles which provide a narrative of Leo's reign find explanations for the abhorrent policy of iconoclasm in the 'wicked' character of the emperor. Both were written about eighty years after his death. Nikephoros who was patriarch from 806 to 815, and Theophanes the Confessor who died in 817 or 818, compiled their texts from a strictly pro-icon (iconophile) point of view. They took no account of the military achievements of the emperor, and instead emphasised his heretical religious policy. Leo III was Saracen-minded, they report; he was influenced by Jewish advisers; he was a heretic and did not understand the orthodox tradition of venerating icons. In the same light, it was possible for them to claim that he was an uneducated soldier who destroyed the traditions of higher education in Constantinople. The emperor was made personally responsible for the persecution of icon-venerators that followed the edict. And for this part of their histories both authors drew on accounts of the suffering of iconophile martyrs, some of whom had died for their faith in icons.

But in the context of the 720s, it is said that the emperor was greatly influenced by a vast underwater eruption which occurred in the Aegean Sea in 726. A volcano below the seabed threw up a new island between Thera (Santorini) and Therasia, an area renowned for tectonic activity, causing the sky to be darkened by solidifying lumps of lava for three days, and provoking tidal waves which washed up more lava on the

40

northern and eastern shores of the Aegean. In the Middle Ages such natural phenomena were understood as divine warnings, and when Leo tried to discover what could have caused God's displeasure, his theological advisers suggested that He was vexed by Christian idolatry, that is by the excessive veneration of icons. This interpretation of the popular cult of religious paintings in all forms was surely influenced by the Arab prohibition of such objects. Under the Islamic revelation of the Qu'ran all human representation was banned, in strict observance of Mosaic law. The same policy was also imposed on Christian and Jewish communities under Arab control. Fighting under a firmly iconoclast policy had apparently inspired the continuing victories of the Saracen heretics, victories which raised an uncomfortable question about the cult of images in Byzantium. Could the profound veneration offered to religious icons be misunderstood as idolatry? And was this the reason why the forces of Islam were regularly more successful in battle than the forces of Christianity?

While there must have been considerable support among the military and the reforming clergy for the new policy of iconoclasm, there is also much evidence that people put great faith in the power of icons to heal, to protect homes, and shield cities from enemy attack. They believed that their prayers to the saints represented on religious images would be answered: would secure fertility, cure blindness and paralysis, and intercede for them in the court of heaven. It was only a short step from praying to icons for intercession to kissing and adoring such material objects, which might indeed be identified as worshipping them as graven images. In a further development, if Christians who had previously placed such secure hope in their cherished images found that these did not protect them, then their disappointment could be extreme. In place of confidence, they turned against the icons that had failed and started attacking them as useless. This was demonstrated in military terms when a soldier is reported to have cursed an icon of the Virgin which had failed to hold off the Saracen forces. Such stories circulated widely, causing more anxiety and distress. For those who already had reason to doubt the powers of icons, inexplicable volcanic warnings merely confirmed their fears: that God was displeased with His chosen people and had transferred His favour to the followers of the one who claimed to be His prophet, Muhammad, inspirer of the forces of Islam.

In 730 when Leo summoned the patriarch to consult him about the problem, Germanos had already been disturbed by reports from other bishops who had removed the icons from their churches in order to avoid idolatrous veneration. He had written to Thomas of Klaudioupolis and Constantine of Nakoleia to protest against this unwarranted action, which he claimed had thrown whole provinces and cities into tumult. So when the emperor instructed Germanos to follow this example and take down the major icons from the cathedral church of Hagia Sophia, he refused. He was therefore dismissed and sent off into internal exile. Leo chose as his successor his former assistant (*synkellos*), Anastasios, who was prepared to agree with the imperial interpretation. The emperor also wrote to the Bishop of Rome warning him of the dangers of idolatry and ordering him to remove icons.

ROMAN REACTION TO ICONOCLASM

The news that Leo III had dismissed his patriarch and appointed a more pliant figure shocked Pope Gregory II, who refused to accept the synodical letter from Anastasios and wrote critically to the emperor. The Roman attachment to religious images could not countenance any suggestion that they might lead to idolatry; on the contrary, icons assisted the faithful in their prayers and brought benefits to those who had faith in them. Had not Pope Gregory the Great identified religious images as 'the Bibles of the illiterate'? His eighth-century successors, who took the same name in an act of homage, understood the important pedagogic role of icons and refused to obey the orders brought from their imperial overlords in the East. While they dated their documents by the year of the emperor's rule, mentioned his name in their daily prayers and used his coinage, they were not prepared to follow the example of Anastasios. In 731 Pope Gregory III went further: in one of the first acts of his pontificate he held a synod in Rome to denounce the Byzantine policy of iconoclasm. This officially opened a schism between Old Rome and New Rome.

Eastern iconoclasm thus provoked extreme disapproval in the West. And the manner in which Leo III announced the reform may have contributed to the violence of the reaction in Rome. In Byzantium the emperor could dismiss the Bishop of Constantinople and impose another candidate more favourable to his own views. But such a policy was anathema to the Bishop of Rome, whose independence from secular authority was a hard-won privilege, especially as he was subject to local military and political pressures. In the see of St Peter, the principle that the bishop should be elected by his clergy, with the popular support of the city's inhabitants, and should hold his position until he died, left no place for such drastic non-ecclesiastical intervention. Popes Gregory II and III also drew on an increasingly assertive practice of refusing to obey imperial decrees which were considered unorthodox, in the way that Pope Sergius declined to accept the canons of the Council *in Trullo* as orthodox.

Under Gregory III, ninety-three Italian bishops were summoned to Rome in 731 in order to condemn the eastern church for its policy of iconoclasm. They denounced the imperial decrees which presumed to identify as idolatry the veneration inherent in the use of images. It is significant that a major disagreement over the emperor's authority lay at the heart of the dispute, namely, his right to intervene in ecclesiastical matters. In Rome, fully conscious of papal claims to primacy within the Christian universe, as well as the bishop's duty to support the traditions of the church, no such secular power was recognised. No civilian could interfere with the election of a Bishop of Rome. The battle lines were thus drawn up on legal grounds, in addition to the obvious matter of the icons and their role in Christian worship. Many years later, at the end of the eighth or early ninth century, a clever forger probably working in iconophile circles close to the Roman *curia* devised three letters, which he attributed to a Pope Gregory. In these, the Roman bishop (presumably Pope Gregory II or III) accuses Leo III of trying to be both emperor and priest, following the Old Testament example of Melchisedek. Putting words into the emperor's mouth, which he 'quoted' from alleged letters written by Leo III to the pope, this unknown author had the Byzantine ruler claim a monopoly of both sacred and secular authority. Against such false claims, the intransigence and courage of the Roman pontiff is praised. It represents the superiority of ecclesiastical over secular power in religious matters. No bishop should ever be subjected to such bullying, which cannot be justified by reference to Old Testament models of kingship.

While the Old Testament provided a constant inspiration for Byzantine rulers, the emperor's interventions in the life of the Church were taken for granted. But now Leo's attention was focused on the need to defeat Islam. Under his rule the entire government of the empire was put on a puritan, war footing. However, like many uneducated career soldiers who attained imperial status, Leo III ensured that his son Constantine received an excellent training in theological as well as in military matters.

The second generation of the dynasty consolidated the vigorous anti-Islamic policy, celebrating numerous military victories and building confidence among the Byzantine provincial forces. In addition, Constantine V enshrined the principles of iconoclasm in a developed theology, which stressed that the only true image of Christ is the Eucharist. Given that God is uncircumscribable and can never be depicted, and that Christ is the Son of God, Constantine argued that no painted images of Him would ever be legitimate. In a series of writings he analysed the most mysterious aspect of Christian belief, the transformation of the bread and wine offered to God (transubstantiation). At this moment, when the priest officiating at the liturgy blesses and breaks the host, which thus becomes the body and blood of Christ, Constantine argued that Christ is indeed visible: His symbolic presence takes form only in these circumstances, and this is the sole way of visualising the Saviour. But such eastern theology only drove a deeper division between Constantinople and Rome.

THE COUNCIL OF HIEREIA

Constantine V's interpretations were endorsed by a large number of bishops who claimed to constitute the Seventh Ecumenical Council in 754. A universal gathering, however, required the representation of all five patriarchs (collectively known as the pentarchy), and Rome did not attend. Nevertheless, at this meeting the assembled eastern bishops declared iconoclasm orthodox and threatened persistent idolaters (iconophiles) with persecution as heretics. Iconoclasm was presented as a reform of the abuse of idolatry, which had grown up within the church under the practice of icon veneration. This was not accepted outside Byzantium. But within the capital and specific areas of the empire, officials loyal to the new iconoclast policy arrested icon venerators, put them on trial and condemned them to death. Their sufferings and martyrdom no doubt strengthened the resolve of many iconophiles, who spread their stories to audiences beyond the imperial frontiers, especially in Jerusalem and the West. On the other hand, many of Constantine's soldiers became tenacious supporters both of the emperor and his iconoclasm, making a firm link between his religious policy and his military victories. In Byzantium the iconoclasts celebrated Constantine V as one of the most successful rulers of the eighth century, while the later iconophile sources condemned him for diabolically inspired heresy and persecution.

The link between a commitment to close observance of the law of Moses and military vigour was to be recreated during the Puritan revolts of the sixteenth and seventeenth centuries, when Protestants quoted exactly the same proof texts as the council of 754. And Cromwell's New Model Army exemplified the same connection between fighting and righteous Puritan theology. Such direct parallels also suggest that both reforming movements developed in comparable circumstances of deep uncertainty and underlying change, when Christians questioned their relationship with God and sought to place a spiritual interpretation above the material means of worship.

Given the tone of the surviving Byzantine sources, most of them written much later than the events of the mid-eighth century, the extent of iconoclast persecution remains unclear. Very few bishops seem to have felt it necessary to resign; many monasteries adopted the new policy, though monastic leaders also led iconophiles into exile and sustained resistance to the policy. Like many other changes in theology, the theory of iconoclasm seemed to most Christians to constitute a new definition of orthodoxy, backed by the authorities, which had to be accepted. In a similar fashion they had generally found it politic not to oppose seventh-century changes in Christological definitions. But there was an additional element to the practice of iconoclasm: the removal and destruction of icons provoked opposition among anonymous Christians apparently deeply attached to icon veneration. They actively circumvented the order to impose iconoclasm by hiding icons and continuing to use them. In many churches, images of both New and Old Testament stories were plastered over. In this way, the Vision of Ezekiel with the four symbols of the evangelists survived in the church of Hosios David, Thessaloniki. In Constantinople, where no pre-iconoclast figural decoration had previously been identified, a fine mosaic of the Presentation of the Christ Child in the Temple was revealed in 1969. It had been walled up at the site known as Kalenderhane Camii so that it would no longer be visible and was thus saved from possible destruction. Its dramatic discovery while the monument was undergoing restoration is due to the skill of the workmen, who realised that the wall was hollow and, feeling around the edge, identified a mosaic on the surface that had been covered.

Popular support for the protection of revered images was encouraged by the domestic setting of much icon veneration, and the personal nature of iconophile prayers even in shrines and churches. Christians addressed the holy person represented on what might be quite a small and portable wooden board as an intercessor, making their own private appeals, pouring out their problems, promising further services and honour should a wish be granted. The rituals of praying before an image, kissing and adoring it, were largely personal; they were available to even uneducated Christians. So, by its nature, icon veneration became particularly significant to those otherwise excluded from ecclesiastical responsibilities – the uneducated and illiterate, women and children, the blind, deaf and maimed, and all those disadvantaged people who gravitated towards churches and monasteries seeking help and charity.

The official policy of iconoclasm instituted by Constantine V was generally supported by the ecclesiastical authorities, but at the same time it generated obstinate opposition among other groups of believers. From 754 to 775, when Constantine V died, the policy seems to have been entirely successful in imperial terms. Serious opponents were brought to trial and punished or driven out of the empire, while the unspoken opposition of lesser people was ignored. But since all the official iconoclast writings were later destroyed, it is impossible to calculate how effective the policy really was. Later iconophile texts claim that for these twenty years anyone found in the act of venerating an icon by the authorities might be arrested and dragged off to be tried by a military court. They provide examples of the risks true Christians were prepared to take: for example, when St Stephen the Younger and his companions were in prison awaiting trial, the warder's wife secretly brought in her own icons so that the iconophiles could perform their prayers. The notion that a mere woman could subvert official imperial policy becomes a commonplace in these later histories and martyr stories. But clearly the idea stemmed from a background of profound attachment to icons which Constantine V and his theological advisers were unable to uproot.

If iconoclasm intensified the separation of Latin Rome from Greek Constantinople, the Lombards drove a further wedge between the two when they conquered Ravenna in 751. The loss of this last outpost of Byzantine power in northern Italy meant that Rome came under much greater threat. Despite numerous appeals received in Constantinople, Constantine V was greatly preoccupied with Bulgarian challenges at the time and could ill afford to spare troops or funds in support of Rome. The popes therefore turned instead to the Franks. As a result, notional Byzantine authority in Italy north of Rome was replaced by the Frankish forces of King Pepin, who defeated the Lombards and assumed the role of protector of the Bishop of Rome. This fundamental shift in the axis of the main papal alliance, from the Byzantines to the Franks, linking Italy with Transalpine Europe rather than with the East Mediterranean, was to have serious consequences. It represented an integration of Christian forces in the West under a western secular power, independent of Constantinople in the East. The break from the traditional Rome–Constantinople alliance was made easier by Rome's opposition to iconoclasm. It was also marked by changes in the dating of papal documents and by the first issue of papal coins. While Constantine V maintained and extended diplomatic relations with the Franks, he was powerless to prevent a realignment of western forces, which was to result in the creation of a western emperor, Charles, regularly identified as 'the great', *Karolus magnus*, Charlemagne.

CONSTANTINE V'S RENEWAL OF CONSTANTINOPLE

As well as consolidating military victories over both the Arabs and Bulgars, Constantine V oversaw a revival of Constantinople (which is barely noted in the surviving sources). After a recurrence of bubonic plague in the late 740s, which had reduced the population of the capital to perhaps its lowest level since the fifth century, the emperor was determined to increase the city's basic resources. People were brought into the city from Greece and the islands. To secure additional water, the aqueduct, destroyed during a siege of 626, was repaired. Markets were also moved to take account of the harbours at which goods, grain and cattle were unloaded. After working on the repair of the aqueduct, the clay potters, bricklayers and plasterers who had been recruited from the provinces, were put to work rebuilding monuments which had collapsed in a serious earthquake in 740. When they failed to return home, their families may have joined them in the capital. But the main stimulus to the repopulation of the capital was the revival of economic activity which attracted adventurers, merchants and ambitious men seeking jobs in a now expanding city.

Since there is evidence of considerable building and redecoration of monuments, artists and craftsmen must have participated in this development. Although it is often assumed that iconoclasm means the destruction of all art, the replacement of figural by symbolic and floral decoration may even have increased the demand for mosaic workers and fresco painters. In addition, it is important to remember that the cathedral church of Hagia Sophia, consecrated in 537, contained no permanent figural art. In sixth-century descriptions of the original construction, the only iconic decoration noted occurs on curtains hung between the columns of the screen, which divided the main body of the church from the apse. These hangings, like portable icons which might be displayed on stands, were temporary fixtures which could easily be removed. So no destruction took place, or was necessary, in the cathedral church of the capital: it had been originally built in an aniconic style (without figural images).

This was the style employed on many monuments which had been devastated in 740, such as the Justinianic church of Hagia Irene, which had to be rebuilt from the foundations. Here, mosaic workers erected a monumental Cross and recorded the event in a long inscription in the apse. They used the finest materials and no expense was spared. While there is no clear evidence for other decoration, the use of polychrome marbles to decorate the floor and lower levels of the walls (as in Hagia Sophia) seems very likely. Possibly the walls of the entrance hall at the west end (the narthex) received mosaic images comparable to the 'Garden of Paradise' or floral style employed at the Great Mosque of Damascus and the Dome of the Rock at Jerusalem. These Muslim structures, erected by Caliphs Abd al-Malik and Yezid of the end of the seventh and early eighth century respectively, were decorated without any use of figural representation. Under Justinian II, mosaic tesserae were collected from the empire and Byzantine craftsmen were sent to set them so as to ensure the most prestigious and exquisite wall coverings in these important mosques. If the decoration of the rebuilt church of Hagia Irene resembled these buildings, to worship in it with the gold and silver tesserae glittering in the light of myriad candles must have been deeply impressive.

This style of decoration was also employed in other eighth-century churches, at Nicaea and Thessaloniki for instance. As well as the all-powerful Christian symbol of the Cross, floral, vegetable and Garden of Paradise-type decoration, secular scenes of horse-racing were put up in place of figurative art. Iconoclast emperors continued to patronise builders, artists and craftsmen, who exploited their knowledge of the classical repertory, such as the Labours of Hercules, as well as traditional geometric patterns and floral borders. There was no disruption to artistic production. The training of ivory carvers, gold and enamel workers continued without a break, as these skills were closely linked to the minting of coins and the production of lead seals, two basic necessities of the state. The silk factories of Byzantium also continued to produce their highly-sought-after materials, decorated with Hippodrome and hunting scenes rather than religious figures. Such silks were used as diplomatic gifts for the Franks, for instance, or as a form of payment to secure the release of prisoners captured by the Slavs.

The turbulence of the period should not be ignored, however. Despite the second Arab civil war, which lessened the Muslim threat after 750, Byzantium enjoyed very few years of peace as Bulgar military threats increased in the Balkans. Almost constant warfare and the urgent military requirements of the state preoccupied Leo III and Constantine V, who appreciated that the survival of the empire was in question. Through their vigorous defence of the city and the extension of provincial government in the western regions of the empire, they strengthened and embellished the Queen City while increasing imperial resources. Their determination to secure the ruling family resulted in a dynasty that persisted until 797. To the confusion of all later historians, they also named their sons after their grandfathers, in the traditional fashion, so that after Leo III and his son Constantine V, Leo IV was followed by Constantine VI. It is often difficult to distinguish all the previous generations represented on the reverse of gold coins (see plate 1a), yet this concept of dynasty undoubtedly strengthened the empire. And in the same process, the Syrian rulers also banned religious images, which had been identified as the instruments of a dangerous tendency to idolatry. Iconoclast reform was part and parcel of their restoration of Byzantium.

At the death of Constantine V in 775 his eldest son succeeded him as Leo IV. Though both Arabs and Bulgars persisted in their ambitions to make the Queen City their own capital, there was no immediate threat to Byzantium. The machinery of imperial administration functioned efficiently. Both provincial and élite guard troops had proved their worth. The church of Constantinople was united in a form of spiritual worship without visual aids of figurative art, even though this iconoclast policy isolated it from the eastern Christians living under Arab rule and from the West. There Charles, King of the Franks and the Lombards, had just confirmed his role as the protector of the pope by an official visit to Rome. In Constantinople the classical Greek tradition of education was available to those who wished to pursue an administrative, legal or ecclesiastical career. Artistic production flourished. Above all, as a result of two long and successful reigns, Leo III's Syrian dynasty was well established and able to deal promptly with any opposition. Byzantium had begun to consolidate its profound reforms and extend its military might. Against this background, the first of the three women in purple emerged from within the ruling family to set Byzantium on a different course.

CHAPTER 2

Irene: the unknown empress from Athens

To arrive at Istanbul by sea is still one of the great thrills of modern travellers to ancient Byzantium. It was far more impressive in the eighth century, especially for those who had never seen such structures as it possessed. So for Irene, who first set eyes on the Queen City as a young girl early in November 769, it must have been extraordinarily exciting. Sailing from the palace of Hiereia on the opposite coast of Asia, Irene saw the profile of the site of Byzantium, the Acropolis hill that juts out into the Bosphoros at the point where it enters the Sea of Marmara, with the Golden Horn, the deep-water port, to the north. Approaching from the sea, she could not have missed the most visible monuments of the city: the huge rising dome of the cathedral church of Hagia Sophia, Holy Wisdom, visible on the horizon from a great distance; the honorary columns topped by statues, which broke into the skyline of the city, marking monuments set up by Constantine the Great, founder of the city, and many of his successors. Irene might have noticed the equestrian statue of Justinian atop his column in the square of Augousteion, or the column of the Goths on the Acropolis. In that era without photographs or postcards, nothing could have prepared her for the grandeur and scale of the Queen City. As her boat and the accompanying flotilla approached the Acropolis headland she could not have failed to observe the strong sea walls stretching for three miles along the shore.

The official announcement of Irene's arrival is reported in laconic style in the *Short History* by Patriarch Nikephoros: 'In the 8th indiction Constantine brought from Hellas a wife for his son Leo, namely Irene, and in the month of December he crowned her Augusta and, after uniting her with his son, celebrated their wedding'.[1] Theophanes comments in greater detail:

On 1 November of the 8th indiction Irene made her entrance from Athens. She came to the Imperial City from Hiereia, escorted by many *dromones* and *chelandia* decorated with silken clothes, and was met by the prominent men of the City and their wives who led the way before her. On the 3rd of the same month of November the patriarch went to the church of the Pharos in the palace, and the betrothal of the emperor Leo to the same Irene was celebrated. On 17 December Irene was crowned empress in the hall of the Augusteus. She proceeded to the chapel of St Stephen in the Daphne and received the marital crown along with Constantine's son, Leo.[2]

So Irene had embarked from central Greece late in October 769 and sailed through the Dardanelles, into the Sea of Marmara and over to the suburban palace of Hiereia, on the Asiatic shore (see map 2). Given the unpredictable weather and therefore sailing times, she disembarked at an imperial residence where she could rest before entering the Queen City. After a few days, when news of her arrival would have been made known, on 1 November she was transported over the Bosphoros, with many boats coming to escort her and ships flying silk sails. All the leading members of the city with their wives went to welcome her at this, her initial reception in Byzantium, which probably took place at the Boukoleon harbour.

Irene's landing at the Boukoleon must have been a very colourful and noisy affair, with the most distinguished citizens as well as a large crowd of local people all trying to get a glimpse of the new princess who was to become their empress. There may have been a musical element provided by members of the circus factions or simply by well-wishers who came to sing and dance in her honour. Irene disembarked to be greeted formally by the welcoming party. To ascend the steep incline to the Great Palace, she was probably carried in a litter preceded by representatives of the leading notables, perhaps accompanied by a military escort of *scholarioi* and an official herald. The less important inhabitants followed along behind while the streets were lined by people all pressing forward to see if she was really a beauty. From later medieval images that depict women being carried on a litter, it is clear that there were no curtains to protect them from the stares of the onlookers. Official Byzantine ceremonies required the participants to show themselves to the people.

Of course, Irene had not undertaken the journey from Greece alone: she was certainly accompanied by her own servants and companions, probably including a female relative who was later married most advantageously. She also brought her own trousseau of clothes, jewels, linen, furniture and so on although she was destined to wear official imperial costumes for a great part of her life. All her party and their baggage must have been transported up the hill towards the centre of the city that was reckoned the largest and most glorious in the world. As she was carried past the villas and dwellings on the slopes of the first district, she would have seen some of the most privileged areas occupied by members of the ruling family and their more distant relatives as well as old, established citizens of the city of Constantine. These were the people qualified to call themselves 'Byzantines', natives of the ancient city of Byzantium. From this district the views out over the Sea of Marmara rivalled the sights of the city: the massive structure of the Hippodrome, a large Roman circus that adjoined the Great Palace complex, and the public baths of Zeuxippos to the north. As they came to the brow of the hill she would again have caught sight of Hagia Sophia, the biggest church not only in the city but also in the entire Christian world of the time. It was then only a short distance to the Bronze Gatehouse (Chalke) of the Great Palace, decorated with imperial mosaics and antique sculpture, which formed its main entrance. Set behind walls which marked off a large area of the city, the palace was closely guarded and protected against assault. Amid the cheers and shouts of welcome, Irene was accompanied thus far, where an official imperial escort was awaiting her. This brief journey from the harbour to the palace in Constantinople constituted her first public appearance, however unofficial, and gave her an impression of the city in which she was to spend the next thirty years of her life, as Empress of Byzantium.

IRENE'S BACKGROUND

There has been no mention of Irene in the sources until this moment in 769, and the chroniclers give no hint as to why she had been selected for this unique honour. Fortunately, her background can be quite well documented and may provide clues to her particular qualifications for the role of the wife of the future ruler of Byzantium.

As we have seen, by the mid-eighth century Irene's homeland of central Greece formed part of the *thema* of Hellas, and both military and ecclesiastical forms of control had expanded to encompass a larger area under the direct control of Constantinople.[3] The general in charge of Hellas probably resided at Thebes, while Athens was one of the important ports through which naval contact was maintained. The fact that Irene embarked from Athens suggests that she may have lived in the city, which was more like a small fortified citadel within the walls of the Acropolis than the ancient city of Perikles. Its Christian character was symbolised by the conversion of the Parthenon into a church dedicated to the Virgin. During the eighth century the names of Bishops Marinos, John, Adamantios and Gregorios were recorded in graffiti on its columns, which marked the dates of their deaths on which special liturgies are held in their memory.[4] The Christian presence in medieval Athens, however, must have been greatly outweighed by the number of classical buildings, even if they were increasingly treated as deposits of good quality building material. Monuments dedicated to the ancient gods were now regarded as haunted rather than sacred spaces.

Through these two arms of central government, the military and the church, Constantinople was drawing the whole area much closer to the capital, making Greece and the islands serve its needs and support its policies. Such control is evident in the policy imposed by Constantine V when he ordered the transplantation of inhabitants from the region to the capital after an outbreak of plague in 747. Further confirmation of the effectiveness of the new *themata* was provided in 766, when the same emperor determined to restore the main aqueduct of the capital, constructed by Valens in the fourth century and destroyed during the Avar siege of 626. The epidemic of plague had been followed by a severe drought, which made this essential. 'He [Constantine V] collected artisans from different places and brought from Asia and Pontos 1,000 masons and 200 plasterers, from Hellas and the islands 500 clay workers and from Thrace itself 5,000 labourers and 300 brickmakers.'[5] All these were set to work under the direction of a patrician and, as a result, the aqueduct was restored and 'water flowed into the city'. The element of compulsion behind the activity is quite normal and was a tradition of imperial government (Diocletian, Constantine I and Justinian I provide similar instances of building mania). To undertake a massive public-works operation involving many miles of aqueduct stretching from the city walls out into the Belgrade forest, it was necessary to import workers. They may have been forced to remain in the city to swell the population.[6] But the most fascinating thing is that Hellas and the islands of the Aegean and the Adriatic, provided five hundred clay workers to form and fire the water pipes.[7] How did the emperor know where to find such a large number of ceramic workers who could make the right sort of water pipes?

Clearly, Constantine owed this knowledge to the thematic administration which had already established a certain amount of information about the skills available in Hellas and the islands. From lists of families who did not provide military recruits but practised other crafts, it would be possible for government agents to go out and press-gang the necessary number of clay workers. So the repair of the aqueduct involved a certain amount of administrative know-how, based on provincial government records. There was no point in setting out with a wish-list of skilled workers; the central administration in Constantinople had to know where it would find them, and did so thanks to the files kept by the *strategos*, or general in charge of each *thema*.

IRENE'S FAMILY

This slow process of reconnecting the regions of central Greece with the centre of Byzantine authority in the capital provides the backdrop against which we must now look at what precisely is known about Irene's family. From information supplied later in the *Chronicle* of Theophanes the Confessor, it is clear that her family was established in the region and known by a family name: the (Tes)sarandapechys (literally, forty pieces, forty cubits, probably a reference to one particularly tall family member, who had given this epithet to his relatives). Such nicknames lie at the base of several family identities in this period, such as Lachanodrakon (cabbage caterpillar) or Koutzodaktylos (short fingers). Others carried a geographical origin, 'Damaskenos', 'Sinaites' or 'Paphlagonites', for instance, or a particular trade, such as soap- or candle-making.[8] But most people, even emperors and high-ranking officials, were identified simply by their Christian names.

When she set out for Constantinople in 769 Irene was not named as a member of the Sarandapechys family, which suggests that her father was probably dead or that this name was not well known or meaningful enough to attract the attention of the chroniclers.[9] This may be confirmed by the fact that she later claimed to be an orphan. Being orphaned, however, did not mean that she was without relatives: she had lost her father, but her mother may still have been alive, though she is never mentioned in the sources. Others accompanied her, including an unnamed female relative who was later married to the Bulgar leader, Telerig. In the early ninth century another relative, Theophano, was chosen as the bride for the Emperor Staurakios. Irene must also have had a brother or sister, for her nephew is later documented. But as the information about all of them is derived from a later period, after Irene's promotion to empress, this says little about the family's previous standing in the region.[10] It was probably not from the highest ranks of whatever provincial aristocracy existed in eighth-century Greece, although in later years members were to fill important positions in local administration (obviously this prominence would have been partly a result of Irene's role as empress).

To assess how Irene came to be selected for such a singular honour, it is helpful to review the way such choices were traditionally made. Imperial princes and princesses were regularly married to representatives of important political allies. Leo III had consolidated a policy of friendship with the Khazars through the marriage of his son Constantine to a young Khazar princess named Čiček, which means flower. Their betrothal took place in 731/2 when both were still children (Constantine was twelve and Čiček was probably much younger as their only child was born nearly twenty years later). When she arrived in Constantinople, Čiček was renamed Irene (peace) on the occasion of her baptism into the Orthodox Church. In 750 she died after bearing a son, Leo. Constantine subsequently married Maria, who also died before 752, and finally his third wife Eudokia gave birth to many sons and a daughter. But Leo was his first-born, the eldest son, who was designated as emperor-elect and heir presumptive by his elevation as co-emperor (in June 751, at the age of eighteen months). Because of his mother's origin, he was known as Leo the Khazar.

In 769, when Leo was nineteen years old, Constantine V set about finding him a suitable bride. Throughout imperial history, such important issues as marriages were arranged by those who knew best (parents) and the children accepted this fact. Any number of foreign candidates might have been considered, or daughters of court officials, who were always anxious to promote their female relatives. In this case it seems that the emperor chose a girl from a family established in a remote area, where imperial control was critical to the empire. Hellas had experienced only two generations of provincial government, its churches had only recently been brought back under the control of the patriarch, but its coastlands were accessible to the capital by sea. The selection must have been the result of serious calculation: an alliance between Constantine V and the Sarandapechys family would bind one local family, and through it a significant part of central Greece, into a firm co-operation with the capital. Since Hellas also had a heavy presence of Slavic tribes, the expansion of imperial control, assisted by loyal orthodox families, would support their conversion and assimilation. Therefore, Irene might help to consolidate a new area of Christian expansion under Constantinople rather than Rome; to provide a base for the conversion of the Slavs; and to reinforce the new link created between immigrant workers and the capital. The choice of a wife from the region of Athens was a well judged move to demonstrate the renewed, expanding ambition of the empire, as well as its Homeric links, which were appreciated not only by the educated sector but by the population as a whole.

The emperor may have learned about Irene from the imperial officials who had visited the area to search for ceramic workers in 765/6.[11] But the key elements in his choice were that Irene was of the right age to marry Constantine V's son Leo, and that her family would strengthen the rule of Leo the Khazar, who would become emperor on the death of his father.

Both the bride and groom were required to give their consent to the marriage which had been arranged for them, even though they had no say in the actual choice of spouse. Since there is no record of her date of birth, we can only guess how old Irene was in relation to her future husband. If Leo was nearly twenty, Irene was probably at least fourteen or fifteen, which suggests that she may have been born between 750 and 755. She gave birth to their first child thirteen months after the marriage, indicating that at the time of their wedding she was probably past puberty, unlike some child brides who were betrothed at a very young age.

One further deduction may be made from the fact that Irene was chosen by Constantine V: she must have come from a family which supported the official imperial policy against icon veneration. Whatever else Irene knew about icons, in 769 when she prepared for her journey, she like the emperor, her future father-in-law, subscribed to the policy of iconoclasm. When she set sail from Athens in late October, knowing that she was destined to become the consort of the future ruler of the empire, what an amazing prospect lay before her. It must have been with great trepidation, as well as immense excitement, that the teenager from the provinces crossed the threshold of the Great Palace into the home of the emperors of Byzantium.

IRENE'S INTRODUCTION TO THE GREAT PALACE

Once she passed through the Chalke entrance and entered this enormous complex of buildings – ancient palaces, villas, reception halls, churches, baths and guardhouses, linked by gardens, corridors, galleries and decorated passages – Irene was entrusted to a group of attendants, ladies-in-waiting, deputed to take care of her, and to help her get used to the very formal, ceremonial life of the court. From descriptions preserved in the *Book of Ceremonies* we can build up a picture of what Irene experienced in her first months in the capital. We can track her as she is guided through the different buildings that together formed the Great Palace, the Kremlin of Byzantium, to the rooms within the women's quarters which had been assigned to her; we can imagine these private apartments, where a staff of female servants and eunuchs appointed to look after the young woman would instruct her about the role she had to perform during the long ceremonies that lay ahead.

After two days of coaching by these court officials, she was conducted to the church of the Pharos (lighthouse), dedicated to the Virgin, where the patriarch, the emperor, her future husband Leo, and most of the court were awaiting her. This was probably the first time that the young couple met in public. It is possible that portraits had been exchanged, so that they had some idea of what to expect. At the official betrothal, her first experience of a Byzantine ceremony, Irene must have gained a sense of the emphasis on formal movements, slow processions, gestures and acclamations, which marked the life of the court. In addition, as the ceremony took place in church, she met the Patriarch Niketas for the first time, and his clergy who subsequently performed the liturgy in the exquisite setting of this new palace chapel recently constructed by the emperor, Constantine V.[12]

Although, as an iconoclast, Constantine is not given credit for building churches by the prejudiced pro-icon authors of the period, it is clear that he had a major impact both within the Great Palace and also in the city. He not only restored the aqueduct but also rebuilt many churches which had collapsed during the earthquake of 740, such as St Irene. He also transformed the decoration of many others, replacing figural painting by images of the Hippodrome, chariot- and horse-racing as well as other secular, floral and vegetal patterns. While descriptions of the interior of the original Pharos church do not survive, this major new construction close to the imperial quarters in the Chrysotriklinos would have been endowed with the most lavish decoration, possibly in the non-figural 'Garden of Paradise' style, with buildings, animals, flowers and streams set in a forest of trees on a gold mosaic background.

Following the betrothal ceremony Irene was accompanied back to her quarters and during the next six weeks she underwent an intensive training in preparation for her coronation as empress and marriage to Leo. Now she had to get used to the heavy official costumes which she would wear in her new role as empress. These were already in the imperial wardrobes, tended by a host of official seamstresses who were probably very active during this period making sure that everything to be worn by the new empress fitted correctly. Irene's behaviour was crucial to the success of the ritual: how she stood and walked, when she made a turn, where she stopped to be acclaimed, to light a candle, or make an obeisance. There were no words to learn, in fact she would remain silent throughout the ceremony, but a whole series of movements had to be memorised, so that she, as the centre of attention, would perform the rites correctly. There is a daunting aspect to such a forced learning process: yesterday, a member of a relatively unknown provincial family, tomorrow the wife of the future Emperor of Byzantium. We can imagine the tension of those six weeks between Irene's arrival and her marriage on 17 December 769.

IRENE'S INAUGURATION AS EMPRESS: CORONATION AND MARRIAGE

Constantine V attached great importance to the marriage of his son because it confirmed Leo's superior status as his first-born son and the heir to the throne. As a baby Leo had been crowned co-emperor, and the position was confirmed in 769 when he was designated the future *basileus* (emperor) and Irene was crowned and acclaimed as *basilissa* (empress). In this way Constantine indicated that his five sons by Eudokia, his third wife, were to be excluded from the succession. These five step-brothers of Leo are known collectively as 'the caesars' because they were all promoted to the high rank of caesar. Despite this status and their mother's coronation as *augousta*[13] the previous March, their older stepbrother Leo the Khazar and his new wife were now singled out for the future glory of ruling the empire. There is no record of the actual marriage of Irene and Leo, or of Irene's coronation as empress, but the *Book of Ceremonies* provides clear and detailed instructions about how such inauguration rites are to be performed.[14]

In 769 the reigning emperor, Constantine V, performs the actual coronation with the help of his co-emperor and son, Leo. It is almost a private ceremony. After the reception of the Senate and courtiers by the emperors, they are dismissed from the Augousteos. The patriarch then enters with his clerical staff; his role is restricted to the blessing of the imperial tunic (*chlamys*), the crown and its pendants. Now the bride and empress-elect is ushered into the hall, wearing an imperial robe (*sticharin*) and a veil, which the emperors remove. The patriarch then presents the blessed objects to the emperors, who clothe Irene in the tunic, place the crown on her head and attach the pendants to it. These are the long strings of pearls clearly visible on pictures of the empress's official crown. Irene is now officially crowned, but her acclamation as empress is the essential part of the procedure. For the Byzantines, the most significant part of this day-long ritual is the following ceremony devoted to receptions at which she is presented to the court, the Senate, all the officials rank by rank, and their wives.

The first of these takes place immediately after her crowning in the Augousteos: when the patriarch and his staff have retired, an additional throne is set up for the newly crowned empress, beside the thrones of the emperors. The entire court is then presented. In turn the different groups of male officials are introduced, make a deep reverence bending down to the ground in *proskynesis*, and kiss the knees of the emperors and the empress. At a sign from the master of ceremonies they acclaim Irene and then leave the hall. Next it is the turn of the female members of the court hierarchy to perform a similar ceremony, making three deep reverences and kissing knees. First come the wives of the highest rank of officers (the *patrikiai*) and so on down to the eleventh-ranked *protiktorissai* and the *kentarchissai*.[15] This idea of kissing knees is embedded in Byzantine ceremonial. It carries all the connotations of extreme respect (*sebas*), constantly stressed in the text, while permitting a distant physical contact similar to the notion of kissing the hem of a garment of a distinguished prelate.

After this first reception the participants move to the portico of the Augousteos, called the Golden Hand (probably because a hand of blessing or welcome was displayed there). All the female patricians and women of senatorial rank accompany the new empress to this point, where the staff of her own bedchamber take over the role of escort, and she moves with them to the area of the Onopodion, the Single Foot. There the patricians are awaiting her, grouped in a semi-circular formation called a consistorium; at her arrival they again fall to the ground and at a sign they acclaim her, shouting 'Many and good years!' three times. In turn they escort her to the Dikionion (the place where a huge curtain is hung between two columns), where yet another group of senators waits to perform the deep reverence and acclaim her, as they move to the final reception on the terrace of the Tribunal (which forms part of the complex of the Nineteen Couches). While the Senate forms up on either side of the steps, the leaders of the élite military regiments (*tagmata*) go up to the terrace of the Tribunal where the Cross, sceptres, military ensigns and banners are all set up. When the Empress Irene enters she is led by two high-ranking court officials to the centre of this terrace. There the circus factions perform the long series of official coronation acclamations.

This is the high point of the coronation ritual for an empress. When she presents herself to the assembled crowds, Irene also performs an important ritual: she advances to the centre of the balustrade and lights candles which she offers to the cross placed here. At the moment when Irene makes her own gesture of ritual reverence to the cross, all the military standards of the armed forces, the banners, ensigns, sceptres and other holy objects are lowered, so that the material symbols of imperial authority imitate the action of bowing low to the cross and the new empress. At this point in the ceremony, Irene appears as an icon of imperial power, suitably regal, imposing, statuesque. But more importantly, she personifies the way that imperial power is transmitted from one generation to the next. She guarantees that the authority of the emperor, her husband, can be legitimately passed on through her children. She promises the continuing rule of the dynasty in power.

For Irene, this is the moment at which her role takes shape. While she stands there in her golden imperial robes, encrusted with precious stones and decorated with gold and silver thread, the factions chant a long series of acclamations in dialogue form. After invoking God's protection for the empire and its people, the chanters and the people repeat, each three times, a long list of acclamations.

This is the great day of the Lord, this is the day of the salvation of the Romans, this day is the joy and the glory of the world, on which the crown of the empire has been correctly put upon your head. Glory to God who is the master of all things! Glory to God who has made you empress! Glory to God who has crowned your head, may He who has crowned you, Irene, by His own hand, keep you in the purple for many years, for the glory and the exaltation of the Romans.[16]

For the first time Irene hears herself identified as *basilissa*, the female equivalent of *basileus* (the most official term for the ruler); she is associated with the purple worn by the rulers, and her own name is inserted into the chant so that the new empress is officially named Irene. After this exchange of acclamations, the empress salutes both factions and the assembled crowds on either side with a low obeisance and leaves the terrace. As she retraces her steps, escorted by the senators, she is again greeted and acclaimed by groups of officials. When she reaches the Augousteos the entire staff of the private imperial quarters, chiefly eunuchs employed in the care of wardrobes and bedrooms, welcomes her with an acclamation in Latin, 'Bene, bene!', a survival from the sixth century when Latin was regularly spoken in Byzantium.

The formal part of the coronation is now over and the empress proceeds to the church of St Stephen in the Daphne Palace where the emperors await her for the wedding service. Leo is already wearing his imperial crown and of course Irene is now also wearing hers. Even though the marriage service is performed in church, involves an ecclesiastical blessing and is considered a sacrament, marriage is not yet viewed as a religious ceremony. The core of any marriage lies in the civil arrangement between two families, represented by the parents of the two partners: the exchange of contracts, accompanied by the dowry and wedding gifts.

During the liturgy, the imperial couple leave the church and only return to receive their wedding crowns, *stephanoi*, from the patriarch. Possibly these resemble gold filets which can be worn in addition to the imperial crowns (*stemmata*).[17] The patriarch probably joins their right hands and rings are exchanged, but there is little of the ceremony associated with modern Greek Orthodox weddings. Once the ritual is over, they emerge from the church to further receptions and acclamations, before making a slow progress through different parts of the palace to their nuptial chamber in the Magnaura. This is quite distant from the Daphne and involves a long procession through the gardens, where there are trees and stables. The factions play their organs, the singers stand on either side and shout greetings and then accompany the imperial couple into their bedroom. Here Leo and Irene deposit their imperial crowns on the nuptial bed and then make their way to the wedding banquet, which takes place in the Hall of the Nineteen Couches. Still wearing their wedding crowns, they participate in the feast together with all the guests, male and female, whom the emperor has invited.

But the ceremony does not end there.[18] For the empress there is one further and highly significant ritual which takes place on the third day after the wedding.[19] This is the official 'day of the bath', when the empress is escorted to one of the many baths inside the Great Palace. On this occasion the factions establish themselves on either side of the passage through which the procession must pass, with three organs strategically placed to accompany the cortège. It is customary for an entire orchestra to accompany the officials who have responsibility for escorting certain objects which are involved in the ceremony – the perfume box, other receptacles, towels and necessities for the laundry – down to the bath and church of St Christina. This complex appears to form an integral part of the Magnaura Palace but the procession from the nuptial chamber is still a lengthy business because of the number of people involved and the noisy musical accompaniment.

Once the objects have been escorted to the bath, the empress comes out of the nuptial chamber followed by the lady-of-honour (*parakathistra*) and two other ladies-in-waiting who all carry ornamental porphyry *granates* (possibly small, carved representations of pomegranates) encrusted with precious stones.[20] Irene's appearance provokes factional acclamations, first by the Blues and then by the Greens, each one in turn shouting and all three organs sounding. Senators escort this unusual cortège on its passage through the Magnaura Palace as far as the platform at the head of the steps which lead down to the bath. There one of the organs is played and the consuls take over the role of escort as Irene proceeds down the spiral staircase to the bath of St Christina. When she emerges from the bath, the senators again accompany her and the factions walk along chanting acclamations all the way back to the nuptial chamber. There they form a consistorium until Irene has gained the right part of the apse of the chamber, and only leave her once the final chant has been delivered. In this way, the aim of the marriage is emphasised and the hope of offspring restated. To an empress, the endlessly repeated slogans,

'Many years, many years, many years!' may carry a very slight threat. Will she enjoy many years of imperial status if she fails to produce the much desired male child?

THE FIRST YEAR AS EMPRESS

On 20 December, the Sunday before Christmas, Irene was at the centre of the court's attention during this ceremony of the bath. The following celebration of Christ's birth and the period of feasting which lasted till Epiphany (6 January) was a joyful one in all medieval Christian cultures, and gave the new empress an opportunity to observe the court in its most brilliant form. In addition to the important feast-days, the New Year was celebrated in almost pagan style by Hippodrome racing. Imperial banquets were given nearly every day. But Irene's new position reminded her of her one overriding duty: to give birth to a son and heir to Leo, to ensure the maintenance of the Syrian ruling family into which she had been married. Leo was expected to spend the wedding night with his bride but since he had his own quarters, they may not have lived together in any normal sense. He visited her, frequently one assumes, until her pregnancy was evident. After about six months Irene knew that she was on the way to fulfilling the primary aim of her marriage. Her health and the health of her unborn baby then became the major concern of the palace.

During this period Irene held sway in her own quarters, most probably in the Chrysotriklinos area. She was mistress of this small part of the palace and the court officials on duty were bound to obey her orders. Although she was probably no more than sixteen years old, this was the time when her will and character were tested to the full. Since Leo shared the more prominent areas of the palace devoted to the senior emperor and empress, she might find herself quite alone. Her husband's five stepbrothers also had their own quarters, each with their own servants. The extended family may not have met together often, but certainly all were involved in the liturgical and secular ceremonies which the court observed at Easter and other major church festivals. For the entire calendar year of 770 Irene participated in these gatherings and observed what occurred. In particular, she watched her mother-in-law, Eudokia, very closely, for the senior empress performed a role that would pass one day to Irene. Whether Eudokia helped Irene or ignored her as a threat to the imperial claims of her own sons, the caesars, the young bride like many another daughter-in-law was learning on the job. By watching what happened, listening to the formulaic acclamations and instructions given by the master of ceremonies, who directed the various stages, she followed the rituals in order to learn about the role which she would in due course play.

On 14 January 771, Irene gave birth to a son, who was born in the Porphyra chamber of the palace.[21] This was only the second time that a child born in the special chamber lined with purple would bear the title *porphyrogennetos* (born in the purple). The Porphyra, redolent with the imperial associations of purple-dyed silk or purple stone, was reserved for female relatives of the ruling emperor. Its dominant colour, obtained through the use of porphyry or purple-dyed hangings, emphasised the most luxurious materials, which were restricted to the imperial family in Byzantium. Although the date of the room's construction is unknown, the title *porphyrogennetos* is first documented in a manuscript of 763 in reference to Leo IV, Irene's husband.[22] Leo himself had been born there in 750. This suggests that Constantine V, or his father Leo III, may have been responsible for building the room or adapting a previous bedchamber to perform this special function. While Leo's half-brothers and sisters may also have been born in the Porphyra, none was regularly identified with this highly prestigious epithet.

Irene's great fortune in becoming the mother of a male child who would inherit his father's power was immediately celebrated by the court and the entire city of Constantinople. Such a happy event was always marked by further public acclamations listed in the *Book of Ceremonies* as appropriate for the birth of an heir to the emperor.[23] In addition, it gave rise to ceremonies connected with the naming of the child in which Irene took no part. These include the Senate congratulating the emperor, a procession to the Great Church for the patriarchal prayer of thanksgiving for the successful delivery, and a reception in the hall of the Sigma, where the factions request that the event shall be marked by games given in the Hippodrome. They then hang out the flag, which is a sign that horse-racing will be held the next day, and to order all the people to gather in the Hippodrome to learn the name of the newborn *porphyrogennetos*. The following day, at the announcement of his name, predictably Constantine, the acclamations are made, and the races held.

Further, the emperor provides a special drink, called *lochozema* (literally, broth of childbed), which is distributed free to the whole population. Within the palace, toasting the new prince takes place at the portico of the Hall of the Nineteen Couches, and members of each rank come in turn to drink the *lochozema*. In the city, moreover, the same drink is laid out all along the main street (*Mese*) from the Bronze Gate of the palace to the Forum of the Ox (*Boos*), and the poor – 'our brothers in Christ' – are particularly requested to come and toast the child for seven days. The emperor provides funds for this distribution of imperial largesse whenever his wife is successfully delivered of a son. Even if Irene was not able to hear the acclamations from her own quarters, these events must have been relayed to her.

Next, the empress must prepare herself for the major ceremony when she will receive the congratulations of the entire court. This is a magnificent celebration prescribed for the eighth day after the birth. The empress's bedchamber is specially decorated for the purpose with golden hangings from other parts of the palace, spread over the bed and hung on the walls, and lamps with numerous candles are lit. The mother is made as comfortable as possible and the baby is dressed in a special robe. Then the staff of the bedchamber, the eunuchs in charge of the private imperial quarters, offer their congratulations. Immediately afterwards the ladies of the court enter in turn, according to their rank (women first, because childbirth is essentially a female business, although the emperor gets the first congratulatory acclamations. Even the widows of past office-holders are allowed in before the men). Each group brings congratulations and greetings for the mother, together with a little gift. Then the men of the court follow suit, starting with members of the Senate and finishing with the lesser officials. This may be only a much grander version of the celebration for a successful delivery accorded to most women, but for Irene it marked the moment at which she had ensured the continuity of the Syrian dynasty.

For forty days Irene, like all new mothers who had given birth, was considered unclean and confined to her quarters. Her gradual return to more public spaces culminated in the church ceremony of her cleansing, when she was readmitted to the ecclesiastical community. This ritual of cleansing was a necessary stage in every woman's experience of childbirth. Once it was over, Irene participated in the baptism of her son, a rite performed again by the patriarch, this time in the cathedral church of Hagia Sophia.[24] Following established tradition the boy was named after his grandfather, Constantine V, the ruling emperor. In his chronicle Theophanes implies that it was quite unusual for a grandfather to witness the birth of his son's son.[25] Rarely did an emperor live long enough to enjoy such a felicitous event – many died on the battlefield, or fell victim to an assassin, often at a much younger age than Constantine V, who had ruled for thirty years. In 771, not only did Irene's son Constantine represent the fourth generation of a highly successful dynasty, but he also held out the promise of a peaceful continuity of its authority well into the future. The future looked bright for Irene as she went in procession to Hagia Sophia for the baptism of her first-born son. She had achieved the first and most important responsibility of an imperial princess.

IRENE AS MOTHER AND EMPRESS

Between 771 and 775 Constantine V's foreign policy was dominated by campaigns against both the Arabs and the Bulgars, while internally he continued to prosecute known iconophiles. He thus strengthened the link between military triumphs (against Arab raiding parties in Syke in 771, Mopsuestia in 772, and against the Bulgars in 773) and official iconoclasm, which gave his soldiers great confidence. Most of the evidence for iconoclast persecution is associated with Michael Lachano-drakon, the general in charge of the Thrakesion *thema*, who was particularly active in this respect. Many monks who refused to accept the Definition of Faith issued by the iconoclast council of 754 were tortured, blinded and exiled; those who did not resist were forced to marry nuns. The official persecution of iconophiles, their illuminated books, paintings, and monastic buildings, was vigorously pursued in this region at least, apparently to the great approval of the emperor. This pattern was broken in 774 when a naval disaster destroyed many warships sent to Bulgaria and provoked a final campaign in 775, which was intended to crush Bulgaria once and for all. But during this offensive Constantine was wounded in the thigh and died as he was being transported back to the capital from Selymbria.[26]

After his death in August 775, Constantine V was reverently buried in the imperial mausoleum attached to the church of the Holy Apostles by his surviving wife, Eudokia, and his sons. The eldest, Leo, was acclaimed as sole emperor. At all moments of succession a number of significant *rites de passage* take place in addition to the obvious replacement of one emperor by another. As a result of Leo's acclamation, Irene now became the senior empress, and the widowed Eudokia was demoted to the status of empress-mother. At such a major change-over, the older empress should make way for the younger one to take possession of the official quarters and bedchambers reserved for the reigning emperor. On certain occasions, this did not happen and the new imperial couple found themselves excluded from their official quarters.[27] In 775 there is no suggestion that Eudokia followed this example, which always led to embarrassing conflicts. She probably moved out and took up residence in a separate palace or a monastery in the vicinity. Her five sons, the caesars, however, may have been less willing to give up their unrestricted access to the Great Palace. Certainly their father's death, Leo's acclamation as sole ruler of Byzantium, and the existence of his son Constantine, reduced the chances of any of them ever becoming emperor.

There is considerable evidence that the military leaders of the provinces were anxious to settle the issue of the imperial inheritance by removing the caesars from consideration. They came to the capital for the celebration of the subsequent Easter feast with a great crowd of people who gathered in the Hippodrome. Throughout holy week of 776, from Palm Sunday to Thursday, the demonstrators chanted their support for Leo and his young son Constantine as rulers. On Good Friday, Leo summoned the Senate, the army and the people and reminded them of the oath they had taken to accept only himself, his son Constantine, and his descendants as rulers. This was repeated by oral acclamation in the presence of the relics of the True Cross which were kept in St Sophia, and also recorded in writing. To ensure family unity and the agreement of his half-brothers, the youngest, Eudokimos, was promoted to the rank of *nobelissimos* on the following day, Holy Saturday. The caesars then accompanied Leo IV to the church of Hagia Sophia, where they performed the prescribed liturgy of changing the altar cloth. All the senators, followed by the military and civilian population, then laid their scrolls containing the written record of the oath that they had sworn, on the altar, the holiest place in the holiest church in Byzantium. Leo went up into the ambo of the church with the patriarch and begged the people present to accept Constantine as their emperor, 'from the Church and from the hand of Christ'. 'Be our surety, O Son of God, that we are receiving the lord Constantine as our emperor from Thy hand that we may guard him and die for his sake!' they all shouted.[28] Little did they know that even the hand of God would not save him from the hand of woman.

By this means a particular imperial succession was decided. All the essential constituent elements: church, army, senate and people, gave their agreement. A novel rite of acclamation was introduced into the

Easter Saturday liturgy in order to designate Leo's son Constantine as the heir to the throne. Once Leo had this approval he asked the patriarch to arrange the coronation ceremony, which took place at dawn on Easter Sunday, 14 April 776. A portable altar was set up in the imperial box overlooking the Hippodrome. Here, in the sight of all who were gathered below and on the seating tiers of the vast racecourse, the patriarch blessed the imperial regalia and Leo IV crowned his five-year-old son Constantine. After this very public act, they all processed to the Great Church to celebrate the most significant feast in the ecclesiastical calendar, the Easter commemoration of the Resurrection of Christ, which promises the salvation of all true believers and their eternal life. A recent analysis of this important achievement emphasises that, in the context of the Easter celebration, the Byzantines would have understood Leo's presentation of his son to the people of Constantinople as a parallel to the divine gift of the Son of God to the world.[29] The patriarch is associated with every stage of the procedure to guarantee the succession of Constantine, to the exclusion of his uncles. The church thereby gives its support to the rights of the eldest son and attempts to remove any claims that might be made by the caesars, children of Eudokia.

It is significant that, as the mother of the infant emperor now designated as the sole heir to imperial power, Irene took part in the Easter service of 776 in the cathedral church. She arrived in the south-east corner of the gallery (*katechoumena*) via the private, raised passage, which linked palace and church, accompanied by members of the imperial guard (*scholai*) bearing sceptres. Of course, her participation would be expected; the emperors always took part in this central feast of the church. But in 776, following the elevation of her son as co-emperor, Irene's presence is noted, as is her arrival independently of the male rulers.

The attempt to bar the caesars from imperial power did not remove their ambitions. On the contrary, they had been plotting throughout their father's reign in a great power struggle to capture the succession. Irene must have been aware of this rivalry and of the fact that the birth of her son had set back their claims. The young prince Constantine's coronation as emperor may have provoked them to try and get rid of their older stepbrother Leo right away. For only a few weeks later, in May 776, Nikephoros the eldest of the caesars was accused of mounting a conspiracy. A council was held and all the brothers were stripped of their titles and exiled to Cherson, because they had broken the oath they had taken to their father, Constantine V. This was only the first of many periods of exile from which the emperor's half-brothers continued to plot against him and, later, against Constantine VI. In 781/2, 792 and 799 they were the focus of revolts, which were all put down. The caesars may have been exploited by other dissatisfied factions within the empire, rather than actively trying to gain the throne. They finally lost all potential as imperial candidates twenty-three years later in 799, when the younger four were blinded on Irene's orders.[30]

Back in 776, however, they were exiled to the northern coast of the Black Sea. In the same year one further event draws attention to the importance that Irene had already attained as empress. When the Bulgarian ruler Telerig sought refuge in Constantinople, he was welcomed by Leo IV. Telerig adopted Christianity, received baptism with the emperor standing godfather to him, was promoted to the rank of patrician and then married to one of Irene's relatives. She is not named, but as the empress's cousin, niece or sister she moved in the most eminent social circles of the court. The alliance brought Telerig a high-ranking wife to match his own new Byzantine status. Such measures are regularly recorded as it was customary for the imperial court to foster rival claims to distant regions.

A similar instance is provided by the case of Adelgis, son of the last king of the Lombards, Desiderius, who was dispossessed by Charlemagne's conquest of Pavia (774). After spending twenty years in Constantinople, where he was known as Theodotos, he was finally sent back to Italy to claim his title (unsuccessfully as it turned out). His son Grimoald also received a bride from Byzantium who was related to the imperial family. In welcoming and supporting such disaffected elements, the emperors hoped these claimants would one day repay their generous hospitality by imposing a pro-Byzantine policy in their own countries. The practice serves as a reminder of the numerous suppliants and foreigners who were maintained by the imperial court, attended most gatherings and thus became influenced by the Byzantine style of rule. Such methods of induction were by no means new; most ancient civilisations had developed similar routines; but in the early medieval period the court of Constantinople was one of the very few that could and did sustain a brilliant cycle of ceremonial life, which outsiders found deeply impressive.

The marriage of a Bulgarian prince to one of Irene's relations thus confirmed the importance of her family (of which so little is known).

Telerig's welcome among the Byzantines appears to have weakened the Bulgars who did not provoke further warfare against the empire for many years. But the eastern regions were repeatedly invaded and devastated by the Arabs. In 777 Leo IV sent the combined forces of all the eastern *themata* against Germanikeia in northern Syria and they won a decisive victory, which was celebrated with a triumph at the palace of Sophianai. This was an imperial residence on the Asian side of the Bosphoros, where the troops traditionally received congratulations after battles and a distribution of the war booty. Young Prince Constantine accompanied his father and both sat enthroned while the spoils were given out. The victory parade in the city came later, and followed the prescribed route, entering Constantinople by the Golden Gate, passing many major monuments and terminating in the Hippodrome, where the emperors again presided from the imperial box.

LEO IV AND ICONOCLASM

In both his foreign and domestic policies, Leo IV appears to have continued his father's traditions and supported iconoclasm, though when Patriarch Niketas died he was replaced by a reader (*lektor*) on the patriarchal staff, Paul, who later claimed to have been critical of iconoclasm. During Leo's reign a few exiled iconophiles were permitted to return. Within the palace, however, when Leo is said to have discovered a plot to make icons available for certain eunuch officials in their private quarters, he took a very hard line.[31] Since icons had been banned and their veneration condemned by the church council of 754, those responsible knew they were running a risk. After investigation, Iakobos, the *papias*, four other *koubikoularioi* (all palace eunuchs) and a number of unnamed pious men were arrested, scourged and publicly humiliated by being forced to walk down the main street of the city in chains to the Praitorion, where they were imprisoned. Their hair was cut off, a sign that they had committed a serious crime. Theophanes, one of their number, later died and was in due course acclaimed as an iconophile martyr.

Irene was not associated with this event.[32] Later sources, however, add her name to the conspirators, and a twelfth-century version by Kedrenos proposes a graphic confrontation between the emperor and his wife, whom he accuses of venerating icons secretly. He denounces her and says that he will never sleep with her again.[33] Recently this account has ingeniously been attributed to a source nearly contemporary with the events it describes. It would thus preserve a true account of Irene's iconophile sympathies before the 780s.[34] According to this reconstruction, Irene was known as an iconophile before her marriage to Leo IV. Her father-in-law Constantine V made her swear on the Holy Gospels that she would never bring icon veneration into the palace, that she would in fact observe his iconoclast policy in perpetuity. But she circumvented all these oaths and stealthily restored the cult of icons. As a result, the eunuchs of the imperial bedchamber were found bringing in icons (at Irene's request). Once her true identity had been revealed, Leo IV, a wicked iconoclast, turned against her. And for her part, in order to hasten her intention of restoring icons, Irene did nothing to prevent Leo's death, which is attributed to carbuncles which grew on his forehead as a result of wearing a particularly beautiful and richly decorated crown.

This description of Irene seeks to identify her from her birth as a devout and pious icon venerator, who clung to the condemned policy despite the opposition of Constantine V and insisted on having her own icons in the palace. It is both highly flattering to the young empress and humiliating for the ruling emperor. Obviously neither aspect is at all likely, but the determination to prove Irene a lifelong iconophile can result in many twists and turns of the historical record. The argument about an eighth-century source which documents Irene's actual words is patently the work of writers who lived much later and sought additional ways to blacken the name of Constantine, seen as the heretical iconoclast ruler. That such a powerful emperor would ever have chosen for his eldest son a bride who supported idolatry (as the iconoclasts conceived of icon veneration) is inconceivable. That he should have tried to win the agreement of a young princess (aged perhaps fifteen) by making her swear on the Bible not to follow iconophile practices, suggests that he was an imbecile and she a headstrong individual. On the contrary, he was the most powerful man in the Byzantine Empire and she the extremely fortunate young woman selected to join the court. Since the choice of bride was in Constantine's gift, Irene represented the weaker party and the one honoured by his choice, which was made for political reasons. The notion that she might have arrived in the capital to disagree with the emperor over such a fundamental theological issue ignores the fact that this would automatically have disqualified her.

There is thus no way that the testimony of Kedrenos, written over three centuries after the events, can be adduced to prove that Irene was always an iconophile. Like all later historians who revised the history of Byzantium in the eighth century, Kedrenos found inexplicable gaps in the surviving narrative of Theophanes and sought to fill them. This process can be plotted from the ninth to the twelfth century, revealing the growth of iconophile traditions, bent on reclaiming Irene as one of their heroines. The invented story of Leo's anger at his wife's veneration of religious images does, however, draw attention to a particularly significant silence in the *Chronicle* of Theophanes. No mention is ever made of other offspring of Irene and Leo; Constantine remained an only child. This situation is not without precedent but it is most unusual. For medieval rulers there was safety in numbers, even if sibling rivalry might result. The accidental death of an only son would be viewed as a tragedy by any emperor, so most wanted to engender many children and their wives normally gave birth regularly every two years or so. Why did Leo and Irene have no more offspring?

Kedrenos found the answer in the story that the emperor was so furious with his wife that he refused to sleep with her ever again. But this cannot be considered a serious explanation. If Irene had indeed been found venerating one of the banned icons, then she, like the palace officials, would surely have been punished. Divorce and exile might have been in order for an empress caught defying the canons of the church in this fashion. Leo could then have remarried and produced many more children, as his father had after the deaths of his first and second wives. But it was only the eunuch officials of the palace who became martyrs for the iconophile cause. Leo would certainly have continued sleeping with his wife, in the hope that she would give birth to more sons.

One possible reason for their lack of further offspring may lie in the skills of those women who knew how to prevent conception or to provoke a miscarriage. Such gynaecological knowledge may have been very primitive but it was practised and was sufficiently effective to be regularly condemned in both civil and church law.[35] It is also possible that Irene simply failed to conceive between 772 (allowing about eighteen months after the birth of Constantine) and 780, when her husband died. The birth of her first child may have been complicated in ways that made it harder for her to conceive a second time. One later piece of information about Irene's health may possibly be relevant. Between 780 and 790 Irene was cured of a haemorrhage by the healing waters of the church of the Virgin of the Spring (*tes Peges*) and set up mosaic images as a thank-offering.[36] Whether this reflected an internal gynaecological problem is quite unknown. But in light of the pressure on imperial couples to have many children, and the expectation that an apparently healthy young empress would give birth at roughly two-yearly intervals, her infertility remains a mystery. It is not resolved by proposing that Leo IV wilfully chose not to have intercourse with her.

A further objection to the additional elements of the story as preserved in Kedrenos is that Theophanes knows nothing of Irene's secret iconophile convictions. And since this chronicler is largely favourable to the empress, had he been able to show how brave and strong she was during her husband's lifetime, he would surely have done so. He makes no comment on Irene's religious beliefs until the middle of the 780s, leaving readers to guess that she observed the iconoclast regulations, as did the vast majority of the population, whatever their private views. During the fifteen-year period from her arrival in 769 until about 784, when the empress appointed her chief secretary as patriarch, Irene witnessed many changes. Her own views were probably formed less by preconceived ideas than by political and social factors. The plot by palace officials may perhaps have been her first exposure to the deep undercurrent of iconophile sympathy that survived the condemnation of icons in 754. Whether it influenced Irene or not, it made her aware of the serious divisions within the Byzantine church and between it and the other patriarchates, where iconophile practice was maintained.

Leo IV's personal views on icons remain unclear. He applied the church's condemnation and his father's theological objections to icon venerators, and he would not tolerate them in his private quarters, at the heart of his own power base. So he dismissed the eunuchs who had challenged his authority and made a public spectacle of their punishment as a warning to others. But there is no evidence that he believed that icons were necessarily idolatrous. The fact that the plotters were not put to death may even signal a slight shift in the application of imperial iconoclast policy. Certain exiled iconophiles are said to have returned to the empire during his reign. Leo, however, was more concerned with the important business of combating the Arabs and extending imperial control to different regions of the empire through the *themata* system of provincial government. He ordered the removal of heretical Syrian Jacobites from the eastern borderlands to Thrace, to strengthen a weakly populated area which was proving increasingly useful for the food supplies of the capital. Theology does not appear to have been one of Leo's major interests.

His reign, however, was brief and his death at the age of thirty sudden and unexpected. Leo is said to have been inordinately fond of jewels and particularly a jewelled crown belonging to the Great Church (Hagia Sophia). But constant wearing induced the growth of carbuncles on his head, and these in turn gave him a raging fever from which he died. This suggests, in its extremely curt and unconvincing fashion, that no one knew why the emperor died; another mysterious development for which later historians sought reasons elsewhere. And, in the light of what Irene was to achieve, her connivance at Leo's early demise was suggested: it might have been encouraged by slow poison, or the refusal of marital relations. Such accusations are not made by the sources compiled close to the period, which provide no clue as to why Leo died and do not even mention Irene.

The sudden death of her husband on 8 September 780 created a totally new situation for Irene. Her immediate concern must have been to secure the succession of her son Constantine, who had been crowned as co-emperor. But at the age of nine and a half he could not rule in his own right and would need guidance for at least six years. As his mother, Irene would automatically be appointed to a Regency Council since she was the individual considered most likely to have his best interests at heart. Irene could also exercise rather more authority as a widow than as a wife, not only over her son, but over her own person. In 780, while she arranged and participated in the funerary rites for Leo IV, who was buried in the imperial mausoleum beside his father, Irene must have considered how to secure her own position and that of her son. She was then about twenty-five years old.

IRENE AS REGENT (780–90)

Under the heading for the 6273rd year of the world since its creation, the writer of the *Chronographia* attributed to Theophanes, makes a grand claim: God now permitted a widow and her orphan son to glorify Him as had once been done by 'the weak hands of fishermen and illiterate folk'.[37] To compare a woman to the apostles was obviously extraordinary, but in his eulogistic account of her rule Theophanes lavishes praise on 'the most pious Irene'. This is, of course, dependent on what she will do later for the church, by restoring the icons to their honoured place. But he reads back into the moment of Leo's death a miraculous and divine intervention.

The Regency Council must have included Patriarch Paul and other leaders of the civilian and military bureaucracies, nominated to rule in the name of the young emperor and to protect Constantine's imperial claims. Irene took her place with them and was acclaimed with her son as joint ruler of the empire. The first coins issued in 780 display Constantine VI to the right of the cross, taking the place of the senior emperor, with his mother Irene to the left. On the reverse the three preceding generations of the Syrian dynasty are depicted: Leo IV, Constantine V and Leo III. In this way all those who handled the new coins could see that the young boy-emperor, who had been crowned by his father in 776, had now acceded to imperial power which he shared with his mother Irene (see plate 1a).[38]

Coin types were a most telling mechanism of legitimating Byzantine rule. Money circulated quite widely; soldiers received their pay in gold coins, taxes had to be paid in the same gold *solidi*, while bronze coins served for everyday use and silver was reserved for commemorative issues. Since official announcements of the change of ruler often took several weeks to reach distant parts of the empire, coins were important bearers of news as well as a vital element in imperial propaganda. The circulation of the new issue of coins reinforced the message which Irene wished to publicise: namely, that the Syrian dynasty was firmly in control, now in its fourth generation, under the joint government of Constantine VI and herself.

As Irene must have anticipated, the caesars reacted to the news of their half-brother's death with renewed hope. Immediately after the forty days of mourning following his burial, they challenged Irene's position by conspiring to elevate the eldest, Nikephoros, as emperor. The plot was discovered, however, and many eminent officials such as Bardas, previously general of the Armeniakon, Gregorios, *logothetes tou dromou* (foreign minister), Constantine, *domestikos ton exkoubitoron* (leader of the crack troops, *exkoubitors*), and Theophylaktos, son of Rangabe, the naval commander (*drouggarios*) of the Dodecannese, were apprehended. Irene had them all scourged, tonsured and banished.[39] For Nikephoros and his brothers she reserved the punishment of forcing them to become clerics (which meant that they could no longer marry) and making them serve in the Great Church at the following feast of Christmas. She also decided that during this celebration she would perform the ceremonial restoration of the crown which had allegedly caused her husband's death to its rightful place. This crown had been further embellished with pearls at her orders. Whether it was the so-called crown of Maurice, which that emperor had suspended above the altar table in Hagia Sophia at Easter 601, or one later presented by Herakleios, it was indeed part of the holy objects (*hagia skeue*) belonging to the cathedral church. So, by bringing it back, the empress restored it to its correct position, having added to its beauty and value.

By using a liturgical event to make a political gesture which brought her prominently into public view while displaying her generosity, Irene demonstrated a particular flair for publicity. It was to become one of the hallmarks of her style of government. Obviously she understood how to make the most of an official function by transforming it into a personal intervention. On this occasion, the Christmas feast required her presence in the cathedral church. Her imperial role in the celebration of Christ's birth was greatly enhanced when those who had recently opposed her were forced, as clerics, to administer the Eucharist to the population. She must have sensed the public impact that her presence would have beside them: the sons of Constantine V, dressed in clerical garb, serving at the altar rail, while she flaunted the most colourful and gold-embroidered imperial costume, and returned the crown to its hallowed place above the high altar. Her grasp of the symbolism involved is exemplary, although it is doubtful whether a contemporary commentator would have thought in those terms. But reading the text of Theophanes today, one cannot but be struck by the masterful way in which Irene disposed of the caesars, who had dared to mount a challenge to her authority and that of her son.

To consolidate her position, Irene appointed military commanders and established her own trusted servants in positions of responsibility. References to 'the eunuchs of her household' indicate that she promoted these representatives of the third sex and used them to reinforce her authority. John the *sakellarios* (treasurer), was made commander-in-chief of the armed forces and led them against numerous Arab raids; Theodoros, a patrician, was sent to put down a rebellion in Sicily, and the patrician Staurakios was made head of the civil administration. In this way Irene deployed the staff of her personal quarters to deal with military and civil problems, though she also maintained other generals who had effectively served her husband. One of these, Elpidios, who had previously been governor (*strategos*) of Sicily, Irene sent back to this post, only to discover two months later that he had supported the revolt of the caesars. So she sent another official to arrest Elpidios, and when the Sicilians refused to hand him over, she had his wife and sons whipped, tonsured as monastics and imprisoned. Elpidios eventually defected to the Arabs in North Africa, presumably abandoning his family. There is no evidence that Irene deposed any iconoclast generals like Michael Lachanodrakon who had not taken sides with the caesars; indeed, she probably needed to maintain all those who had military experience, given the number of conspirators who had been arrested.

Her handling of the challenge displayed a skill that few would have predicted in the young 'Irene from Athens'. She had had no previous experience of politics, although over the past eleven years she must have observed how emperors dealt with opposition. On Leo's death in 780 many high-ranking officials thought that they could dispose of her quickly and establish Nikephoros as a male ruler more to their liking. In this they assumed she was a weak woman, and not a highly ambitious Regent with a strong sense of self-preservation. By her decisive action against the plotters and their dispersal to various places of exile as clerics, she demonstrated sound judgement and a determination to protect the imperial inheritance for her son.

MARRIAGE NEGOTIATIONS WITH THE FRANKS

In the second year of their official joint rule, Irene dispatched ambassadors to the West to negotiate a bride for Constantine. In 781 they had met with Charles in Rome and established the first contacts between the Byzantine Regency and the Frankish monarch. One year later they had to make the longer sea journey to Venice and then by land over the Alps to wherever the king was residing. After successful discussions with Charles, one of his daughters, Rotrud (rendered in Greek as *Erythro*, Red), was betrothed to the young Byzantine emperor. As Constantine was just eleven years old, Rotrud may have been about the same age or younger. A court eunuch, the notary Elissaios, remained in the West to teach her Greek.[40] The plan was for him to instruct Rotrud in 'the customs of the Roman Empire', which were preserved in Constantinople, so that she would have some grasp of the Byzantine world when the time came for her to travel to the East.

Embassies had been going to and fro between the Frankish and Byzantine courts for years, and with greater frequency since the Frankish conquest of northern Italy, which left Byzantium with no outpost there.[41] Constantine V had even proposed a marriage alliance of the type that Irene now hoped to realise for her son. But it was an ambitious scheme for Irene to ally herself with the most powerful ruler in the West, who had just captured Pavia and crowned himself King of the Lombards using their traditional iron crown. Charles was also on very good terms with Hadrian, the Bishop of Rome, who still refused to accept the iconoclast council of 754. Further, Irene was aware of Frankish ambitions in Italy: Charles was well placed to launch attacks on the Lombard duchies south of Rome, a policy which might threaten the Byzantine provinces of southern Italy and even Sicily.

Through a marriage alliance Irene hoped to deter Charles's military ambitions. She may also have considered the possibility of easing the schism with Rome, since Charles and Pope Hadrian both opposed the iconoclast position on religious images. But the chief aim of the embassy of 782 was to secure a bride for Constantine, a suitable girl who would one day become empress, just as Irene had. On the return of the embassy, Constantine learned about his fiancée and perhaps what she looked like. While her advisers may have suggested the policy, it seems clear that Irene was responsible for making it happen. Usually, it was the emperor who concluded a foreign alliance by such a marriage. Now Irene took over this responsibility, planning her son's future in the normal imperial fashion.

In other aspects of foreign policy, Irene also appears to have taken initiatives. After the fiasco in Sicily, she sent off a major naval force under Theophilos, another eunuch and patrician, to punish Elpidios. When the latter fled to Africa, Byzantine control over this important island was restored. Meanwhile, in the east, the Arab leader Madi sent his son, Harun al-Rashid, into Byzantine territory. In 781 the Arabs had been defeated by John the *sakellarios* and now reacted by mounting a larger force which advanced all the way to the Asiatic shore of the Bosphoros, opposite the capital. While hostile forces had been seen in Chrysopolis before, this invasion was particularly threatening. Fighting continued behind the advance force: Lachanodrakon was defeated; Tatzatios, an Armenian general in charge of the Boukellarioi, went over to the Arabs. A peace treaty was proposed but the Byzantine officials mishandled the negotiations and the terms eventually agreed were most unfavourable to Byzantium. Tribute was to be paid (a great deal) although the Arabs withdrew without capturing any cities. In the narrative of this disastrous campaign, Theophanes emphasises that the empress and the Arab commander, Harun, sealed the treaty with many gifts and personally agreed to the terms. They did not meet, but Irene took responsibility for the treaty on the Byzantine side and rescued her wayward officials.

Through this action she displayed particular concern for her chief minister Staurakios, who was 'at the head of everything and administered all matters'.[42] This appreciation was not shared by Tatzatios, whose hatred of the eunuch provoked his defection to the Arabs. Staurakios' powerful position and intolerant manner is said to have provoked this extreme action. It suggests that Irene's determination to put her own servants into positions of authority cost her support among the military. In addition, Staurakios was one of the two officials captured by the Arabs after their unsuccessful negotiations. He thus displayed qualities that might have made another ruler doubt his ability. Irene, however, sent him off in the following year to campaign against the Slavonic tribes settled in Thrace and Greece. When he returned, after marching as far south as Peloponnesos, bringing much booty and many captives, she accorded him a triumph in the Hippodrome in January 784.[43] So, despite his failures in 781/2, Staurakios regained her favour and Irene would keep him in important posts until his death.

The alliance between a female ruler and her eunuch servants was of a different nature to other relations. Irene felt that she could rely on those who had previously served in her own household. She counted on their loyalty because they owed everything to her alone. In most cases, this assumption seems to have been borne out. Her eunuch advisers remained consistently loyal and supportive of her rule. In the case of Staurakios, whose military expedition to the *Sklaviniai* was hardly as testing as a campaign against the Arabs, it is interesting to note that Irene insisted on granting him a triumph. This involved not only the display of booty, captives, and a victory march-past by the troops, but also gave emperors who had not participated in the campaign a particularly glorious moment. Standing in the imperial box overlooking the Hippodrome, they received the cheers of all, for God granted victory to the rulers as well as to the generals who fought the battles. We can be sure that Irene took this opportunity to make another impressive public appearance. Perhaps that is why she considered a triumph appropriate, when in fact such an honour was normally reserved for a major military victory rather than what may have been a prolonged raid into territory claimed by the empire and nominally under imperial control.

THE OFFICIAL TOUR OF THRACE AND MACEDONIA

As a result of Staurakios' campaign in the western provinces of the empire, Irene and Constantine made a spectacular royal progress through parts of Thrace in the following May (784). The description of their tour, with musical accompaniment, suggests a festive occasion but it also had a serious aim: the rebuilding of cities destroyed during the recent Bulgar wars. The first was Beroia, which was fortified with strong walls and renamed Eirenoupolis, the city of Irene. This was a typical imperial conceit, to honour the empress in the manner of many foundations named after famous rulers, such as Helenoupolis, Arkadioupolis, Hadrianoupolis. The pun on Irene's name, by which Eirenoupolis was also declared to be the city of peace, was probably intended to draw attention to the calmer situation in the region. Only twenty years earlier Constantine V and the Bulgars had fought over these places, leaving them devastated and empty. The refortification of Beroia was intended as a means of persuading the population to return, or to attract loyal new settlers.

The second stop on their tour was Philippoupolis and the third Anchialos on the Black Sea coast where, in 765, Constantine V's fleet had been destroyed. Emperors had rarely been seen in these places unless they were on campaign, so the stately arrival of Irene and Constantine with organs and musicians must have been a wondrous surprise to the locals. At Anchialos, an important port and base of military operations, rebuilding was undertaken, probably of the harbour and city fortifications but also perhaps of monuments within the walls. On this royal progress, Irene and Constantine VI showed themselves to the inhabitants and confirmed their authority as rulers over an area of vital importance to the capital: Thrace supplied Constantinople with grain if military activity did not disrupt the harvest. The western areas of Thrace, however, had not been under efficient imperial control for nearly two hundred years and the claim staked by Irene and Constantine in 784 would shortly be realised in the creation of a *thema* with the designation Macedonia.

As their trip is characterised in the *Chronicle* of Theophanes, they went to Philippoupolis with complete impunity and returned in peace to the capital.[44] The progress permitted them to display the imperial emblems of government: the rulers of the empire in person and their entourage, with organs as well as the dancing and acclamations which always occurred whenever musicians were in attendance. Such an un-military visit presumed that peaceful relations had been restored and that the local population would be more closely linked to Byzantium as a result. Since none of the three cities visited – Beroia, Philippoupolis and Anchialos – sent a bishop to the council of 787, if there was any Christian presence in these places it was still very limited.[45] But through such demonstrations of imperial power, it would be increased. Once again, Irene had shown how ingeniously she could further her own claims as empress while constructing a new imperial duty. The element of performance and public display is all too evident.

Although Theophanes makes no mention of Thessaloniki, it seems likely that Irene and Constantine also concerned themselves with this important city, even if they did not extend their ceremonial tour to the west in order to visit it. An imperial presence is confirmed by the archaeological discovery of monograms of the two emperors in the apse vault of the city's cathedral church, also dedicated to Holy Wisdom (Hagia Sophia). While its early history as a five-aisled basilica is no longer visible, in the late seventh century, probably when Justinian II visited Thessaloniki, it was converted into a domed church with three aisles. This may be connected with the endowment of a salt-pan and its revenues to the church of St Demetrios. Recent cleaning confirms that the extension and redecoration of the church's apse and transverse vault in front of it must be attributed to Irene and Constantine, or at least to their patronage. The high-quality gold tesserae of the apse reveal the shadow of a large cross (such as the one preserved in St Irene, Constantinople). This too may be due to the imperial visit of 784. If this monumental cross is indeed the consequence of Irene's patronage, it conforms perfectly with the prevailing views of the time, when iconoclasm was the official policy of the church. Irene's investment in Thessaloniki, which may also be related to the extension of provincial administration to Macedonia, reveals that the empress was continuing to introduce effective government to areas previously not under imperial control. This was part of the slow process of bringing back the Balkans with their largely Slavic population into the orbit of Constantinople. She may also have endowed churches in Greece, though none that can be associated with her rule service.

So the actions of her first three years as Regent suggest that Irene had a firm grasp of imperial government. She placed her own supporters, often eunuchs of her household, in dominant positions and rewarded those who carried out their duties successfully. Her reliance on these servants, in addition to experienced iconoclast generals like Michael Lachanodrakon, leaves no place for her own family. Apart from her female relative who married Telerig the Bulgarian leader, none are mentioned until much later. She certainly did not encourage them to come and join her in Constantinople. Her choice of an alliance with the King of the Franks and Lombards, also patrician of the Romans, was a bold move which promised to acquire a suitably high-ranking bride from the West for her son, and reopened contacts with iconophiles there. Irene's decision to promote her household eunuchs draws attention to their increasing power, but also to her own desire to maintain control.

During this period there is no indication of Irene's personal attitude towards icons. She maintained iconoclasts in their positions, and there was no change in the official policy of iconoclasm. Whatever her own feelings on the matter, however, she could not overlook the fact that this policy had divided the church and driven many into exile. The unease became openly apparent in the summer of 784 when Patriarch Paul fell ill and retired to a monastery. In anxiety at what he felt to be his approaching death, Paul wanted to resign from his position as leader of the church and die as a monk.[46] When the empress and her son went to visit him, to protest against this highly irregular act of abdication (since patriarchs, like popes, are always expected to die in office), he claimed that he had been promoted unwillingly. He now wanted to state his disapproval of the official policy and express his sincere belief in the icons. The patriarch told the emperors that he was ashamed to have governed the church of Constantinople when it was condemned by the other leading Christian sees, and that a universal (ecumenical) council should be held to reverse iconoclasm. These sentiments, expressed in the *Chronicle* of Theophanes and reinforced in later sources, fit neatly with iconophile history. But whatever Paul actually said, there must have been a significant trend in favour of reversing the council of 754, which had established iconoclasm as official policy. Irene may have sensed a way to reunite the opposing factions and consolidate her standing with the church.

THE RESTORATION OF ICONS

The visit to the patriarch was a turning point in Irene's role as Regent. She realised that she needed to persuade all the members of the Regency to support what Paul recommended. So she sent the Senate to his monastery to listen to his arguments. In amazement they protested at his *volte face*. Had he not been appointed patriarch to support the prevalent iconoclast policy? Yes, he replied with chagrin, 'but I only remained silent and did not preach the truth from fear of your fury'.[47] Knowing that the Senate followed the official line on icons, he now wanted to be left alone to weep and repent. Shortly after this Paul died, creating a gap which Irene had to fill with a man who was responsive to her own position.

Her method of stage-managing the replacement follows the same pattern that has been observed in her previous public appearances. She invited her advisers to propose a candidate, having planted the name of the one she favoured, Tarasios, who was then in charge of part of the civil service (*protoasekretis*). But when they duly suggested that Tarasios would be the best person, she complained that he refused to obey imperial instructions to accept the appointment. Invited to explain his reluctance, he did so first in personal terms (the required statement of his unworthiness, which in the circumstances was more truthful than usual), and second, in the terms laid down by Paul on his deathbed. Without an ecumenical council which carried the approval of the whole pentarchy of the Christian world, it would be impossible to root out the evil heresy of iconoclasm.[48] The speech stressed the danger of Byzantine Christians remaining excommunicated and anathematised by the other churches, and the need therefore to restore Christian unity in relation to the holy images.

Everyone present agreed that this should be done, which was what Irene wanted. There is no mention, of course, of iconoclast opposition in the biased sources that survive. So measures were taken, in the name of the young emperor Constantine VI and his mother Irene, to invite the leaders of the pentarchy, the five patriarchal sees and apostolic foundations: Alexandria, Antioch, Jerusalem and Rome, in addition to Constantinople, to attend an ecumenical council which would undo the work of 754 and reinstate the icons in their honoured place. The letter sent by the emperors to Pope Hadrian I immediately after this meeting dates from September 784.[49] It would be interesting to know if Irene had a hand in drafting it, though she may well have left this to Tarasios who was still a civilian bureaucrat with particular skills in precisely this field. He was eventually ordained Patriarch of Constantinople on Christmas Day 784, and then sent his official letter of appointment and declaration of faith to Pope Hadrian.[50] The latter replied favourably, but criticised the procedure whereby a layman had been promoted rapidly through the necessary clerical grades.[51] In addition, because the peace treaty was still in force, it was possible to send embassies to the patriarchs under Arab political control, and they agreed to send their representatives to the ecumenical council. When they heard the news, many iconophiles who had taken refuge in distant regions to avoid persecution hurried back to Constantinople.

The replacement of the patriarch had thus opened the way for a change in religious policy, which Irene saw as a method of increasing her power and consolidating relations with the West. The iconophiles who had been exiled and persecuted would always be grateful to her. She may have already had contact with some of those permitted to return under Leo IV. With their help Irene would be able to handle the obdurate iconoclasts. Perhaps she also anticipated that the icon venerators would hail her as a saint, for this is how she is described in some of the iconophile sources. Yet there is no evidence that she herself practised or believed in the cult of icons; she had probably been brought up as an iconoclast. Irene did not remove the most virulent iconoclasts from their official posts, although she expected those holding bishoprics to blow with the wind.

While Irene's personal views on iconoclasm remain unknown, her policy appears to be in line with the general subordination of theological matters to political needs in Byzantium during the eighth century. When the emperor developed sophisticated theological arguments against the representation of Christ in human form, a majority of office holders and state appointees supported his opposition to icons. In general they did not express strong views either for or against icons. Their Christian belief was not greatly altered by a renewed emphasis to worship in spirit and in truth. Bishops similarly could agree that images might encourage an idolatrous attitude in the uneducated, those usually identified as 'simple-minded' in ecclesiastical texts (in other words, women and children). Would the new patriarch Tarasios be able to reverse the position? Many middle-ranking, nominal iconoclasts may have readied themselves to change sides, to follow the official line, whatever their personal opinions.

So preparations were made to gather representatives of the pentarchy and all the bishops subordinate to the see of Constantinople for the Seventh Universal Council of the church. Tarasios and Hadrian, the Bishop of Rome, refused to recognise the meeting summoned by Constantine V to establish iconoclasm in 754, which had already identified itself as the Seventh. But the plan was to counter the claims of that meeting by refuting its Definition of Faith (*Horos*). The new council was to open in September 786 in the church of the Holy Apostles in the Queen City. The agenda of its business was drawn up by Tarasios, taking some account of Pope Hadrian's official letter of support for the end of the schism, which had stipulated certain conditions: iconoclasm had to be declared a heresy, its adherents had to confess their errors and renounce their past belief. All this was planned.

The new patriarch and the empress, however, had underestimated both the allegiance of certain bishops and, more importantly, the loyalty of the army to the policies of Constantine V. The military-political identification of iconoclasm with victory was still very strong and manifested itself at the very opening of the Seventh Ecumenical Council. As representatives of the pentarchy took their places in the presence of the rulers, who observed the proceedings from the gallery, the *scholarioi*, *exkoubitors* and leaders of the professional corps of *tagmata*, unsheathed their swords and threatened to kill the patriarch. Supported by iconoclast bishops, their action was clearly planned in advance and proved effective. Chanting the iconoclast Definition of Faith, they advanced on the patriarch and his supporters in the apse of the church and refused to stop, even when the empress sent down men of her household to intervene.[52] So instead of the well-ordered session planned by Tarasios, a chaotic riot occurred inside the church. Rather than stay to witness any further disorder, Irene and Constantine abandoned the council and returned to the palace. Only the iconoclast bishops loyal to the Definition agreed in 754 remained, together with the military who chanted 'Victory!' (*Nika!*, a word which had such significant associations in the capital city).[53] In highly unsatisfactory circumstances, the council was cancelled. The bishops set off back to their provincial sees, assuming that there would be no change in the official policy of iconoclasm.

Tarasios may have been unaware of this deep commitment to iconoclasm sustained by the military; his previous experience as a civilian official in the capital gave him limited exposure to that section of Byzantine society. Irene, however, should have been informed by the mass of servants and officials, whose duty it was to track sentiment among the military, of a firm current of support for the doctrine associated with Constantine V. For whatever reason, the council revealed that she and the new patriarch had not paid adequate attention to potential opposition. And the débâcle in the church of the Holy Apostles must have made

Irene realise that ecclesiastical unity would not be imposed without more stringent preparations. She therefore arranged for the offending units of the professional army (*tagmata*) to be disbanded, a drastic step. But first she had to secure the military defence of the capital. For this, she ordered Staurakios to win over the potential forces of the Asiatic *themata* currently stationed in Thrace. Once their support and their ability to control the city was secured, she ordered the *tagmata* commanders to proceed to Malagina, the traditional meeting point for military campaigns against the Arabs. To confirm the seriousness of her plans, all the imperial equipment required for such an undertaking was also transported to Asia Minor. There, instead of receiving orders to advance against the Arabs, she had the troops dismissed and paid off. Their wives and children were expelled from Constantinople and told to go back to their original homes.[54]

Having dispersed the most committed iconoclast troops, Irene then appointed military commanders loyal to herself. In May 787, when she was confident of the support of the army, she sent out invitations for a second meeting of the council, which was now to be held in Nicaea. In eight months she had quelled the fiercest opposition by obliterating the collective presence of military regiments who had always been loyal to her father-in-law, Constantine V. Her own servants and household eunuchs helped to realise this turnaround, which then made possible a more considered attempt to restore the official veneration of icons. The papal legates had already reached Sicily on their journey back to Rome, but were persuaded to return to the East; the representatives of the eastern patriarchates had been detained in Constantinople. All the bishops were also informed that they had to journey to Nicaea. In addition, a large number of monks were invited to attend, both as representatives of iconophile groups and as individuals who had been exiled by the iconoclasts.

THE SEVENTH ECUMENICAL COUNCIL

The choice of the provincial city of Nicaea in western Asia Minor as the venue of the council was brilliant. As the site of the first ecumenical gathering summoned by Constantine I in 325, it was associated with the basic declaration of Christian faith, the Nicene creed, and the condemnation of heresy. Constantine had presided over its deliberations, setting the pattern for imperial control over the church in the East. In addition, Nicaea had resisted many sieges and retained its classical urban form, enclosed within impressive city walls. It had a large imperial palace which would serve as the meeting place and a church dedicated to Holy Wisdom, Hagia Sophia, where the restoration of icons could be celebrated. The participants would have the model of the 338 Fathers of the Church, as the bishops of the first council are known, before them, and this would emphasise their duty to strengthen orthodoxy. Unfortunately, the metropolitan of the city was a known iconoclast, but the local *strategos*, Petronas, who was loyal to Irene, was put in charge of the arrangements.

Preparations for the second meeting of the Seventh Ecumenical Council left nothing to chance. Every move in the procedure of readmitting repentant iconoclasts, suspending the obdurate, marshalling the arguments against iconoclasm and in favour of iconophile veneration, and the final decree, was well planned. Irene did not participate in person, but her officials Petronas and John, previously *sakellarios*, now *logothetes*, organised the proceedings, even to the point where they upstaged Tarasios. One of Irene's trusted eunuchs, Niketas Monomachos, who may also have been a relation, represented her.[55]

From 24 September to 13 October 787, seven main sessions were held in Nicaea.[56] By the penultimate session, 365 bishops and 132 abbots and monks were present. The delegates of the church of Rome took precedence and representatives of the eastern patriarchates played a prominent role. With such numbers the council could claim to represent the entire Christian universe (*oikoumene*), although the Frankish church was later to complain that it had not been invited to participate (its representation being subsumed within Rome). The monastic contingent did not participate on the same level as bishops; they approved two dogmatic declarations issued by the council but did not sign the final Definition of Faith. During the proceedings, however, several leading abbots joined in the debate over the readmission of previous iconoclasts, taking a markedly stricter line than Patriarch Tarasios.[57] This distinct difference prefigured divisions between the imperially selected leader of the church and those iconophile monks who had suffered for their cause.

For the final session all the participants were summoned to the Magnaura Palace in Constantinople, where Irene and Constantine presided. The empress thus arranged to take full credit for the success of the council, and made the rulers appear as the authorities in charge. They endorsed the Declaration of Faith by which the icons were restored, probably signing the document in the red ink reserved to Byzantine rulers, and Irene appended her signature before it was passed to her son for him to sign. In imitation of Constantine I at the first Council of Nicaea in 325, Constantine VI and his mother Irene were now acclaimed as a new Constantine and Helena, and were thus granted a similar status as saints of the church.[58]

The council had successfully accomplished a revolution in orthodox theology. Searching through scriptural and early Christian patristic writings on icons, Tarasios and his team of researchers had produced a few not very convincing justifications for the veneration of icons. Much greater authority was found in saints' lives, which drew attention to the miraculous powers of icons, their role as intercessors and their ability to inspire greater Christian devotion. God clearly approved of the icons and worked miracles through them, for cures of the blind, paralytic and comatose were effected only by divine power. Several monks and bishops who participated brought their favourite stories and read them out to remind the council of these wonders.[59] Particular attention was given to testimony cited at the council of 754, which turned out to be of dubious value. The iconoclasts had read out short excerpts from authorities such as St Neilos of Ankyra, taking them out of context in order to emphasise their own interpretation. When the participants at Nicaea heard them placed in their true setting, such *pittakia* (little boards) were condemned. Although John of Damascus had been singled out for condemnation (anathema) by the iconoclasts at the earlier council, no use was made of his *Three Treatises on Holy Images* in 787. In fact, the theological content of the Seventh Ecumenical Council was rather thin; more time was devoted to the punishment of iconoclast bishops than to the elaboration of a well-documented justification of icons. None the less, by relying on hagiographical sources, the Byzantine iconophiles found the material they needed to argue that icon veneration was an ancient tradition in the church, to circumvent the Mosaic prohibition of images, and to condemn the iconoclasts as heretics. The council of 787 thus elevated the holy images to a novel position and generated a devoted iconophile interpretation of the role of ecclesiastical art.

ICONOPHILE ART RESTORED

Irene's removal of the most fervent supporters of iconoclasm meant that the reversal of her father-in-law's policy was not openly opposed. Even the firmest, such as Michael Lachanodrakon, stood by silently while the icons they had scorned as idolatrous were restored. Though underpinned by a rather flimsy theological foundation, religious images were now hailed as a central part of orthodox faith, one of the basic features of Christian worship, which had an important role to play in the liturgy. As a result artists, often monks, began to copy older images that had survived the persecution, to recreate those which had been destroyed and to develop new styles of decoration. Icons from this period onwards depict the Crucifixion, showing the suffering Christ flanked by His mother and St John.[60] This new stress on the Good Friday scene may have its roots in the liturgical poems, such as the *kontakia* (religious poems) of Romanos which had become an integral part of regular worship. Newly identified iconophile texts were also copied and illustrated in scriptoria, like the one attached to the monastery of St John the Baptist, more often identified by the name of Stoudios, the fifth-century senator on whose property it had been built. Irene appears to have granted the newly reconstituted iconophile community an imperial stipend. Monks, scribes and artists were encouraged by two particularly forceful iconophiles, Abbot Platon of Sakkoudion, and his nephew Theodore, who later became leader of the Stoudios monastery. The latter wrote epigrams on Byzantine works of religious art, which were commissioned to decorate the Chalke Gate, the main entrance to the imperial palace.[61]

The cross remained the most potent Christian symbol, as it had done under the iconoclasts. So no change was made to the mosaic cross which still adorns the apse of churches such as the one dedicated to St Irene in the capital city. In one of the major churches of Constantinople, the foundation dedicated to the martyr St Euphemia, restoration work was undertaken. According to the source which describes this task, the shrine had been converted into an arms depot by Constantine V. Whether true or not, after 787 the shrine was returned to its primary ecclesiastical function as the church hallowed by the famous relics of the saint who had helped to define orthodox theology at the Council of Chalcedon in 451. Elsewhere, figural images were returned to places of prominence. The empress restored or erected a mosaic image of Christ on the Chalke entrance of the Great Palace, a clear indication of her own support for iconophile art. After 787 she may well have commissioned artistic decoration for the buildings she restored, notably the church of the Virgin of the Spring, as well as new constructions she patronised (see below). Iconoclast decoration of particular churches and monuments such as the Milion, the central milestone of Constantinople from which distances were measured, was replaced by appropriate figural images of church councils, individual saints and holy persons. By thus demonstrating the primary didactic purpose of such images both in churches and on the streets of the capital, Christians were invited to emulate the example of the saints. In a tradition going back to the earliest justification of images, realistic art was singled out as the great educator of the illiterate.

Throughout the 780s, Irene regularly claimed the position of senior emperor over her son. On some of the coins issued in their joint names, Irene is shown holding the sceptre of office; she took precedence over Constantine at the council of 787, and she insisted that her name precede his in certain acclamations. At the time of the council the young man, now nearly seventeen years old, was certainly of an age to claim his rightful position as emperor. There were probably officials in his own entourage who encouraged him to insist on his superiority and who denigrated his powerful mother. She, however, persisted in keeping Constantine under strict control and so prevented him from coming into his inheritance. Her wilful style is evident in the way she broke off his engagement to Rotrud, the Frankish princess, and insisted on him marrying a girl called Maria from the village of Amnia in the region of the Armeniakon. This major upheaval in Constantine's life occurred as a result of a switch in foreign policy, from the alliance with the Franks to a hostile opposition to Charles's projected expansion into southern Italy.[62] Whether it was Charles who cancelled the engagement, by refusing to allow Rotrud to leave the West, or his own mother, who made and imposed alternate plans for his marriage, is immaterial. Constantine was married to Maria in November 788 (see the detailed description in chapter 3) and he is said to have resented the change.

Irene, however, plunged into a more aggressive campaign against Charles's policy in southern Italy which was seen as threatening to the Byzantine province of Calabria. She now called on the Lombard prince Adelgis, who had spent many years in Byzantium under the name Theodotos, to reclaim his patrimony. He was sent back to the West with Byzantine forces under the command of John the *sakellarios*, and the extra support of Theodoros, the general in charge of Sicily, to curb Charles's plans and win over some of his Italian supporters.[63] In the event, this expedition of 789 proved disastrous. Worse still, it coincided with renewed Arab raiding in the East, from September 788, and a military victory won by the Bulgars on the Strymon. Irene had not foreseen the dangers which resulted when the empire was threatened simultaneously on three widely separated fronts. This was a strategic error that most emperors and their military experts consistently avoided. It was foolish to risk troops in Italy when forces were needed in eastern Asia Minor, and particularly dangerous when the Bulgars were laying claim to the area only recently declared a pacified zone by Irene and Constantine's royal progress. Irene had been poorly advised, her generals had been outflanked and defeated, and her foreign policy had failed dismally.

CONSTANTINE'S BID FOR SOLE RULE, 790

In these circumstances Constantine was propelled to claim his rightful position as emperor in 790. His resentment of his junior position and his mother's autocratic behaviour was doubtless encouraged by the men of his own entourage, though they are said to be few in number. Now in his nineteenth year, Constantine is described by Theophanes as 'vigorous and very able', an ambitious young man who was frustrated by his lack of authority.[64] His determination to rule in his own name now took a more tangible form: he decided to try and arrest Staurakios, the eunuch who still exercised a broad control over the government. These plans must have filtered back to Irene who informed Staurakios. Together, they resolved to curb Constantine's ambitions. Taking advantage of an earthquake in February 790, which obliged the court to move out of the capital to the suburban palace at St Mamas on the European side of the Bosphoros, Irene ordered the arrest of her son's entourage. In the uncertain conditions of after-quakes, all Constantine's advisers were rounded up, flogged and tonsured, then exiled or subjected to house imprisonment.[65] Even her own son was flogged and imprisoned, while she reproached him for his threats to Staurakios (and to her own controlling grip on imperial power).

This battle of wills at the apex of Byzantine government is characterised in the chief source, Theophanes' *Chronicle*, as the work of evil men inspired by the Devil to set mother against son and son against mother. Claiming that ancient prophesies had established her right to rule, Irene's supporters fanned her ambitions and flattered her abilities.[66] Whether she was persuaded by them, or their confirmation merely reinforced her intention to rule independently of her son, she perceived that control of the army would be crucial to her success. Since she had already appointed commanders loyal to her, she now tried to compel all the armed forces to swear that they would never accept Constantine as their rightful emperor.[67] So while Constantine was confined in the St Mamas Palace after the failure of his plot against the chief eunuch, his mother tried to win over the support of the army.

But this power struggle produced echoes among the military. The forces of the Armeniakon *thema* refused to swear the oath: indeed, they had sworn previously to maintain the authority of Constantine and Irene, in that order, and would not accept any change. Further, they must have considered her actions improper as they expected Constantine to become the senior emperor. From the eastern regions of Armeniakon came news of a serious revolt: the troops had imprisoned their own general, set up a new leader and proclaimed Constantine as sole emperor.[68] Their example was followed in other areas and the rivalry between mother and son took on a military character that threatened civil war. In this situation of increasing tension, Irene withdrew. She recognised the threat posed by troops loyal to the imperial dynasty of Leo III, who expected the young emperor to lead them in battle and would not countenance his continuing subordination. In October 790 Constantine was acclaimed as sole emperor by many of the provincial armies, who had marched to Atroa in Bithynia (western Asia Minor) to ensure that Irene would step down.[69]

With this firm declaration of support behind him, Constantine now took immediate steps to consolidate his hold on power. He sent an order to the capital that he was taking over as sole emperor with instructions that it should be announced in the Forum of Constantine.[70] This was the usual place for the citizens of Constantinople to gather whenever the prefect of the city had news to disseminate. Heralds were sent through the different regions to inform the population of an impending announcement, or fliers posted up in prominent places with the actual news. On this occasion, the Greens and the Blues would have delivered the official acclamations of Constantine as emperor and everyone would have understood that the empress-mother and Regent had retired from the political scene. Meanwhile, in Atroa, Constantine confirmed the appointment of a new general of the Armeniakon force, Alexios Mousoulem (Mousele, an Armenian name), and insisted that the soldiers swear never to accept Irene as their emperor. He then returned to the capital and arrested the chief eunuch, Staurakios, the *logothetes*, Aetios, Irene's confidant, and all the other eunuchs of her household. They were flogged, tonsured and exiled to different places, Staurakios being sent to the Armeniakon *thema*, so that the soldiers there would understand that Constantine meant business. The emperor confined his mother to the palace of Eleutherios, which she had built, on the understanding that she would remain there.[71]

THE REIGN OF CONSTANTINE VI, 790–7

As a result of this denouement, Constantine finally came into his inheritance in 790 and assumed imperial power as the only son of Leo IV, grandson of Constantine V and great-grandson of Leo III, the founder of the dynasty. He and his wife moved into the official imperial quarters of the Great Palace and in due course Maria gave birth to a daughter named Irene after her paternal grandmother.[72] The entire court must have prayed that the next time the emperor would be blessed with a son. Aided by experienced generals like Michael Lachanodrakon, who had served his grandfather, and those whom he placed in charge of the provincial and professional forces, Constantine VI prepared to rule without his mother. His first efforts in the field were not brilliant: against both the Bulgars (April 791) and the Arabs (the following September) he failed to secure a victory. He also failed to sustain the loyalty of the Armeniakon troops, who resented the fact that their general, Alexios Mousoulem, was detained in Constantinople with nothing active to do. So in the first year of his sole rule the emperor neither displayed successful military strategy nor made particularly good use of his officers.

Irene, meanwhile, pressured her son to restore her to her proper place as empress-mother. In January 792, following appeals by many highly placed persons, he acceded to the request that she be reinstated at court. The occasion was marked by acclamations shouted in the form made familiar by their joint rule in the previous decade: 'Long live Constantine and Irene!'[73] Once again the Greens and the Blues made public the official shift: the empress-mother was no longer in disgrace, confined to her own palace, but had reasserted her position as co-emperor with Constantine. As her favourite eunuch official turns up in the capital again shortly after her reinstatement, it appears that she was also able to insist upon the recall of Staurakios from exile. Since Constantine could have insisted on the acclamation of himself alone, the joint acclamation was a concession to Irene's past authority which boded ill for his own. When the new acclamation was made known to the military, it angered the troops of the Armeniakon army who refused to add Irene's name. In addition, they demanded the return of their general, Alexios Mousoulem. Constantine however sensed that this would be a dangerous move and had Alexios thrown into prison. The Armeniakon army then rebelled.[74]

Perhaps as a distraction from this unco-operative section of the army in the East, the emperor ordered a further campaign against the Bulgars in July 792. In the company of many distinguished generals he advanced to Markellai, which was refortified, and then attacked the Bulgars under Khan Kardamos without a clear battle plan. In the ensuing disaster, many Byzantines were killed, and the Bulgars carried off the whole imperial baggage train, all the money, horses, supplies, even the imperial tent, while Constantine fled back to the capital in disarray.[75] Such a notable defeat, which cost the lives of Michael Lachanodrakon and several other prominent generals, provoked the professional forces, *tagmata*, to support another revolt in the name of the former caesar Nikephoros, Constantine's uncle. Although he had been reduced to clerical status by Irene after 780, this third attempt by the caesars had serious support and challenged Constantine to take decisive action. In an effort to terminate their imperial ambitions, he ordered that Nikephoros should be blinded and the other four caesars mutilated.[76] At the instigation of his mother and Staurakios, Constantine also had the Armeniakon general Alexios Mousoulem blinded, so that he could never be a candidate for imperial power.

While he showed in this way that he could deal harshly with rivals, Constantine unwittingly played into the hands of the opposition, for when the Armeniakon troops learned of the treatment of their general, Alexios, their rebellion developed into out-and-out war against Constantinople. They effectively monopolised the emperor's attention for nearly a year, forcing him to mount two expeditions against them and concentrating his attention on an internal struggle to the detriment of all else. Eventually he succeeded in defeating the Armeniakon revolt, and marched one thousand prisoners in chains through the Blachernai Gate of Constantinople in a humiliating parade. The words 'Armenian plotter' were tattooed on their foreheads and then they were exiled to Sicily and other places.[77] But he did not reward those who had supported him, and thus failed to win the enduring loyalty of that section of the troublesome provincial army.

CONSTANTINE'S SECOND MARRIAGE

In 793, therefore, after three years in control, Constantine had not succeeded in establishing his own authority or in winning the sort of victory which could be celebrated with a triumph. Crucially, he had readmitted his mother and her courtiers to governing circles and still took her advice. Whether she sowed the seeds of the decision which was to cost him his throne is not clear. But the remaining period of Constantine's sole rule is dominated by another error of judgement which could so easily have been avoided that contemporaries suspected Irene's hand in it. As Theophanes puts it, the emperor conceived an aversion to his wife Maria 'through the machinations of his mother' and looked for a way to divorce her.[78] He may have tired of her following the birth of their second child, another daughter, some time in the early 790s. Needless to say, this birth is not noted by any contemporary historian. Yet the second female *porphyrogennetos* born to Maria, who was christened Euphrosyne, was to play a critical role in the third and fourth decades of the ninth century. She is indeed the second of the women in purple who are the object of this study. And the first thing known about her is that she shared in her mother's disgrace.

By January 795 Maria had been forced to become a nun; with her hair cut short and wearing monastic costume, she was exiled with her two small children to a nunnery founded by Irene on the island of Prinkipo in the Sea of Marmara.[79] Since there were no legal grounds for divorce, such as proven adultery or conspiracy to murder, this act was immediately criticised by the ecclesiastical authorities, who pointed out that marriage was for life. But the divorce was necessary if Constantine was to remarry, and it rapidly became clear that this was his intention. Only seven months later, in August, he had crowned his new empress as *augousta*, a title Maria had never held, and in September 795 their marriage ceremony was held in the palace of St Mamas. The forty-day celebration was denounced by a strict disciplinary party within the church, who protested against what they believed to be an adulterous marriage. They also refused to hold communion with Patriarch Tarasios because he had allowed one of his clerics, Joseph, to bless the union.[80]

The emperor's new wife was named Theodote. She had previously held the position of *koubikoularia*, a lady-in-waiting at court, and was related to Platon of Sakkoudion and his nephew Theodore, two leading monks who were great supporters of Empress Irene. She had clearly attracted Constantine's attention at a point in his life when he wanted to assert his own authority and manage his own affairs. The idea of divorcing Maria, whom he had not chosen, and marrying Theodote must have been enticing, but any prudent adviser would have warned him of the dangers of offending the church. He none the less insisted on the divorce and so antagonised another sector of the court. Far from trying to assist her, Theodote's relatives led the opposition to her imperial marriage. They played a major part in what became a ten-year dispute known in Byzantium as the 'Moicheian schism' (from *moicheia*, adultery in Greek). By condemning the emperor's second marriage, they set up their own strict, puritanical interpretation of the canons governing divorce, in opposition to Patriarch Tarasios' more lenient attitude. In particular his refusal to excommunicate the priest who had blessed the imperial union was branded as 'oikonomia' (literally, economy, in the sense of being economical with the truth, in this case of the canons). The church in Byzantium was thus divided by an internal disagreement which threatened to engulf the central players in imperial government. The patriarch found himself increasingly isolated by a sea of opposition, which swelled and grew from the conviction that Constantine's second marriage was illegitimate. Although the emperor had been poorly advised, he must have realised the more serious, long-term danger: any children Theodote might bear him would not be considered legitimate and would be unable to inherit.

Irene's role in all this is never made explicit. But with her monastic supporters upholding the strict interpretation of the canons against permitting divorce, she must have distanced herself from Tarasios' more flexible policy towards the emperor's remarriage. It is known that she granted stipends to various monastic communities including that at Stoudios. Theophanes claims that Irene 'was yearning for power and wanted him [Constantine] to be universally condemned'.[81] Given that the scenario was quite predictable, the emperor's entourage does not seem to have taken a measure of the potential opposition. Once Tarasios' assent had been secured, they probably hoped that the rest of the church would fall into line, following the patriarch's judicial exercise of 'oikonomia'. But they underestimated the monastic party's authority. Many iconophile monks had returned to Byzantium after the restoration of icons; Platon and his followers had been promoted and welcomed into Irene's circle of advisers. Of course, she supported their opposition to

Tarasios, playing one sector of the church against another. She also observed the popular sympathy for Platon and his nephews, who had been flogged and exiled on Constantine's orders. The righteous self-justification of the monastic's party further reduced the emperor's following and made his position less tenable.

Although he might have redeemed himself by acting in a truly imperial fashion, by allowing his mother to return to the ruling circles of the court Constantine left himself open to her experienced calculations. He did win various campaigns against both the Bulgars and the Arabs during the years 795–7, but his image was tarnished by the divisions over his divorce. In the autumn of 796, he accompanied his mother and the entire court to Prousa (Bursa in western Asia Minor) to bathe in the hot springs. While they were there, news came from the capital that Theodote had given birth to a son, and Constantine rushed back to the city. The baby was named Leo after his grandfather, Leo IV.[82] In Constantine's absence Irene was able to bribe all the commanders of the *tagmata* and courtiers gathered in Prousa. She instructed the men of her household to persuade them that Constantine would never make a good ruler. Setting herself up as the only person capable of governing, she conspired to get rid of him. Over the course of the next year, Constantine gradually became aware of these schemes but he had alienated too many sectors of the church, court and military to sustain general support. Then, on 1 May 797, his baby son Leo died aged seven months, a disaster that deeply affected Constantine. The grieving parents buried him in a tiny marble sarcophagus in the mausoleum attached to the church of the Holy Apostles.[83]

In these difficult circumstances, Irene drew the net tighter around her son, isolating him from his military supporters among the eastern *themata*. None the less, the two rulers participated in certain ceremonial events such as the return of St Euphemia's relics to her church in central Constantinople, probably in July 797. The translation of the famous relics, which exuded a healing liquid, into the restored church constituted a major event to mark its rededication as an iconophile shrine.[84] Several loyal iconophiles were rewarded by gifts of the bones: Niketas the eunuch and patrician received the right hand of the saint, and Constantine's two daughters by Maria, his first wife, also benefited. It seems more likely that Irene would have been the person responsible for arranging this gift, as there is no evidence that Constantine paid any attention to his former family, who were all living in the monastery on the island of Prinkipo.

This is the only mention of his two surviving children during his lifetime. It was also to be one of his last official duties.

Rumours of what Irene had said to the military leaders at Prousa must have circulated, as Constantine gradually realised that it would come to a showdown with his mother. In August 797 he fled from the city, instructing Theodote to make her way to the eastern coast of Marmara. But his mother's friends outwitted him and had him arrested as he attempted to seek refuge with the Anatolikon forces. They brought him back to Constantinople. And on 19 August 797 Irene ordered that Constantine, her son, should be blinded in the Porphyra, the purple chamber where she had given birth to him twenty-six years before.[85]

Despite its repugnant nature, blinding was considered a merciful option in comparison with death, the normal punishment for plotting against the emperor. Depriving an opponent of his sight was a common method of removing political rivals, both in Byzantium and the West. As we have seen, it had been used by Constantine VI in 792 when he faced a plot, the third, mounted by supporters of his uncles, the caesars: Nikephoros was blinded and the four others had their tongues cut out. At the same time Alexios Mousoulem was blinded to prevent his aspirations to the purple. Blinding was also imposed on ecclesiastics accused of high crimes and political misdemeanours: in 705, when Justinian II re-entered the capital to reclaim his position as emperor, he had Patriarch Kallinikos blinded and exiled to Rome.[86] Kallinikos later returned to Byzantium, one of the rare examples of survivors of this operation. In 799 Pope Leo III narrowly escaped a plot to blind him.

So the punishment imposed on Constantine at Irene's orders conforms with the normal style of disabling a political rival. It suggests that she conceived of her son's ambitions to rule without her as an intolerable challenge to her own authority. Theophanes cannot excuse the action, which he claims was designed to cause Constantine's death. He reports that the sun was hidden for seventeen days, the unexpected darkness mirroring the loss of sight Irene had inflicted on her son. This is a common metaphor, for the emperor was always likened to the sun. Despite these portents, Constantine lived on for several years, the controversy over his marriage continuing to divide the church. Theodote looked after him until about 805, by which date he seems to have died, and she appears to have retired into a monastery.[87] By a curious twist of fate, quite unintended by Irene, Constantine was to outlive his mother.

IRENE AS SOLE RULER, 797–802

Irene thus assumed control of the empire. As co-emperor she already held the imperial title so the change only required an announcement to the effect that Constantine was no longer able to rule. Irene appears to have offered no explanation other than the fact that her son had been deprived of his sight and therefore could not be emperor. Her sole rule is documented by new coin forms which emphasise her as the only official ruler. The gold *solidi* present her as *basilissa* (empress) with her own image on both sides. The obverse and reverse are clearly struck from nearly identical dies, so that whichever side falls uppermost Irene is the only ruler depicted in her imperial robes, bearing the sceptre of office. She felt no need to draw on the authority of her husband, Leo IV, now long dead, or his ancestors, members of the Syrian dynasty which had been in power for eighty years. Through these newly minted coins she proclaimed the change of ruler, and in 797 the citizens of the empire and all those who traded with Byzantium could have been in no doubt about her authority (see plate 1c).

While the title on the coins was the perfectly correct feminine form, *basilissa*, empress, on her legal documents the masculine form for emperor, *basileus*, was employed.[88] Since the emperor was the source of law, it was customary for legal regulations to be introduced with the authority of the 'great emperor, faithful in Christ'. Neither Irene nor her legal advisers saw any reason to change this formula, which guaranteed authenticity. The two new laws, *novellai*, issued in her name, were devoted to the question of oaths and remarriage – topics which had already proved extremely important in her rise to full power. The first stressed that oaths were taken in the presence of Christ himself and should not be lightly broken, while the second prohibited third marriages as a practice akin to bestiality. These additions to the penal code were signed into law by Irene as emperor, the *autokrator*, supreme ruler.[89] She did not want anyone to misunderstand the nature of her authority. Everyone would respect and treat her as the sole emperor, for there was no other.

In this way she indicated to those foreign powers to whom she wrote, to the Bishop of Rome, to her loyal officials in the provinces and also to the people of Constantinople, who heard her laws read out in public, that she was no mere consort, but the real emperor. In this respect, the Byzantine court, church, army and people, who all had ways of expressing their disapproval of new developments, may have understood that the office of emperor was distinct from the person who occupied that office. For the empire to flourish, it had to be ruled by an individual who held the title of *basileus*. This title had been bestowed on Irene as co-emperor with her son Constantine VI, who confirmed his mother's share in authority when he readmitted her to imperial power in 792. They had both been jointly acclaimed as rulers and the evident dominance of mother over son had accustomed people to think of her in imperial terms. It might have been unusual for a woman to hold a position defined in the masculine case but there is no evidence that in Byzantium Irene's position as sole ruler and emperor caused particular outrage. She was accepted as the emperor. The only comparable use of a male title is found in the late tenth century in the West, when Theophano, the widow of Emperor Otto II, who was herself of Byzantine origin, would sign some of her acts using the male form, *imperator*, rather than the more common female, *imperatrix*.[90]

As co-emperor and previously Regent, Irene had all the necessary qualifications to assume total control, however unprecedented the means. The surprise is that more sectors of Byzantine society did not protest. Undoubtedly she had prepared for this development for some time, by carefully winning over to her side most military leaders. If those disaffected supporters of her son sought to honour his memory, they did not take immediate action. Constantine now lived in isolation with Theodote and their few servants, who put up no opposition. Irene's own staff from the Eleutherios Palace and the eunuch officials still loyal to her helped to reinstate her in the Great Palace. She replaced those officials whose loyalty to her might be in question: by 799, her own men were in charge of the units of Thrakesion, Opsikion, and Sicily, and her own appointee, also named Nikephoros, had taken over the finance ministry (*logothesion tou genikou*).[91] Similarly, she had won much support among the monastic party in the church, by promising an end to the persecution imposed by the adulterous emperor. The leading abbot, Platon of Sakkoudion, his nephews, Theodore of the Stoudios and Joseph, and all their followers who had been humiliated, punished and exiled for their opposition to the imperial divorce returned to the capital to seek favours from the new ruler. Many of them were appointed to bishoprics, others to monasteries which were now favoured with imperial patronage.

IRENE'S IMPERIAL PHILANTHROPY: BUILDING ACTIVITY

Throughout her long association with imperial authority, and particularly after 797, Irene demonstrated an increasing sense of the imperial duty to patronise ecclesiastical as well as civilian buildings and to practise philanthropy. This is one aspect of her rule which is noticeably different from her husband's. Like her father-in-law, Irene paid particular attention to the capital. Under Constantine V, major steps had been taken to increase the population of the city and restore buildings damaged by the earthquake of 740. Irene followed this pattern, restoring churches and monasteries which had fallen into ruin or been adapted for other uses, and building new ones with enthusiasm. The record of this activity has to be pieced together from a variety of sources, some less reliable than others, but it forms a conspicuous contribution to the beautification of the capital. Most of it is attributed to the empress and her son Constantine, indicating a date before 797 if their two names are taken as a serious marker. But since there is no independent evidence that Constantine was concerned with building, I think we can safely assume that the empress took most of the initiative. And a few constructions are specifically said to be due to her, which suggests at least the personal involvement of the empress rather than her son, even if none are dated after 797.

The most notable construction of Irene and Constantine in Constantinople was of a new palace, called the Eleutherios in the centre of the city, south of the Amastrianon on the slope leading down to the port of Theodosios. In the late eighth century this may not have been densely populated area but it was to become the base for many involved in trade who settled near the main commercial port. The area had to be cleared of earlier constructions, one of which was supposed to have been a hippodrome built by Theodosios the Great. Whether this is accurately identified or not, it seems that quite a large area in this part of the city was redeveloped, initiating construction work and employment for local people. The Eleutherios complex sustained its own identity for centuries, eventually becoming linked with another one. In the tenth century its hostel, *xenon*, is recorded in a list of similar institutions mentioned in the *Book of Ceremonies*. Historians often describe the Eleutherios as something of a 'vanity' construction to please the empress, but it formed part of a large complex associated with workshops including bakeries, *lamia*, which provided work for the local population.[92]

At a later date, *ergodosia* including silk-weaving workshops, were added. During a thunderstorm which took place on Christmas Day, 792, the offices of the Chrysion, where gold thread was woven, were struck by lightning and went up in flames. Since silk weaving was an imperial monopoly and the secrets of production were closely guarded, they had been attached to the Great Palace.[93] The building of new workshops attached to the Eleutherios after 792 raises the tantalising possibility that Irene wished to keep control of the place where imperial skills were produced. During the eighth and ninth centuries large numbers of extremely valuable purple silks were woven – the charioteer silk, for instance, used as a shroud for Charlemagne (see plate 5). Constantine V may well have extended silk production at the old workshops for many diplomatic gifts of silk are recorded during his long reign. Irene appears to have continued this activity, perhaps sensing how highly Byzantine silks were valued in the West, where the secrets of silkworms had not yet been mastered. At her new residence, craftsmen continued to weave and decorate the fabrics worn by secular rulers and churchmen alike on ceremonial occasions. Smaller pieces of silk were also used to cover liturgical vessels and icons, and to wrap the most precious relics. The survival of Byzantine silks today is due to this high regard, and nearly all of them are to be found in western cathedral treasuries.[94]

The empress had access to many other palaces within the city and in the immediate vicinity: the palace of Hiereia on the Asian coast of the Marmara, where she stayed when she first arrived from Greece; the palace of Therapeia on the European shore of the Bosphoros, which was also used as a place of detention; the St Mamas Palace, again on the European shore, which became associated with Constantine VI and Theodote who celebrated their wedding there. But it seems that Irene particularly enjoyed her new palace of Eleutherios and liked to spend time there. Ignatios the deacon records a story of an official accused of embezzling money, who was tortured in the Eleutherios Palace where the empress was residing, a clear indication that the new structure functioned as a centre of government.[95] In 790 Constantine had confined Irene under guard in her palace of Eleutherios while he tried to rule alone.[96] This was obviously a convenient way of keeping her out of the Great Palace, so that Maria could occupy the official imperial quarters. It seems very likely that Irene had insisted on occupying these rooms after the death of her husband, and perhaps even beyond 788 when Constantine and his first bride should have moved in. The structural problem of an older empress refusing to make way for a younger one was not uncommon, as we have seen. Later, when the emperor divorced Maria and installed Theodote as empress, it also seems likely that they continued to exclude Irene from the chief imperial residence. But it was probably from choice that she was still living at the Eleutherios Palace in 802, when her opponents were to plot their final coup against her.[97]

The other major building associated specifically with Irene was the monastery of the Virgin, on the island of Prinkipo in the Sea of Marmara, to which she was first banished in 802, and in which she had asked to be buried. In the *Life of Irene* there is an indication that the community of nuns was especially committed to her well-being; after her death in 803, they welcomed her body and laid it in the chapel of St Nikolaos, within the monastic church dedicated to the Virgin.[98] While there are no further details of when and how the monastery was built, it fits perfectly the type of retirement home that élite women regularly constructed for themselves. It must have been one of Irene's first constructions as it was already functioning as a nunnery in 780/1.[99]

From the later text of the *Patria* of Constantinople, there are many legendary accounts of Irene's building activities, but some seem to fit well with her known philanthropy. The most significant account centres on a complex attached to a church of St Luke: 'Eirene the Athenian ... built three most important [monuments] for death, life and health. And for death she built the cemeteries for strangers (*xenotaphia*) and for life she built the dining halls (*triklinous*) of Lamias of Pistopeion, and for health she built the hostel (*xenon*) called the Eirene (*ta Eirenes*).'[100] The text specifies that burial for the poor was provided free of charge, as well as for foreigners, strangers and visitors to the city who had the misfortune to die there. Eating places for the elderly (*gerotropheia*) are listed in addition to houses where they might live, soup kitchens and retirement homes. The empress's piety and virtue are linked to the fact that she also reduced the burden of taxes (*phoron bare exekopsen*).

This extraordinary combination of life, health and death with clearly philanthropic aims and public functions, embodies Irene's concern for the well-being of the city. It may not have been an entirely unselfish charity, for through these institutions she made a useful contribution to poor relief which ensured that her name was associated with such structures. The reduction in taxes (dated to her sole rule, 797–802) may also have been a move designed to win public support rather than a considered intervention in the city's economy.[101] The hostel, however, survived into the tenth century when its manager is named along with others based in the capital.[102] One can imagine that the empress inaugurated her new buildings with the type of public ceremony that drew attention to her generosity. This complex of St Luke, in fact, may serve to symbolise her notion of the imperial calling. It would also become a model for other emperors, who were not solely preoccupied with structures within the Great Palace.

In a more problematical reference, the *Patria* attribute to Irene the foundation of 'a monastery of Euphrosyne called ta Libadia ... built by Eirene the Athenian, small and poor (*penichra*)'.[103] While this claim presents difficulties, it is quite possible that she did establish a monastery in a region of the city that was undeveloped, in the fields (*libadia*). It seems to have fallen on hard times after her death in 803 and was then restored by Euphrosyne, her granddaughter (see chapter 3). Two much more legendary attributions suggests that Irene and her son built the church of St Anastasios the Persian, and one dedicated to St Eustathios. But for these churches there is no confirmation from other sources.[104]

Further to these three or four major foundations, which all appear to be new constructions, Irene paid attention to important buildings in the city which were in need of restoration. The most important is probably the church of St Euphemia with its very holy relics which form the object of a detailed description by the iconophile bishop, Constantine of Tios. According to the *Patria*: 'Constantine the Great built the church of St Euphemia, the "all-well-named", in the Hippodrome ... Many years later, at the coming of the God-hating Kopronymos (Constantine V), he made this an arms dump and the dung heap and he threw out the remains of the saint in the coffin into the depths of the sea. And after another 37 years Eirene the most pious queen (*anassa*), the Athenian, restored it again and finding the remains brought them there.'[105] The date would be 796 and the destruction might have been caused by the earthquake of 740. Constantine V would have used the ruined structure to store arms, military supplies and horses, hardly the offensive misuse described by the *Patria*. Nevertheless, the restoration of the church of St Euphemia returned a significant collection of relics to Constantinople and gave Irene another opportunity to distribute some of the bones to worthy officials and relations.

She also restored the church of the Virgin of the Spring (*tes Peges*) built by Justinian I outside the city walls, in Thrace, with wood left over from the building of Hagia Sophia. The source of the water was a healing spring to which she personally attributed a miraculous cure. Irene and her son donated new golden curtains, a crown and liturgical vessels set with pearls and gems, as well as commissioning mosaic portraits to adorn the shrine.[106] This is a particularly significant type of reconstruction in that it formed a secure structure for a shrine already famous for miracles. By giving funds for its reconstruction, Irene provided not only the local population but also people from far away with a church complex to which pilgrimages were made. It thus constitutes another aspect of her concern for facilities for the sick and her attention to social services.

While the same source preserves a particularly unreliable account of Irene's building at the Chalke Gate of the Great Palace, she does appear to have been associated with its redecoration. Irene 'the Athenian' is held responsible for restoring the icon of Christ set in mosaic cubes which was displayed on the principal entrance to the palace. To shed light on this, it would be necessary to know what type of decoration preceded it: an image of Christ at the Chalke Gate is alleged to have been the focus of iconoclast attention in the first stages of the reform of icons. Sources of a much later date elaborate the heroic role of women who are supposed to have defended the image and killed one of the soldiers sent to remove it.[107] If indeed the iconoclast rulers had set up non-figural images at this key point, Irene is quite likely to have replaced them. But the history of this structure is very unclear. Leo III is said to have installed new images of the saints and Fathers of the Church holding scrolls with long biblical quotations, and if these remained in situ throughout the 750s and 60s, there would have been no need for action.

Once this construction activity in the capital is added up, Irene appears as quite a lavish builder, more concerned with charitable institutions and churches in the city and its environs than most emperors.[108] When records of imperial building resume in the ninth century, Theophilos, a dedicated and extravagant builder, spends most of his energy constructing grand reception halls and additional rooms and chapels inside the Great Palace. This had been the main activity of Justinian II, the last emperor to add to the primary imperial residence and to its fortifications, and of Constantine V, who built the new church of the Pharos and possibly the Porphyra. Irene's artistic patronage creates an impression of a more public-spirited concern for the needs of the city, a point which always brings enhanced popularity. Although there are references to Leo III and Constantine V in connection with building in the city earlier in the eighth century, Irene seems to have set a new trend, which was picked up by others, such as John Pikridios who was appointed as a tutor to

Constantine VI. He became *protospatharios*, a loyal supporter of the emperor, and built the *mone ta Pikridiou.*[109]

From the buildings in particular, we get a very different picture – that of a pious ruler dedicated to good works and the relief of poverty in the capital which was probably growing as the city expanded. While such activity is the duty of every Christian emperor, Irene revived the tradition on a grand scale, another aspect of her publicity-seeking nature, no doubt, but with beneficial results. Her patriarch Tarasios was similarly devoted to poor relief and is specifically associated with lists of deserving persons, who received monthly subsidies in silver, the establishment of poorhouses, food and winter clothing for those who sheltered in the porticoes of Hagia Sophia wearing nothing more than a loincloth. He too participated in public functions at which the poor banqueted, and he personally served the wine at the annual Easter feast to commemorate Christ's resurrection.[110] Together the pious empress and her leading churchman committed funds and their personal interest to improving the lot of the poor, probably attracting new inhabitants to Constantinople due to the consequent improvement in public services.

In conjunction with this expansion of imperial investment in religious structures and provincial control, Irene also developed imperial ceremonies in order to make new public appearances for effect. Though no record of the inauguration of her buildings survives, such rituals must have occurred. The *encaenia* of other monuments is clearly described and Byzantine emperors performed these ceremonies with lavish exhibitions of imperial symbols and distributions of largesse. If a religious consecration was also required, the patriarch added his entire clergy to the procession that would solemnly walk to the site and bless every corner of the church. Irene would certainly not have let such an opportunity pass. Her eye for publicity and her flair for ceremonial self-presentation would have ensured a brilliant ritual.

IRENE'S EUNUCH SERVANTS

Another aspect of Irene's government, regularly cited as specific to her unusual situation, is her employment of palace eunuchs to fill important positions. Historians have often commented on the close association of imperial women, especially widowed empresses, with the eunuchs who were in charge of their private quarters within the Great Palace. As empresses were surrounded by these beardless men throughout their lives, this is hardly surprising. From the moment when Irene arrived in Constantinople as a young bride, she would have become familiar with the officials who maintained court ceremonial. Whether she became dependent on them is another matter. It is a common charge that women and eunuchs could conspire together more easily than women and bearded men. In nineteenth-century China, such alliances permitted women to rule a vast empire from 'behind the curtain'. But in Byzantium, when an empress wished to see one of the male officials of the army, civil service, church or court, she only had to summon him. The eunuchs of her bedchamber and wardrobe, however, were always there on duty and could come and go with much less restraint than other men. Given their physical proximity, it is natural that Irene often used them to carry her secret orders (a task also documented in most aristocratic households).

There is thus a structural reason for the association of women and eunuchs in the Byzantine court. The existence of this third gender, and the particular ranks of the court hierarchy reserved to beardless men, meant that a large number of officials heavily dependent on their patrons were always anxious to please the ruling emperor and his consort. There is also evidence that the legal prohibition of castration within the empire was regularly flouted in circumstances where a particular family wished to create a eunuch son. The operation could be safely performed, without threat to the life of the usually young male child, and would ensure his career either as an ecclesiastic (many clerics and patriarchs were eunuchs) or as a high-ranking court official. Examples are provided by Niketas and Leo, eunuchs from Paphlagonia (see chapter 4).

In contrast, a significant number of eunuchs were created by the Byzantine imposition of castration as a punishment for political opposition. In this case the operation might be speedily or carelessly performed with the result that the victim died (as did the youngest son of Leo V and Theodosia in 829, and many others). Castration in these circumstances was intended to debar the individual from any capacity to engender heirs – to put an end to a dynastic line, for example. It was also considered an effective way of removing from imperial status the sons of a deposed emperor. Early in the ninth century, the sons of Michael I were castrated and, seven years later, those of Leo V. Patriarch Germanos had suffered a similar punishment for his father's opposition to Constantine IV in the late seventh century. Such mutilated men frequently entered monasteries, which might also contain eunuchs who embraced the monastic life. Within religious communities eunuchs were considered fortunate, in that their condition was believed to spare them some of the sexual temptations visited upon 'whole' men. This reveals one of the many elements of misinformation that circulated about eunuchs. However, in contrast to the prejudice against eunuchs in the medieval West, there was no objection to their promotion to ecclesiastical careers in Byzantium. In the eighth century, Patriarch Niketas was a eunuch of Slavic origin; in 847 one of the castrated sons of Michael I became patriarch as Ignatios, and several other leading members of the church hierarchy are so identified.

The acceptance of eunuchs, and their presence in some of the well documented early Christian monastic communities, also gave rise to a particular connection with women. For by cutting their hair and adopting male dress, women were able to escape their biological destiny, disguised as beardless men. Their lack of body hair and high-pitched voices were interpreted as a confirmation of this status, which must therefore have been common enough. In this way, Christian women using the disguise of the eunuch pursued their dedication to the spiritual life. In the numerous stories written about them, they fled from arranged marriages, repented of their previously unchristian lives as prostitutes, and sought refuge in monasteries of men, where their angry relatives were least likely to come looking for them. Such disguise leads to some bizarre situations: the man who is not a man meets 'his' father in circumstances where their natural roles are reversed; the isolated hermit, whom all the local monks respected, dies and turns out to be a woman after all; the woman disguised as a man is accused of making a nun pregnant and suffers ostracism, until the deceitful nun is stricken with remorse.[111]

From the many versions of such stories, ending with a good Christian moral, it is evident that they had tremendous appeal. Not only were they written down, they were also translated into many languages and circulated widely throughout the medieval world. The misadventures of eunuch women, such as St Eugenia and St Euphrosyne, make exciting reading. In a different category but equally compelling, the Lives of reformed prostitutes, such as St Pelagia, who also passed as a eunuch, survive in many languages. Numerous examples were preserved in the *Synaxarion* of Constantinople, thus ensuring that these Lives were read on the name-day of the saint.[112] The popularity of such stories may account for a most unusual addition to the literature about such eunuch women. In the fourteenth century, Nikephoros Kallistos Xanthopoulos wrote a life of St Euphrosyne the Younger, whom he placed in the late ninth century and endowed with a highly adventurous life, complete with disguise as a eunuch. This construction is typical of the early Christian period but, as there were no more saints in this older mode by the ninth century, probably totally fictitious.

Yet such inventions reflect one obvious way for women to get round the social prohibition of activities considered inappropriate for them in the medieval period. And references to the use of such a well-known disguise persist. In the Life of Tarasios, Patriarch of Constantinople from 784 to 806, miracles that occurred at his tomb in the monastery he had founded at Stenon on the Bosphoros, include the healing of a woman with an issue of blood. Like the New Testament figure, she believed that she could be cured by the patriarch's relics, but women were not allowed to enter the male monastery. So she and some friends craftily disguised themselves as eunuchs and thus gained admittance. She was, of course, miraculously cured and she and her friends escaped to tell the tale. In this case the author, Ignatios, seems to approve of their inventiveness and determination to get close to the holy relics.[113] Later hagiographic texts are less indulgent: St Neilos of Rossano could sense the mere presence of a female, and male saints were generally hostile to the device.

By the eighth century, the pattern of creating female Byzantine saints had changed radically and early Christian opportunities for travel, pilgrimage, or pursuing a solitary or communal life disguised as a eunuch had been gradually removed. Women could still be sanctified by martyrdom, by demonstrations of excessive piety and good works, especially if miracles occurred at their tombs, but it was no longer considered suitable for them to adopt the disguise of the eunuch. So the third gender of the eunuch became the preserve of the mutilated man or a male born without adequate physical characteristics to perform the act of sexual penetration and procreation. These were the advisers on whom all empresses were said to rely for support and help in managing their affairs. Does Irene fit into this model?

As the reader will have noted, from the beginning of the Regency in 780 Irene had placed the beardless men of her household in key positions. This is in marked contrast to her husband's rule, and that of her successor Nikephoros I, when few eunuch officials of note are recorded as being active in the political direction of the empire. Irene, however, used these loyal servants to fill important military and civilian roles. Some performed adequately, others quite brilliantly, so there is no need to assume an unrealistic favouritism which took no account of their abilities. But obviously the empress found support among eunuch officials who were already known to her for their personal service and loyalty, just as any ruler on coming to power relies primarily on administrators and officials whom he knows and can trust. At other times in Byzantium it is possible to document the dependence of male rulers on their eunuchs. But Irene became Regent for her young son after a succession of military emperors whose rule had been characterised by annual campaigning in the field. Since 717, the dynasty of Leo III had devoted its energies to holding off the Arab threat in the East and subduing the Bulgars in the Balkans. This had involved considerable administrative reforms, in which eunuch officials may have played a role. But the overriding importance of defending the much-reduced borders of the empire had drawn attention particularly to military skills and the importance of military victories.

In 780 this was a role that neither Irene nor her young son could fill, so the Council of Regency must have appreciated the need for military leadership from non-imperial circles. Irene chose to employ her own eunuch servants for the task, and this makes a dramatic change in the record of her years as Regent. She also kept the veteran generals such as Michael Lachanodrakon, who had remained aloof from the plot against her in 780, in their commands. Others who conspired with the ex-caesars were severely punished and replaced by men loyal to Irene. From the outset she appears to have gained and held the support of her eunuchs, so it seems excessive to suggest that they manipulated her and took over the management of the empire.

As an instance of this claim, it is instructive to read Theophanes' account of Constantine's attempt to establish his own authority in 790. Vexed because everyone ignored him, the crowned emperor, and treated Staurakios as the ruler, who 'had everything in his power',[114] Constantine decided to remove the eunuch from this position, banish him to Sicily and then rule the empire with his mother. So the first object of his hostility was not Irene so much as Staurakios. And the chief eunuch's prominence was due to Irene's advisers, or seers, who had been informed by prophesies that she alone should rule, and that it was ordained by God that her son should not obtain the empire. Theophanes comments: 'Deceived, like the woman she was, and being also ambitious, she was satisfied that things were indeed so, and did not perceive that those men had offered the above pretext because they wanted to administer the affairs of State.'[115] In this explanation of the rivalry between mother and son, Theophanes manages to imply that the empress was entirely led by her courtiers, who played on her natural feminine weakness as well as her ambition, and allowed Staurakios to assume the role of emperor. Thus, when Staurakios learned of Constantine's plans, he 'roused the Augusta against her son'[116] and, as a result, it was Constantine's men who were banished as far as Sicily, rather than the other way round.

The chronicler has correctly identified the structural problem which provoked Constantine VI, then aged twenty, to try and assume his rightful position as emperor. The Regent, his mother, had ruled during his minority with the help of eunuch official, many of whom had previously been employed in her household. They were linked to her by rather special bonds and obviously had a vested interest in the continuation of her rule. So they concocted a prophesy that she alone should be in charge, to the exclusion of her son, to safeguard their own prominent roles in government. After a decade of exercising such power through the empress, they were not likely to tolerate a change of ruler. If, as seems clear, Staurakios was the leader of this faction of the court, then young Constantine correctly identified the individual he had to remove from power. But, Theophanes continues, the emperor intended to assume control of the empire 'together with his mother'.[117] So he did not believe that Constantine considered it necessary to rule alone, without Irene. He blamed her ministers for depriving him of his imperial position.

In this account of the first outbreak of direct rivalry between Constantine and his mother, the chronicler falls back on what I have termed a stereotypical method of analysing women in power. He does not consider the possibility that Irene herself spotted the restlessness in her son and attempted to quell it by a harsh demonstration of her own authority. Instead, because she was a woman, she was deceived by blatant inventions about her God-given role; she was unable to understand that this was a ruse designed to allow her advisers to sustain their own place in imperial administration; and she did what Staurakios proposed in order to counter her son's plot. When it comes to the final part of the story, Theophanes has probably preserved a reliable element: namely, that her chief minister warned her of Constantine's plans and urged her to make a pre-emptive strike. That was his duty as her adviser. But it seems unlikely that Irene had not already thought about her son's growing desire for independence when her determination to keep army commanders loyal to herself, rather than him, reveals such foresight. Theophanes recognises this when he records the difficulty that Irene had in persuading some of the military units to renege on the oath of loyalty they made to Constantine in 775.

The assumption behind the writing is, however, of a predictable style: women are weak and need advisers more than men. They are moreover likely to believe all the flattery that is poured on people in power. They can not perceive the hidden agendas of such flatterers. All this is due to their position as women, condemned by the sin of Eve to be inferior to males. Some women may on rare occasions rise above this feminine weakness and take on manly strength and courage. Irene manifests these qualities when confronted by the *coup d'état* of her finance minister, Nikephoros. Theophanes characterises her response as the product of 'a brave and prudent mind', adding 'though she ought to have been overwhelmed by the misfortune of her sudden change (especially since she was a woman)'.[118] The speech which is then put into her mouth reveals precisely this manly courage. Irene takes full responsibility for her actions, praising God for having raised her to the imperial throne and accepting the same divine judgement which now elevates Nikephoros in her place. In this brief address, Theophanes shows how a woman in purple behaves with a man's strength and an imperial training, in marked contrast to his previous claims about the inherent and unavoidable incapacity of the female sex. Bearing in mind this contradiction which infuses the written records of the period, let us examine what Irene achieves as emperor.

IRENE'S POLICIES AS EMPEROR 797–802

Once Constantine has been removed from power, Irene issues an announcement to the effect that he is no longer emperor. Within the empire, this news immediately provokes two more attempts to replace Irene by the sons of Constantine V. In October 797 Aetios, one of her eunuch advisers, quelled the first of these efforts and banished the ex-caesars to Athens. But the following year some forces attached to the *thema* of the *Helladikoi* (Hellas) collaborated with a local Slavic chieftain, Akamir, to try yet again. On this occasion Irene finds her own kinsmen useful: her nephew Theophylaktos Serantapechos, who held the title of *spatharios*, is sent to ask his father Constantine, Irene's brother to put down the plot. The four sighted caesars are then blinded.[119] Yet even in this miserable condition they are still the focus of other rebels' attention: in 811/12, during the reign of Michael I, a further plot to install the

brothers, then imprisoned at Panormos, revealed a continuing attachment to the sons of Constantine V.[120] Despite the slight difference of
name, on this occasion two male members of Irene's own family are
mentioned for the first and last time. Perhaps her much younger brother
Constantine had been left in Greece when she began her career in the
capital and had only recently been promoted to the patriciate together
with his son, the *spatharios*. But if they hoped for far greater prominence,
they were to be disappointed. Irene was not concerned to favour her
relations.[121]

She is, however, very anxious to establish a stable foreign policy and
to this end, in 798, she sends embassies to both the Arabs and the
Franks. The news of Constantine's mutilation and removal from power
is announced in these two missions, both dedicated to the same end:
peace. Harun al-Rashid declines to cease his military operations against
Byzantium, which are going well. Instead he sends Abd al-Malik to
devastate Cappadocia and Galatia, and the following year raids the
imperial stud, based at Malagina, capturing the entire camp equipment
of the Opsikion *thema*. Hostilities with the Arabs thus seem fated to
continue. In the West, however, the announcement is better received.
Irene specifically requests the release of Sisinnios, brother of Patriarch
Tarasios, who had been taken prisoner by the Franks in 788, and this is
granted. Charles also returns the peace embassy and East–West contacts
are reopened after a long disruption.[122]

Even if the Arabs and Franks accept Irene as sole emperor in Byzantium, her assumption of power causes some misgivings. Some of Charles's advisers in particular question who is really governing the empire.
For western leaders, both secular and ecclesiastical, who had previously
maintained diplomatic contacts with Byzantium, Irene is more clearly
identified as a woman, who has for a long time been empress and co-
emperor with her son. Some even suggest that because she is not a male
emperor in the same sense as Constantine VI, the imperial position is
somehow vacant. Of course, in Constantinople Irene has no doubt about
her own role and title as emperor and indicates that she considers herself
the equal of her predecessors. The court also accepts her use of the title
basileus, however anomalous.

As if to forestall any possible criticism, Irene makes another spectacular
appeal to the loyalty of the inhabitants of the Queen City as their emperor.
After the celebration of Easter in 799, she rides from the church of Holy
Apostles in a gilded chariot drawn by four white horses, with four

patricians holding the reins, and distributes largesse all the way back to the palace. This ceremony, which is prescribed for Easter Monday in the *Book of Ceremonies*, was cleverly adapted for a female emperor so that the traditional distribution of coin would not be missed.[123] Normally, the male emperor would ride a white horse decked out in the richest equipage and his chief officers would ride beside him, preceded by foot soldiers and palace officials all wearing their best uniforms and Sunday costumes. It is a day-long ceremony with numerous stops at different monuments in the city where the ruler is acclaimed by the factions and distributions of coin are made. As a female emperor, Irene prefers to ride in a carriage but she adds four of her chief military officers, Bardanes Tourkos, *strategos* of the Thrakesion, Sisinnios of Thrace, and his brother, Niketas, *domestikos* of the *scholai*, and Constantine Boilas, in the subordinate role of walking beside the horses throughout the long procession.

Taken together with Irene's previous building activity, her decision in 799 to appear in public in the traditional philanthropic role of the ruler lavishly throwing money to the crowds lining the streets, fits a clear pattern. She manifests the same policy when she decides to reduce the so-called civic taxes paid by inhabitants of Constantinople and the commercial taxes levied on all goods entering or leaving the empire. These *kommerkia* were collected by officials named after them, stationed at Abydos (at the southern entrance to the Dardanelles) and Hieron at the north end of the Bosphoros (which controlled the entrance to the Black Sea). As tax reduction is always a popular measure, the emperor calculates that it will consolidate her position and expand her support, which is still drawn largely from iconophile and monastic circles. This concentration on securing the approval of the city's growing population reflects the all-important position of the capital within the empire. Given the hostility of Harun al-Rashid and his military success, Irene can do little to relieve the suffering of those who live in the path of invading Arabs armies in Asia Minor. But she is determined to strengthen the popular support of the Byzantines.

Although it is difficult to date other measures precisely, Irene seems to have pressed on with the policy of extending imperial administration to parts of the Balkans and the western regions of the empire. Here there were fewer serious military threats, though Arab pirates were already causing problems for those living on the shores of the Aegean. In the last decade of the eighth century or very early in the ninth, new *themata* were established in key areas: Macedonia, covering the regions of western

Thrace subdued in the 780s and visited by Irene and Constantine in the regal progress of 784; Kephalonia and Zakynthos, two key islands from which the Christianisation of mainland Greece was being undertaken; and Dyrrachion, further north on the western coast of Greece.[124] The creation of these new provincial units is frequently attributed to Irene's successor, Nikephoros, but the dates of the first appearance of thematic officials suggests that she is more likely to have been responsible. From her first-hand experience of visiting northern Greece she may well have considered this a priority.

The importance she attaches to the area is also evident in her decision to elevate the episcopal see of Athens to metropolitan status.[125] In making this promotion, she overrode the regular policy of permitting only one metropolitan see in each diocese, as well as honouring the church of her own home town. While the list of church leaders of Athens does not establish a distinct date for this change, Irene is traditionally associated with the move. In this way historians have revealed their own assumptions that a female emperor would be more concerned to elevate the position of the church of Athens than to tackle the much more fundamental problem of expanding effective, centralised control over regions previously beyond imperial authority.

In her new position as sole emperor, Irene also has to consider her future. As mother of the heir to the throne, she had protected her son's claim since 780 and the question of her remarriage had not been publicly discussed. But being a widowed empress, who has eliminated her son as a successor, she is now in a position to confer imperial status on a husband of her own choosing. Such a policy might have limited her proven appetite for power, and it does not seem to have appealed to her. She has certainly refused all the proposals made by her eunuch advisers, especially Aetios who consistently tries to promote his brother Leo. In 797 Irene is over forty years old and quite possibly past child-bearing age, so that any husband who outlives her will automatically have a very good chance of inheriting her power. But she resists the idea that she might marry Leo or adopt him as her successor. The prospect of ruling alone for many more years is probably far more attractive and will, of course, ensure that Irene is laid to rest in the imperial mausoleum beside her husband Leo IV.

Aetios's manoeuvrings, however, spark an increased rivalry between the two highest-ranking eunuchs in the Byzantine government, which eventually becomes a matter of public knowledge. It disturbs Irene's first two years as a sole ruler and grows more dangerous when Irene is taken seriously ill in May 799. The possibility of her dying with the succession undecided intensifies the competition between Staurakios and Aetios, her supposedly most loyal servants. As Theophanes puts it, they openly display their enmity, for now 'both aimed at securing the empire for their own relatives after her death'.[126] Staurakios plots among the resident *scholarioi* and *exkoubitors* stationed in the capital, bribing their officers with money and gifts, while Aetios makes an alliance with Niketas Triphyllios who holds the key military post of *domestikos* of the *scholai*. Irene attempts to control this in-fighting by summoning a council at which she prohibits any men in government service from approaching Staurakios, but the battles are only brought to an end by the latter's death in June 799.

In the event, Irene recovers her health though not her previous control over Aetios, who blatantly promotes his brother Leo. As governor-in-chief (*monostrategos*) of two western provinces (Thrace and the newly created *thema* of Macedonia), Leo holds power in the European areas closest to Constantinople, while Aetios himself combines the command of Opsikion and Anatolikon, two of the most important eastern provinces. Displaying an increasing amount of confidence, grandeur and rudeness, Aetios alienates all those outside his family power game. While she must be aware of the danger of these developments, Irene is unable to prevent them.

IRENE'S PROPOSAL TO CHARLEMAGNE

In these circumstances Irene investigates a dramatically different course of action, namely that of making a marriage of convenience to a husband who would not interfere with her sole rule. There is just a hint in the sources that Irene seriously considers this possibility. The evidence is recorded only in a very brief Latin text known as the *Kölner Notiz*, which describes how a Byzantine embassy arrived at the Frankish court from Sicily and proposed to hand the empire over to Charles.[127] Since the exact nature of this mission is very unclear, its aim is revealed in just four words, and Irene is not identified as the authority responsible for sending it, many interpretations have been suggested. One would trace the mission to Irene, who wanted to find out somewhat unofficially what attitude Charles might take to the idea that they might form a peaceful alliance cemented by a formal marriage. Alternative readings might suggest that a fifth column of discontented citizens had taken the initiative to make Charles their ruler, but this would constitute a totally improper invitation to declare outright war on Byzantium and the Franks would have understood it as such.

If, on the other hand, Irene is correctly identified as the source of the proposal, it would fit perfectly with *her* idea – namely, that through a political marriage of convenience, Charles would rule over his territories in the West and she would rule over Byzantium in a union that ensured peaceful co-operation rather than tension and potential warfare. Whether this proposal would also have involved some recognition of Charles's position – bestowing on him the imperial title, for example – is not clear.[128] But the choice of a delegation from Sicily fits well with the status of the island, a region where both Latin and Greek were known, which had always been a sensitive listening post for western developments, and whose governors regularly participated in both diplomatic and military activity in southern and central Italy. A delegation from Sicily would also have understood the importance of securing peace in the island.

Although it was highly unusual for a female sovereign to propose such an arrangement to a male ruler in a distant region not subject to her rule, we must remember that Irene expresses no interest in extending her authority over the West, nor does she expect Charles to march into Constantinople and take over in the East. Both of them are experienced rulers, who have negotiated a betrothal, broken it off, and sent troops to fight over the rich lands of southern Italy. In her new circumstances as sole ruler, Irene could now view the prospect of securing peace in this way.[129] One of her first acts had been to send an official delegation to negotiate an end to military activity. The unofficial mission which set out from Sicily a little later brought the same message within a different framework. And to this suggestion Charles responded favourably.

WESTERN OPPOSITION TO ICON VENERATION

In order to understand how this new initiative had developed, it is necessary to recall the framework of East–West relations since the council of 787 which had restored image veneration. Relying on an inaccurate Latin translation of the Greek text which they had been sent, Frankish theologians had refused to accept the acts of the council. They identified the Byzantine practice of icon veneration as the idolatrous worship of material objects. They found fault with the Byzantines on biblical grounds and disapproved of the proof texts adduced to justify figural representations. None of the eastern arguments put forward at the Council of Nicaea in 787 was accepted by western experts. In the *Libri Carolini* prepared by Theodulf of Orleans, all the Byzantine claims concerning icon veneration as an ancient tradition were fiercely condemned.[130] Instead, at the Synod of Frankfurt held in 794, arguments in favour of a middle way between the overt veneration of icons and their use as instruments of teaching and inspiration, were propounded.

As a result of the court theologians' critical analysis of the acts of 787, Pope Hadrian found himself in a particularly awkward situation. The Bishop of Rome had been happy to celebrate the restoration of church unity occasioned by the successful conclusion of the council of 787. But his acceptance of the *acta* placed him midway between the extreme iconophile resurgence in the East and the very measured and often hostile interpretation of it by the Franks. In 795 Pope Hadrian died and a new bishop of Old Rome was elected from an established aristocratic family. Taking the name Leo III, the pope inherited from Hadrian a number of problems both in relation to the Franks and to the Byzantines.[131] His election was not unanimous either, so he also faced opposition from within Rome.

THE IMPERIAL TITLE

Pope Leo III was, however, in possession of a forged document entitled the *Donation of Constantine*, which purported to record the arrangements made by Constantine I (306–37) when he left Italy to establish his eastern capital of New Rome on the Bosphoros. Constantine the Great had allegedly been converted to Christianity by the Bishop of Rome, Sylvester, to whom he had entrusted control over the western regions of the empire. This document was probably fabricated in Roman clerical circles during the middle of the eighth century.[132] It conveniently overlooked the fact that for several centuries after Constantine I's move to the East, emperors in the West had been appointed by their senior colleagues in Constantinople. It also held that the imperial title and imperial control over the western half of the old Roman Empire were within the gift of the Bishop of Rome. Armed with this forgery, Leo III could reinterpret the process by which Charles had already been acclaimed *patricius Romanorum*, patrician of the Romans. The title adopted as a result of Charles's victorious campaign against the Lombard kingdom of northern

Italy became a preparatory step towards the higher one, which Leo III as pope was in a position to bestow.

Among some of the Frankish courtiers also, the idea that Charles might accede to the title of emperor, which was more elevated than all his previous ones, was very appealing. Alcuin, a scholar from York, was especially keen that the king's political control in Europe, extended by his recent triumph over the Avars in Hungary and his promotion of Christianity among the pagan Saxons, should be recognised in some formal way. Charles's role in uniting many territories within the European continent thus gave rise to the epithet 'Europae pater', father of Europe. This new entity also represented a transformed version of the Roman Empire in the West, a most Christian 'imperium' which should be ruled by the most Christian 'imperator'. Further, this same Charles was in the process of constructing a capital city which was already known as the Second Rome, or the Rome of the future. Aachen was intended to replace the older, pagan Romes, both the one on the Tiber and the one on the Bosphoros. Reasoning in this way, Alcuin and others prepared a more glorious role for Charles than the Frankish monarch may have dreamed of.[133]

Then, unexpectedly, in April 799 Pope Leo was attacked by a gang hired by a rival aristocratic family, which hoped to blind and mutilate him so that he could no longer perform the function of bishop. In the event, the perpetrators failed to remove his eyes and cut out his tongue, and he was able to flee north and across the Alps to Charles's court at Paderborn.[134] This was only the second time that a bishop had left Rome, the first being when Stephen II made his decisive appeal to Charles's father to become the secular protector of the Roman church against Lombard military threats. In 799, as in 753/4, the Frankish king responded favourably to the pope's plight. After entertaining him at Paderborn for several months, Charles had him escorted back to Rome later the same year. Despite the difficulty of settling matters in which Leo had been accused of serious moral wrongdoing, the pope was restored to his see. While Charles remained in Saxony and supervised defensive fortifications in the early part of 800, discussion continued in Rome about whether, and if so, how, to honour him.

CHARLES'S CORONATION AS EMPEROR

After an assembly held in Mainz in August 800 Charles set out for Italy, visiting his son Pippin in Ravenna on the way to Rome. Pope Leo came out to meet him at the twelfth milestone at Mentana, and on 24 November Charles made his ceremonial entry into the city and visited St Peter's.[135] It was in these highly charged circumstances, as Charles presided over the assembly which devised a way of reinstating Pope Leo, and planned legal proceedings against those who had attacked him, that the Christmas feast approached. For the occasion it was appropriate for Charles to put on the costume of a Roman *patricius*, some form of toga, and to attend mass at St Peter's where the pope would officiate. This provided the context in which the Bishop of Rome placed a crown on Charles's head and had him acclaimed as 'imperator Romanorum' by the choir and clergy of St Peter's. The imperial coronation ceremony had obviously been prepared in advance, perhaps for as long as eighteen months, since Leo's journey to Paderborn. Yet Charles may have been angered at the way it was performed, which established Pope Leo as the authority with power to endow such an ancient title. The king perhaps did not want to be indebted to the Bishop of Rome in this way. The Frankish court had only recently seen how insecure was Leo's hold on political power in Rome.

The precise motives and expectations of the participants in this crucial event, which took place on Christmas Day, AD 800, are still difficult to reconstruct fully and there are many hypothetical explanations.[136] For certain western contemporaries who recorded the ceremony, it was the absence of a male ruler in Constantinople which meant that the imperial title could legitimately be claimed by another. For these writers, the title in question was the one previously held by Constantine VI, whose blinding disqualified him. They refused to consider the imperial claims of Irene as *basileus*, for how could a woman be emperor? For Pope Leo III, whose predecessor had already given Charles the title *patricius Romanorum*, the possibility of elevating him to imperial status would fill this gap. He would be crowned *imperator Romanorum* by the Bishop of Rome, and his new status would entrench papal claims according to the *Donation*.

In his record of the five-year period of Irene's rule as sole emperor, Theophanes devotes most space to Charles's coronation by Pope Leo III. It is mentioned on two separate occasions in the *Chronographia*.

Drawing on a Roman source, Theophanes accurately presents the imperial coronation as a consequence of rivalries between the aristocratic families of Rome, which put the pope's life in such jeopardy that he fled north across the Alps to the Frankish court. But neither of his entries gives any explanation of what the parties involved thought they were doing.

The first description is entered under the year of the world 6289 (797) and follows on from the story of the attack on Pope Leo III and his escape to the Franks. When he later returned and was reinstated as Bishop of Rome, the pope 'repaid his debt to Charles' by crowning and anointing him with oil from head to foot, investing him with imperial robes and a crown, on 25 December of the ninth indication (AD 800). Theophanes has the correct date but has inserted his account three years too early. When he reaches the year of the world 6293, which corresponds to AD 800, he repeats the crowning in a second entry, and on this occasion connects it with Charles's proposal of marriage to Irene, which was brought to Constantinople by Frankish ambassadors. So, in this account, he also looks forward in time to the arrival of the embassy in 802. Theophanes here claims that Charles had first considered mounting an expedition against Sicily, an aggressive move against a Byzantine province, which would have caused Irene great concern. But he changed his mind and instead decided to make an alliance with her.

BYZANTINE REACTION TO THE CORONATION

As far as the Byzantine court was concerned, for Charles to claim the title 'emperor of the Romans' was an insult. The only emperor of the Romans was the one who resided in Constantinople, New Rome. There could be no other. It was a fundamental aspect of imperial ideology that the Emperor of the Romans resided in the capital named after Constantine I, the first Christian emperor, from whom Irene and all other rulers traced their authority. If, in one year of the world 6293, Irene held the title of emperor, it was an exceptional situation which the court had accepted. However, it is possible that Irene's advisers sought to revive the Late Antique traditions by which the senior emperor in the East had regularly named a colleague, who served as the junior emperor in the West. In this case, Irene could have devised the plan of elevating Charles to the position of emperor in the West. If, in addition, Irene herself had proposed the marriage alliance in her secret embassy from

Sicily, she might have developed a dual policy of political and matrimonial alliance with Charles.

A thorough examination of the circumstances going back to the time of Constantine I, when eastern emperors appointed their junior colleagues in the West, has recently shown that if Irene had made such a proposition it would have been 'constitutionally correct'.[137] Several factors, however, argue against this interpretation, not least the acclamations by which Charles was accorded his new title. Instead of being identified as emperor ruling with Irene, the senior emperor, he was simply called *imperator Romanorum*. This was in agreement with Leo's notion of a secular authority based in Rome, and reflected the progression from *patricius Romanorum* to *imperator*. But Charles himself revealed an ambiguous relationship to this title, preferring to use the circumlocution, 'governing the empire', *gubernans imperium*, which is documented in his first legal acts issued in Ravenna from 801 onwards.[138] He never alluded to the joint authority of the two emperors or deferred to Irene as the senior emperor.

Further, if Irene had indeed supported Charles's acclamation as emperor over the western parts of the empire, she would not have been satisfied with the way in which the ceremony was performed. Normally the senior emperor would have participated in the crowning of the junior partner. But since Irene could not be present in person to perform this role in the traditional fashion prescribed in the *Book of Ceremonies*, she ought at least to have sent her court officials to establish the correct procedure. This could have been easily done, had she so wished. Eunuchs familiar with the coronation ceremony would have set off for Rome with the proper imperial insignia (a crown, an imperial *skaramangion*, the gold tunic worn by the emperor at his coronation, the red slippers of imperial power and so on). A precedent had been set only recently when Byzantium decided to recognise the claims of Adelgis' successor as Duke of Benevento. The imperial costume and regalia were sent to him as confirmation of imperial approval (though it arrived after his death and was therefore of no use). So there were established methods of awarding high-ranking titles of the Byzantine court to deserving rulers in the West.[139]

An additional anomaly in the ceremony as performed by Leo III concerns the use of holy oil to anoint the new emperor. Unction, as it is called, was never a part of the Byzantine imperial coronation, but it had become a central feature of the enthronement of bishops and rulers in the West.[140] The Byzantine chronicler, Theophanes, misunderstood the ceremony when he described the unction as anointing with oil from head to foot. In fact, a tiny amount of consecrated oil was used in the ritual. By this specifically western addition to the imperial coronation procedure, the Bishop of Rome revealed that he was employing the established practice of consecrating rulers in the medieval West. Clearly, he had not received instructions from the East about how to perform a Byzantine imperial coronation in the name of the senior emperor.

On the contrary, Pope Leo III had to persuade Charles to put on some form of Roman attire, while a suitably imperial crown had to be found and a coronation ritual had to be devised. It is unclear what procedures had been agreed. Whatever the Frankish king anticipated on Christmas Day 800, his acclamation as *imperator et augustus* only partly answered Alcuin's proposals for a grander title and did not please the Frankish theologians. They did not consider that the Bishop of Rome had any right to bestow an imperial title and thus assume a crucial role in the ceremony. The Franks did not perceive of Roman ecclesiastical authority as something overarching which covered the whole of Charles's territories. Within northern Europe, papal authority was hedged by the claims of many archbishops to an equal power. They may have been ignorant of the alleged *Donation of Constantine* and therefore mistrusted papal motives. Much later Charles's biographer, Einhard, would claim that the king had been surprised by Leo's initiative, taken apparently without mutual agreement on Christmas Day.

On balance, therefore, the idea that Irene herself initiated the coronation of Charles seems less likely than that Leo III took advantage of the king's presence in Rome to have him acclaimed *imperator Romanorum*. Of the three powers involved in the coronation event of 800, the Roman pontiff emerges as the clear winner in the triangular contest over imperial authority. By seizing the initiative and crowning Charles in his own way, Pope Leo claimed the superior authority to anoint an imperial ruler of the West, which established an important precedent. Drawing on ancient traditions of acclamations of rulers and papal protocol used when Charles had been elevated to the position of *patricius Romanorum*, the ceremony of coronation was completed by the additional feature of unction with holy oil, which had been used for the anointing of kings and bishops in the West for centuries. The events of 25 December 800 were thus put together as the opportunity presented itself. Of course, through this composite ceremonial the pope expressed his gratitude to the monarch who had saved his life and restored him to his episcopal throne.

If Charles's attitude towards his new honour remains unclear, his decision to abandon the proposed military campaign against Byzantine provinces in the West is inexplicable. Perhaps he saw it as a way of wining over Irene's support. For whatever reason, Charles gave up an earlier idea of attacking Sicily, one of the most important Byzantine possessions in the West and a key area for monitoring western developments. Instead, he announced that he would seek to marry Irene and thus reunite the two halves of the old Roman world, which had been separated for so long. As a result of this change of policy, he appointed ambassadors to travel to the eastern capital and negotiate a marriage alliance with the empress. The decision was supported by Pope Leo III, who added his own legates to the party.

Meanwhile, in Byzantium, news of Charles's imperial claims gradually became known in more than one version. For eighteen months, however, Irene chose to ignore these accounts and waited to learn what Charles would say in response to her own proposals. When finally the western embassy arrives, she reveals herself not ill-disposed towards the idea of an alliance. The marriage proposal is presented as coming from Charles, who perhaps sees in this ploy a method of sharing imperial authority with Irene. He would keep his new title as the ruler of the western half of the empire, while the empress retained hers in the East. For Irene the idea may not have been at all new, if she herself had proposed the same policy to Charles. It seems unlikely that she has considered what would happen when either of them dies. Despite her ill-health she has not yet taken steps to resolve the succession issue in Byzantium; Charles has many potential heirs but has not yet designated the one to succeed him. For Charles to 'inherit' the eastern empire by marriage probably seems as inconceivable as Irene laying claim to his western territories. But to the empress's courtiers and advisers, the threat of a western ruler having any role in the government of the Roman Empire of Byzantium may be a future too dreadful to contemplate. For the moment, in 802, Irene listens to the embassy with interest and might have agreed to its proposals had not Aetios, the chief eunuch, intervened.[141]

IRENE'S DOWNFALL

In the summer of 802, therefore, a combination of circumstances challenges Irene's control. Domestically, Aetios' stranglehold on the military is provoking some dignitaries in positions of authority, who have already been insulted by his behaviour, to plot against Irene. While she counts on her own support in the capital, she is obviously not warned of the dangers posed by these developments. And this internal dissension is deepened by the arrival of the Frankish and papal ambassadors proposing a 'foreign' alliance which some courtiers find very threatening. Both raise the issue of the succession, a matter which Irene chooses to ignore. Possibly Aetios now realises that he would never win imperial power and urges the finance minister, Nikephoros, to rebel. It is notable that he continued in high office under the new ruler; they both died on the battlefield in 811.

Irene's refusal to settle the question of the succession proves her undoing. The first of our three women in purple is overthrown in a governmental *coup d'état* executed by Nikephoros and a group of like-minded courtiers, with military support. They trick the guards on the Chalke Gate of the Palace into opening its doors just before dawn on Monday 31 October 802, and send soldiers to surround the Eleutherios Palace where Irene is living.[142] Not only the two Triphyllios brothers, who had participated in the Eastern procession of 799, but also the *sakellarios* (treasurer), Leo of Sinope, and the *quaestor* (chief legal officer), Theoktistos, take part. They are joined by two of the disaffected generals whom Irene had sacked, Gregorios, previously Count of the Opsikion, and Petros, commander of the *scholai*. This was quite predictable. The involvement of Leo Serantapechos, presumably another of Irene's relations, is more problematic. Nothing is known of this figure prior to his participation in the coup against Irene, but given her refusal to promote family members to positions of prominence, there may have been several Serantapechoi who felt cheated of the handsome salaries and honorific posts which they anticipated might come to them.

Later the same day, Irene was moved to the Great Palace and Nikephoros was proclaimed emperor and crowned in a bloodless revolution. Patriarch Tarasios may have tried to ensure that she would be well treated, but certainly he did not delay the coronation ceremony necessary to legitimise the revolt of Nikephoros. The change of government was witnessed by the Frankish and papal ambassadors who returned home shortly afterwards. Whatever understanding Charles and Irene had hoped to set in place immediately disappeared. The new Emperor of Byzantium had no time for the Franks and their imperial pretensions. Although Nikephoros had promised Irene a quiet life in her palace, as soon as she revealed where all her treasure was stored, he had her banished to the island of Prinkipo. And in November 802, when the winter was particularly severe, she was sent even further away to the island of Lesbos, to a secure exile where her guards were ordered to make sure that she received no visitors. Eight months later she died there and her body was transferred back to Prinkipo. According to the very favourable *Life of Irene*, probably written for the community at Prinkipo, it was during her last visit to the foundation in 802 that Irene expressed her desire to be buried there.[143]

Theophanes gives no warning of the conspiracy; Nikephoros' role as finance minister dates back to 799 but his imperial ambitions are not mentioned previously. But it is notable that Irene had tried to secure local support by cancelling taxes, thus reducing imperial revenues and perhaps provoking concern in the ministry of finance. The quarrels between Aetios and Staurakios drew attention to their concentration of powers, which both divided the court and excluded other officials from the centre of government. In addition to financial and political issues, there may have been other factors involved which were not recorded by the chronicler, such as military concerns: several of the leaders of the 802 plot had previously held army posts. Military matters in the East had not been going well since Harun al-Rashid had extracted one of the most heavy tributes as the price of peace with the Arabs. Even this treaty had been broken by the negative response to Irene's first mission of 797 and was followed by further Byzantine military defeats. So doubtless there were many other disaffected civilian and military officials who found the idea of a change of leadership appealing. Under Nikephoros I not all of them would find the change to their liking, but in 802 they were not to know that.

Once the new Byzantine emperor had been installed, Irene's chief officials quickly abandoned her and pledged their loyalty to Nikephoros. In retrospect, the main reason for her failure to sustain her rule longer probably turns on her understandable refusal to remarry and thus name an heir. This must surely have been one matter to which she should have devoted much greater attention. For neither in the proposal to Charles nor in her indecisiveness over Leo, Aetios's brother, did she manifest the determination which had brought her to supreme power. Her failure to tackle the question of the succession was to prove disastrous. But even if she foresaw the challenge mounted by her finance minister, she was unable to pre-empt it.

CONCLUSION

After five years at the apex of the Byzantine Empire, Irene's downfall and exile brought to an end the rule of the first female emperor. She was probably about fifty years old. Modern historians are quick to point out that this was an unfortunate experiment, doomed to failure. But to judge Irene by the last five years only, the period of her sole reign, is to ignore her formative influence in the government of Byzantium since 780. For over twenty years she had been the dominant figure in the imperial court of Constantinople. It was her initiative that led to the successful staging of the council of 787 and the restoration of icons. Towards the end of the century, as she began the negotiations with Charles, she became embroiled in a process that spun out of her control. What might have resulted in a marriage of convenience and a useful political alliance became complicated by the desire of Pope Leo III to take a more notable role in western medieval politics. As a result of his own plots, the Bishop of Rome is the one person who emerges from the events of 800 with additional powers. Leo III took the main role in the dramatic act of coronation – and his motives were very different from Irene's. For the pope saw in the crowning of Charles a clear demonstration of the sacral power of the church to bestow the imperial title on a worthy candidate, in accordance with the forged *Donation of Constantine*. Such a factor could not have been anticipated in Constantinople, although it was to have momentous consequences for the eastern empire.

Its consequences were equally significant for the Franks. Later Charles would insist on crowning his own son Louis as emperor, without papal intervention. He thus designated his successor and, in due course, Louis inherited his father's authority. But the notion that a western ruler could not be a real emperor without a papal coronation and acclamation in ancient Rome grew out of the ceremonial devised by Leo III in 800. Subsequent claimants of the imperial title, especially the weaker ones, would all make the pilgrimage to Rome, to try and acquire some greater kudos and authority by virtue of a papal ritual of coronation. Many of the stronger claimants could have dispensed with the performance of

Roman bishops but even the tenth-century German rulers, Ottos I, II and III, were anxious to deepen this association. They also marked the symbolic importance of the coronation by dedicating grander and more extravagant imperial regalia, which remained in Rome when they returned to northern Europe. Thus, over time, still exploiting the invented arguments of the *Donation*, bishops of Rome were able to assert that without a papal coronation no one could be emperor, certainly not a Holy Roman Emperor (as the title became).

In this way the medieval West strengthened its sense of Christian identity under the leadership of bishops of Rome. While this gradually excluded Byzantium from imperial power in the West more effectively than at any earlier period, it also had the effect of preserving imperial traditions in the East unchanged. The government in Constantinople deepened its own sense of purpose, perpetuating ancient Roman patterns of administration in their transformed Greek medium which characterised Byzantine culture. Irene made her own contribution to this long process most notably through her ecclesiastical policy, both iconophile and pro-monastic, her patronage of buildings and her development of social services maintained by the church. Despite the disruption of the Syrian dynasty provoked by her blinding of Constantine VI, she ruled in his place more effectively, and sustained eastern traditions of imperial dominance through her innovative foreign policy. As supreme legislator, Irene paid due attention to major problems, revealing her grasp of the established traditions of Roman imperial authority securely based on the Bosphoros. She extended provincial government in key areas of Greece and the western half of the empire.

As a woman, Irene was bound to be challenged. Her anomalous claims to supreme power were without precedent and hardly established before she became caught up in foreign forces beyond Byzantine control. None the less, she managed all aspects of imperial government, handling negotiations with Harun al-Rashid and Charles the Great, the two leading statesmen of her era, and left many lasting monuments to her rule. It is notable that she reigned alone for a longer period than her husband, Leo IV (775–80). And in the long overview of history she not only made a greater impression than he did; she also reversed the policy of her three male predecessors, the most powerful leaders of the Syrian dynasty, who had initiated and sustained iconoclasm. Perhaps the most telling part of her inheritance was that it created a vital precedent. In due course this would be taken up by her ultimate successor, Theodora.

CHAPTER 3

Euphrosyne: a princess born in the purple

We have already met Euphrosyne, a daughter of Constantine VI and his first wife Maria of Amnia and so a granddaughter of Irene. She was probably the second of two children, both female, born to the imperial couple in the early 790s. The arrival of Euphrosyne instead of the much-wanted son may have sparked the ensuing disaster. For if Euphrosyne had been a boy, Constantine would have had a male heir to inherit his imperial authority. One can predict that such a son would have been named Leo after his grandfather, Leo IV. More importantly, his birth would have guaranteed the survival of Maria as the mother of the heir apparent. But this was not the case. Euphrosyne was another girl. After two daughters it seems that Constantine ceased to regard Maria as the woman who could provide him with a successor. And once he had discovered Theodote, it was only a matter of time before Constantine tried to remove his legal wife in order to remarry. The issue of his divorce from Maria, whether or not it was legitimate and valid, bedevilled the rest of his life and can fairly be said to have caused his downfall. Why, then, did he persist?

THE MARRIAGE OF CONSTANTINE AND MARIA

A possible answer is provided by the original circumstances of Constantine's first marriage. When Irene had planned his betrothal to Rotrud, she had treated him as a pawn in the dynastic alliance she wished to make with the King of the Franks. This was perfectly normal. The decision was one of the first of her Regency and the young prince grew up knowing that this highly prestigious marriage had been arranged.[1] When Rotrud was old enough to be married, however, Charles would not let his daughter leave court and the engagement was broken off.

Irene immediately found another bride for her son, this time from a family established in the village of Amnia in the *thema ton Armeniakon*, where the young girl's grandfather, Philaretos, was respected as a very Christian man. In due course Constantine was married to Maria of Amnia. Since this too was an imperial alliance, the young couple were not consulted; they were merely required to give their consent. Through their marriage a large extended family of once wealthy landowners from a region repeatedly overrun by Arab raiders arrived in Constantinople as the imperial in-laws. Maria's mother, Hypatia, her sisters, Myranthia and Evanthia, her brother Petronas and uncle John were all accommodated and found jobs at court. Her grandfather was entertained by the patriarch. The empress clearly saw some value in this alliance.

In contrast to Irene's personal experience, Maria was not crowned as *basilissa* before her wedding in November 788. While the marriage must have been celebrated in identical style, the young bride from Amnia was not raised to the higher status of empress. Imperial wives often had to wait for this honour, which was sometimes bestowed after the successful delivery of a male child. But since this occasion had been masterminded by Irene, she made sure that Constantine and his young bride remained subordinate to her.[2] Indeed, Irene's domineering style is held responsible for most of her son's efforts to attain a measure of independence. Yet Constantine seems to have been unable to sever his links to his mother. There were probably psychological reasons for his inability to break loose. Irene's maternal skills were certainly put to effective use to keep him dependent, to encourage him to rely on her in what appears to us today a very unhealthy fashion. Did she already sense his weaknesses, in comparison with which her own strengths were so overwhelming?

Since most marriages between members of élite families in Byzantium were conducted in this manner, the official announcement preserved in the *Chronicle* of Theophanes provides all the basic information: the empress sent an official to bring Maria from Amnia and she was joined in marriage to Constantine.[3] But the same source claims that the prince had become attached to Rotrud, or to the idea of marrying Rotrud, and grieved as if over a loss when the engagement was broken off. This may help to explain the later failure of his marriage, which Theophanes witnessed (his *Chronicle* was compiled in about 814). There is, however, another dimension to the arrangement that united Maria with Constantine. According to a slightly later source, the bride was selected in a manner quite peculiar to Byzantium at this time: she was chosen in a beauty contest or bride-show. The extremely full details of this procedure are found in the *Life of Philaretos*, written by his grandson Niketas in about 822.[4] As a relative of the family elevated by this event, everything claimed by Niketas should obviously be questioned. As many commentators have shown, he writes with ulterior motives.[5] The marked difference between the two sources has given rise to much critical analysis of Niketas' version. His fascinating account of how the contest was organised is regularly dismissed as a literary fiction, a fanciful reworking of the story of the Judgement of Paris. This ancient myth records how Paris was invited to choose the most beautiful among three powerful goddesses, and presented an apple to the one he judged the winner.

THE LIFE OF PHILARETOS

In order to evaluate the evidence, the circumstances in which Niketas wrote the *Vita Philareti* must be examined: he was in exile in *ta katotika mere* (the southernmost parts, a reference to Peloponnesos). Throughout the text he stresses his close relationship to Euphosyne and all the other descendants of Philaretos, many of whom had made careers in the capital and were buried there in different monasteries. After setting the family in their rural context and documenting the extreme generosity of Philaretos, Niketas describes the event which propelled his cousin Maria and her siblings and other relations to great fame and fortune in a manner designed to remind the reader of the family's origins. In the concluding paragraph of his story, he gives the date of composition, AM 6330, that is AD 822/3. So, thirty-four years after the event, he decided to write an account of his family, in which the bride-show plays a key role.[6]

After introducing the family, Niketas devotes the central part of the *Vita* to the bride-show procedure. Imperial officials arrived in the region, having been sent on a search for the most beautiful young girls in the empire, who were to compete in the contest to win the prince's hand in marriage. They were equipped with an ideal portrait (*lavraton*), a measure to establish vital statistics, and even a shoe to check foot-size. In this way they were supposed to find the right type of beauty. Their search in other parts of the empire had been unsuccessful until they made their way to Amnia and found the house of Philaretos. Eventually, after some persuasion they were permitted to look at the women of his household (secretly, to avoid embarrassing them) and immediately realised that the granddaughters were potentially excellent candidates for the contest. A further ten were also found in the area and all were invited to accompany the imperial team back to the capital. Maria excelled herself in modesty and refrained from boasting when another contestant expressed her confidence in being chosen because her family was so wealthy. Once in the Great Palace, their mothers presented the girls and Hypatia's three were considered the most attractive by a reviewing committee. Maria was of course selected and the marriage was celebrated immediately. Her sisters made good matches too and all the other girls were rewarded with many gifts before being sent home. Hypatia remained in Constantinople living in a grand villa near the Palace. Philaretos also spent several years there before he died and was buried in the monastery of St Andrew *in Krisi*.

A very thorough survey of the problems of the text has recently concluded that it was put together to elevate the holiness of Philaretos, despite his married status and secular preoccupation with family life.[7] The arrival of the imperial officials with their ideal measurements constitutes an obvious break in the narrative. This eruption of the metropolitan into the rural backwater of Amnia allows Niketas to adapt various myths for his own ends, to show how Maria by her virtue and the beauty of her soul, as much as her body, was destined for an imperial future.[8] Using the myth of the Judgement of Paris, Niketas has invented this story, perhaps with echoes of the way the marriage of Theodosius II and Athenais was set up by his sister Pulcheria in 421. The author adapts these devices to serve his purpose, which is to account for his family's meteoric rise into the highest court circles, while emphasising how worthy they were of this promotion.

An explanation for the description of the bride-show in the *Vita* turns on the literary genre employed by Niketas: encomium, or the extravagant praise of the subject according to specific categories. This style, often based on a speech given in honour of the person glorified, goes back to Hellenistic models and was never forgotten in Byzantium. Previous examples were to hand in the tradition of Procopius' praise of Justinian (in the *Buildings*) or Corippus' of Justin II. In addition, the alternative, a piece of invective designed to demonstrate the despicable and wicked character of a villain, constituted another literary model also available. Recently it has been suggested that both types of characterisation were employed by writers of the early ninth century to associate individuals with positive or negative features.[9] And in this process of elevation or condemnation the bride-show features as a key illustration.

The first description of an alleged bride-show is that arranged by Emperor Nikephoros I for his son Staurakios in 807. It is preserved in the *Chronicle* of Theophanes, who was extremely hostile to this emperor, and emphasises all the worst qualities of that ruler.[10] By attacking his sexual activities, it vilifies Nikephoros, implying that he availed himself of the most beautiful young women who had been assembled for his son to choose from. Since Staurakios was also obliged to select a woman who had to be forcibly separated from her fiancé, his father's role is assimilated to that of an adulterer. In fact, the woman so chosen was a relative of Irene's from Athens called Theophano. Clearly, whatever else she represented she had important family links to the previous ruler. And Nikephoros wished to consolidate these. So the 'choice' was dictated by political considerations.

In the second instance of a bride-show, Niketas took over the genre but in a positive sense to enhance the status of his own family. In contrast to Theophanes' use of invective, Niketas transformed his grandfather Philaretos into a saint. His cousin Maria of Amnia became the most beautiful woman in the empire, and her selection as the bride of Constantine reflected the family's Christian dedication. In both cases the episode of the bride-show is employed as an element in a rhetorical exercise but to quite different ends. Neither author describes what actually happened and the bride-show itself may be no more than a literary fiction. Theophanes may well have used the issue of Staurakios' marriage to build an even more negative image of Nikephoros, by condemning his alleged indulgent sexual habits.[11] In his turn Niketas adapted the bride-show to reflect Maria's moral qualities and the family's traditions of piety.

When writing his colourful account of the process of selection, Niketas had several models to hand, including the Old Testament story of Esther. The account of the marriage of Theodosios II to Athenais in 421 was, however, the most useful precedent. The original version of the story, as preserved by Malalas, was recorded about 130 years after the event and stresses the young emperor's insistence that beauty should be the only criterion for the choice.[12] His sister Pulcheria, who had looked through the ranks of suitable candidates, imperial relatives, daughters of senatorial families, highly placed officials of state and so on, now widened her search. And by chance she was introduced to two ladies who were taking care of their niece Athenais. In this roundabout way, the empress found a girl who was not only very beautiful (Theodosios insisted on having a secret look at her while she slept), but also very well educated: her father had been a professor of philosophy in Athens. She was not even a Christian, but that did not matter because Theodosios had found the one whose beauty was overwhelming. She was therefore baptised, given the Christian name Eudokia and married to him. A compelling combination of natural beauty in a previously unknown family, of no social, political or economic distinction, thus made its way into the legend.

It was well known in Byzantium and surfaces in a curious collection of usually fanciful historical stories about different monuments in Constantinople, the *Parastaseis syntomoi chronikai*, probably written down in the late eighth century.[13] In this version, after Athenais 'found good fortune through her beauty', her brothers, who were also philosophers, follow her from Athens to Constantinople and offer their skills in interpreting Late Antique monuments. They confound several philosophers who are unable to fathom the meaning of certain obscure sculptures in the Hippodrome. The element of the bride-show is here subordinated to the supposed brilliance of a famous philosopher's daughter, as if her genes qualified her to marry the prince. In both versions the problem of how Pulcheria, a deeply Christian princess dedicated to virginity and the cult of the Theotokos, could have allowed her only brother to marry a non-Christian, is simply not addressed. Athenais-Eudokia's pagan background is ignored as if either the bride's outstanding beauty or her family's reputation for philosophical reasoning provided the justification for her promotion.

In neither of these versions, however, is there a description of a bride-show. According to the earliest (Malalas), once Theodosios has set eyes on Athenais, he does not want to see any further candidates. But, prior to this happy moment, Pulcheria had inspected a lot of beauties and found them all wanting. In spite of the absence of a selection process, the event thus encapsulates the central elements of the beauty contest and the selection criteria: the extreme beauty of the young girl, and the complete insignificance of her background. The later version ignores this. But both provide certain legendary elements which are woven into the story of a beauty contest. Niketas also sets the qualification of beauty within the hagiographical tradition, thus elevating the family of Philaretos to the status of sanctity. By transforming his secular, lay ancestor into a holy man, and characterising Maria as a supreme example of ninth-century views of beauty, Niketas manages to combine the two elements. In a properly Christian fashion he stresses the beauty of Maria's soul as well as her physical charms. Her poor background was caused by her grandfather's endless good works and charitable gifts, which had reduced the family to poverty. But in the skilful presentation by Niketas, the fundamental message of the myth was that any true beauty could compete for the privilege of marrying the future emperor of Byzantium.

Despite the uneasy way that the *Vita* is put together, its account is confirmed in one key respect: Philaretos *was* greatly honoured by the marriage alliance, and Maria *did* marry the prince. Her sisters also made good marriages; her brother was promoted, and her relatives' residence in the capital are all part of the story. These elements are also documented by other sources. The family from Amnia, whose inherited resources had been almost totally depleted by Philaretos' irrepressible charity, made it to the summit of Byzantine society by this unexpected marriage. So whether or not Niketas' fairy-tale version of Maria's selection represents a reworking of the legend in the style of encomium, Empress Irene did alight upon the person she considered appropriate for her son and the marriage was concluded. It was Irene, assisted by her chief minister, the eunuch Staurakios, who reviewed the girls and insisted on Maria. But according to the *Vita*, the young prince played a major role in the selection, was very happy with his bride and showered her family with gifts, including magnificent houses near the Great Palace.[14]

Whatever the circumstances of his marriage, of one thing we can be sure: Constantine was obliged to agree. Imperial children played no part in the negotiations, which were handled by their parents. The parents in turn had other motives for insisting on one alliance rather than another. To this extent all high-ranking marriages represented family interests and economic and social concerns. Whether the bride-show had any foundation in reality or not, the outcome of the occasion was not in doubt: Constantine was to marry Maria, and that was that. For her own reasons, which are not clear at all, Irene had decided to bring the family of Philaretos into a closer alliance. The story of the bride-show permits Niketas to establish his family's side of the alliance and is used as a delightful way of covering over a hard-nosed political strategy. Why then bother with it?

THE PURPOSE OF THE BRIDE-SHOW

One of the key functions of a beauty contest was to keep all provincial families with daughters of the right age vying for the idea of taking part.

They may have realised that it was statistically impossible for more than one of the many thousands available to be selected. But even the poorer members of the provincial aristocracies, every mother and perhaps a good many fathers, must have hoped that on this occasion their young daughter's beauty would result in fame and fortune for the entire family. In addition, they guessed that there would be compensation prizes for the runners-up. Those who were not selected might yet make a good marriage at court, and thus gain access to the highest ranks of Byzantine society. For families anxious to promote their male relatives, the opportunities which followed from presenting a daughter at court were also very powerful. So whether the event actually occurred or not, this idea of a bride-show inspired families from a regional base to imagine a metropolitan fame. The function of this Byzantine adaptation of the Judgement of Paris was to attract the loyalty of local élites, to keep them looking towards Constantinople as the most important centre of patronage and self-advancement. This focus on the imperial court, where fortunes could be gained overnight, concentrated the attention of all ambitious provincial families.

Irene knew how to use this force to extend the magnetic field of the court's range of loyal support outside the capital. She did not need to announce that there would be a beauty show in the manner described by Niketas, for once it became known that the engagement to the Frankish princess had been broken off, then every family with a girl of the right age wanted to be considered. Courtiers in particular were always anxious to bring their daughters to the attention of the prince. To gain the entrée to the women's quarters of the Great Palace as a trainee lady-in-waiting was a most desirable method and also one of the most common ways of seeking a position at court. But from the empress-mother's point of view, unless there were pressing reasons for an alliance with a family already established in the capital, the alternative – to make the prize open to all inhabitants of the empire – could prove far more valuable. So Irene found in this rumour a means of recovery from the implicit rebuff to her foreign policy. If Charles would not allow his daughter to make the journey to Constantinople in order to marry the prince, even after her lessons in Greek and Byzantine customs, then Irene would incite all provincial families to yearn for the chance to do so. By letting it be known that Constantine's previous betrothal was cancelled, she encouraged the belief that any local beauty might now win his hand.

In reality, the deciding factors turned on the political, economic or social benefit to be realised by any such alliance. Irene, like previous rulers, wanted to strengthen her rule by bringing members of the provincial aristocracy into a closer relationship with the capital. Through a marriage, she could tap into a source of loyal support which would always be entirely dependent on her own patronage. Since she herself had come from precisely this sort of background, she must have understood the forces involved. From the time of Athenais in the fifth century, no one from central Greece had married into the ruling family before 769. And until Irene selected Maria, no one from Amnia had previously been chosen. But by even suggesting that one family was to be so honoured, she not only raised great expectations in all these unvisited and unloved areas, but she also extended the potential number of allies. Why she finally decided on Philaretos remains a mystery, partly because the story of the bride-show hides the real alternatives from us. But it is likely that a distinct choice was made, other candidates were rejected, Amnia won the prize. As a result, Maria was brought to the capital and married to Constantine. In addition, of course, the selection ensured that no faction within the court or the Queen City would be strengthened.

EUPHROSYNE'S BIRTH

In contrast to 'Irene from Athens', Euphrosyne was a true imperial princess, a child probably born in the Porphyra, the purple chamber, to the reigning imperial couple, Constantine VI and Maria of Amnia. She was the second daughter, a younger sister to Irene, who had been named after her grandmother. As the traditional naming pattern of imperial children applies to girls just as much as boys, the first-born female is normally named after her paternal grandmother, in this case Irene, the empress-mother. Strictly speaking, Euphrosyne should have been named after her maternal grandmother, but this did not happen, perhaps because Maria's mother was called Hypatia. Now Hypatia is also a very old Greek name which predates the Christian era. In Byzantium it recalled the Alexandrian philosopher and mathematician Hypatia, a known pagan. Philaretos' wife is called Theosebo, which in that form is another pre-Christian name. Further, many members of this large group have names based on the Greek for 'flower', *anthos*.[15] The men are called Anthes, Anthimos, the girls Myranthia, Euanthia, Anthousa and other derivatives. In a brilliant note Auzépy has observed that this may reflect a desire to avoid naming children after the Christian saints, which would correspond to the Protestant development of flower names in contrast to the more familiar Christian names used by Catholics. In the case of Philaretos it may be connected to an iconoclast criticism of the cult of saints often centred on images. There is no evidence in the *Vita* that this very Christian family ever venerated icons.

Anyway, when Euphrosyne was born, she was not given the name Hypatia.[16] Instead, she was christened Euphrosyne (literally, gladness, joy). That she was the younger of Maria's daughters is confirmed in a letter written to them both by St Theodore of the Stoudios, in which Irene takes precedence as the eldest, over her sister Euphrosyne. As noted previously, there is no official record of their dates of birth. But Irene cannot have been born before August 789 at the earliest, i.e. nine months after her parents' wedding, in which case 791 would be a likely date for the birth of Euphrosyne. Both events could have occurred a few years later, however, at any time between 789 and 794. And if Euphrosyne arrived towards the end of this time period, in 793 or 794, her birth may have proved the last straw for the emperor who needed a male heir.[17]

EUPHROSYNE'S CHILDHOOD: THE EXPERIENCE OF EXILE

Given these indeterminate factors, it is impossible to tell how many of her early years Euphrosyne spent in Constantinople – between four (maximum) and even less than one (minimum). In neither case is the environment of the women's quarters of the Great Palace going to make much impression before Maria and the two little girls are banished from the capital. But her mother and older sister will later tell her about the highly privileged, imperial life they used to lead at court, before the emperor expelled them. As this story is developed by Theophanes, Constantine VI spreads an accusation that his wife is trying to poison him, which is akin to planning to murder him (a crime for which divorce is legitimate). In addition this is an attack on the emperor, which therefore falls into the highest offence of *lèse-majesté*, punishable by death. In his *Life of Tarasios* (a composition by Ignatios the deacon dating from after 843), the patriarch is said to have found the accusation shameful and untrue.[18] At the time, however, people did not voice their suspicions about Constantine's real motives. Tarasios did refuse to tonsure Maria against her will, but he could not save her from the monastic exile to which her husband committed her. Following the denunciation as a poisoner and potential murderer, Maria and her daughters are forced to leave Constantinople in January 795 and enter a monastery. Seven months later, as we have seen Constantine VI married Theodote, one of the *koubikoulariai*, a lady-in-waiting, and crowned her empress, *augouste*.[19]

In this manner Constantine got his way, but at a price. Maria's failure to produce a son and heir resulted in a divorce on dubious grounds and the remarriage of the emperor, which was almost immediately denounced as illegitimate by Platon, abbot of the Sakkoudion monastery, and his nephew Theodore, who were closely related to Theodote.[20] Family connections, however, made no difference to their objection to the marriage on canonical grounds. Yet no protests appear to have been directed against the emperor on Maria's behalf. Where were all her relatives, who had come with her to Constantinople in 788 only seven years earlier and stayed in the capital? They did not come to her support at this time of greatest need. Nor is it clear where Maria and her daughters were initially enclosed. One late source claims that the ex-empress first retired to her own foundation, the monastery of the Ladies (*ton despoinon*) but was not allowed to remain there. Others have suggested that she was sent to *ta Gastria*, a monastery 'in the outlying part of Constantinople'. Her lifelong imprisonment in fact took place in a monastery founded by Irene the empress-mother on the island of Prinkipo before 780.[21] By 795 it was quite a famous iconophile institution under Irene's patronage.

MARIA'S LIFE AS A NUN

From a tender age, Euphrosyne's life is thus one of unbroken and obscure monastic imprisonment. Her mother Maria had been tonsured against her will by the patriarch's catechist; her hair was cut off and she was forced to join a religious community on the largest of the Princes Isles, lying in the Sea of Marmara not far from Constantinople. The island is small, there is no way of escaping except by sea. A Byzantine Alcatraz? But for Euphrosyne and her older sister Irene, Prinkipo with its pine forests, red rocks and delightful vistas may not have been a dreadful place. As children they would have lived in the monastery with their mother, probably in quarters better furnished than normal, with servants to attend to them and provide some sort of education. When they reached the age when they too could take their vows, they may have joined the community. But not necessarily. Irene appears to have died young; she is not mentioned after *c.*816 and did not live to share the family's rehabilitation.

There is no reason to doubt Theophanes' claim that Empress Irene established this prominent monastery on Prinkipo, in which Maria was housed. Not only was he an eyewitness of her reign and death, but his own wife, Megalo, entered the same community allegedly with the empress's support. Irene's role as patron is also confirmed by the fact that when she was first exiled from Constantinople, she spent a short time at Prinkipo in 802 (see chapter 2). In the *Life of Irene*, a much later compilation, she delivers a speech of appreciation addressed to the abbess (*hegoumene*) on the eve of her departure to Lesbos. The nuns all gather round weeping as Irene leaves them. After her death in 803, her body was transported with due ceremony back from Lesbos to Prinkipo and laid to rest in a new sarcophagus of Proconnesian marble in the chapel of St Nikolaos on the left side of the monastic church.[22]

It is hard to guess whether Maria's status as an ex-empress entitled her to a more privileged existence than that of ordinary nuns, or condemned her to a harder life. In the late sixth century, aristocratic women who were loyal to the Monophysite church were forced to wear the plainest robes of coarse material and to clean the latrines of the monastery in which they were confined. The imperial princess Anthousa, who became a nun in the late eighth century, devoted herself to fetching water and serving the sisters in the refectory.[23] Another almost contemporary text of female monastic life stresses that very dedicated nuns never permitted others to serve them or to pour water over their hands. Their diet could be extremely sparse. Athanasia never tasted fruit; Irene of Chrysobalanton ate only bread and water with some green vegetables in the evening. Their basic clothing was made of rough goat hair; they only had one robe and it was changed once a year at Easter. Sometimes they reclined on stones at night, not even lying down.[24]

A slightly later ninth-century text confirms that women who had led an easy life prior to becoming monastics were required to demonstrate humility by undertaking particularly strenuous or tiring work. In this way Theodora of Thessaloniki made herself 'a worthless servant', doing all the most menial domestic tasks: grinding grain, making bread, cooking, shopping, fetching wood and weaving. Her claim to sainthood was confirmed by her total obedience to her spiritual mother, the abbess, Anna, whom Theodora cared for in her last years. When Anna was bedridden and had lost her mind, Theodora carried her to the bath, fed her and turned her in bed so that she would be more comfortable, even when Anna cursed and hit her. In this way she manifested the signs of true sainthood, later confirmed by miracles that occurred at her tomb after her death.[25]

If this general principle prevailed, Maria must have been expected to show humility by doing such chores. For her, the monastery of the Virgin may have felt more like a place of detention than a religious institution. Others may have shared her exile: condemned adulteresses, heretics, ex-wives of bishops, and the insane were regularly committed to monasteries. The most common way of punishing such women was to force them to adopt a monastic existence. In an era when there were no prisons in the modern sense of the term, isolated monasteries might serve the same purpose. The *praitorion* (official residence of the prefect (*eparchos*) of Constantinople) had cells where rebels were regularly incarcerated. But it was also quite common for them to be detained in secure places attached to churches and within monasteries, even in the basements of the Great Palace. When married priests were elected to bishoprics, they had to divorce their wives, who were legally obliged to enter monasteries at a distance from their ex-husbands. Those convicted of sexual crimes or heresy were similarly punished. Men too were sent to ecclesiastical institutions. Deposed emperors and empresses normally ended their days in monasteries where they were certainly kept under surveillance, if not actually locked up. In the early eighth century, Philippikos was blinded and then confined in the monastery of Dalmatou, a pattern which would be repeated many times over (see the fate of Bardanes Tourkos below). Many, of course, sought refuge in a monastic retirement from the secular world once they realised that their imperial ambitions could not be fulfilled.[26]

While there is no way of measuring the percentage of common criminals normally detained in nunneries, and they may have been few in number, the dedicated nuns who joined out of a serious Christian devotion and commitment to the contemplative life had to get along with them. So it was possibly rather a mixed group in which the ex-empress found herself confined. How the abbess directed such a community is not documented, but stories preserved in contemporary and slightly later sources draw attention to problems which might arise. Some young girls were seeking a refuge from over-enthusiastic suitors, others had serious mental difficulties, while some became possessed by evil spirits.[27] As in every small community, petty jealousies and personal rivalries required

142

the abbess's attention; her judgement was final, and her punishments could be severe.

On the other hand, one of the dedicated sisters in the monastery on Prinkipo was Megalo, formerly the wife of Theophanes, who wrote at least parts of the *Chronographia*. The story of their engagement when very young, their subsequent brief marriage, which was not blessed by children, and their decision to separate, follows an established pattern. According to the panegyric composed by St Theodore of the Stoudios for Theophanes, he settled Megalo in the monastery of the Virgin on Prinkipo with Empress Irene's encouragement, and she took the monastic name of Irene. Then he was tonsured on the nearby island of Kalonymos and thus began his long monastic vocation which included mastering the skills of the scribe (*kallitechnia*) and compiling the famous history, so often cited in this study. They agreed not to see each other any more. While Megalo-Irene may have taken her own dowry with her into the community, for Patriarch Methodios claims that she came from an extremely rich family, Theophanes also made suitable benefactions to the community on Prinkipo. We can assume that his wife had embraced the life of a nun voluntarily and that her dedication observed the liturgy for the entry of women to the monastic life.[28]

As Megalo and Theophanes had decided to separate in c.780/1, she was one of the older sisters in the community when Maria arrived with her two small children, about fourteen years later. She lived on through the early years of the ninth century and received the news of her ex-husband, Theophanes', death from St Theodore of the Stoudios in 818. It is very curious that this letter of condolence is addressed to Megalo-Irene and Maria, and tempting to see in this a friendship between the two women otherwise undocumented.[29] If so, it would suggest that within her enforced monastic confinement Maria had found companions and made alliances with other well-born women. This is just what one would expect. Given their circumstances, which did not seem likely to change, those who were restrained in monasteries for political reasons, might yet find congenial company amongst those who had sought a refuge from the world in female communities.

The irreversible devotion to Christ is marked by the ceremony of hair-cutting, putting off the world and all its finery, in order to adopt poverty, obedience and chastity. Parents often considered the taking of vows a spectacular event, and dressed their daughters in rich silk clothing and jewels. This practice was condemned at the Council *in Trullo* as an unnecessary display of wealth, which may have had the effect of making the young girl regret her decision. Similar condemnations of inappropriate clothing and conspicuous demonstrations of wealth occur in connection with both lay and clerical people. Clearly, if some girls were observed weeping instead of smiling with joy at the prospect of becoming 'brides of Christ', their tears might be misinterpreted. So the canon recommended modest clothing which would not draw attention to any sense of loss.[30]

The idea that taking monastic vows was indeed a ceremony equivalent to a secular marriage is made abundantly clear in references to the heavenly marriage ceremony documented in female saints' lives. An elaborate wedding ritual with Christ as the bridegroom, complete with wedding dress, feast and bridal chamber, make it evident that girls taking their vows were making a commitment for life and did so in a complex ritual of abandoning the world in order to embrace Christ. Truly dedicated nuns then adopt a perpetual virginity and stability of place, which was manifested in the 780s by Anthousa, the daughter of Constantine V, who had refused her father's numerous attempts to force her to marry. Although Empress Irene is said to have exerted pressure on her to stay in the Great Palace, she always wore a tattered hair-shirt under her imperial robes and eventually retired from the world. After distributing her entire inheritance to the poor, to churches and pious institutions, she was tonsured by Patriarch Tarasios.[31] Anthousa's withdrawal from the world was understood to include the fact that she would never go out into the world again, or even move from one nunnery to another.

While she was confined in the Prinkipo monastery, the ex-empress Maria was allowed to receive letters, and St Theodore of the Stoudios wrote to her and to both her daughters, Euphrosyne and Irene.[32] This implies that Maria could write back and indeed Theodore's letters make it plain that his female correspondents (and there are quite a number) sent him information, asked his advice, and assisted the iconophile cause in different ways.[33] So she was not completely cut off from the world. In addition, after Empress Irene's fall from power, Maria and her daughters probably witnessed her arrival at Prinkipo; her departure for Lesbos in 803, and the return of her coffin. If so, this would constitute the only meeting of the two empresses between January 795, when Maria was banished, and November 802, when the same thing happened to Irene.[34]

TRADITIONS OF RELIGIOUS LIFE FOR WOMEN
IN THE LATE EIGHTH CENTURY

Few female communities of nuns shared the settled traditions associated with the most famous male monasteries then concentrated on Mount Olympos in Bithynia.[35] There is a striking contrast between the religious houses established by the parents of St Theodore in about 781. While his mother Theoktiste and his sister converted their house in Constantinople into a nunnery, where Theoktiste was probably the first abbess, Theodore's father and brothers established a male house at Sakkoudion, on a rural family property, which became a famous centre of iconophile devotion. His uncle, Platon, was the first abbot and in turn he became the second. Its traditions were transferred to the Stoudios when Theodore became abbot there. Under the patronage of Empress Irene important reforms were introduced, which set new standards of monastic observance. During the second period of iconoclasm the iconophile community was dissolved on imperial orders and monks loyal to the official theology were installed. After 843 the process was reversed and Stoudios continued to act as a beacon of reformed monastic practice. In comparison with this developed history, nothing further is recorded about the nunnery founded by Theoktiste. Female communities rarely preserved a long existence; they were often founded by one pious, wealthy patron and failed to survive her death.

For Byzantine nuns of the period, the commitment to celibacy as brides of Christ was coupled with poverty and obedience. They owned nothing; their diet was very limited, and they took turns at preparing food, fetching water, weaving, cleaning and so on. They rose to chant the services at set hours and devoted themselves to learning the Psalter and the Gospels by heart. Occasionally visitors were allowed access and nuns might attend the funeral of a close relative, otherwise there was very little contact between the outer world and the community. Many communities are documented because a future saint, a wealthy patron or empress chose to favour them. In some of these sources an unofficial class barrier seems to have existed between the wealthy independent women who voluntarily adopted the monastic life and their servants who did the work. But there are so many accounts of individuals refusing to allow their past status to buy them privileges that it is hard to generalise. The most devoted seem to have shared in the regulated life of the community, whatever their background.

During the eighth century, however, monasteries of both men and women were subject to political surveillance, especially those close to the capital. When iconoclast rulers were in power, all monastic communities had to observe the official policy on icons (images should be removed, whitewashed, or even defaced). St Anthousa (not the imperial princess), who directed a large double monastery near Mantineon, was pursued by officials sent by Constantine V to persuade her to adopt the iconoclast view. When she refused, she and her nephew, who was the administrator of the male house, were tortured. Anthousa was stretched out and whipped and had burning icons put on her head, while glowing coals were placed on her feet.[36] While this treatment may not be typical, it confirms that iconoclast tortures and beatings of women occurred. After 787 all monastics were expected to return to the iconophile devotion to icons. Abbesses therefore had to bend with the wind or risk punishment. As we have already seen, some women are singled out by iconophile authors for special praise; their courage is mentioned in circumstances which indicate a strong loyalty to icons and a determination to relieve the sufferings of victims of persecution. So, among Maria's 'sisters', there may have been some who had suffered and were now reaping the rewards of their commitment to iconophile practice. It seems reasonable to assume that between 795 and 815 the nunnery was observing the iconophile regulations set in place in 787.

EUPHROSYNE'S UPBRINGING

What did Maria and her two daughters do during the seven long years that separate their unwilling arrival in 795 and Irene's exile in 802? Despite their seclusion it is likely that they have learned about developments at court: Constantine VI's remarriage, his deposition and blinding (797), Irene's sole rule and patronage of monks such as the Stoudites, and her further support for institutions like the Prinkipo monastery in which they are confined. On one occasion there is evidence that the court took into consideration their situation: after the restoration of the church of St Euphemia in Constantinople, small parts of the relics were sent to Prinkipo for the two children. This gift, probably organised by Irene, constitutes their grandmother's sole recorded contact with her granddaughters. For Euphrosyne and her sister, these seven years will witness their growth from small children into young girls, fully aware of the theological battles over icons, familiar with the correct forms of veneration, probably educated to read and write by older nuns or a special tutor. Even though they are shut away from the world, Maria is able to correspond with important iconophile supporters, such as St Theodore. And as the division between Stoudites and supporters of Tarasios over Maria's divorce continues to deepen, it is clear that her party keeps her informed of the situation. For them she is a woman wrongly accused and improperly exiled, which must be her only consolation. Moreover, the news that Theodote's marriage to Constantine has been denounced as adulterous, and then the birth and rapid death of their son Leo, followed by the mutilation of her ex-husband, all these changes would have confirmed her sense of righteous indignation at the injustice she continues to suffer.

During her childhood Euphrosyne may not understand all this, but she learns about iconophile theology and practice and acquires some basic education. In her adult life she will display good sense and certain skills in handling her relatives. She also manifests the imperial qualities perhaps imbued by a conscious emulation of her illustrious ancestors (even if they were iconoclasts). She remains the legitimate daughter of Constantine VI, the granddaughter of Leo IV and Irene, and the great-granddaughter of Constantine V, the outstanding military leader. Her destiny lies in this inheritance. For, after the death of her older sister Irene, Euphrosyne is the only living descendant of Leo III, the last surviving member of the Syrian family established in the eighth century, which ruled so brilliantly. In the troubled years of the early ninth century, such a connection is going to prove most valuable.

THE REIGN OF NIKEPHOROS I (802–11)

In order to follow the next stage of Euphrosyne's career, it is necessary to make yet another short detour into the history of Empress Irene's successors. After the *coup d'état* of 802, the finance minister Nikephoros reigned for nine years. In the *Chronicle* of Theophanes he receives the least favourable treatment of almost any Byzantine emperor (see above). Neither his efforts at financial reform, necessitated by Irene's lavish gifts and remittance of taxes; nor military reforms, designed to put more men under arms; nor administrative improvements (clear from the expansion of *themata* and the extension of imperial control) are treated as worthy achievements. His rule was challenged early on by the Anatolikon forces who revolted and proclaimed their commander Bardanes Tourkos, under the pretext of restoring Irene to power.[37] It proved unsuccessful but was important in bringing together a group of junior army officers, whose ambitions were to determine the course of Byzantine history from 813–29 (see below).

Nikephoros I was not a gifted military commander. His campaigns against the Arabs in 804–6 resulted in defeats, and peace was only concluded on terms so humiliating that apparently they surprised even Harun al-Rashid. So in this respect the new emperor provided no relief from the foreign policy failures of Irene's rule. The Arab threat to Byzantium only declined after the death of the caliph in 809, when the Muslims became divided among themselves.[38] An uprising of the Bulgars occurred immediately, ensuring that there would be no respite from military threats. Nikephoros now displayed his worst talents: he flattered himself that he could put down the Bulgarian rebellion and led the combined Byzantine forces into the most disastrous campaign for many years. At the battlefield of Markellai in 811, he was initially victorious and set fire to the Khan's encampment.[39] But he refused to withdraw peacefully and the Bulgars eventually found his tent and killed him, together with many leading generals and the flower of his troops. The Bulgar leader, Khan Krum, is said to have taken his skull and had it mounted in a silver cup, so that the Slavonic tribes could be forced to drink to further triumphs over the Byzantines from the coupe made of the emperor's head.

In keeping with the generally bad press accorded to Nikephoros, one matter that directly concerned Euphrosyne and her mother reveals his determination to override ecclesiastical opinion. When Patriarch Tarasios died in 806, the emperor chose another layman, also called Nikephoros, to replace him. Like his predecessor, the new patriarch had been trained as a civil servant and contributed greatly to the revival of classical learning and culture which began to develop in the late eighth century.[40] The monks of the Stoudios transferred their hostility to the new patriarch and refused to communicate with him, allegedly on the grounds that a layman should not be promoted to the leadership of the church. The emperor then tried to settle the matter of Constantine VI's divorce, which still dragged on. He asserted his right to readmit to communion Joseph of Kathara, the priest who had blessed Constantine's marriage with Theodote in 795, and summoned a synod to approve this.[41] While the new patriarch concurred, the monastic party objected, thus deepening the rift between them. The stand-off continued until 808, when

Joseph's return to the clergy of Hagia Sophia provoked a revolt which Nikephoros put down with customary severity. The emperor's claim to be above the laws also had repercussions in the Stoudios monastery, now said to number seven hundred monks, and stimulated the abbot Theodore to firmer opposition. As a result he, his brother Joseph and uncle Platon were all banished from the capital.

In 809, therefore, an influential group of clerics who had taken Maria's side in the divorce, were punished for their support of the ex-empress. By a coincidence Theodore was sent into exile on the Princes Islands, to a similar situation and much greater proximity to Maria. Whether the two were already in correspondence or not, she must have been relieved that some part of the church continued to support her marriage to Constantine VI as the sole legitimate one. After the emperor's death in the military disaster at Markellai (811), Patriarch Nikephoros healed the schism by summoning a fresh council to reverse the decisions approved in 809. Finally, the church united behind the monks' firm resolve: the marriage of Constantine and Theodote was declared illegal. The 'Moicheian schism' was thus brought to an end. The patriarch excused his previous weakness, claiming that he had been forced to agree under political duress. While this was no more than a posthumous condemnation of Constantine's second marriage, it may have comforted Maria a little. The implication of the judgement was that she had not been guilty of planning his murder; she *had* been unjustly divorced and forced to adopt the monastic life on Prinkipo. But no one suggested that she might be released from this banishment. That would have been too embarrassing, too awkward for the court. So whatever her personal views, she remained on Prinkipo with her daughter Euphrosyne.

Owing to the very serious injuries he sustained in the Byzantine defeat of 811, Nikephoros' son and co-emperor Staurakios was evidently not likely to live for long. His sister Prokopia advanced her own husband Michael as a suitable candidate for the imperial position, but Staurakios' wife Theophano seems to have clung to the idea that she might rule in the same way as Irene.[42] During the summer of 811 while different factions of the court were fighting over the imperial title, we can already sense the legacy of Empress Irene. Whether Theophano, who was her kinswoman and came from Athens, really intended to rule alone, or the chroniclers merely note that they feared she might want to, the example had been established. On this occasion the model set by Irene provoked comment and anxiety. Obviously, the anxiety was dominant among male chroniclers, while Theophano might have had a very different reaction. It would be too simple to deduce that when women found imperial power within their grasp they found it appealing, while men were horrified. But Irene had clearly made her mark as an unusual ruler and later imperial woman would always have her achievement in mind.

THREE JUNIOR OFFICERS AND THEIR 'PLOT'

Eventually Prokopia won the argument and her husband Michael Rhangabe became emperor. During his brief and unglorious reign (811–13) she is said to have been a dominant force at court, while Michael I was better known for his piety and generosity to the church. He certainly proved no more successful than Nikephoros in the Bulgar wars which continued every year without respite. Khan Krum moved ever closer to Constantinople, devastating Thrace and the outlying regions which provided its food supplies. Among the military, such repeated defeats constituted a serious threat to the empire as well as a humiliating experience. And following the rout of Byzantine forces at Versinikia in June 813, Patriarch Nikephoros also seems to have worried about Michael I's capacity to rule. The immediate danger of a Bulgar siege of the capital propelled Leo, *strategos* of the Anatolikon, to prominence. Encouraged by another officer, Michael of Amorion, with whom he had served under Bardanes Tourkos in 802–3, and a third figure Thomas, sometimes identified as a Slav, Leo the Armenian assumed the purple. Michael I abdicated, adopted the monastic robe and sought refuge in the church.[43]

In this way the three military officers who had been associated with the revolt of Bardanes Tourkos in 803 began to play a leading part in Byzantium. Much later sources preserve a legendary story that, shortly before their rebellion, all four had been to consult an elderly seer, who claimed to be able to foresee the future.[44] According to his prophesy, two of the three younger men were destined to rule the empire, while Bardanes was warned that he would fail in his attempt and would be blinded. This consultation at Philomelion is ignored by Theophanes and is not emphasised by Genesios. However, in the mid-tenth century version preserved in the Continuators of Theophanes it assumes a pivotal role. The prophesy is mentioned no less than six times in the first fifty-two pages of the history, giving it undue prominence. In this reconstruction we can see what had been no more than a rumour being developed into an important and firmly documented event. Of course, such later justifications for subsequent rebellions against imperial authority were common enough.[45] But there is more evidence that the three officers who had served together under Bardanes shared the same aspirations, though they avoided his fate.

During the summer of 803 Bardanes failed to raise any substantial support for his revolt and therefore negotiated a safe conduct to his own monastery on the island of Prote.[46] Leo the Armenian and Michael of Amorion both helped to secure a peaceful end to the uprising of the Asian *themata*. They were rewarded by grants of high military positions and houses in Constantinople, while Thomas fled across the border to the Arabs and plotted his own rebellion. The other two appear to have kept in close contact and both eventually made advantageous marriages: Leo to Theodosia, daughter of another Armenian, Arsaber, who rose to become head of the judiciary and by 808 held the position of *quaestor*; Michael to Thekla, the daughter of Bardanes and his wealthy wife Domnica. Despite a romantic legend that both men were 'duped into marrying Bardanes' daughters', at the time of the alleged prophesy, Michael was the only one who did so and there is no evidence that the alliance was made during the coup of 803.[47]

After the failure of his revolt, Bardanes sought refuge as a monk in the monastery he had founded on Prote where, on the orders of Nikephoros I, he was blinded despite the safe-conduct.[48] He lived on for many years and his wife, Domnica, and her daughter were forced to become nuns and retired to their house in Constantinople which they transformed into a retreat known as the Resurrection (*Anastasia*).[49] Leo and Michael both followed successful military careers until 808, when Leo appears to have been exiled for participating with his father-in-law in the unsuccessful coup of 808. Michael of Amorion may also have been implicated since both men, and their colleague Thomas, were recalled after the death of Nikephoros in 811. The date of Thekla and Michael's marriage is not known, but when their first child was born (probably between 811 and 813) Michael invited Leo to be his godfather.[50] The two men thus formed an additional spiritual relationship around the infant who was named Theophilos.

In the wake of repeated Bulgar triumphs inflicted by Khan Krum, Leo the Armenian was asked by other military and ecclesiastical leaders to accept the position of emperor. Patriarch Nikephoros realised that if Michael I abdicated quickly and his family all entered monasteries, the empire might be saved from the Bulgars. He therefore demanded a guarantee of Leo's orthodoxy and then accepted him as emperor; Leo was acclaimed at the Tribunal outside the walls by the army, and was crowned in Hagia Sophia on 12 July 813.[51] Michael of Amorion assisted his entry into the capital and accompanied him into the palace, a measure of the close relations they sustained. For this support he was promoted to the rank of *patrikios* and commander of the *exkoubitors,* while their older companion-in-arms, Thomas, was made *tourmarch* of the *Foederatoi.* Both these troop formations represented élite military units: the *tagma* of the *exkoubitors* was composed of crack forces stationed in the capital, while the *Foederatoi* had been created by Nikephoros I to boost the imperial guard.[52] The initial threat of a Bulgar siege was thwarted by strengthening the fortifications of the city; Leo V built a new curtain wall around the shrine of Blachernai. After devastating the suburbs with impunity Khan Krum was eventually forced to retreat, causing further devastation throughout Thrace. A year later while he was planning another major attack on the city, Krum suddenly died.

THE REIGN OF LEO V (813–20)

During Leo's reign his two military comrades co-operated in military campaigns which did much to salvage the honour of Byzantine forces. To conform with the successful Syrian dynasty of the previous century Leo changed his eldest son's name to Constantine, from the Armenian Smbat (hellenised as Symbatios), and crowned him as co-emperor. Ordering the people to acclaim them with the traditional cry, 'Long live Leo and Constantine', he clearly intended to establish his family in the same prolonged exercise of power.[53] He also wished to benefit from the deep-rooted loyalty to the memory of Constantine V, which had never been erased among the regular troops attached to the *themata.* During the disastrous Bulgarian campaign of 813, Constantine V's supporters had infiltrated into the church of the Holy Apostles in Constantinople during a liturgy and staged an opening of his tomb there, calling on their hero to rescue the empire. Theophanes says that they were Paulicians, who blamed the orthodox faith and monastic school of godly philosophy for the empire's defeats. 'Inspired by the Devil, they clamoured for their prophet, the Jewish-minded Constantine, and like him they denied the incarnation of Christ.'[54]

THE REVIVAL OF ICONOCLASM

Leo V interpreted this demonstration as justifying a return to the icono-clast policy of his model, claiming that by imitating the eighth-century rulers he too would live long and rule with success.[55] The revival of iconoclasm provoked the retirement of Patriarch Nikephoros. At a synod held in Hagia Sophia in 815 icons were again officially condemned as idols and banned; Christians were required to demonstrate their correct observance of the official policy of the Byzantine church.[56] In the Defin-ition of Faith issued by the synod, most of the theological arguments derive from the eighth-century experience of iconoclasm. But a greater sophistication is observed, the result of a prolonged debate within Byzan-tium and between Byzantium and the West, which had intensified since 787. To what extent people outside the military cared, is impossible to gauge. But Leo V felt that the reintroduction of iconoclasm would guarantee the support he needed to win battles against the Bulgars, which would in turn establish his dynasty on the throne for many generations.

For Euphrosyne and her mother Maria on Prinkipo, as for the monks of the Stoudios and other iconophile houses, this revival threatened their traditional devotion to the icons. Although it is nowhere mentioned, the abbess of the nunnery on Prinkipo must have taken account of the official change. In order for the foundation to avoid investigation, it had to subscribe to the Definition of Faith issued in 815. A nominal acceptance of iconoclasm, including the removal of icons, must have occurred. When the leaders of the strict iconophile party refused to comply, the most prominent were persecuted, beaten and sent into exile. The mon-astery of Stoudios was disbanded, the iconophiles were moved out and a new iconoclast community established. It was during this second period of iconoclasm that Theodore established a network of opposition linked by letters, a virtual community of icon venerators bound to resist per-secution by his vivid appeals for solidarity. As we have seen, women were also involved in this network and some are singled out for their courage. Although Maria does not appear to have been one of these, she may have learned of this secret circle of opposition which sustained iconophile traditions. Theodore's death in 826 weakened it but the community in exile survived.

In Leo's belief that the revival of iconoclasm would secure military success, he had overlooked the ambitions of both Michael of Amorion and Thomas the Slav, his companions-in-arms. During the course of

820, Michael threatened to challenge him, using the command of the *exkoubitors* in Constantinople as his military base. By the end of the year Leo recognised the challenge and had Michael imprisoned.[57] His wife Theodosia, however, prevented him from imposing the death penalty on such a holy day as the Feast of the Nativity, urging him to investigate Michael's allies more fully. But through careful plotting, which involved some of the court officials in charge of the cell where Michael was imprisoned in the Great Palace, the planned conspiracy against Leo V was put into operation. As the emperor sang the Christmas liturgy in the palace chapel on 25 December he was assassinated by Michael's allies, who had disguised themselves as members of the choir. Once Leo was dead they rushed to release Michael and carried him, still wearing his iron fetters, into the Augousteion. There he was clothed in the purple and acclaimed emperor. He then proceeded to Hagia Sophia, where he was crowned by Patriarch Theodotos and thus assumed supreme power. Leo's four sons were exiled to the Princes Islands and castrated so that they would never have children to challenge Michael. As a result, the youngest Theodosios died; Basil and Gregorios lived on as monks until at least 847.

THE ACCESSION OF MICHAEL THE AMORION

In 820 Michael II, who was held responsible for the murder of Leo V, lacked any imperial connections. He was uneducated, spoke with a stammer and was associated by some commentators with the heretical sect of the *Athinganoi*, related to the Paulicians. It was not an auspicious start to a reign which, he must have known, would be challenged sooner or later by Thomas, the last of the trio. So Michael found himself in a difficult situation when Thomas declared his bid for imperial power. The rival was not a murderer and he commanded significant support among the Anatolikon troops, who were loyal to him even though he was not their *strategos*. In contrast, Michael had only the definite support of the professional *tagmata* based in the capital and his relatives whom he placed in high positions.

The revolt of Thomas the Slav was a long-drawn-out business which involved a major siege of the capital, attacks on important castles, pitched battles, complex troop movements and declarations of theology by the parties involved.[58] At one stage Thomas appears to have promised to restore the images, which won him support from covert iconophiles, especially monks who had been exiled by the resumption of iconoclasm in 815. In spite of a long siege of the capital, Michael was able to hold out, thus confirming the Byzantine proverb that he who rules in Constantinople rules the world. But the length of the revolt weakened the whole empire and left even the victor with reduced resources to deploy against renewed Bulgar and Arab challenges.

At the height of these unfavourable circumstances Michael suffered a further loss when his wife Thekla died and was buried in the imperial Mausoleum of Justinian attached to the church of the Holy Apostles. It is said that he grieved greatly at her passing and vowed never to remarry. When the Senate heard this, however, they tried to persuade him to change his mind; their wives demanded a mistress to supervise their part in court activities.[59] To overcome his distinctly unimperial credentials the upstart military man from the lower ranks of officers, whose immense ambition had already made him emperor, now opened marriage negotiations with Euphrosyne. How and when this was done remains unclear. But Michael sought to use the significant connections that she represented. In the same way as Leo V, Michael II was consumed with the ambition of establishing his own family. But he also wanted an association with the Syrian dynasty of the eighth century, and found it in Euphrosyne.

EUPHROSYNE'S MARRIAGE

As the sole surviving descendant of Leo III, Euphrosyne seems an ideal choice. She alone can bring to Michael of Amorion a genuine link with all those highly successful military rulers whose reforms had secured the survival and consolidation of Byzantium. Her genes are her fortune. As regards their ages, Michael II may be about forty years old in 820 and Euphrosyne is probably between twenty-six and thirty. The fact that she has been raised as an iconophile is overlooked as an inconvenience. In Euphrosyne, Michael also sees a wife who is aware of her imperial birth, who will probably learn the ways of the court much better than he ever can, and who will perform the role of consort and stepmother to his son and heir Theophilos. From the point of view of the calendar of court ceremonies, he needs an empress to accompany him on official engagements, at palace rituals, religious services and so on, in other words a truly imperial wife. Euphrosyne provides the perfect solution. The only problem is that she is living in a nunnery and may not agree to leave her monastic seclusion and play out this imperial role.

The first hurdle in the proposal is to get Euphrosyne out of the monastery on Prinkipo. Since nuns are expected to remain cloistered for life, this poses difficulties. How it is negotiated remains a mystery. Presumably the abbess, her spiritual mother, is required to give permission for a nun to be released from her vows. An appeal is made to the patriarch, Antonios Kassymatas, who will presumably agree to the emperor's request.[60] Although it is never supposed to happen, Euphrosyne's dedication to the monastic life may not be a 'normal' one, and in her case the 'nun' may not have freely chosen to take 'vows'. Her mother Maria had been tonsured against her will, that much is clear, but what about Euphrosyne?

We do not know if Euphrosyne exercised any choice in the matter, whether she adopted the monastic habit voluntarily, or felt pressured to follow her mother. She may have been obliged to take vows in order to remain enclosed, but the way this had been done might have a bearing on the possibility of her release. In any case Euphrosyne must be summoned to see her abbess to discuss the unexpected proposal. At this point Theodore of the Stoudios, who is once again in exile because of the resumption of iconoclasm, writes to Maria to urge her not to allow this wicked development to take place. In his third letter he insists that Euphrosyne should not even consider agreeing to Michael II's suggestion, and on no account should Maria consider leaving her monastery to accompany her daughter back to Constantinople.[61] From the other side, the abbess of the community which is now observing the iconoclast definition of 815 does not want to anger the new emperor who has selected one of her nuns as his future wife. Presumably she can sense that further imperial patronage may well be forthcoming. But Theodore forcefully states his own position: a monastic devotes herself to Christ for life. There can be no change in Euphrosyne's status as a dedicated nun. In this battle of wills it would be so interesting to know what Euphrosyne herself thought.

The problem can be put another way. To which strand of Euphrosyne's past life can Michael appeal? Does Euphrosyne still consider herself an imperial princess, despite monastic confinement? Probably yes, because of her mother Maria and their shared fate. So the call to duty would be in some ways pleasing, a true fulfilment of her birth and privileged upbringing. The marriage would realise yet another of those potential roles laid upon Byzantine princesses, however surprisingly. Alternatively, Euphrosyne could have become a truly penitent nun adopting the ideology of humility and self-abasement appropriate for a member of a persecuted religious community. Theodore of Stoudios' disapproval of the proposed marriage may also imply that Euphrosyne is in this situation, but regardless of the degree of her ascetic commitment he obviously thinks she should remain in the nunnery.

Although he does not raise the issue, there is another unspoken matter – the question of Michael's adherence to iconoclasm. At the beginning of his reign, the emperor refused to countenance any change in the policy decreed at the Council of Hagia Sophia in 815, and is reported to have told the iconophiles who petitioned him that matters of faith were an individual matter. Responding to ex-Patriarch Nikephoros, he ordered 'a profound silence as regards any mention of icons'.[62] It is notable, however, that there was no further persecution of icon venerators in the fashion adopted by Leo V. In official records Michael defends his predecessor's resumption of the iconoclast policy. Within this context Euphrosyne may believe that her duty lies in persuading Michael to restore iconophile practice ... so *she* may have a hidden agenda as well! But there is no evidence that the iconophile party has perceived this opportunity to influence the emperor.

The resolution of this battle, or tug of war, can only be gauged by the fact that in the early 820s, at an unspecified date, Euphrosyne leaves the nunnery in which she has passed twenty-five years or more, and is duly married to Michael II and crowned empress.[63] By this political marriage, she becomes stepmother to the young prince Theophilos. Her resurrection as an imperial wife may also permit Maria, her mother, to renounce their long enforced exile and return to the capital. If, as a result of whatever negotiations occur, Maria is able to accompany her daughter back to the palace she knew so well, she would finally experience some sense of justice.

This would form an extraordinary culmination to her life, which graphically encapsulates the tremendous potential of being plucked out of obscurity to become an imperial bride, and of the horrendous consequences of the breakdown of such a marriage. Maria experienced the extreme highs and lows of a Byzantine empress. That she could also win the satisfaction of returning to the palace to witness her second daughter installed as empress, and herself as empress-mother, seems too good to be true. Yet it may have happened. As we have seen, this denouement is precisely what Theodore of the Stoudios foresees, fears and condemns.

It will come as no surprise to the reader to learn that nothing whatsoever is recorded about Euphrosyne's activities as empress during the reign of her husband Michael II (820–9). The date of her marriage, her role as stepmother of the young prince Theophilos, her management of the women's quarters of the Great Palace, her participation in court cere-monial – all are ignored. This is partly a consequence of the dearth of contemporary historians. While some ninth-century writers correctly note the emperor's second marriage, other iconophile sources do not mention it, either out of ignorance or prejudice. Some are unaware of Thekla and make Euphrosyne the mother of Theophilos. Several attrib-ute Michael's failures as emperor to this illicit union, which had removed a dedicated nun from her monastic house and overridden her original marriage to Christ.[64] None considers Euphrosyne's views.

Through a different set of sources, however, it is possible to observe at least some of her actions. The most significant one, which Euphrosyne probably took quite rapidly, concerns her creation of a family shrine in which she would be buried. This is not entirely surprising since wealthy individuals usually planned their tombs and left their relatives strict instructions about their burials. Among emperors, it was the custom for funerary plans to be made very early: Herakleios was barely established on the throne in 610 before the guild members responsible for burials came to consult him about what colour of marble they should use for his sarcophagus. Once he had chosen it they went away to prepare his tomb, though in the event he was to reign for another thirty-one years. Michael II had already interred his first wife Thekla in the imperial mausoleum of the Holy Apostles, and planned to be buried beside her, barring some hideous revolt which might banish him to a monastic retirement. So Euphrosyne may have realised that she was very unlikely to find a corner in the Holy Apostles. She therefore took steps to ensure her own tomb was in a place she approved.

According to the *Patria*, a generally unreliable collection of stories about monuments of Constantinople, and somewhat later sources, two monasteries in the capital were endowed by Euphrosyne. The first is *ta Libadeia*, a monastery founded in the fields (*libadeia*) by Empress Irene, which had fallen into ruin and poverty (see chapter 2). Euphrosyne rebuilt it and renamed it the monastery of Lady (*Kyra*) Euphrosyne. By endowing it with imperial funds, she transformed it into her own foundation.[65] The second is a house which she purchased from Niketas the patrician 'in the outlying part of Constantinople', and then converted into a nunnery called *ta Gastria*.[66] From other sources it is thought that this Niketas may have been one of Empress Irene's most trusted eunuchs. By this date he had become an iconophile monk and later, under Theophilos, he suffered for his dedication to icons.[67] While both monasteries are associated with Euphrosyne, the second became more closely linked with a later empress, Theodora, the wife of Theophilos. However, it is clear that Empress Euphrosyne was known as the founder of a monastery which took her name and housed her tomb. It survived into the tenth century and is recorded in the *Book of Ceremonies*.[68]

THE MONASTERY OF LADY EUPHROSYNE

The monastery of the *Kyra Euphrosyne* was located near the walls of the city in what had probably been an area of gardens and vegetable plots in the ninth century, less densely populated than other parts of the capital. Even more important, it housed a remarkable collection of tombs, which suggests a determined policy to bring together in death the immediate members of Euphrosyne's family of origin. The fact has not gone unnoticed but Euphrosyne's responsibility for it has not been sufficiently stressed.[69] In addition to planning her own tomb, Euphrosyne also took care of her mother's final resting place, not wishing her to be buried in the monastery in which she had unwillingly spent so many years of her life. It is likely that Maria died at some point during Michael II's reign, though this event is of course not noticed by any surviving source. If she was born *c.*770–4, and married in 788 aged between fourteen and eighteen to Constantine VI who was then nineteen, she might have lived till 830, when she would have been around sixty years ago. Although this is old for a medieval woman, a good monastic diet might well have kept her healthier than some, and determination to win back her imperial status and have her marriage validated is a powerful motor for survival. When she does die, Maria is buried by her daughter in the monastery of the *Kyra Euphrosyne*, recently established by the new empress as her own shrine. She may have been in fact the first of the family to be interred there. Euphrosyne then adds her father's remains and those of her sister Irene.

Constantine VI had died quite some time after his blinding (outliving his mother Irene) and his second wife Theodote buried him, probably in the establishment where they had lived.[70] As we have seen, their remarriage had continued to divide the church, with the monks of Stoudios taking a strict line against the priest who had blessed the union. For their opposition Theodore, his brother Joseph and his elderly uncle Plato were all sent into separate places of exile and were only recalled after the death of Nikephoros I on the battlefield in 811. Once the united church upheld the sole legitimacy of the marriage of Maria and Constantine VI, Theodote was branded as an adulterer. In these adverse circumstances her decision to retire into a monastery seems even more natural. The palace in which they had lived since 797 was converted into a monastery allegedly called the monastery of Repentence (*Metanoia*), but this may just be a rumour. It was also identified as 'the monastery of Theodote' as well as by the name of the original owner, Isidore. How long Theodote remained there is unknown, but at least in her retirement she may have managed to avoid the horror of imperial, ecclesiastical and social disdain.

So when Euphrosyne decided to transfer the relics of her father to her shrine, she had to find out whether they remained at Theodote's monastery of Metanoia or had been sent back to Maria on Prinkipo. Since her older sister Irene appears to have died young and had probably been buried in the monastic church on Prinkipo, there was already one tomb to collect from there. Finally, one of her step-granddaughters, Anna, is also known to have been buried in the monastery of the *Kyra Euphrosyne*, perhaps by choice. It provided a suitably imperial context and the step-grandmother may have suggested it. In due course, again at an unrecorded date, Euphrosyne herself will be buried among them, according to her wishes.

Such attention to the creation of a family shrine is all the more striking because Euphrosyne's family was already well represented in other monasteries in the capital. Her maternal grandfather, Philaretos, had purchased a burial plot in the nunnery of St Andrew *in Krisi*, and his widow Theosebo was later laid to rest beside him. Four other relatives had tombs elsewhere: two uncles in the monastery of St George *ta praipositou*, and two aunts who had adopted monastic life at the Theotokos *tes portes Pemptou*.[71] Once Euphrosyne and her mother had been liberated from their exile on Prinkipo they could have planned to expand one of these family establishments. It would have been quite in order for them to arrange additional space at St Andrew *in Krisi*. But this was not done. On the contrary, Euphrosyne wanted to construct her own family shrine in which the divorce which had blighted her life could be undone retrospectively. Once more, and for the last time, the hand of woman was to decide Constantine's fate.

FAMILY COMMEMORATION

In this way we can observe Euphrosyne attending to the matter of gathering her relatives into a family tomb, where her parents may be commemorated in an appropriate fashion and finally allowed to rest in peace. Because honouring the graves of ancestors is a serious duty of later generations, such a policy constitutes a vital part of the historical record of any great family. It is also intimately connected with the preservation of memory, in which women traditionally play an important role. Through their devotion to the deceased they preserve some knowledge of family history, the names of those who died young, the achievements of others. So Euphrosyne's aim in creating this shrine is perfectly in keeping with the methods used by many noblewomen to ensure that their kin receive proper respect. Elderly relatives, soldiers cut down in battle prematurely young, even children, male and female alike, they are all remembered on the days of their births and deaths, when candles are lit, liturgies said and charitable distributions made in their names.[72] In performing this task, Euphrosyne physically effaces the experience of her own family as separated into hostile camps; she reunites her parents in death. The monastery of the *Kyra Euphrosyne* thus becomes identified as a family shrine in which she and her immediate relatives are commemorated annually.

Since she is the last of the line and has no children, her task is all the more pressing. The first three generations of the Syrian dynasty produced emperors who were all buried in the imperial Mausoleum of Justinian, attached to the Holy Apostles, alongside Justinian I, Justin II, Herakleios and so many others. Their tombs were visited by reigning emperors on fixed dates such as Easter Monday as well as others. But due to the vicissitudes recounted above, Constantine VI, representing the fourth generation of the ruling family established by Leo III, had been denied his place beside his father, grandfather and great-grandfather. Euphrosyne could therefore appreciate that the fourth and fifth generations of the dynasty, in which she was numbered, had to be endowed with an appropriate shrine. She therefore decides that her father, his first wife and two legitimate daughters will be commemorated in her own foundation. In this way, while other imperial dynasties may come and go, each attempting a similar claim on posterity, her family would remain enshrined in its own distinctive burial place. In Constantinople the process undertaken by Euphrosyne serves as a model for later imperial women.

Of course, the imperial Mausoleum of Constantine I, founder of New Rome, was the prime example of a burial area attached to a church. Later Byzantine emperors assumed that they would join their predecessors in this consecrated space at the church of the Holy Apostles. Justinian had added another mausoleum when the number of tombs expanded and these benefited from the same veneration and commemoration already laid down in ecclesiastical and court ceremonials. But many rulers perished on the battlefield or met an untimely death at an assassin's hand. Others, like Irene, did eventually find a resting place there, but only after a period of condemnation and later rehabilitation.

By the early tenth century, Romanos I Lekapenos could plan a different mausoleum for the new dynasty which he hoped to found. In his construction of the church of the Myrelaion (Holy Oil) he clearly intended this, shifting imperial associations to his own foundation where his wife Theodora was buried in 922. Although his dynastic plans were thwarted by the perseverance of Constantine VII, there is no doubting his aim. Similarly, the Phokas family appears to have established a dynastic shrine in Cappadocia. The process reflects the growth and dominance of aristocratic groups, wealthy families established on landed estates in the provinces, who always had an eye on imperial power. Their numerous unsuccessful rebellions also mean that they rarely attain the summit of Byzantine society and have to settle for local shrines. But these in turn can become very significant foci of political ambition and regional commemoration.

OTHER IMPERIAL ACTIVITIES

Euphrosyne seems to have performed the role Michael II had wanted her to undertake; at least there is no suggestion that he was dissatisfied. Whether he had seriously intended to father more children or not, his second wife produced none. Perhaps she was unable to conceive. This certainly seems more likely than an assumption that the marriage was merely one of political convenience.[73] Men normally marry in anticipation of regular sexual relations and resulting children. Theophilos, however, remained Michael's only child and had been crowned as co-emperor in 821. Euphrosyne presumably attended to her stepson's needs as a stepmother should. Since he was about ten years old at the time of her marriage to his father, it is difficult to evaluate her possible influence over him. None the less, at all major court events the imperial couple must have appeared with young Theophilos in attendance, and Euphrosyne would certainly have been in a position to develop a close relationship with him. The events of his rule a decade later suggest that this may have been the case.

For the most part Theophilos was trained in imperial skills by male tutors, court eunuchs and specialists in all the matters he would need to master. Since Michael II was an uneducated man, like so many military usurpers, he was determined that his son should have the best teachers and learn from leading scholars. The emperor therefore put John the Grammarian, a very scholarly cleric, later patriarch, in charge of Theophilos's education. This figure is known from his theological expertise; as a reader in the church of Hagia Sophia in the early ninth century, he had been employed by Leo V to search the libraries of Constantinople for iconoclast texts to support the revival of this policy prior to the council of 815. He played a key role in the reintroduction of iconoclasm and made sure that Theophilos had a correct grasp of iconoclast theology.[74] In addition to his theological training, John seems to have encouraged in Theophilos some knowledge of the law, which the young prince combined with great enthusiasm for building ever more elaborate and fancy palaces and churches. These particular characteristics may date back to his early education.

Other aspects of Euphrosyne's life as empress which can be assumed turn around her official position as the imperial consort. In this capacity, we know that every empress had access to particular funds, which she used to perform her charitable roles; to finance gifts such as *solemnia*, annual donations to monasteries, like those granted by Irene to the Stoudios; to entertain high-ranking women as well as the wives of senators; and especially to meet the needs of the female side of the court, which had its own dinners, grand receptions and promotions to official positions (when the wives of officials gained the appropriate title, *spatharissa, tourmarchissa, strategissa* and so on). Many of these activities are documented indirectly from the existence of the seals of courtiers, for instance those responsible for the empress's table, or of women identified by their husbands' titles.[75] By the middle of the tenth century when the *Book of Ceremonies* was written, the ranks of court wives constituted a major body, distinguished according to the position of their husbands in the military or civilian hierarchy. There is evidence that such positions were becoming more significant at precisely this time.[76]

In her position as empress we can also assume that Euphrosyne played the role expected of her in the diplomatic receptions of the court. There is one further task for which she would have to take responsibility: the selection of a suitably impressive gift to send to the wife of Louis the Pious, Charlemagne's son and heir, when her husband dispatched a friendly embassy in 827. Diplomatic relations with the West had been interrupted by the murder of Leo V and the long civil war between Michael II and Thomas the Slav. So in 824 the first Byzantine embassy to Frankia carried ten different types of silk as gifts to Louis from his brother emperor.[77] On his return the ambassador, Theodore Krithinos, informed Michael II that the Carolingians were very interested in the writings of a Christian author identified as Pseudo-Dionysios, whom they equated with St Denis. So with the next embassy of 827 the emperor sent a de luxe manuscript of this work, highly appropriate for a ruler whose Merovingian predecessors were all buried at the monastery dedicated to St Denis, north of Paris.

On this occasion the Byzantine empress was expected to initiate her own version of the diplomatic exchange by selecting a gift appropriate for the wife of the foreign ruler. Euphrosyne had a specific role, though we have no record of how she executed it. It seems possible that one of the many Byzantine silks preserved in western cathedral treasuries might have been considered a suitably luxurious gift for Empress Judith, Louis' wife.[78] If the workshops established as part of the complex at the Eleutherios Palace were devoted to silk production (see chapter 2), Euphrosyne may perhaps have taken some responsibility for supervising them. This would not have been incompatible with her residence in the women's quarters of the Great Palace, since the Eleutherios continued in use for many years. The weaving and decoration of silks intended for export as diplomatic gifts demanded continuous production so that there would always be enough of these precious bolts in store to meet the empire's needs.[79]

MICHAEL II AND ICONOCLASM

Regardless of the fact that Euphrosyne had been brought up as an iconophile by her mother, who had kept in contact with St Theodore of the Stoudios (and perhaps with others who supported the veneration of images), she was probably obliged to conceal her childhood training in the emperor's court. Michael II adopted a position of mild support for the policy reintroduced by Leo V, declaring that the law must be observed (meaning that all must adhere to the Definition of Faith of the 815 council). Although some iconophiles were permitted to return to the capital from exile, the community at Stoudios was replaced by a loyal iconoclast group of monks. This form of substitution, which favoured those monasteries prepared to support the official position, may well have been widespread – communities of iconoclast monks and nuns certainly dominated the well-established centres. From the letters of Theodore of the Stoudios, the behaviour of iconophiles during the second period of iconoclasm was rather circumspect, avoiding direct confrontation with the iconoclast authorities wherever possible. His web of correspondents reflects a scattered but sustained opposition to Michael II's official approval of iconoclasm.

A more detailed exposition of the Byzantine position is laid down in the letter carried by the first embassy to Louis the Pious, in 824. It may have been written by John the Grammarian, for it certainly pours scorn on the faith which people used to put in their icons: believing that they could act as godparents, lighting candles and burning incense in front of them, and so on. It reports the Council of Hagia Sophia in 815 which had restored a moderate iconoclasm and plays down the number of iconophile opponents, who had fled to Rome among other places. This position probably reflects the intense discussion at the court of Charlemagne and his son, sparked by a faulty translation of the Acts of the Seventh Ecumenical Council (see chapter 2). The Synod of Frankfurt held in 797, the composition of the *Libri Carolini*, in which Charles himself took a prominent part, and subsequent debate over the appropriate use of religious art, had rehearsed, extended and finally condemned Byzantine iconophile arguments.

The letter of 824 also explains why Michael II has not been in communication with 'his brother emperor' before – the rebellion of Thomas, who is accused of sexual impropriety and apostasy, is held responsible for cutting off Byzantium and preoccupying the emperor. Assuring his colleague of his best wishes, Michael assumes that they both share the same moderate iconoclast policy. He then requests help concerning the iconophiles who have apparently sought refuge in Rome. The letter appears to take into account the breach that had opened between the papacy (loyal to the memory of Pope Hadrian and his understanding of the council of 787) and the moderately iconoclast Carolingian court. Reminding Louis that he too venerates the relics of the saints and wishes to strengthen the true faith in every way, Michael's letter proceeds to condemn practices that had developed before 815, ignoring the Carolingian commitment to images as a means of instruction. The key texts of Pope Gregory the Great on pictures as 'the bibles of the illiterate' do not seem to have been well-known in the East.[80] Similarly, the letter opposes superstitious customs associated with icon veneration that were unknown in the West. Each party thus neglected arguments considered essential by the other, a reflection of the different circumstances in which iconoclasm was regarded in East and West.

None the less, at the Synod of Paris held in 825, Louis the Pious instructed his bishops to endorse this new approach and to condemn excessive devotion to images. They also reaffirmed the conclusions of the Synod of Frankfurt held in 794, which had established an independent Carolingian theology of images. They criticised Pope Hadrian for endorsing the council of 787 but emphasised the value of images as a means of teaching. By approving this policy midway between the excesses of both icon destruction and icon veneration, the Carolingian theologians opposed successive bishops of Rome and aligned themselves more closely with the official Byzantine policy.[81]

WOMEN AND ICONS

From the many letters written by Theodore of the Stoudios during the reign of Michael II, it is clear that he thinks some women may be able to support the cause more effectively than men. This derives primarily from his praise for particular nuns, favourably compared with monks who have gone over to the enemy and become iconoclasts. Certain abbesses are singled out as examples of steadfastness under threat. In addition, the number of wealthy widows and women who are mentioned as assisting the iconophiles in prison, bringing them food, clothing and even smuggling in icons, recalls the anonymous wife of the jailer who had performed similar tasks for St Stephen in the mid-eighth century.

The role of particular women in indirectly supporting the cause of icon veneration is repeatedly mentioned and suggests that some were prepared to oppose the official policy on icons. In the second phase of his exile, when Theodore was sent to central Asia Minor in 818, he was protected by a wealthy lady named Irene, who was a member of the Tourkos family. On her estates at Bonita she made his exile comfortable until officials from Constantinople arrived to make sure he was being punished. This Irene is only one of several women who put themselves and their resources at the disposition of the iconophile leadership.[82]

While these are no more than hints, they raise the question of whether icon veneration was specifically meaningful to women, whose roles in the organised church were so limited. Apart from the position of abbess, which might prove the culmination of a young girl's dedication to the monastic life, there were very few recognised ways in which women could contribute to ecclesiastical life. We hear of a *thyroros*, doorkeeper, who might also sweep the steps of the church, remove the spent candles and so on, in the manner of so many dedicated female helpers today. But outside of the nunnery, it was very rare for a woman to attain a position of influence. And even communities of nuns were dependent upon an ordained priest for the Eucharist. Unlike the official services of the church, however, the act of praying to an icon was a personal matter which could be undertaken at the convenience of the individual Christian. It did not require the intervention of a priest and could be performed at any time when the icon was visible. From numerous accounts of women who were devoted to the icon of the Mother of God at the Blachernai shrine in the north of the capital, it is evident that they sustained a personal relationship with the icon. One woman participated in the Friday evening vigil every week, developing a strong belief that the image actually communicated with her. Others owned their own icons which they venerated in the privacy of their domestic space. Such stories are quite common and suggest that individual women secured a particular comfort from prayers they addressed to such well-loved images.[83]

Icons almost certainly played a similar role in the early part of Euphrosyne's life. The extent to which she disagreed with Michael II on the question of icons is not revealed by the sources, so silent on the thoughts of women though ever eager to condemn female weaknesses. As she had lived through the change of 815 and knew what persecution entailed, she understood the political necessity of keeping her feelings to herself, whatever their nature. If she did assist the imprisoned and persecuted iconophiles, Euphrosyne managed to preserve her anonymity in this role. After his unsuccessful protests against Euphrosyne's imperial wedding, Theodore of the Stoudios seems to have abandoned his efforts to influence Maria and her daughter: no further letters to them are preserved. Nor does he appear to have tried to use the empress's influence with her husband. With Theodore's death (from natural causes) in 826 the iconophile party lost its most effective organiser, and modern historians their best source of contemporary and immediate information. No other letter-writers emerge to fill the gap he leaves, and the Lives of several iconophile saints and martyrs tend to record their heroes' resistance long after the events they are supposed to have experienced.[84]

Like others, Euphrosyne could have maintained her iconophile faith privately while conforming outwardly with the official policy. But there are no hints in the surviving sources about her position, no suggestion that the foundations she established might have been less than enthusiastic in their support for the official policy on icons. It would be easy to imagine that the court of Michael II was rather a divided one, with John the Grammarian and the iconoclast Patriarch Antonios maintaining iconoclasm, while Euphrosyne and her ladies-in-waiting kept their own counsels. But since there is no evidence, speculation can be avoided. What may be deduced from the silence is that Euphrosyne performed her imperial duties in the manner expected of her. To that extent, Michael II's choice proved highly successful.

Indeed, unlike his predecessors, Michael of Amorion, the soldier-emperor with a stammer and most unimperial qualifications, is the only one who dies in his imperial bed. In contrast to Constantine VI and his mother Irene, who both died in exile, and his three immediate predecessors Nikephoros, Staurakios and Leo V, who were killed in battle or brutally assassinated, Michael II had a peaceful death. On 2 October 829, he succumbed to a kidney disease after a reign of eight years and nine months, leaving his young son and heir already established as co-emperor and well trained for imperial rule. This constitutes the first peaceful transition between rulers for nearly fifty years. One may legitimately ask if Euphrosyne played any part in making sure that on her husband's death his son would inherit his position unopposed.[85]

THE ACCESSION OF THEOPHILOS

As the widowed empress, Euphrosyne's first task is to bury her husband in the tomb prepared for him next to Thekla in the Mausoleum of Justinian attached to the Church of the Holy Apostles and to secure the elevation of her stepson Theophilos to the imperial purple. Her role is noted by some of the tenth-century chroniclers, such as Leo the Grammarian, who mistake Euphrosyne for the young emperor's mother: 'After him [Michael II] his son Theophilos held power with his mother Euphrosyne'.[86] Others, like Genesios, simply record that Theophilos inherited the throne from his father. This discrepancy is probably due to the fact that he was around sixteen years old in 829, just on the cusp of manhood and thus able to rule without a regency council. Only Theophanes Continuatus claims that Theophilos was of man's age and took over from his father.[87] But this source, as we shall see, is most aggressively opposed to the iconoclast emperors of the ninth century and may wish to attribute all the errors to Theophilos alone.

Among the first actions of the new ruler, two merit comment: several histories recount how Theophilos summoned the Senate to the Magnaura Palace and enquired of them what had happened to the men who had conspired with Michael II to kill Leo V on Christmas Day 820. When he was informed, the emperor accused them of murder and ordered the city eparch to inflict the due punishment (death), claiming that he had promised his father to do so. The severity and unfairness of this retrospective judgement may be interpreted as a sign that the new emperor, however young, was not going to tolerate any plots on his own life. Since the emperor was approved by God, no attack on his person could be permitted to go unpunished. But if Leo V had also been Theophilos' godfather, the need to avenge his spiritual father may have played a part.[88] The second act concerns the emperor's appreciation of his tutor, John the Grammarian: he was appointed imperial representative to the patriarch, holding the post of *synkellos*, which effectively designated him as the next head of the church. He was also sent on an important and sensitive diplomatic mission to the Arabs. In this way a renowned iconoclast scholar was placed in a prominent position, which could leave no doubt that the emperor would continue the ecclesiastical policy of his father and suppress icon veneration.

On the military front, also, Theophilos continued his father's policy of opposing Arab forces who had attacked and occupied Crete during the last years of Michael II's reign. These were pirates driven out of Muslim Spain, who were seeking a new base in the eastern Mediterranean. After Alexandria refused to accept them, they attacked Crete, killing the Christian leader, the Metropolitan of Gortyna, and others in their attempt to establish a separate Arab kingdom on the island. Despite several campaigns Byzantine forces had failed to dislodge this most unwelcome force, so Theophilos inherited a serious problem which had to be addressed. He was therefore preoccupied by military matters from the beginning of his reign and the surviving sources devote most attention to them. Several, however, record another notable event that occurred early in the reign: the emperor's marriage, which was arranged by his stepmother Euphrosyne.

THE MARRIAGE OF THEOPHILOS

Although accounts of the marriage arrangements vary from one source to another, there seems no doubt that Euphrosyne initiated the process. In 829 her stepson was probably sixteen years old, just the right age to marry, and she set about finding him a suitable bride. Here we come to the third account of a bride-show. As we have seen, the first to be recorded was in connection with the marriage of Staurakios, the son of Nikephoros I, in the first decade of the ninth century. The second account was composed slightly later, but relates to the earlier marriage of Euphrosyne's parents, Maria of Amnia and Constantine VI, which was arranged by Empress Irene and took place in 788. The third is this one, in which Euphrosyne selected a group of most striking young beauties and invited Theophilos to choose his future wife. According to some versions, she even gave him a golden apple so that he could act out the ancient role of Paris.[89]

There is every reason to doubt the elaborate details of versions of this bride-show preserved in tenth-century histories but for the fact that the young lady who won the competition and became empress was later recognised as a saint of the Orthodox Church. To commemorate her achievements, a Life was composed in the style of a panegyric in the late ninth or early tenth century, probably before these chronicles were written.[90] Following the rules for such imperial *enkomia*, normally addressed to emperors, the unknown author emphasises the empress's natural beauty, moral qualities and outstanding iconophile character which marked her out for imperial fame. Writing as he does long after the event, his account is elegantly put together to demonstrate the empress's superior qualities, for he wishes to belittle the wicked iconoclast, Emperor Theophilos. He makes clear that Euphrosyne, whom he identifies as the emperor's mother, was responsible for gathering a group of undisputed beauties, in preparation for the marriage.

So here, it seems, Euphrosyne takes an initiative. According to the Life, messengers are sent out to identify a select number of young women of the appropriate age and attractions.[91] This is the moment at which the heart of every father throughout the empire with a suitable daughter begins to beat faster. Each imagines, What if *my* child were to be chosen as empress? That mechanism for drawing the provincial nobility into the life of the metropolis, perhaps into the centre of the imperial court itself, moves into operation. From all corners of the Byzantine world well-informed and ambitious parents try to find a way of making their child available. Euphrosyne, of course, has her own plans. She is not going to allow Theophilos to choose an unsuitable bride, and her criterion of suitability may be quite unusual. While beauty may be a factor, the bride's potential as a mother, her family's standing in the country, and their attitudes towards religious images may all be significant. At any event, if the stories may be believed, among the young beauties considered appropriate at least two devout iconophiles had been assembled by Euphrosyne. Theophilos rejected the first, Kassia, and then 'chose' the second, Theodora. She is our third woman in purple.

The ceremonies of her coronation and their marriage took place on 5 June 830 according to the prescribed rituals (see chapter 4). In this way yet another provincial beauty was elevated to the highest position any woman in Byzantium could aspire to hold. Like Irene, Maria and Theophano before her, Theodora was transformed from a 'nobody' into the most important female figure in the empire. Her family accompanied her to the capital in expectation of related rewards. And in contrast to the lowly status accorded Maria after her marriage into the imperial dynasty in 788, Theodora is immediately raised to the position of empress. Euphrosyne has no ambitions to frustrate her stepson's new bride or to continue in occupation of the imperial quarters. Indeed, she will retire from the court almost as soon as the ceremonies are over (see below). So Theophilos' choice of Theodora is celebrated in the most obvious way, by the replacement of the older generation by the younger generation. The newly wedded couple accede immediately to full authority within the Great Palace.

All the surviving accounts of this bride-show present their evidence in such a way that those who venerate religious icons are always victorious, and their opponents who destroy icons are defeated. What they claim is that Euphrosyne set up the bride-show for her stepson in such a way that he could only select an iconophile bride: Kassia, who became a nun after the competition and devoted her life to the composition of hymns and religious poems, was a fine writer, one of the few female authors in Byzantium, or Theodora, who turned out to be an iconophile saint. And the person responsible for this bride-show was the daughter of Maria of Amnia, granddaughter of the Empress Irene who had restored the veneration of icons at the Council of Nicaea in 787. The obvious implication is that Euphrosyne was a secret iconophile who carefully disguised her loyalties and managed to deceive her stepson. This conveniently makes him look a fool who unwittingly selected a committed iconophile to be his wife.[92]

Such a definite theological interpretation overlooks the fact that Euphrosyne was also a *porphyrogennetos*, born in the Porphyra ('in the purple') to a ruling couple and raised with a thoroughly imperial aura, despite the unimperial conditions of Prinkipo. Through the unexpected proposal of marriage, she was able to return to secular life as the empress at the head of the Byzantine court. And as the wife of Michael II she realised her imperial destiny, reaffirming all the Byzantine ruling characteristics which her mother Maria must have inculcated in her. Euphrosyne was not a provincial beauty like Theodora; rather she came from the very apex of Byzantine society and returned to it quite naturally. Her identity as a member of the empire's inner ruling circle was just as strong as her iconophile commitment.

So when the time came to arrange her stepson's marriage, Euphrosyne was well prepared. She knew that it was important to select a girl whom she could influence, so that in the fullness of time she would be able to count on her support. The chief qualifications were that she should be of an age to bear many healthy children and come from a not too powerful (or not very well connected) provincial family, which would be eternally loyal to Empress Euphrosyne and would do nothing to challenge her. While some sort of parade of suitable young women may well have been arranged, and Euphrosyne may have vetted the families involved, it would have been difficult for her to ensure that undeclared iconophiles monopolised the event. It seems more likely that she only permitted young women whom she considered suitable to take part.

In the event Theophilos made the final decision and Theodora became his bride (see the detailed analysis in chapter 4). In rapid succession she bore him three daughters and a son, who died young; two more daughters, and finally in 840 a son, Michael, who inherited his father's power in 842. The marriage that Euphrosyne had arranged in 830 proved lasting. The couple appear to have been well suited by medieval standards and even after her husband's death Theodora displayed conspicuous devotion to him. Whether it had involved any element of a beauty contest or more simply an alliance between two families of unequal status, the significance of the marriage is confirmed by the success of Theodora's family in the capital. Her mother, Florina, her three sisters, who contracted advantageous marriages, and her two brothers all made good in the anticipated fashion.

Theophilos seems to have taken care of his wife's large family. In particular, he honoured his mother-in-law by creating for her an entirely new title: that of *zoste patrikia* (patrician of the girdle, named from the highly decorated girdle, *zoste*, of office). By elevating her in this way, he established a much higher position restricted to women at the Byzantine court: the emperor's mother-in-law attained the fifth place in the imperial hierarchy. There is little evidence for the impact of this new title as Florina had already adopted the more Christian name of Theoktiste and preferred a monastic environment to the life of the court. She established her own quarters within the monastery called *ta Gastria*, which came to be associated specifically with her and her family. However, the creation of a new and very distinguished position for the empress's mother meant that a title reserved solely for a woman was inserted into the system of ranking titles and government positions held by men. Perhaps Theophilos saw it just as a way of honouring his wife's mother, but he may have recognised the needs of the female members of the court and decided to consolidate his control over them.

BYZANTINE COURT HIERARCHY

As we have already seen, the system of ranking honorific titles and official posts was essentially linked to the notion of order (*taxis*).[93] Such order had to be preserved for court ceremonial to be carried out correctly. But it also controlled access to the imperial presence at banquets, documented in four surviving lists (*taktika*), which preserve seating plans for these long celebrations, one of the most important elements in court etiquette.

After the patriarch, who ranks first in these lists, the *kaisar* (caesar, heir presumptive) comes second; the *nobelissimos*, third (a title reserved to members of the imperial family), and the *kouropalates*, fourth (another title usually reserved for a son-in-law and heir, if the emperor has no son). Directly behind the *kouropalates*, the *zoste patrikia* takes her place. In this way, the imperial family became more firmly ensconced at the apex of court society. After the mother-in-law come the highest-ranking courtiers, the *magistros* (a high-ranking adviser), *raiktor* (rector, leading lawyer), *synkellos* (the emperor's personal representative to the patriarch) and the *praipositos*, the chief eunuch officer in charge of court procedure.

The earliest of these *taktika* is dated to the last years of the reign of Theophilos, indicating a court initiative to commit to writing what may have been preserved in oral traditions before.[94] The development suggests that within the Byzantine court it was considered necessary to record the now more complex ranking system. New *themata*, reflecting the expansion of imperial control both in eastern and western regions; new honorary titles, such as the *zoste patrikia*; new administrative posts to cope with the increase in record-keeping – all these changes receive indirect commentary in the seating arrangements for imperial dinners. With upwards of four hundred regular guests, a clear sense of order is essential. In addition, when there may be visiting ambassadors, honoured hostages being kept in the gilded cage of the Byzantine court, and sons of Venetian, Bulgarian and local aristocratic families, learning to be imperial pages, the correct priorities have to be established. Proximity to the emperor and a place at the high table is eagerly sought and rarely given.[95] The survival of this particular seating list (known after its editor as the Uspenksy *taktikon*) suggests that Theophilos paid attention to the orderly administration of his court, which enclosed a vaster and more complex machinery of government than ever before.

EUPHROSYNE'S RETIREMENT

Euphrosyne turned her back on all this when she decided to move out of the Great Palace. After successfully organising Theophilos' wedding, Euphrosyne withdrew, leaving the young couple in occupation of the official imperial quarters. In such transitions between generations, empress-mothers had to decide whether to retire to their own palaces within the city, where their lives would not be so dominated by the court, or to remain in the Great Palace. By moving out, they avoided the structural difficulty which occurred if the younger generation were prevented from taking up residence in the official imperial quarters. In such cases, the succession was marred by often lengthy wrangling, a well-known feature of the transition between rulers. Euphrosyne seems to have appreciated this potential for division and to have decided to leave Theophilos and his new wife on their own in the Great Palace. The implication of her quite rapid departure from the court is that she did not feel it necessary to remain close to Theodora, that she could rely on Theophilos and the eunuch staff to teach her the basics of court ceremonial, and that the young couple should be left alone to grow into their new roles as emperor and empress.

Some historians claim that Euphrosyne was expelled from the palace by her stepson, thus hinting again at the possibility that she opposed his religious policy. The Continuators of Theophanes support this view, insisting that Euphrosyne was obliged to leave court. Others present the opposite view: that she left of her own free will, presumably because she wished to reside elsewhere.[96] The key term is *hekousios*, without constraint, voluntarily, used in the *Life of Theodora*.[97] What does seem clear is that the two widowed ladies – Euphrosyne and Theoktiste – both preferred a monastic setting to the official life of the Great Palace. Their close relationship and distance from the court are interpreted by some later historians as a shared dedication to iconophile practices. But this need not be the case. Indeed, for Theokiste there is little evidence of it. The Life of her daughter, Theodora, presents a predictable iconophile position, stressing the family's courage in assisting those who resisted persecution. In Euphrosyne's case, we can suppose that her upbringing had induced a definite commitment to the veneration of icons. But there is no evidence that she tried to dissuade Theophilos from following his father's policy. She had a measure of the official imperial attitude towards icons and was not going to jeopardise her position as empress by openly pressing an iconophile position. This was part of her calculation in accepting the offer of marriage to a known iconoclast back in the 820s.

Constantinople was well supplied with palaces, suburban villas and official residences which could be used by such an eminent grand lady. As an ex-empress, Euphrosyne, like the mother or the mother-in-law of a ruling emperor, was guaranteed an imperial standard of retirement; through her titles and pensions, she received distributions of money, silk vestments appropriate to her rank, and clearly would not want for anything. Similarly, the empress's mother, Florina-Theoktiste, would have been offered suitable accommodation once she had decided not to reside in the court with her daughter. But both the mothers-in-law chose to spend their last years in private quarters attached to religious institutions. As we have seen, Euphrosyne had patronised certain monastic foundations which are linked with her name. The monastery of the Lady Euphrosyne was probably already established as the shrine of her parents and her sister. She may have encouraged Theoktiste to select the monastery called *ta Gastria*, which was also associated with Euphrosyne. Here Theoktiste could establish her own quarters as an entirely self-contained small palace appropriate to someone of patrician rank and considerable resources, and plan her own burial space in the monastic church.[98] After 830 Euphrosyne seems to have been a regular visitor and spent much time with Theoktiste at *ta Gastria*. In their retirement they probably did what most old people do: sat around, gossiped, exchanged stories of times past and devoted time to the routines of daily life.[99]

EUPHROSYNE'S WARNING OF CIVIL WAR

Even in retirement Euphrosyne retained a developed sense of her imperial inheritance, her commitment to the well-being of the empire and her own identity as a member of the ruling élite. Under pressure she could still behave with considerable political acumen, as an event in 838 demonstrates. In the summer of that year Theophilos suffered a humiliating military defeat when Caliph Mutasim captured the birthplace of his father, Amorion. While Michael II's origins did not suggest that this was a particularly fine place, the Arabs considered it an important fortification on one of the main routes to the capital and had tried to take control of it several times before. It served as the residence of the *strategos* of the Anatolikon and was strongly defended. Mutasim set out with massed armies determined to force the city to surrender, in reprisal for the Greek slaughter of Arabs taken prisoner at Zapetra in 837. In a double attack he also sent one army to besiege Ankyra, capital of the Boukellarion. Since these plans were not kept secret, Theophilos was in no doubt as to the seriousness of the campaign, and he left the capital to plan his own campaign in June 838. It was during the initial fighting for Amorion that a rumour spread among the Byzantines that the emperor had been killed. Instead of fighting on, many soldiers fled and sought a way to escape back to the capital.

Their arrival in Constantinople with this entirely incorrect news

1. Coins: (a) gold *nomisma* (solidus) of Constantine VI and Irene (780–97), with Leo III, Constantine V and Leo IV on the reverse; (b) copper *follis* of Constantine VI and Irene (792–7); (c) gold *nomisma* of Irene alone (797–802); (d) gold *nomisma* of Michael III with his older sister Thekla, and Theodora on the reverse (842–55).

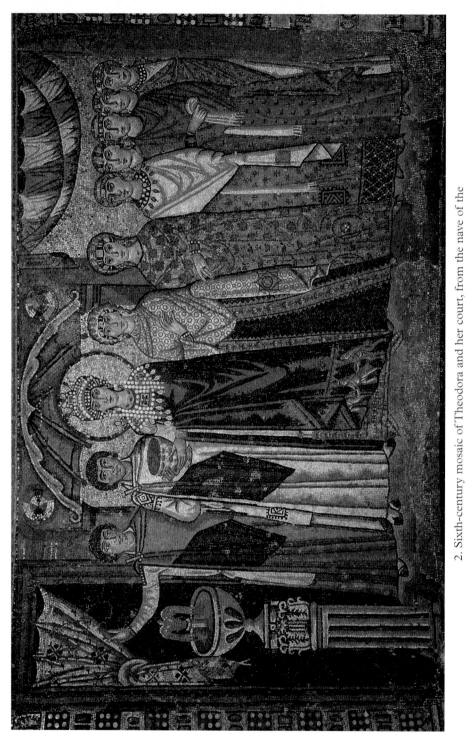

2. Sixth-century mosaic of Theodora and her court, from the nave of the church of San Vitale, Ravenna, dedicated in 547.

3. Mosaic from St Sophia, Thessaloniki (late eighth century), showing the monogram of Irene (EIPHNH) in the centre, from the south side of the barrel vault in front of the apse. The inscriptions, which begin on the north side (not shown) read: 'Lord, help the master (*despotes*) Constantine'; 'Lord, help the lady (*despoina*) Irene'; 'Christ, help Theophilos, the humble bishop' (ΤΑΠ(Ε)ΙΝΟΥ ΕΠΙΣΚΟΠΟΥ).

4. The front of the Fieschi-Morgan cloisonné enamel reliquary, early ninth century, Metropolitan Museum, New York (10.2 x 7.35cm), depicting the Crucifixion with 14 saints all identified by name. The inscriptions in gold above Mary, called Theotokos, and John, Ioannes, read: Behold, thy son, Behold, thy mother (John, 19: 26–27).

5. Charioteer silk, late eighth century,
from the Musée de l'Hôtel de Cluny, Paris,
which was used as a shroud for Charlemagne
when he died in 814.

6. *Right*:
sixth-century
encaustic icon of
the Virgin and
Child, from the
Museum of Western
and Oriental Arts,
Kiev.

7. *Below*: Illustration from
the *Chronicle* of Skylitzes,
MS. Vitr. 26-2, Biblioteca
Nacional, Madrid, folio 44v
(late twelfth/early thirteenth
century): the five daughters of
Theophilos and Theodora,
identified by name (from left
to right): Thekla, Anastasia,
Anna, Pulcheria and Maria,
are instructed in image
veneration by their
grandmother Theoktiste.

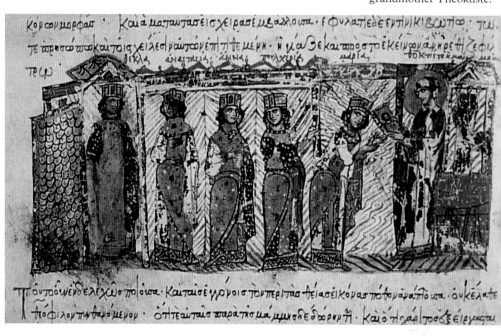

8. Eagle silk from the Cathedral
Treasury at Brixen/Bressanone,
eighth/ninth century.

9. The Triumph of Orthodoxy icon,
British Museum, fourteenth century, with Theodora
and Michael III (upper register, left) and Patriarch Methodios
(right) flanking an Hodegetria icon of the Virgin and Child.
In the lower register are iconophile saints and martyrs,
including the fictitious St Theodosia (extreme left)
holding a small icon of Christ.

provoked a plot to elect a new ruler. Senators and officials opposed to Theophilos began to consider alternative imperial candidates. News of these plots came to Euphrosyne's knowledge. In these dangerous circumstances she had the presence of mind to send a messenger to her stepson with the warning that he should return immediately.[100] And this cannot have been a simple matter. She had to arrange for a reliable and trusted servant (probably one of her eunuchs) to ride as fast as possible, using the imperial facilities for changing horses, to find the emperor wherever he was and to gain access to him. To validate the oral message the emissary would need to carry an authentic sign from Euphrosyne, probably her ring, an *enkolpion* or a cross identified as hers. To facilitate the journey he would need sufficient funds to bribe his way out of any difficulties, as the Arab forces encircling Amorion were surely policing all the surrounding roads. But her planning proved successful.

Euphrosyne's message is reported in graphic terms by much later Arabic and Syriac sources: 'The Romans who have come have reported that you are killed and they wish to appoint another king; come quickly!'[101] This is why Theophilos abandoned the campaign, and rode immediately back to Constantinople. The change of tactic is quite unexplained in the Greek sources.[102] Despite military problems the emperor followed his stepmother's advice and appeared in the capital to show that he was by no means dead and to punish the perpetrators of the false news. But in his absence the Arabs breached the defences of Amorion and eventually forced their way in. Stories of betrayal did nothing to relieve the emperor's guilt and sense of shame. For, after burning the main church, in which many had sought refuge, the caliph took thousands prisoner. Only the most high-ranking officers survived the return journey to Samarra, and despite many efforts to negotiate their release, Mutasim held them captive for seven years. Finally, in 845, a group of survivors of the disaster of 838 were beheaded on the banks of the Euphrates: the forty-two Martyrs of Amorion.[103]

None the less, in the summer of 838 Euphrosyne's initiative may have saved his throne. It also protected Theodora's position as empress, as well as her own standing. The measures taken by Euphrosyne indicate that she retained her political sense. As an imperial princess who had survived a long exile, and had unexpectedly been restored to public life, she could evaluate not only her own best strategy, but also what was best for the empire. In acting as she did, she revealed an awareness of the danger of civil war, which would follow the proclamation of a rival emperor in Constantinople. She may also have wanted to help her stepson, but her own feelings towards him are not recorded. Judged by this action, she considered him a better ruler than those who might try to take his place.

EUPHROSYNE'S COVERT PROMOTION OF ICONOPHILE PRACTICES

It is Euphrosyne's opposition to Theophilos' religious policy, however, that is held responsible for sparking off the last recorded action of the empress-mother: this centres on what is presented as her sustained commitment to iconophile practices. According to the writers who make this claim, Empress Theodora used to take her children to visit their grandmother, Theoktiste, and their father's stepmother Euphrosyne. There are two versions of the story.[104] Both agree that the imperial family used to ride out from the Great Palace, suitably accompanied by guards, almost all the way to the walls of the city where the old ladies had established a sort of private iconophile retreat within the Gastria. Inside the monastic walls and within the private quarters occupied by Theoktiste, the little girls were instructed in the correct forms of iconophile devotion, in the approved ways of honouring the holy images. Theodora approved of this clever device by which her children could be properly brought up in the iconophile tradition. The icons were stored in boxes and only brought out when no official was present. There the girls learned how to pray in front of icons, and to kiss them as a mark of respect, as is still done in orthodox countries today. And this took place under the nose of an emperor who actively persecuted known iconophiles.

There is of course nothing inherently unlikely in the story that the imperial children were taken to visit their grandmother. If Theodora wished to maintain links with her mother, such visits would have been quite normal. After her death and burial at *ta Gastria*, they would also have continued to visit her tomb. Euphrosyne's participation in the visits is confirmed by the fact that when Theophilos discovers that his children have been receiving illicit iconophile indoctrination, he holds his stepmother partly responsible. It is the youngest daughter, Pulcheria, who lets slip to her father that they have been playing with Theoktiste's 'dolls'. The emperor immediately forbids any further activity of this kind. He also identifies Euphrosyne as an iconophile presence and forces her to move away from *ta Gastria*. Since she has lived through long periods of imperial disapproval before, she returns to her own foundation of *Kyra Euphrosyne*. Nothing more is known of this alleged incident, which is clearly designed to subvert the iconoclast order of the day, but one of Theodora's daughters, Anna, who had perhaps participated in the lessons in iconophile veneration, would eventually be buried beside Euphrosyne. Her sisters and their mother Empress Theodora would continue to visit these graves, especially on the important days associated with the lives of Euphrosyne and her step-granddaughter Anna.

Bearing in mind the motivation of the authors, what is to be made of this fascinating claim? Can we believe the suggestion that the empress-mothers used this cover to ensure that Theodora's five daughters were trained as iconophiles, and thus learned the customs so strongly denounced as superstition by the emperor? Several factors make this inherently improbable, most obviously the supposed date of the discovery. This is said to have occurred before the birth of Prince Michael in January 840, and at a time when all five of his older sisters could take part. The dates of birth of the imperial daughters are not documented, but since the fourth eldest, Maria, died in about 839 at the age of four, Pulcheria, the fifth, cannot have been more than about two years old. If the supposed trip to *ta Gastria* occurs in 839, Pulcheria is two or three years old, barely of an age to babble about dolls.[105] The other difficulty is that by 839 there is no evidence that Theoktiste is still alive, so Euphrosyne is most likely to be the older woman responsible.[106]

By the mid-tenth century, however, Theoktiste has become the grandmother in charge of the lessons in iconophile devotion, a scene depicted in the magnificently illustrated version of the *Chronicle* of Skylitzes (decorated in the late twelfth century).[107] Theoktiste is identified holding the icon, Theodora's five daughters bow their heads in reverence at the sight. This is the way iconophile behaviour is transmitted between generations: the older women instruct the children in showing due reverence. Even the youngest can learn how to kiss and honour the holy images, which have been removed from all public churches. In the secrecy of their grandmother's private quarters, children learn how to maintain iconophile traditions (see plate 7).

For the Continuators of Theophanes, writing when icon veneration was an utterly fixed point in the ritual of the church, and the painting of icons a source of inspiration for all religious art, the notion that women had sustained a particularly fervent devotion to the holy images conformed to patriarchal expectations of the female sex. It contained both an element of praise and a firm put-down. The idea that the older generation of imperial ladies would secretly transmit the correct forms of image veneration to the five little princesses behind Theophilos' back had a tremendous appeal. It could be used to make the heretical emperor look even more foolish and unable to control his female kin.

It also carried a germ of truth, which lay in the fact that elderly women are often the carriers of such unwritten traditions. They form the chain which links the generations, teaching younger women and their daughters how to perform the rites of veneration with appropriate devotion. Of course, this is not limited to religious cults; over the centuries grandmothers, mothers and other female relatives have trained the next generations in the fields of medicine, child rearing, sewing, cooking and housework. The French term for midwife, *sage femme*, draws attention to this wisdom which is always transmitted orally. Nor is the method of teaching limited to women. In medieval societies most practical skills are similarly transmitted: care of animals, farming techniques, carpentry and more complex building operations were all learned by observation. Even monks learned asceticism by apprenticing themselves to experienced older experts. But for women, whose access to knowledge was always more restricted than it was for men, this style of education might be all they would ever get.

With this long history of feminine education in mind, we can appreciate that Theodora needed to visit her mother Theoktiste and mother-in-law Euphrosyne, not only for guidance in sustaining correct methods of icon veneration but also for other practical advice. While the former may have been specially skilled in domestic matters, the latter represented knowledge of court activity, ceremonial, competence in political and diplomatic matters, which would have helped the inexperienced Theodora. There is, therefore, no need to force the account of her visits to the monastery of *Kyra Euphrosyne* into a purely religious mould: along with the veneration of icons Theodora and her daughters probably received much more significant elements of education and knowledge. But this is of little interest to the tenth-century writers, who wish to elevate the female members of the Amorion dynasty into champions of icon veneration, largely in order to reduce the power and status of its male representatives.

A MYTH IN THE MAKING

In the famous cartoon of the five princesses learning how to venerate icons, Euphrosyne is nowhere to be seen. Her importance has dropped away – only the iconophile myth is sustained through this image. Based on elaborate reworkings of earlier records, eleventh- and twelfth-century versions of the plot, all seek to trace a predisposition to resist iconoclasm back to women of the ninth century. Knowing that Theodora has been acclaimed a saint for her reversal of the heresy, they associate her with a secret and heroic devotion to icons. This also supports their emphasis on a gendered attitude towards religious images. Such valiant female opposition intensifies the heretical iconoclast rulers' wickedness and draws attention to the impossibility of their task. By heightening the division between the sexes, the chroniclers also magnify the significance of the visual in religious devotion to icons. This in turn helps to create a bogey of the destruction of images which may not have loomed as large in the mental universe of participants. Here we can begin to observe the making of a myth: that iconoclasm was a most dangerous heresy, and that it utterly divided Byzantine society. Photios (patriarch 856–7, 877–86) must certainly bear some responsibility for feeding the flames of intolerant iconophilism: in his repeated condemnations of iconoclast practice he elevated Theophilos' persecution to an exceptionally high profile, which permitted later commentators to see in Theodora's opposition a firm feminine commitment to icon veneration.

Euphrosyne has no role in this imagined reconstruction of the reign of Theophilos. In later iconophile elaboration Theoktiste takes all the credit. Yet, of all the participants, Euphrosyne had greater experience of iconophile practice and had suffered for her identification with the cause of images. If anyone in the 830s had the motivation for such an extraordinary plot, it is she. She has avoided making an issue of her personal faith throughout the period of her most unexpected return to public life. While there is no record of her views, she is neither praised nor blamed until this moment. The implication of Theophilos' reaction, however, is that Euphrosyne is guilty.

If the story is to be believed, it is indeed tempting to see Euphrosyne's hand in it. But further doubts are cast by the fact that the revised account preserved by the Continuators of Theophanes is followed by a very similar story involving the court jester, Denderis, and icons which he alleged were hidden by Theodora in her private apartments within the

181

Great Palace.[108] In this version of female iconophile devotion, the empress venerated her icons, which she called dolls. When the emperor was informed of this by the jester, she explained that Denderis had merely glimpsed her ladies-in-waiting in a mirror reflection and had mistaken them for icons. Here is an obvious echo of Leo IV's fury in the 770s when he discovered that palace eunuchs were secretly venerating icons in their own quarters. As we saw in the previous chapter, Theophanes, who records the story, makes no mention of Irene in connection with this covert expression of iconophile devotion. Only in later sources is the empress associated with the eunuch officials, who were publicly humiliated and imprisoned for their actions.[109] The similarity is so close that I think we should assume that the tenth-century authors, knowing of a court jester called Denderis, and wishing to endorse their conviction that women love icons while men destroy them, have elaborated a new version of the well-known trope. The clown makes an amusing accusation about the empress's dolls, the emperor reacts in horror and anger, and Theodora skilfully deflects the charge by claiming that it was all a question of mirror images.

THEODORA'S DEBT TO EUPHROSYNE

It is the case, however, that Theophilos persecuted male icon venerators and would surely have been greatly exercised by the knowledge that his own wife and female relatives were consciously undermining his theology. He would perhaps have taken firmer steps to control them, to prevent their opposition to the official definition of orthodoxy. At the very least, we can imagine that John the Grammarian would have been summoned to persuade Euphrosyne, Theoktiste and particularly Theodora of their egregious errors and to terminate their activities. Having exiled the leaders of the iconophile opposition, Theophilos could have done the same to his stepmother, if not his wife and mother-in-law. But no action is recorded, beyond Euphrosyne's first banishment from the Great Palace, which is documented only in later sources. Perhaps this concealed veneration of icons never occurred or was never discovered?

Theodora will learn from her association with Euphrosyne and will become the saint and heroine of the second reversal of iconoclasm. She has to wait until Theophilos is dead before she can act. Her commitment, however, will turn out to be his salvation. Yet her debt to Euphrosyne is only partly linked to the iconophile tradition – Euphrosyne also represents the survival of a woman whose destiny had been decreed by her parents' divorce, who was a pawn in the highly political battle which continued to resonate for years. To have sustained a sense of imperial pride during a childhood spent in exile, an identification as a *porphyrogennetos*, and to have commemorated all that in the construction of a family shrine at her foundation, the monastery of Lady Euphrosyne – these aspects of Euphrosyne's life also contain important lessons for Theodora. In turn, she will enjoy the fruits of power, followed by exile from court, and will experience political impotence, though not quite as severely as Maria of Amnia and Euphrosyne. The example of her stepmother-in-law may well have helped Theodora to hold on to her imperial inheritance. For she too will create a family shrine like Euphrosyne, to ensure the commemoration of her own relatives. In sum, there is much more in Euphrosyne's history to inspire the Paphlagonian empress than just a shared opposition to iconoclasm.

In the absence of any knowledge of Euphrosyne's personal views, what she really thought will be forever hidden from us. But her action in warning her stepson of a possible revolt against him suggests loyalty and political courage; the decision of a woman who identified herself with imperial responsibilities and was not swayed by personal religious convictions. In this she seems to have remained true to the marriage arrangement she had made with Theophilos' father, Michael II, which had transformed her life. While her withdrawal from the court probably reflected a desire to enjoy a life of retirement, she did not forget the skills of political manoeuvre which had assisted the astonishing changes she had experienced in the transition from an exiled princess who was apparently destined to die in the monastery on Prinkipo, to Empress of Byzantium, and finally stepmother to the emperor of the day. And she stood by Theophilos when his own fate looked grim.

EUPHROSYNE'S DEATH

Like so many other aspects of Euphrosyne's life, there is no mention of her death, though we can be sure that her will provides for special services to be said and distributions of money to be made to the deserving poor. The nuns established at her monastery will perform the required liturgies on the third, ninth and fortieth days after her death. When her body is laid to rest in the tomb of Bithynian marble, it joins those of her parents and sister already buried there.[110] In death the last representatives of the fourth and fifth generations of the Syrian dynasty are reunited. By creating this shrine to her parents and her sister, Euphrosyne achieves a permanent and lasting centre for her family's cult.

Theodora will surely bring her children to say farewell to the step-grandmother who may have taught them a lot more than icon veneration. By her example, Euphrosyne has demonstrated that individuals can sustain an imperial identity through great adversity. While she was born with this, she promoted Theodora to the same high station and expected her to live up to the most demanding traditions of Byzantine rule. It is a paradox that Euphrosyne, the last surviving member of the Syrian dynasty which had introduced iconoclasm, should bequeath to Theodora an iconophile understanding of the significance of religious images. This is because she links the ruling family of the eighth century with the dynasty of Amorion into which they both married. Because of their public place in the court hierarchy, Euphrosyne and in turn Theodora must uphold the imperial traditions which guarantee the survival of empire. But in their personal lives, both may have favoured the use of holy images which suited the private devotions so greatly appreciated by women. They have to combine two very different practices: the imperial exercise of authority (which in this period is largely defined by iconoclast reform) and their own commitment to icon veneration. Euphrosyne's ultimate gift to her successor may lie in her capacity to handle the resulting tensions. How well Theodora learned the lesson, and proved herself able to continue the example, will form the subject of the next chapter.

CHAPTER 4

Theodora: the Paphlagonian bride

With Theodora, our third empress comes to centre stage – the daughter of a couple from rural Paphlagonia, whose family acquired fame and fortune through her beauty. For, as we have seen, she was chosen by young Theophilos to become his wife in a bride-show. Since there are some aspects of early ninth-century history which illuminate Theodora's background, let us first examine what is known about her place of birth and family.

PAPHLAGONIA IN THE EARLY NINTH CENTURY

Paphlagonia was a mountainous region of northern Asia Minor bordering the Black Sea. Then, as now, it was a source of timber which was used to construct boats and its coastal population was a seafaring one. It also supplied the capital with grain, pork 'and the necessities of life'. According to the *Life of Theodora*, Paphlagonia had its own special bounty, from which all parts of the world benefited.[1] It lay between the *thema* of the Boukellarioi in the West, and the vast *thema* of the Armeniakoi, which stretched as far as the border of the empire in the East. There is some doubt about whether the region had previously formed part of one of these two bigger *themata*, or had been divided between them.[2]

Paphlagonia was established as a separate province with its own general in 819/20. The reason behind this subdivision lay in the numerous revolts led by soldiers inscribed on the military lists of the Armeniakon. In the late eighth century they had rebelled against Constantine VI more than once, and displayed their rivalry with the troops of the Anatolikon. By 819 Leo V, who had previously commanded the Anatolikon, was determined to curb their potential power as king-makers. He therefore created two new provincial units on the territory of the Armeniakon: the duchy of Chaldia in the far east, and Paphlagonia in the west (see map 3). This reduced the size of the Armeniakon to approximately one third of its original extent.

While the general in charge of the new Armeniakon retained his place in the hierarchy of military ranks, and earned a much larger salary than those in charge of the recently created provinces, he now had responsibility for a particularly sensitive part of the border with the Arabs, centred on Kamachos, and a much smaller length of Black Sea coast. Chaldia, with its central control at Trebizond, took over a long strip of coastline, and Paphlagonia, with a substantial hinterland south of its capital, Gangra, had responsibility for a central section. Both the new *themata* had naval forces and were intended to patrol the sea lanes so vital for trade.[3] These were under threat from hostile forces from the northern littoral where the 'Rus', Vikings from Scandinavia who had penetrated through the river networks of Russia, were now in a position to venture south across the Black Sea. Accounts of attacks by the Rus on coastal sites like Amastris in Paphlagonia, stress their unexpectedly terrifying nature, but these seem to have ceased by 839. The appearance of sea raiders from the north gave added significance to the new *themata* along the Black Sea coast.[4]

PAPHLAGONIA'S SPECIALITIES

In the mid-tenth century the region of Paphlagonia was famed for its pig industry, pork being a standard meat consumed in Byzantium, and especially for its bacon. It was also known as a source of eunuchs (not foreign but native-born Byzantine eunuchs). This combination led to bad jokes at the expense of the Paphlagonians (who were called pigs' arses), and drew attention to their illegal practice of castration. By c.900 Paphlagonian eunuchs were attaining very high positions at court. But the mutilation which prepared younger sons for careers at court or in the church seems to have been established in the region considerably earlier.[5] Niketas, who was to play a prominent role in late-eighth- and early-ninth-century history, was sent by his parents from Paphlagonia to the court of Irene in the 770s.[6] They had had him castrated. An association of Paphlagonia with the supply of local eunuchs can therefore be traced to exactly this moment in eighth-century history.[7]

Niketas was born in 761/2 and arrived in Constantinople in about 778 at the age of seventeen. He entered Irene's household as a young eunuch servant (*oikeios*) and attended the council of 787. He later rose to high positions in the military under her rule. She favoured him with an important part of the relic of St Euphemia when these were translated into the church near the Hippodrome. By 797 Niketas is recorded as a general in Sicily, and it is tempting to link him with the construction of a church on the island dedicated to St Euphemia. But this is attributed to a Niketas who bears the family name Monomachos.[8] While he was serving in the West, he visited Rome and acquired an icon of Christ. At the relatively advanced age of fifty he was tonsured and joined a monastic community in the capital, apparently of his own volition. Although many aspects of his career are unclear, his support for the iconophile cause is not in doubt. Niketas was persecuted by Leo V and Theophilos for his stand and probably died in exile in 836.

A similar career was guaranteed another eunuch from Paphlagonia, Leo, who is known both by the name of the post he held for many years as 'Leo the *sakellarios*' (treasurer) and Leo from Sinope.[9] While Sinope on the Black Sea coast became part of the *thema ton Armeniakon* in the ninth century redivision, it is only just over the border from the new Paphlagonia, and can hardly be distinguished from it. Like Niketas, Leo was also promoted by Irene and had reached the top position in the finance ministry by 802 when he supported the *coup d'état* of Nikephoros I. His iconophile sympathies are evident from his friendship with Theodore of the Stoudios and his attempt to reconcile the exiled abbot with Michael II in 824. Theophilos retained his skills in the same post and in this capacity Leo is known to have requested the prayers of St Ioannikios in about 838 when he visited the holy man in Bithynia. Like the later Paphlagonians who made a habit of castrating their sons, the parents of Leo and Niketas had already identified a career path which became a long-lasting tradition. However, this was not a pattern followed by Theodora's family.

THEODORA'S BACKGROUND

Theodora's parents came from the village of Ebissa and her father Marinos was inscribed on the military catalogue. At some time he had held the position of *tourmarches* or *drouggarios*, the official in charge of a subdivision of a province (either the Armeniakon prior to 819 or Paphlagonia itself). But by 830 Marinos was dead, which may account for the vagueness over his precise role in the military. Theodora's mother, Florina, had six children, of whom Theodora was probably the fourth. As none of the dates of birth are recorded, the ages of Theodora and her siblings must be calculated from other data recorded about them, where dates of marriage form a significant pointer. The widowed Florina may have dedicated herself to a monastic style of life, adopting the name Theoktiste ('creation of God') in place of her rather unchristian baptismal name.[10]

Elements of the family's status can only be pieced together from stray references: they may have had experience in Black Sea trade, even to the extent of owning boats used for commerce. They associated with certain Armenian families of the capital and formed part of the 'mafia' of easterners who found a natural environment in Michael II's military and iconoclast court. One of these was an uncle of Theodora, Manuel the Armenian, who had held an unusual command as *strategos* in charge of all five Asian provinces for a short time in 819/20; Michael II retained his services, but on Theophilos' accession in 829 Manuel was accused of treason by Myron, the *logothetes tou dromou*, and fled to the Arabs. After considerable plotting, he managed to return to the empire and was restored to the post of chief military adviser to the young emperor.

It seems that the family shared in the Paphlagonian identity as 'people of enterprise', and were not tarnished by the association with pig farming.[11] Apart from Manuel, it is not at all clear whether the family was important and well-connected before 830: *drouggarios* is not a very high rank in thematic terms, and Marinos was already dead. But to be enrolled on the military catalogue with any title was already an indication of resources and resourcefulness.[12] Theodora's two brothers may have been intended for army careers following in their father's steps: Petronas later proved himself an able commander, and the other, Bardas, in due course attained very high office. Her sisters were to make excellent marriages but it seems rather more likely that these alliances with the high society of Constantinople were a consequence of Euphrosyne's planning, rather than a prior achievement. There is no indication why Theodora's family rather than any other should have been selected for the highest honour of marrying into the ruling dynasty of Amorion.

THEODORA'S UPBRINGING

Since nothing is recorded of Theodora's childhood, we can only assume that she had been brought up in the traditions of 'spindle and distaff', to spin thread and weave cloth, the proper skills of girls. What else did one learn in Ebissa? A certain knowledge of the seasonal work of farmers, for Byzantium was predominantly an agricultural society, plus, in the case of Black Sea Paphlagonia, some awareness of activities connected with sailing and fishing. The Christian liturgy must have dominated the lives of most provincial people for it established their days of rest (Sundays and the great feasts of the church) and taught them the stories of the Old and New Testaments, as well as the lives of the saints, through regular readings in church. Despite the iconoclast supremacy of Theodora's childhood there is no reason to doubt that she too learned all the basic elements of Christian education and was as well informed about theological definitions as any other girl raised in a rural settlement.

Her Life dutifully records that her parents sustained their iconophile devotion through the periods of official iconoclasm, and always aided people who were oppressed by persecution.[13] If this is so, Florina also permitted two of her daughters to marry men who totally supported the iconoclast policy of the Council of Hagia Sophia (815). One of Theodora's sisters, Kalomaria, who may have been older than her, was married to Arsaber, a brother of John the Grammarian, the tutor appointed to ensure that Theophilos received a developed and iconoclast education. This alliance suggests that the family was known as reliable supporters of the official policy on icons that had been in place since 815.

So when Euphrosyne sends out the summons for beautiful young ladies to attend her in the Great Palace, we are not told of any special characteristics that qualify Theodora for the most prestigious marriage of all. But her family's fecundity and good health may help her towards the imperial role she is to fulfil so well: the production of children. This she does with great regularity, enduring seven pregnancies in less than ten years, until January 840, when her son Michael is born. For this task no training is required, but genes may help, and Euphrosyne may well have considered Florina's precedent a useful guideline. It is also interesting to note that, like Irene from Athens and Maria of Amnia, an orphaned girl has just as good a chance as others. Does this suggest that an incoming imperial bride might actually be hampered by an active or powerful father? Constantine V in 769, Irene in 788 and Euphrosyne in

830 may all have preferred a girl whose chief male relative was no longer alive to demand the rewards of a successful father of the bride.

THE 'BRIDE-SHOW'

Once Theodora and her family arrive in the capital, together with the other young beauties, Euphrosyne presents them to her stepson and invites him to choose his wife. Unlike Constantine VI, who may have had little choice, Theophilos at least gets to play the part of Paris. Two distinct versions of the event are preserved. In the *Life of Theodora*, Theophilos has a first inspection of the contestants and distributes apples to them all. Their embarrassment when he asks for the apples back the following day draws attention to Theodora who alone has not eaten hers. Much is made of her visit to Isaiah, a holy man leading the life of a stylite saint on top of a tower near Nikomedeia. She tells Theophilos how *he* also gave her an apple and prophesied her success. As a result, she is able to present two apples to the emperor, which she says represent her virginity and her fertility (the promise that she will bear him a son), two key requirements for any imperial bride.[14]

In another account, it is Theophilos' brief conversation with Kassia, another of the contestants, which dominates the selection. When the prince opens the conversation with the statement that woman is the fount of all evil – an unfortunate way to engage a future wife's affections – Kassia reminds him that woman is the source of greater good. The exchange is part of a well-known couplet which contrasts the roles of Eve and the Virgin Mary.[15] Through Eve's first sin of disobedience, women are condemned to be inferior to men. Yet by the extraordinary role of the Ever-Virgin Mother of God, they are given a second chance to redeem themselves, following her example of purity and dedication to Christ. Not wanting to be reminded so quickly of the saving power of Christian women, Theophilos proceeds to the second contestant, Theodora, to whom he gives a golden apple. No conversation is recorded though the beauty of both the girls is emphasised.

In both versions of the bride-show, with highly unlikely exchanges recorded between the young emperor and his potential brides, the function of the contest dominates the form. The bride-show is fleshed out, given detail and specificity in order to strengthen popular belief in this method of selection. Every family's expectation of winning the prize, against all the odds, is to be encouraged. Previous occasions when a young prince has been married in this fashion are thus confirmed and in turn these accounts will continue to inspire provincial notables with great ambitions in later centuries. Probably both the alleged conversations are elaborations on the process of selection, invented partly to fill out an event which cannot be accurately documented because it never took place. Or perhaps, to borrow a modern cliché, we can say that a bride-show is not an event, it is a process. What part family qualifications or individual character traits played in the final selection is impossible to judge. We are left with the distinct impression that the marriage was certainly arranged, but that Euphrosyne allowed Theophilos the gesture which gave him a sense of choice. Theodora was crowned empress on 5 June 830 in the prescribed manner and the wedding celebrations followed.

EMPRESS THEODORA (830–42)

As far as Theodora is concerned, the early part of Theophilos's reign is entirely given over to child-bearing. She appears to have conceived and given birth regularly almost every year, though no birth dates are recorded either for her three daughters or her first son. But allowing for the few events which are datable in the decade 830–40, Theodora must have been fairly preoccupied by her offspring. The first-born, Thekla, is named after her paternal grandmother, Theophilos' mother, who had died many years before and was buried with her husband, Michael II, at the Holy Apostles. Young Thekla is celebrated on coins issued to mark her arrival and crowning. Later, her father would suggest her as the possible wife of the western emperor Louis II, son of Lothar and grandson of Louis the Pious. While this diplomatic proposal did not reach a successful conclusion, it reminds us of the importance of emperors having many children, female as well as male. Indeed, unlike Constantine VI, Theophilos appears to have taken great pride in his daughters. By 833 he orders the next two, Anna and Anastasia, to be recorded on the reverse of his gold issues, while Theodora and Thekla flank him on the obverse.[16] He thus presents himself with four females, a highly unusual imperial coin type.

Finally, the joy of his first son's arrival in about 834 is also noted on the coinage. While the male child should have been named Michael after his paternal grandfather, Theophilos breaks the rule and gives him the name Constantine, perhaps to honour both the founder of

Constantinople and the great iconoclast emperor, the fifth of that name. The emperor crowns his son as co-emperor and fully expects him to inherit the throne. Sadly, however, Constantine is not destined to survive babyhood, for in about 835 he crawls away from his nurse's care, falls into a cistern in the Great Palace gardens and is drowned. This tragic event is marked by a ceremonial burial in the Mausoleum of Justinian attached to the church of Holy Apostles, where Constantine's small sarcophagus is laid close to those of his grandparents, Michael II and his first wife Thekla. The grieving parents still hope for another son, although the next two children are both female: Maria and Pulcheria. Their patience is eventually rewarded when Theodora gives birth on 9 January 840 to another male child, christened Michael and crowned by his father probably at the following Christmas feast.

During this decade Theodora also has to bury her fourth daughter Maria, who dies in about 839 and joins her brother Constantine in the imperial mausoleum. Her mother Florina-Theoktiste dies at a date which is not recorded, and is buried in the monastery where she had made her home, *ta Gastria*. The empress may already be thinking of turning this foundation into a family shrine, following the example set by Euphrosyne. While her father Marinos must have been interred in Paphlagonia, and her sisters will probably find tombs with their husbands, it is quite remarkable that so many of Theodora's relatives end up in *ta Gastria*.

Privately, Theodora seems to have continued certain activities of which her husband did not approve. The most unusual concerns her supposed interest in trade, which turns on the story that Theophilos ordered a commercial ship and its cargo burned after learning that it belonged to his wife.[17] If any credence can be given to this, it implies that the commercial interests of Theodora's family were carried over into her married life and allowed her to make money from trading. The emperor condemned this as an activity incompatible with imperial status. However, it seems more likely that the story is invented to demonstrate the emperor's lack of judgement. It is a curious incident none the less, as it implies that commercial shipping was not so well established that the emperor could turn a blind eye to heavily laden cargo boats on the Bosphoros. If it did represent Black Sea trade with the Aegean and East Mediterranean, this should have been cause for celebration, inasmuch as a revival of trade marked a positive development for the empire of Theophilos. The coins of his reign circulated much more extensively than previous issues, indicating a wider economic contact between the provinces and the capital.[18]

A less alarming activity was the empress's devotion to the Blachernai shrine of the Theotokos to which she used to make visits, both for prayers and to use the famous baths there.[19] This is recorded both in the chronicles and in the *Patria*, and may feature as a sort of parallel to the emperor's weekly visits to the same church. On the way he allowed petitioners to approach him and appeal against any miscarriages of justice. His availability seems to have been appreciated and he was regularly asked to intervene. As a result, some high officials were apparently punished for taking advantage of their positions, or for not imposing the law correctly. Theodora's visits to the Blachernai shrine had no such public function as far as we know, but were probably an aspect of her faith. Like many women, she may have felt an affinity with the cult of the Virgin. In addition, the two visits supposedly connected with pregnancies were more likely to have been generated by the important relic, the *zone* or girdle of the Virgin, which had special healing properties. In particular it was sought by women in childbirth and might therefore assist Theodora in her numerous deliveries.[20]

The most serious aspect of Theodora's private life, however, is her alleged commitment to religious images which, if true, would have divided emperor and empress. We have already noted that Theoktiste, Theodora's mother, is supposed to have maintained iconophile practices at her residence in the Gastria (see chapter 3). She is also given a prominent role as a female supporter of iconophile champions such as Methodios, who resisted Theophilos' persecution. But this identification is made in later iconophile sources anxious to perpetuate the gendered stereotypes observed earlier. Theodora in her turn is said to have taken her daughters to visit their grandmother for iconophile instruction, and tried to relieve the sufferings of the victims of iconoclast punishment. Later in the reign she persuaded her husband to allow Lazaros, an iconophile painter, to recuperate from torture in a monastery where several heroes of the resistance were held (see below). Since the sources emphasise the extent of iconoclast repression, and the corresponding role of imperial women in countering it, in quite different fashions, a slight detour is necessary here.

THEOPHILOS AND ICONOCLASM

Although the young emperor confirmed his father's policy towards icons by promoting John the Grammarian, there is little evidence that he initially thought any further persecution of iconophiles to be necessary. Many monastic leaders had been arrested and were imprisoned in a variety of locales – distant rural castles, monasteries under firm iconoclast control, even in cells attached to the Great Palace. Following the death of Theodore of the Stoudios in 826, no major leader had emerged to take his place. The imperial authorities may well have considered that their policy was sufficiently well established.

Late in 831, however, scurrilous pamphlets about Theophilos' imminent death began to circulate. Similar 'prophesies' had preceded the deaths of Leo V and Michael II, so there seemed to be a distinctive iconophile pattern to the trend. In official circles it was assumed that these originated with Methodios, a native of Syracuse in Sicily who had been chosen to act as papal legate for Pope Paschal I in Rome's attempt to influence Michael II over the issue of icons. Methodios had been imprisoned for suggesting a return to iconophile traditions and the restoration of ex-Patriarch Nikephoros, but was released in 829 when the emperor realised that he was about to die. Now Theophilos had him arrested again, together with Euthymios, the former (i.e. iconophile) Bishop of Sardis. During their interrogation Euthymios claimed that the emperor's mother-in-law Theoktiste had visited them in their confinement. The claim was only one reason for a violent beating, which was so severe that the seventy-seven-year-old bishop died.[21] His death is said to have upset the empress. Methodios survived his physical attack and was exiled again to the island of Aphousia where he spent the next seven years.

Through such measures taken against individuals, the resistance seems to have been bullied into submission. Theophilos tried to prevent the teaching of iconophile veneration by removing icons from Constantinople and its environs and forbidding the production of images. In June 833 he ordered the patriarch Antonios Kassymatas to hold a synod and reaffirm the iconoclast Definition of Orthodoxy of 815.[22] Other notable iconophiles, Joseph of Thessaloniki and Niketas the patrician (the eunuch sent from Paphlagonia to the court of Irene), were exiled at this time, as well as leaders of the monastic opposition, including John of Kathara, Makarios of Pelekete and Peter of Atroa.[23] But by 837 all of them had died of natural causes rather than severe persecution. Most of the iconophile bishops were also dead.

Under John the Grammarian, who was consecrated as patriarch on 21 April 838, the Sunday after Easter, a rather more serious persecution of determined opponents was ordered.[24] The well-documented punishment of two monks who had originally come to Constantinople as envoys of the eastern patriarchs, the brothers Theophanes and Theodore, and Lazaros, a Khazar painter and monk, reveals the iconoclast authorities' determination to prevent further icon painting. For their stubborn resistance, the brothers from Jerusalem were severely beaten and had iambic verses tattooed on their foreheads before they were exiled to Apamea in the province of Opsikion.[25] Lazaros in his turn was branded so that he could not use his hands to paint. At this stage Theodora is supposed to have intervened to make sure that he would at least be imprisoned in a more sympathetic environment – she got him moved to the monastery of Phoberos on the Bosphoros, which was known as a place of detention for iconophiles.

At the same time Theophilos ordered the release of Methodios from his imprisonment on Aphousia; he was brought to the capital to advise the emperor on astrological predictions. It may have been the Sicilian monk's skill in Latin that was particularly appreciated. Certainly, both men seem to have shared an interest in the occult. So, despite their theological differences, Methodios was lodged in the newly built Sigma Palace where he had many serious conversations with the emperor. Did he also meet the empress and discuss quite other matters with her? This may well have happened for, after 842, Theodora had a very clear idea of the person she wished to see installed as patriarch in the place of John the Grammarian. Her conviction that Methodios was the right man may well date back to this period when he was held at the Sigma.

POPULAR SUPPORT FOR ICONOCLASM

From this brief survey, it should be clear that we do not know whether Theophilos was seriously concerned about the role of icons among his subjects, or whether Theodora was seriously committed to iconophile practices. So the extent to which the issue divided them is hard to evaluate. Later sources of the mid-tenth century play up an antagonism, setting the cruel heretic against the saintly empress for reasons that have already been elaborated. At the time, however, the strength of feeling both for and against iconoclasm may not have been widespread. Conforming to the emperor's will was one thing; a passionate commitment to iconoclast theology quite another. Such a middle way may be observed in the behaviour of one of Theophilos' most trusted officials, the *logothetes* Theoktistos, who like many a skilled courtier took care not to offend the emperor. Whatever his personal views, he and other officials like Leo the *sakellarios* sustained an important role under iconoclast and iconophile rulers alike. In the fourth century the pagan philosopher Themistios had demonstrated a similar ability to please Christian rulers, while Talleyrand would transform this expertise into a new art.

In the light of this very considerable sector of the population bending with the political wind, it is possible to gauge the seriousness of feminine commitment to icon veneration? Leaving aside the traditional slur that women are incapable of understanding theology and therefore need visual aids to inspire their Christian belief, were they more likely to persist in following a policy condemned by both church and state as idolatry? Surely not. Those for whom icons had become a necessary part of worship may have hidden them, in order to sustain the familiar ways of praying before holy images. Within the private quarters of an enclosed community like *ta Gastria* Theoktiste and Euphrosyne would also have been able to conceal their own icons (see chapter 3). Their privileged position, financial resources, and respected old age would all assist such a secret habit. But when the rest of the population heard or saw what happened to the brothers Theophane and Theodore, called the *graptoi* because of their tattoos, the risks may well have seemed too great.

THEODORA'S PATRONAGE

In the poorly documented decade of the 830s, there are few hints as to what Theodora achieved as empress. One particular institution, however, seems to be clearly associated with this period because it is related to the empress's repeated pregnancies. Whether the text of the *Patria* can be given any credence or not, the story goes that on more than one occasion when the empress was on her way to visit the shrine of Blachernai, her horse slipped as she passed the portico (*embolos*) in front of the *narthex* of the church at the Diegesteas. On both occasions the jolt made her realise that she was pregnant. After the successful delivery of her daughter Anna, she constructed a church in that place which was dedicated to the same saint.[26] This tale encapsulates a complete methodology employed by generations of writers: when they discovered a monument with no known founder, they looked for a story that could be associated with the area and invented an etymology or motive. Since other churches dedicated to St Anna are also attributed to Justinian II and his wife Theodora, daughter of Tervel the Bulgarian (*Patria* III, 79), or to Anna, the supposed wife (in fact, daughter) of Leo III (*Patria* III, 107), there is obviously room for doubt about Theodora's role. But it is interesting that among these quite unreliable stories the compilers knew that the ninth-century empress made regular visits to Blachernai, in addition to the formal trips made in the fulfilment of ceremonial duties.

With the second of the foundations attributed specifically to the empress, there is less confusion. The *Patria* record that she rebuilt the monastery of St Pantaleimon, called Armamentaris because it had been an arms depot under Maurice: 'after 247 years Theodora made it a monastery and endowed it with many properties'.[27] As Maurice reigned from 582 to 602, the date would lie between 829 and 849, which fits perfectly but gives no indication of whether Theodora undertook the work before or after her husband's death. No further building activity is recorded, suggesting that the empress was not such an active patron as either of her predecessors.

THEOPHILOS' PATRONAGE

This is very likely due to the fact that Theophilos was an avid builder, whose constructions and restorations make the work of most previous emperors pale into insignificance. The emperor was responsible for a veritable extravaganza of construction work within the Great Palace, with new reception halls, entire new complexes of rooms, a new throne room and adjoining chapel; outdoor terraces for demonstrations of dancing, and magnificent fountains to adorn the newly-laid-out gardens. He also embarked on a complete redecoration of the Magnaura Palace, which included a throne room filled with gold – two gold organs, gold lions that roar and birds that sing in a golden tree – as well as new golden robes for the emperor and empress to wear there. Between 834 and 836 the Pentapyrgion, a five-towered display case containing such precious things as imperial wedding crowns and costumes, was added.

Another new palace complex, called the Karianos after the flight of steps made of marbles brought from Caria, was built to please Theophilos' unmarried daughters who lived there. He also founded a completely new palace complex on the Asian side of the Bosphoros at a place called Bryas, where recent investigation has revealed the foundations of a church with three apses, which corresponds to written descriptions of the palace. Islamic palaces in Baghdad are said to have provided the model for this site.[28] After the first embassy of Theophilos to the Caliphate, John the Grammarian returned with accounts of the splendour of Islamic buildings in the new Muslim capital, which the emperor was keen to rival with his own magnificence. In addition, Theophilos restored and strengthened the sea walls along the Marmara coast, which carry inscriptions recording his role, and constructed a new hostel for visitors to the city, known as the *xenon* of Theophilos.[29]

In some of these activities the empress was specifically associated and named. For instance, when Theophilos ordered new bronze doors for the south-west vestibule of Hagia Sophia in 838, her monograph accompanied those of the emperor and patriarch. Two years later, however, on the occasion of the coronation of his son Michael at Christmas 840, the emperor ordered that the monograph of Patriarch John should be replaced by Michael's. The inscriptions now read:

Lord, help Theophilos the ruler; Mother of God, help Theodora the augousta; Christ, help Michael the ruler, From the creation of the world (*apo ktiseos kosmou*) 6349, indiction 4.[30]

This date corresponds with AD 840/1. More than a millennium later, in 1975, these doors were restored and rehung in their original location. Ernest Hawkins, who was responsible for the expert restoration of many Byzantine mosaics and frescoes in Constantinople, took me to witness this difficult operation with a massive hoist to raise the heavy doors and slot them on to their original hinges. The work was rendered more complicated by the fact that the pavement within Hagia Sophia has risen about four feet since the ninth century. Deep trenches had to be made on either side of the porch and the doors had to be lowered into these trenches as well as on to their hinges. Fortunately the doors can remain permanently open with the monograms on view, though the lower quarter is almost buried in the trenches parallel with the side walls of the vestibule.

The chief activities which bring the imperial couple together are, of course, the annual round of ceremonies stipulated by the court and ecclesiastical calendar. Although Theodora has barely witnessed any of these before she performs them, there is no evidence that she fails to master the required actions, perhaps with the help of Euphrosyne. She also takes part in the military achievements of her husband that are fêted with triumphal celebrations in 831 and 837.[31] Her public role in the former includes a special reception for Theophilos and his generals at the palace of Hiereia on the Asian side of the Bosphoros after their first victory. This is a private welcoming ceremony with participation restricted to the highest court officials and the imperial family. Once the Arab prisoners arrive to take part in the victory parade, this constitutes the public celebration.

The triumphant Byzantine troops bearing booty lead the procession, with all their captives, followed by the emperor at the head of a separate cortège. They circle the city in order to enter it by the ancient triumphal arch built into the Golden Gate. The victory is celebrated along the Mese in typical style with receptions and acclamations at different stations all the way to Hagia Sophia, where prayers of thanks are offered. Theophilos addresses the assembled citizens on the successful campaign and promises military promotions and horse races in the days to come. A new bronze coin may have been issued with the inscription: 'You conquer, O Augustus Theophilos', which shows him wearing an ancient triumphal headdress called the *tufa*. For the inhabitants of the capital, however, it may be the races, games and public entertainments in the Hippodrome which make the most impact. For the first time in recorded Byzantine history there is something resembling a joust, when the eunuch Krateros challenges an Arab captive and of course succeeds in unhorsing him.

To what extent Theodora participates in all this is unclear, but her presence in the welcoming party, which greets the victorious emperor on the Asian side of the Bosphoros, is noted. By summer 831, if this is indeed the date of the triumph, she is either expecting their first child or has just been delivered, and may well not review the entire military parade and the games in the Hippodrome. During the second triumph, however, she probably takes part in the reception at the Bryas Palace, Theophilos' new construction on the Asian side, which is followed by another triumphal entry with children bearing flowers going out to greet the troops. On this occasion, probably in 837, Theophilos not only celebrates with major games in the Hippodrome, he also decides to compete in the first of the horse races, wearing the colours of the Blues. Driving a team of white horses (*armati leuko*), the other charioteers allow him to win and the two factions acclaim him: 'Welcome, peerless champion!'[32] There is no record of who crowns the winner, but it would be entirely appropriate for the empress to perform this imperial function from the *kathisma*. Indeed, Theodora's participation in Hippodrome entertainments provokes special comment from an Arab emissary, who was astonished at the public appearance of the ruler's wife in such a context. In this unguarded moment, a quite impartial source confirms that Empress Theodora attended such victory games and so may well have crowned her husband the victor on the occasion of his military triumph in 837.[33]

We owe several fascinating insights into the imperial court under Theophilos and Theodora to such Arab emissaries. One from Cordoba, the capital of Muslim Spain, was Yahya al-Ghazzal, a poet sent to the court of Theophilos in 839–40. In his fascinating account we see the imperial couple in circumstances that are less ceremonial. The poet was deeply impressed by Theodora's beauty. Not only was he unable to take his eyes off her when she was in the same room, but he made a detailed description of her features, 'saying she had captivated him with her black eyes'.[34] Modern commentators point out that he may not have been used to seeing women unveiled and perhaps stared at the empress quite rudely. Since Arab women in the Spanish Caliphate were never veiled at home, this must be incorrect. Instead it seems reasonable to take the ambassador's testimony at face value, even if it was designed to flatter her husband. Theodora *was* beautiful, though this was not the chief reason for her selection as empress.[35]

It is much more interesting to note that Yahya records the empress's presence in meetings between her husband and foreign ambassadors without adverse comment. Along with the interpreters and other courtiers, she might join in such official, diplomatic occasions. He notes that she entered wearing all her finery, 'a rising sun in beauty', perhaps her formal new golden costumes designed by the emperor to be worn in the recently redecorated golden Magnaura Palace. But even if she was wearing less ceremonial costume, it is also possible that the envoy from Spain had simply never seen the imperial silks and gold-embroidered and bejewelled outfits. In either case his admiration knew no bounds, and it has preserved a delightful picture of the emperor taking pride in his beautiful wife.

THE LAST YEARS OF THEOPHILOS

The reason for Yahya's visit to Constantinople was that in the previous year, 838, Theophilos had suffered the loss of Amorion in circumstances that threatened his rule (see chapter 3). It was in the light of the city's destruction and the capture of so many distinguished military leaders that Theophilos opened negotiations with the Umayyad Caliphate of Spain and the western emperor Louis the Pious, in hopes of persuading these rulers to join forces with the empire. Neither embassy proved successful in the short run. Later on, forces led by the western emperor did participate in campaigns in southern Italy aimed at frustrating the expansion of Arabic control there. And although the mission to Cordoba did not lead to similar combined military activity, the diplomatic initiative produced the embassy led by Yahya and established good relations between Constantinople and Spain.

In January 842 the Arab victor of the campaign against Amorion, died, thus bringing to an end a period of hostility between the Caliphate and the empire. Whether Theophilos was able to savour the good news is not clear for he himself felt death approaching in the same month. When he realised that he was dying, although he was still so young, Theophilos summoned his courtiers, the Senate and military officials and made a speech in the Magnaura. He stressed to all present how important it was to observe his son's rights and appointed male regents to serve with Theodora during Michael's minority. In addition to the court eunuch Theoktistos, who held the post of *epi tou kanikleiou* (keeper of the ink-pot), two of the empress's male relatives are named: Manuel her uncle (although some sources have already recorded his death in 838), and Bardas her brother.[36]

THEODORA AS REGENT (842–56)

On 20 January 842 Theophilos dies of dysentery; he is nearly twenty-nine or may have just celebrated his birthday. Theodora is probably twenty-seven or twenty-eight, her five children range from Thekla, eleven, down to Michael who is just two years old. Her son will need to be protected for a minimum of fourteen years, until he is sixteen and gains his majority. And indeed in 856 he will claim power. But in January 842 Theodora's problem is to ensure that no one will usurp her son's imperial rights. Theophilos is buried in the imperial mausoleum close to his baby son and daughter, and his family and court observe the period of official mourning marked by commemorations on the third, ninth and fortieth days after death. Theodora's first task is to proclaim the accession of Michael III through gold coins designed to publicise this fact. The first coins issued display little Michael on the right of the cross with his oldest sister Thekla on the left, looking much older and bigger than him, and Empress Theodora on the reverse. With this truly dynastic coin type, she confirms the arrangements made for Michael III, the new emperor. She and Thekla are associated in imperial power and Theodora will rule in his name (see plate 1d).

As we have seen, this is the regular method of informing both the inhabitants of the empire and its allies and neighbours of a change of ruler. Like Irene before her, Theodora makes clear that the family she has married into remains in control although Michael is very young and the Regency will be even longer than that of Constantine VI. Still, the succession follows the same pattern. Michael has been crowned by his father Theophilos twelve months earlier, his older sister Thekla has also been crowned, and their mother Theodora, Augusta since 830, is in charge. While there are no legitimate rivals, Michael does have over-mighty uncles and Theodora must sense their ambitions. In John the Grammarian, however, she has a powerful supporter who is committed to the dynasty and will support Michael's claims and educate him as an iconoclast. And in Theoktistos, named as Regent, she has a trusted and reliable eunuch official who has served her husband well. In 842 he seems to be the most powerful male Regent on whom Theodora can rely.

THE REVERSAL OF ICONOCLASM

Since the restoration of icons occurs in March 843, just fourteen months after the death of Theophilos, it is generally assumed that this is a matter of the greatest importance to Theodora, the most urgent task to which she addresses all her energies. Clearly, if she is going to reverse the iconoclast policy of her husband, she needs to be sure of majority support – in the army, in the court, among the populace at large, and most obviously in the church. Under Patriarch John, the hierarchy of bishops is thoroughly iconoclast and observes the Definition of Faith going back to the council of 815 (which had been confirmed in 833 and 838). Iconoclast monks occupy the major foundations, although out in the mountains of Bithynia opponents of the official policy survive.

There is little evidence for the religious affiliation of the chief army units. But their failure at Amorion in 838, coupled with the loss of so many officers and regular soldiers taken prisoner by the Arabs, and their prolonged captivity, had taken its toll among those most enthusiastic about iconoclasm. Despite reforms undertaken by Theophilos to restore confidence among the military, the intimate link between iconoclasm and victory had been broken. The detention of so many prisoners of war in the Caliphate and stories of the pressure put on them to convert to Islam were a constant reminder of the disaster. Despite many efforts to secure their release, many senior officers were imprisoned until their martyrdom in 845. It seems likely that those who had fought at Amorion remained depressed by the extended absence of their comrades-in-arms, while those newly promoted to positions of authority lacked the old-fashioned belief in the power of iconoclasm. By 843, Constantine V's policy is no longer a guarantee of triumph over the forces of Islam.

On the contrary, those who support iconophile practice can point to the sins of the Christians as a more serious reason for the failure. God would punish those who refused to venerate the holy images. And among the persuasive voices arguing this case, Theodora must be listening to Methodios, as well as to the iconophile monks who take the death of Theophilos as a catalyst of change. Those who had been imprisoned by her husband are now set free: monks like the brothers Theophanes and Theodore; the icon painter Lazaros, whom she had helped; and Ioannikios, Arsakios and Isaiah, named in her Life as prominent supporters. Isaiah is the stylite saint who had supposedly prophesied her triumph in the imperial marriage stakes.[37] References to the 'many, many more … holy fathers' who remain anonymous sheds doubt on their existence. There are not that many enthusiastic iconophiles to whom she can turn, while the opposition of Patriarch John is bound to be firm, well-argued and difficult to handle.

In these circumstances, Theodora proceeds with great care. Because the sources which purport to document the restoration of icons are notoriously biased, full of later interpolations, and more legendary than factual, it is difficult to identify the steps she takes to ensure a successful change of religious policy. To cite just one instance: many authors are only too keen to attribute to the empress initiatives which they consider appropriate to a female regent. Following the gendered assumption about weak women loving icons and tough men hating them, the mainly tenth-century sources give Theodora considerable credit for arranging things. They want to see in the young widowed empress a dedicated iconophile who has patiently bided her time while her husband persecuted the icon venerators. They allow her much more responsibility for the new policy than normal. Their testimony is thus suspect and has to be checked wherever possible against other accounts, written closer in time to the events of 843, or with less evident bias.

Allowing for this tendency, I think we can see Theodora doing something quite original. She foresees not only the problems of making a fundamental change in the religious policy of the empire, but also the implication of such a change for the status of her young son. If iconoclasm is to be condemned as a heresy, a non-orthodox teaching, a false doctrine, her deceased husband will be held partly responsible. Because of the pattern established in 787 and 815, it may be possible to avoid having him denounced by name as the initiator of persecution, or condemned as a wicked heretic. At the previous changes of policy, the ecclesiastical authorities found it more effective to denounce categories of wrong belief and authors of particularly influential texts, they also preferred to name the patriarchs (good and bad) rather than the leaders of the state. So Theodora knows that the real danger in the proposed change of policy is that her husband will simply not be mentioned; his name will neither be recorded among the heretics nor will it feature among those to be commemorated as upholders of orthodoxy. He will not be remembered in the official diptychs which record prayers for all the orthodox. This leaves a dangerous gap which may adversely influence her son Michael and his chances of claiming his inheritance.

In order to remove any possibility of this happening, Theodora resolves to find a way of excusing Theophilos' behaviour. She may have additional fears: that her husband's support of heresy may cause unknown damage to his immortal soul, that he may go to hell and suffer terrible torments for his iconoclasm. What this implies about the Byzantines' belief in the afterlife, the threat of hell-fire and eternal damnation, is not easy to establish. Given Theodora's devotion to the Theotokos, who plays such a significant role in accounts of the Last Judgement, could there be a connection here between iconophile veneration and post-mortem fate?[38] Would such a view lead the empress to consider a pardon to be the most important aspect of Theophilos' Christian destiny? In 842, Theodora's strategy is to devise a way of pardoning her late husband's support for iconoclasm.

THE REPENTANCE OF THEOPHILOS

The saga of Theophilos' deathbed repentance is the answer. It is presented as the prior requirement before any restoration of image veneration can be discussed. As she works out how to deal with John the Grammarian, Theodora takes steps to put about the pious rumour of Theophilos' conversion to icons just before his death. She hopes to ensure a post-mortem pardon so that he does not suffer and his reputation is not impugned. This clearly involves a rehabilitation of Theophilos, identified by contemporaries as a fervent iconoclast persecutor.[39] It begins with accounts of the emperor's deathbed agonies of doubt and anxiety, the nightmares he suffered of being flogged for his persecution, the frenzy of his last days, moaning, screaming, quite unpacifiable. Theodora herself watched over this dreadful experience, imploring the Theotokos to help her husband. When Theoktistos entered wearing his *enkolpion,* a necklace on which a miniature icon was suspended, the emperor gestured frantically and babbled in an incomprehensible fashion. Theodora could not think what it meant. But as the eunuch approached the couch, her husband grabbed the image on the chain and brought it to his lips and kissed it. At that moment his torments ceased and he dropped into a peaceful sleep, convinced of the value of venerating the holy icons![40] By the time he dies a few days later, Theodora claims that he had fully recanted his previous support for iconoclasm, had truly repented and converted.

In the propagation of the story, dreams and visions feature prominently; for example, when Theodora fell asleep at the bedside of her husband, she saw the court of heaven and witnessed the punishments that her husband was receiving. Iconophiles who had not been impressed by the saga later received heavenly signs indicating that they should accept it. In a further elaboration of the story of the pardon, Theodora appeals to Methodios and the assembled bishops to spare her husband. They draw up a list of iconoclast heretics, including the emperor, lay it on the altar of Hagia Sophia overnight, and miraculously the next day Theophilos' name has disappeared from it. Such reliance on unprovable events, witnessed only by the parties concerned, reveals a weak basis in fact. But belief in oracles, prophecies and other signs which require expert interpretation is widespread not only in Byzantium but also in most medieval societies. Such stories underlie many of the fantastic claims recorded in contemporary histories and saints' Lives.

Since the texts of Theophilos' repentance were written down much later, tracing Theodora's part in the process is bound to be inconclusive. But she alone had a special interest in this part of the rehabilitation of her husband.[41] She is thus the chief person with an interest in the creation of this pious invention. It is quite clear that her anxiety may be genuine, in that he stands to be condemned to eternal damnation for promoting heresy and persecuting the faithful. She alone is anxious to spare him such a fate, and the text probably reflects her determination. This quality is also displayed in the *Acta* of Saints David, Symeon and George, in the section written to demonstrate what a significant part Symeon played in the restoration of icons.[42] In this version, Symeon angrily condemns the funds which Theodora claims her husband had set aside on his deathbed by way of compensation for those who had suffered from his persecution. This fills the empress with grief and hostility. Symeon's brother George and Methodios, the future patriarch, have to persuade him to change his mind (which he does, partly as a result of a dream in which Theophilos appealed to him, saying: 'O monk, help me!'). As a result Symeon accepts Theodora's request that her husband be spared.

While such pious legends are devised to counteract the weight of condemnation which lies on the emperor, all the iconophiles who have suffered for their faith, all the exiled monks and humiliated bishops are determined to see the heretic denounced. Although Patriarch John and convinced iconoclasts would oppose such a development, they are now in a difficult position, for they must sense that they may be on the losing side. In the first year of her rule, the empress's determination to spare Theophilos warns them that a fundamental change in the status of the holy images is under way. And in her insistence on the last-minute conversion of her husband, we have a clear indication of female agency exercised by the wife of an emperor. Her concern underlies the invention. And she must then convince others that it really happened.

THE SECOND RESTORATION OF ICONS (843)

In overseeing the process of change, Theodora finds a willing ally in Theoktistos, whose wearing of the *enkolpion* (a sign of his secret devotion to images) is held responsible for Theophilos' conversion. But it takes more than a year for the actual mechanism of restoring the icons to be sorted out. The final achievement does not occur until 11 March 843, reflecting the complicated negotiations which have had to be made. As is so often the case, when these sensitive issues are eventually written down, many quite different versions of what happened are recorded. There are allusions to discussions that preceded the ceremony; meetings at which the essential prerequisite of removing John the Grammarian from the patriarchal office is debated. He is to be replaced by Methodios, who is one of the obvious candidates and also Theodora's choice. Methodios will be entrusted with the task of confronting the iconoclast clergy. In addition, he will compose a new liturgy which will formally celebrate the end of iconoclasm and restore the holy images to their revered place in ecclesiastical cult and ritual.

Despite the confusion of many variations on this theme, it seems that the restoration was achieved largely by direction from the Great Palace, with much input from the empress. A fairly neutral account describes how the emperors (Michael III and Theodora) recall the iconophiles from their exile and imprisonment, and summon a council to meet in the residence of Theoktistos. At this 'holy local council' John the Grammarian is removed from office and Methodios appointed as patriarch. The seven ecumenical councils are confirmed and the sacred icons restored.[43] The brief description seems to telescope a number of additional events, for instance, the fact that Methodios was elected to the patriarchal throne on 4 March and installed at the ceremony held in Hagia Sophia one week later. It does not mention an imperial banquet given by Theodora during that week. It fails to describe the night vigil held at Blachernai before the clergy processed to the cathedral church, where they met the emperors and all the court carrying icons, candles and crosses. It says nothing about the long liturgy that Sunday, the first in Lent, on which the restoration was formally celebrated. In this version Theoktistos, the court eunuch, plays a key role as the official responsible for arranging a meeting which takes place in his house. A similar account is given in the *Life of Theodora* although the council itself is not mentioned.[44]

A completely different version of the event accords the Stoudite monks an important role and attributes greater authority to the empress's uncle Manuel. He pressures Theodora to restore the icons but she remains reluctant out of loyalty to her husband's policy. In this later version, iconophile monks previously associated with the Stoudios force the issue. Once John is ejected and Methodios becomes patriarch, monks from all the major communities, including Mounts Olympos, Athos, Ida and even Kyminas, come to the city on the first Sunday of Orthodoxy for an assembly at which they proclaim the true faith.[45] Clearly this version wishes to elevate the heroic role of iconophile refugee monks, previously dispersed and greatly weakened by repeated exiles and punishments.

Amidst these conflicting claims every hagiographical text, about each and every saint of the period, preserves its own record of what exactly happened, and these very unbalanced accounts influence later chroniclers. Theodora's *Vita*, designed to magnify her central role, provides a clear example. While its chronology is insecure, it stresses that the major steps in the process of restoration were taken by official decrees. Iconoclasm was condemned by an imperial decree; similarly the recall of 'all the fathers who had been exiled or subjected to harsh imprisonment ... together with large numbers of monks and further, quite a few laymen whom the impious Theophilos had banished after high-handedly confiscating their property and mutilating them' is achieved by imperial decree. Finally, the decree of the orthodox emperors and holy fathers declared the restoration of icons. All these official orders imply that Theodora was actively involved.[46]

It may never be possible to establish an undisputed account of the second restoration of images, but all the elements noted above converge in praising the God-inspired rulers (which can only mean Theodora, given that Michael is three years old in 843), and the devotion of those who had suffered for their faith, the persecuted monks.[47] Since Theodora is not confident of success at first and wishes to be sure that her own views will prevail, she instructs Theoktistos to hold a meeting in his house, to get a sense of the feelings of the returned iconophiles and to find a way of removing John the Grammarian. Once it has been agreed that Methodios will take his place at the head of the church, the next major meeting can be arranged. Rather than permit any further debate over the role of icons, the Seventh Ecumenical Council of 787 will be invoked as proof of the ancient traditions of image veneration. Then a new liturgy will anathematise iconoclasm and restore the holy icons.

THE TRIUMPH OF ORTHODOXY

On 10 March 843, the Saturday before the first Sunday in Lent, Patriarch Methodios holds a nocturnal vigil in Blachernai with all his clergy, and the following morning processes to Hagia Sophia via the church of the Holy Apostles. Early on Sunday, Michael III and Theodora and the court set out from the palace to meet them at the Great Church, all holding crosses, icons and candles. The new liturgy was performed for the first time on 11 March 843. In this way iconoclasm was overturned. And this service is still celebrated on the first Sunday in Lent in the Orthodox Church.[48]

It opens with a prologue which summarises the overthrow of impiety and the approval of correct dogma with the grace of God. After nearly thirty years, persecution is at an end and the divisions within the church are to be replaced by harmonious agreement. Then follow two lists. The first is a positive appreciation of the good iconophiles, who are to be celebrated eternally; the second a negative condemnation of the bad iconoclasts, who are to be anathematised. Each list has an impersonal theological section, e.g. all those who deny the Incarnation of the Word of God, the approval of making images, or the distinction between idols and images, and then a short section naming individuals, which emphasises the iconoclast patriarchs and bishops responsible for introduction and sustaining the heresy. The *Synodikon of Orthodoxy* does not mention Leo III by name, although his patriarch Anastasios is roundly condemned for the introduction of the doctrine; and Irene and Constantine VI are given less praise than Tarasios for its condemnation in 787. The anathemas issued by the council of 787 are repeated.[49]

The continuity of orthodoxy is confirmed in acclamations called *euphemia* (praises) and *polychronia* (wishes for many years) accorded to the rulers, beginning with Michael and Theodora, his mother, the patriarchs and on through the clergy. A final doxology, based on that of 787, includes a prayer not only for the Senate and state officials, but also for the most faithful army and all the citizens (*panti politeumati*) as well as those already listed.

By opening his new service with the liturgical recapitulation of orthodoxy and continuing with a condemnation of all known heresies, ending with iconoclasm, the patriarch establishes a method of repudiating the previous policy and returning to the traditional veneration of icons. Because the restoration of holy images is by no means a new policy, there is no innovation (a key word of disapproval in the Byzantine church). So this ecclesiastical ceremony can take the place of a church council and can undo the synod of 815. Instead of any further debate over the role of religious images, it reaffirms the decrees of the Seventh Ecumenical Council of 787, which constitute the traditions of the church. In later years, the patriarch invites the emperor to dine with him after the conclusion of the liturgy.

All those who refuse to attend this liturgical definition of the heretical nature of iconoclasm thereby confess their sin and stand condemned. Although it is impossible to calculate the numbers of iconoclast bishops who remained loyal to the doctrine, the figure of 20,000 and more dismissed in a great purge should not be taken literally. In the context of the Life of Methodios, this is surely a literary exaggeration for 'a multitude'. Similarly, the suggestion of 'two to three thousand' is no more than a guess.[50] The key aspect of this problem lies in the fact that Methodios found it hard to fill all the vacant positions and was obliged to reappoint previous iconoclasts who made a public confession of their former heresy. This was the issue which provoked another schism between the patriarch and the monks of Stoudios. In a repetition of their quarrel with Patriarch Nikephoros earlier in the ninth century, they refused to remain in communion with Methodios and thus sowed the seeds for yet another major division within the church.

Despite its significance for Byzantium, for the future of ecclesiastical art, and for the development of monasticism, the reversal of policy does not appear to have been treated as such a major event at the time. No foreign, non-Byzantine powers seem to attend or to witness the change. It is not announced to the rest of Christendom as a matter of urgency.[51] Contemporaries do not comment at any length on the issue except to claim individual responsibility. This is yet another reason to doubt the alleged opposition of a very large number of iconoclast bishops. By the end of Theophilos' reign, iconoclasm appears to have become a spent force. True, Methodios had difficulty finding enough iconophiles to take all the available posts, but that is not surprising after a generation of quite severe persecution. His successor Ignatios hardly seems affected by the dispute. Only his replacement, Photios, expresses immense anxiety about a possible resurgence of iconoclast heresy. This may be because he had personally experienced the toughest period of hostility, when his father Sergios and family had been exiled. Since he was also related to Theodora's family, he may have had additional reasons to continue to recall her orthodoxy in comparison with Theophilos' heresy.

THE RENEWAL OF FIGURATIVE ART

While it is reasonable to suppose that Theodora immediately restored icons to the churches of the Great Palace and iconophile monks did the same in their monasteries, there is little indication of public patronage of religious figural art for several years. Not until the end of the first patriarchate of Photios (858–67) was a major change made to the decoration of the Great Church. Of course, the cross was equally sacred to iconophiles and iconoclasts alike and in 843 there was therefore no immediate need to remove it. None the less the time delay in the redecoration of the cathedral church of Constantinople is quite striking.

In his sermon delivered at Easter 867 in the presence of Michael III and his co-emperor Basil, Photios describes the newly installed mosaic in the apse of Hagia Sophia which replaced a massive ornamental cross.[52] It depicts the Mother of God enthroned with the Christ Child on her knee and survives to this day. In Photios' description of this important monument of iconophile art, the Virgin's maternal care for her Son is described as if she were looking at him with particular tenderness. She is said to be so lifelike that the viewer expects her lips to move at any moment. Visitors to Hagia Sophia today may find this perplexing, as both figures gaze down into the church from their great height in the apse without displaying any discernible human emotion. But if Photios is in fact describing the inner emotions of Mother and Child, his description corresponds more closely to what one might expect from an *ekphrasis*, an analysis of a work of art according to the intentions of the artist, rather than the visible result. Like other literary genres, it imposes a rather formulaic style of description.[53] The condemnation of the wicked heretics, who had stripped the church of her beauty, and exposed her to their scorn and wounds, does not follow the same restrictions, and Photios is outspoken. The iconoclast cross was thus replaced by a Virgin and Child, the first figurative mosaics to feature in the church of Holy Wisdom.

Eventually a similar replacement occurred at Nicaea and Thessaloniki, where the arms of the previous crosses are even more visible. Whether iconophile figural decoration was renewed sooner in other public churches is unclear. There is no evidence that Theodora and Michael III celebrated the events of 843 through artistic commissions. But their historic role is probably reflected in an icon type, identified as a commemoration of the Triumph of Orthodoxy, which may date back to the ninth century. Today the most celebrated example in the British Museum is a fourteenth-century creation, one of very few that survives. It displays the heroes of iconophile practice venerating an icon of the Mother and Child of the 'Hodegetria' type.[54] They stand arrayed on two levels, imperial and patriarchal figures on the upper level and saints below.

Wearing their imperial robes of office, Theodora and her young son are prominent to the left of the icon to be venerated, with Methodios and other iconophile confessors, identified by their names written in red above them, to the right. Below, careful analysis has established the figures whose names are very worn: at the bottom left stands a female saint holding a small icon; she is the mythical Theodosia, an invented heroine of the first introduction of iconoclasm in 730. More familiar and better-documented saints fill out the lower level (see plate 9).[55] While this type of icon cannot be traced back to 843, the scene certainly originated in the restoration of orthodoxy under Theodora and Michael III. It is tempting to see in it the chance survival of a much larger number of similar icons devoted to the same event. But the five centuries or more that separate this example from the Triumph itself suggest that there may have been many intermediaries.

In manuscript illumination the use of figural decoration seems to have been renewed more quickly after 843. As we have noted, the importance of scriptoria like the one attached to the Stoudios monastery in Constantinople or the Bithynian communities close to the capital, had grown in the period between 787 and 815; a new minuscule handwriting had been developed, and manuscripts of a different nature continued to be produced during the second phase of iconoclasm. In these circles where scribes had been copying texts and illustrating them with floral and animal designs, mythical symbols and other colourful decorations, it was easier to return to the drawing of human figures. The impulse can be seen in illuminated Psalters, in which the text of the Psalms is illustrated by scenes of historical persons and the recent persecution of iconophiles. Patriarch Nikephoros is driven out of the church by iconoclasts, who whitewash the icons. Another element in the illustration of the Psalms develops a cycle of images associated with the story of David; it also makes use of personified Virtues, depicted as the Muses in classical dress, while Moses and the Prophets take their place as forerunners of Christ. The survival of several Psalters made after 843 suggests that texts with figural illustrations were some of the first products of iconophile art after 843.[56]

Among these, the *menologia*, which record the calendar of Orthodox saints celebrated each month, preserve an image of Empress Theodora as saint. The famous *Menologion of Basil* of *c.*1000 has such a portrait of her, depicted with a halo and holding a small round icon. This clearly commemorates her name-day in the church cycle of feasts. Whether or not it goes back to a much earlier original, this is one of the few remaining images of the empress, and shows her stiffly conforming to the way saints should stand. Nothing personal survives her metamorphosis from empress to saint. But the type of portrait may date back to an earlier manuscript painted after her death to confirm the day on which she is celebrated.[57] And this regular celebration suggests that other icons of her may have been painted. It is, in fact, her role in the restoration of icons that determines her saintly status. Theodora's cult is an official one introduced without any signs of sanctity, such as miraculous cures effected by her relics.

PUNISHMENT OF CONSTANTINE V AND ELEVATION OF IRENE

To mark the restoration of icons Theodora and Michael III effected one symbolic change. The remains of Constantine V, the arch-heretic and champion of iconoclast theology, were removed from his tomb at the Mausoleum of Justinian attached to the Holy Apostles. His bones were burned and the ashes scattered so that in the future no site would ever be associated with his burial. His green Thessalian sarcophagus was broken up and pieces were later used for the redecoration of the church of the Virgin at the Pharos (which was also a creation of Constantine V).[58] This left a space in the imperial burial chamber, which was extremely full by the mid-ninth century. A later list of all the tombs there records one of Empress Irene, although as we have seen she had been buried in her own foundation on Prinkipo shortly after her death in 803.[59]

This anomaly can only be explained by the fact that someone had moved Irene's sarcophagus of Proconnesian marble from Prinkipo to Constantinople. In the context of the obliteration of Constantine V, which signalled the end of iconoclasm, it seems very likely that Theodora undertook this task. In an act of *translatio*, she may have arranged for the mortal remains of Irene to be interred in the vacant place in the imperial mausoleum. When such movements involve holy relics, as for example in the case of St Euphemia in 797, the Patriarch of Constantinople and his clergy are always present to bless the new reliquary. In this case, the imperial sarcophagus did not contain the bones of a saint, although that was how some regarded Irene. But in a similar ceremony, it was solemnly removed from the monastic church of the Virgin on Prinkipo, brought over the Sea of Marmara to the city and installed in the imperial mausoleum.

In this way Irene finally joined her husband Leo IV the Khazar and took her rightful place among the rulers of the empire.[60] The empress who had arranged the first restoration of icons in 787, and thereby served as a model for Theodora, was ceremoniously returned to the most honoured burial place in Byzantium. A ritual humiliation of the iconoclast heretic was balanced by the elevation of an iconophile hero. While Theodora is not identified as the empress responsible for this exchange, it fits so perfectly with the achievement of 843 that it seems unnecessary to look any further. I think we may conclude that in this highly charged act of translation Theodora honoured both her predecessor and the cause of the holy images which she had recently restored.

In the aftermath of 843 other iconophile champions who had been exiled and buried without due honours were also returned to more suitable tombs. The relics of Patriarch Nikephoros, now declared a saint, were solemnly translated from the place where he died in exile and returned to the church of Hagia Sophia.[61] Theodore of the Stoudios and his brother Joseph were both returned to their community. Perhaps other champions of icon veneration were so honoured.[62] Conversely, iconoclasts may have been removed. The patriarchs who were held responsible for the heresy are named in the *Synodikon of Orthodoxy*: Anastasios, Constantine and Niketas in the eighth century (sparing Paul, who abdicated rather than sustain iconoclasm), and Theodotos, Antonios and John in the ninth.[63] Many patriarchs were not buried in the cathedral church but in their own foundations; for instance, Tarasios' tomb was at his own monastery on the Bosphoros; Ignatios later found peace in his foundation at Satyros. So it is possible that it was not necessary to punish the iconoclast leaders by rejecting their relics from prominent tombs in the capital. But in the process of bringing back to Constantinople those who had suffered for the cause of icons, a visual as well as a ceremonial reckoning was undertaken. Theodora played a part in it, even if Methodios and later Ignatios presided over these public rites.

THEODORA'S RULE DURING THE MINORITY OF MICHAEL III (842–56)

During the fourteen years when she is ruling the empire, while Michael is too young to assume any imperial responsibilities, are there any policy decisions which can be attributed to Theodora rather than to her advisers? At this point most sources fall back on stereotypical generalities:

her *Vita* merely records that she was 'managing the affairs of her subjects in this meet and fitting manner'.

In terms of diplomatic contacts with the western empire, we have noted that Theodora does not seem to have considered it necessary to inform the religious or civil authorities about the 843 restoration of icons. She waits until 847 when the election of Ignatios as patriarch, in succession to Methodios, is announced to Pope Eugenius in Rome.[64] Although Ignatios had been consecrated in the normal fashion, uncanonical practice was later detected. And Pope Nicholas I would use it as a means of interfering in Byzantine affairs in the 860s. Nor did the empress pursue the alliance proposed in 841/2 between Theophilos and Louis the Pious for the marriage of one of her daughters. The embassy arrived too late to be effective, for Louis died in 841. She may have learned from the ambassadors who returned that this caused profound divisions among his three sons, who patched up their disagreements at Verdun in 843 but only temporarily. The redivision of the empire and the existence of several claimants to the imperial title greatly reduced the effectiveness of Charlemagne's legacy. In comparison with the wrangling that dominates the West until Charles the Bald wins stronger control in 869, the Byzantine system of government looks infinitely more secure, despite the existence of a female regent for a minor son.[65]

Because the Regency was finely balanced between family and unrelated figures, it is interesting to observe how Theodora handles her male colleagues. From the beginning she appears to rely more on Theoktistos than on her brothers Petronas and Bardas. Perhaps she senses the ambitions which Bardas nurtured for she did not object when Theoktistos found an excuse to exile him in 844. As a result he harboured a grudge against the court eunuch which developed into a serious resentment even after his return from exile. Theodora ignores this and entrusts the main task of government to her favourite, Theoktistos. Up till 856 he is still carrying official papers through the palace of Lausiakos, where the main administrative offices are located, to Theodora for her approval. While she relies on his experience, she does not hand over all the decisions to him or neglect the business of government. Her Regency may take on its own character, independent of the courtiers who put it into effect.[66]

In this respect her administration represents continuity with that of her husband, despite the major shift to iconophile religious practice. Theoktistos, who had held high office for many years during the iconoclast persecution, continued to do so after the restoration of icons. Other supporters of iconoclasm had to go, notably the bishops and monks who had occupied major posts. None the less, the civilian bureaucracy continues in place; many of the military simply adapt to the change. Theodora appoints ministers and handles matters of state, including diplomatic negotiations with foreign powers, sending embassies to Bulgaria, Samarra and Rome in 844, 845 and 847 respectively. When Methodios dies in 847, she appoints Ignatios to head the church, one of the sons of Michael I, who had been tonsured and castrated under Leo V. Unlike the Sicilian, the new patriarch is a completely other-worldly figure who has been living in quiet ascetic retirement since 813. The cultural developments associated with the second period of iconoclasm, the expansion of education and the copying and editing of classical manuscripts, have not touched him; indeed he has a profound distaste for such 'external wisdom'. While his qualifications may seem impeccable, the empress has not chosen a strong leader who will impose unity on the church.

The weakness of Theodora's administration lies in her determination to exclude her brothers, who have been nominated to the Council and anticipate a role in the Regency. Instead, they are neglected, if not physically removed from government circles by exile. This development is dangerous, since Petronas in particular has already proved his military capacity and will confirm his brilliance in the field later on. In contrast, the chief eunuch's efforts as a military leader lead more often to failure. To sideline her brothers from the Regency may be a natural reaction on Theodora's part, but it proves a serious miscalculation.[67] She does not appear to foresee the danger of allowing her administration to become so unbalanced.

FOREIGN POLICY OF THE REGENCY

In relation to the Caliphate, Theodora upholds the military truce achieved in 841, which is sustained by regular exchanges of prisoners of war.[68] The many taken prisoner at Amorion in 838 remain in captivity for years, so there are regular embassies to try and secure their release. In the meantime, in March 843, Theoktistos leads a campaign against the Arabs occupying Crete and fails, allegedly because rumours are spread about that Theodora is going to appoint a rival to rule with her and her son, and he rushes back to the capital empty-handed.[69] Even so, Theoktistos is entrusted with several other campaigns, which are all similarly unsuccessful.[70] Crete will remain under Muslim control for another century, a constant thorn in the flesh of Byzantium despite numerous efforts at reconquest.

In the West during the 840s the Arabs from Africa extended their hold on Sicily from Panormos, which had failed in 831, to Messina, provoking a Byzantine response. In 845–6 Theodora sent a force which was defeated with great loss, and the Greek *strategos* failed to relieve Leontini when it was besieged. This process of slow but inexorable conquest of the island which had been so important to Byzantine–Western relations, continued through the 860s.[71] Simultaneously, the Arabs advanced up the east and west coasts of Italy, capturing Bari in 841 and plundering Ostia in 846. On this occasion they sacked the churches of Saints Peter and Paul outside the walls of Rome. This provoked King Louis 'the German' to campaign in southern Italy (847–9). Eventually he made an alliance with Byzantium and secured a victory over the Arabs, but not under Theodora's Regency, which was marked by a reduction in the Byzantine presence both in the island of Sicily and in southern Italy.

If the 'feast of orthodoxy', as the 843 restoration of icons was rapidly dubbed, inspired harsher policies against heretics within the empire, it was certainly going to spill over into extended warfare with the Arabs sooner or later. While the loss of Crete was a serious setback to Byzantine control of the East Mediterranean, Arabic sources record several naval attacks by imperial forces during the 850s. The most striking was a daring attack on Damietta in May 853, under a naval commander identified only as Ibn Qatuna. He may be the mysterious Sergios Niketiates. The raid was highly successful: Damietta was pillaged and burned, a large depot of arms, military equipment and supplies destined for Crete and Iraq was captured, six hundred Muslim or Coptic prisoners were taken. After two days the Byzantine navy sailed off to Ustum, where they were able to destroy more ballistic machines before returning to Constantinople unharmed.[72] There were probably victory celebrations as a result of such an evident triumph but no account of them survives in the Greek sources.

So there is little evidence that Theodora and Michael had many victories to review while he was growing up, apart from the naval one at Damietta. In contrast, once the brothers Petronas and Bardas were allowed to lead the troops, they won campaigns and encouraged Michael III to fight in person. As *strategos* of the Thrakesion, in the summer of 856 Petronas led a successful attack against the Paulicians in the area of

Melitene. And seven years later, in 863, he witnessed the death of the Emir of Melitene Omar on the battlefield at Poson, a major victory celebrated in a great triumph in the capital. It is quite noticeable that the young emperor followed his uncles' example with alacrity once his mother was removed from power.

MISSIONARY ACTIVITY

In contrast, there is one area of military activity initiated under Theodora's Regency which appears to have been quite successful: the subjugation of the Slavs of Peloponnesos under *strategos* Theoktistos Bryennios in *c.*847–50.[73] He had previously been governor of Dalmatia and had probably served as Theodora's ambassador to Bulgaria. She now gave him large detachments from the *themata* of Thrace and Macedonia to assist in the campaign, which reduced Slav opposition and imposed terms on the independent Ezeritai and Melingoi. This process of conquest, conversion and assimilation may have inspired the long engagement of Byzantium and Bulgaria which came to fruition after Theodora. But its roots may be traced back to an embassy of 844 led by the same Theoktistos, which transmitted letters to Khan Boris. A monk named Theodore Koupharas may also have participated, or he may have been captured in a raiding party. According to the later tenth-century sources he was detained by Boris and tried vigorously to persuade his new master of the superiority of the Christian revelation. In another, even more legendary story, Boris's sister is alleged to have been taken captive and brought to the Great Palace where Theodora converted her to orthodoxy. Eventually the two captives were exchanged; Boris was reunited with his sister who deepened his curiosity about the Christian faith, while the missionary monk Theodore Koupharas returned to Constantinople.[74]

The possibility of spreading knowledge of Christianity among the Slavs was to reach a high point later, under Patriarch Photios, when two brothers with brilliant linguistic skills were commissioned to devise a Slavonic alphabet so that spoken Bulgarian could be written down. Once Saints Cyril and Methodios had developed the new medium, they began the task of translating the Scriptures, theological and liturgical material, into Old Church Slavonic in order to assist the process of conversion and Christian education. The critical moment probably occurs in 866 and Photios, appointed to head the church in 858, will take the credit.[75]

But this missionary effort began with Theodora and her contacts with the Bulgarian leader, Boris, in the 840s.

A further area of missionary activity is found in the remote eastern parts of the empire although it does not involve a pagan people but a heretical sect, identified as followers of Paul of Samosata. And rather than an attempt to convince them of the superiority of the Christian faith, this took the form of a campaign of persecution, to force them back into the fold from the errors of their dualist heresy. Theophilos had moved against the Paulicians before 842, but his efforts were now relaunched with orthodox zeal. In 843/4 a certain Karbeas, who had held military commands in Byzantium, went over to the Arabs to avoid Theodora's efforts to convert him and his five thousand followers. This provoked a series of retaliations which built up into a massive campaign. For many years it absorbed large numbers of troops in battles against fanatical Paulicians, who were prepared to die rather than to submit to orthodoxy. The rivalry was only finally resolved by Basil I's punitive conquest in the 870s.[76]

Against this military record, however, we must set the general impression that Theodora's administration was prudent and successful. In a probably legendary account of her careful government, she summoned the Senate in 856 and showed them the financial resources accumulated during her Regency. Listing the quantities of gold and silver amassed in the Treasury, she informed them that part had been inherited from her husband, Theophilos, while part she had added during her rule (*emen archen*).[77] It would be reasonable to link this claim to Theodora's family interest in commercial activity. But while Theophilos may have condemned her investments in trade as totally unsuitable for one of imperial status, the empress may possibly have extended an acquired interest in making money from trade to the care of government finances.

One possible motive for the circulation of such a story lies in the fact that her son Michael is presented by these late and hostile sources as a wastrel, who squandered the finances of the state on quite trivial and unsuitable matters, such as baptismal presents for the children of his friends among the charioteers. In this case, the administration of the mother is to be contrasted with that of her son, to his disadvantage. But behind such stories there may lie a grain of truth: no one accused Theodora of mishandling the empire's resources; on the contrary, her Regency is marked by her own skill in administration.[78] And her brother Bardas was a beneficiary of this care, for it helped to finance his patronage of higher education and major missionary initiatives. During the decade of his effective rule (see below), Bardas invested in teachers, built up libraries, constructed important buildings and ran the imperial administration efficiently with no reference to financial worries. While he would never have admitted as much, he may have owed part of this achievement to his sister Theodora.

MATERNAL RESPONSIBILITIES DURING THE MINORITY OF MICHAEL III

The *Life of Symeon*, one of the brothers from Mitylene, preserves an account of the saint visiting the court to debate with John the Grammarian. In a delightful scene Theodora presides at this theological event, accompanied by all her children. The daughters stand behind her throne while three-year-old Michael plays at her feet. The text records that the baby could none the less tell the saint from the patriarch; he pushed John away, saying 'bad grandfather' in lisping baby talk, and kept calling Symeon 'good' and grasped his knees. He appeared 'to embrace and talk to and take pleasure in a strange and unfamiliar man who presented a disagreeable appearance to children because of his asceticism and his garb'.[79] Such discrimination as a child was not, however, a guarantee of Michael's future good judgement. But the pious invention reveals that contemporaries thought it quite normal for the empress to hold court in the company of her entire family. Even the young prince is not sent away with his nurse. Indeed, the participation of all members of the imperial family at public events is confirmed by many ceremonies, which emphasise the presence of even babes in arms.

Since Michael is the youngest of her five surviving children and the only boy, he will have male tutors and be taught in a manner appropriate for a future emperor. Theodora will play an important role in his education as she presides over the court, setting an example of imperial behaviour, and eunuch officials will train him in the formal ceremonies. A *paidagogos* (tutor) is mentioned, but he does not appear to have formed a close and lasting relationship with Michael. If the ease with which Basil the Macedonian later insinuates himself into the young man's affections suggests isolation, Michael may lack close friends as he is growing up.[80] However, there is a charming account of the imperial family participating in the vintage, pressing of grapes, at an imperial estate up the Bosphoros. They all set off in the imperial barge with a picnic to watch the pickers and pounders making the wine. This looks suspiciously like the ancient festival at which Bacchus's name is still evoked (cf. the Council *in Trullo*), a thoroughly pagan pleasure that dies hard despite repeated ecclesiastical censure.

In contrast to Michael, no mention is made of the education of his sisters, although they were all crowned. They must have learned what was necessary for imperial princesses. Theophilos was evidently proud of his daughters and had built them an extravagantly decorated palace, the Karianos, which was situated in the Blachernai district of the city. The four surviving sisters lived a life of ease in their special, private residence, if rather separate from the court, presumably with their own servants and imperial staff. But Michael's birth removed their chances of succession. Thekla, the eldest, had been associated in imperial power almost from birth and may have grown up with ambitions. Yet despite negotiations with potential allies, neither she nor any of her younger sisters were married.[81] While Theodora was busy with affairs of state, she may have neglected them. She certainly failed to find suitable husbands for her daughters.

But this may also be a considered policy, due to the fact that she realises the danger of Michael acquiring older brothers-in-law. If Thekla, Anna, Anastasia and Pulcheria are married to well-qualified husbands, his rights of inheritance may be threatened. The empress may consider it safer not to allow them to marry because any adult and competent relatives of the young prince might become potential rivals. This perhaps helps to explain their sisters' unmarried status. The parallel with Empress Pulcheria in the early fifth century is striking: she even forced her sisters to adopt celibacy so that their brother's inheritance would not be challenged. Whether anyone in the ninth century thought of such a precedent is unknown. But the resumption of this ancient name in a ruling family is an odd coincidence.[82] It is usually explained by Theophilos and Theodora's devotion to the shrine at Blachernai, which was founded by the fifth-century Pulcheria. It seems that Pulcheria herself, the fourth daughter of the imperial couple, may well have learned the history of her namesake. Would she have thought it appropriate to take a similar vow of celibacy, to refuse to marry for the sake of her younger brother? This seems inherently improbable. But if her mother Theodora imposed such a policy, she would have had no option but to concur.

THE MARRIAGE OF MICHAEL III

Once he is old enough, Theodora does what we now know to be the responsibility of all good mothers: she arranges Michael's marriage. At the age of sixteen he is almost ready to assume full authority and has taken a mistress, Eudokia Ingerine, the daughter of Inger, a Viking in imperial service. According to certain sources, Theodora and Theoktistos disapproved of her, and she disliked them heartily, so the arranged marriage was partly motivated by maternal desires to see her son settled with an appropriate wife.

As can be expected, the historical chronicles record only the barest facts: in 855 the Empress married her son to a different Eudokia, the child of a court official identified by his regional origins as Dekapolites (of the Dekapolis). Eudokia Dekapolitissa was duly crowned and married following the established rites, which we have noted in relation to all similar unions. In contrast, two later sources provide a quite different version, which include the literary element of a bride-show. The most developed account is in another saint's Life, a biography of a certain Irene, known as Irene of Chrysobalanton because she became abbess of a nunnery by that name. This hagiographic text was written towards the end of the tenth century and uses the *Life of Theodora* as a model.[83] As may be anticipated, it provides details of the mechanism for organising a bride-show for Michael: letters were sent out to all parts of the empire under Byzantine control to find the right girl (qualifications are spelled out). And all those with suitable daughters got ready to send them to Constantinople to participate.[84]

At this point in the *Life of Irene*, it is clear that there is an ulterior motive for the account of the 'bride-show': it provides an excuse for Irene to move from Cappadocia, where she was born, to Constantinople, where she will become a nun. Her parents use the beauty contest as a pretext to send her off to the capital with her sister and an escort. But unlike Kassia she is not going to be passed over in the contest, because she arrives too late to take part. This is due to her insistence on interrupting her journey in order to pay a visit to St Ioannikios (para. 6). Now, not only has the saint been dead a long time, but this detour has suspicious echoes of Theodora's consultation with the holy man Isaiah. In both cases, a holy man will predict the young girls' future, but in Irene's case it does not involve marriage to the emperor. Once she reaches the capital and finds out that the bride-show has already taken place,

Irene is filled with joy. The author concludes: she was destined for a better bridegroom, viz. Christ (paras. 8–9). The only incongruous element in this pious fiction is that her sister, elsewhere named as Theodosia, later married none other than Empress Theodora's brother Bardas (para. 6). So there may be a kernel of reliable historical evidence hidden deep within the Life.

The second account of Michael's marriage is equally untrustworthy, this time because it occurs in the *Funeral Oration* composed by Leo VI for his father Basil, who plays an utterly central role in the reign of Michael III.[85] It was delivered at Basil I's funeral in 888 and has a very particular aim. Its description of the bride-show, Theodora's collection of beautiful young girls from whom Michael is to choose his bride, also concentrates on another contestant who is not going to win the prize. Leo's purpose is to record how the emperor did not choose Eudokia Ingerine because she, too, was fated to marry a better man. Here he alludes to the fact that this Eudokia was later married to Basil. So he is documenting the marriage of his own parents, for Eudokia Ingerine was his mother and Basil I his father.

At least, this is what Leo VI declares most emphatically in his account of the bride-show held over thirty years earlier. But, again, it is clear from other sources that this is not the whole story. Michael's attachment to his mistress was to prove the most lasting commitment of his life. Eudokia Ingerine was not only a very beautiful woman, she was the central woman in his life, it seems. So when he 'chooses' the other Eudokia, she becomes empress but not wife. For Michael has no intention of giving up his mistress.

BASIL THE MACEDONIAN

The key to understanding the complex result of the bride-show lies in the role played by Basil, known as the Macedonian, who becomes a friend of Michael III at about the same time. Confusions and contradictions abound in the stories surrounding this figure. Removing the later accretions designed to show that he was related to the ruling dynasty of Armenia, that he was always destined for an imperial role, that he saved Byzantium from an indulgent and weak ruler, his origins seem to have been undistinguished. His parents had been transplanted from Armenia to the area of Macedonia, which was created a *thema* under Empress Irene and used by Nikephoros I to protect the western frontier with the Bulgars. Sensing the lack of future in the provinces, Basil, like many ambitious young men before and after, sought his fortune in the capital. His skills as a horse-breaker and his strength in wrestling and other physical sports brought him to the attention of people of senatorial rank. And from these humble beginnings he was introduced to the court, specifically to tame an extraordinarily fine but wild horse. His success in this task ensured an appointment in the imperial stables, and from this point on he commanded the attention of Michael III.

How he managed to win and sustain Michael's affections is unknown. Theories have been constructed of their alleged homoerotic life together.[86] But what is clear is that at the point where the young emperor is embarking on his adult life and has been obliged by his mother to choose a wife, Michael turns to his friend Basil. He now proposes that Basil will help him to continue enjoying the company of his mistress by divorcing his own wife, Maria, and then marrying Eudokia Ingerine. This arrangement will permit the emperor's marriage to Eudokia Dekapolitissa to exist in name only. Similarly Basil's marriage to the other Eudokia may be one of convenience, for Michael intends to sustain his relationship with her. Behind these empty unions lie complex agreements designed to allow Michael and Eudokia Ingerine to continue the relationship of which Theodora disapproves. But appearances will be maintained; the decision taken at the bride-show will be carried out, Prince Michael will marry a woman of great beauty selected by his mother, and he will also enjoy the company of his mistress, now conveniently wedded to his best friend.

Of course, Leo does not mention any of this in his eulogy of Basil. But it is clear that contemporaries observed some rather confusing developments and were not clear what was going on.[87] The first step in the process is for Basil to divorce his wife, Maria, who is sent back to her own people in Macedonia laden with appropriate gifts in compensation. Presumably some reasonable grounds are adduced in order for him to free himself of his first wife, who may have accompanied him to Constantinople, although she has never been mentioned before this time. Basil then marries the woman whom everyone in the court knows to be Michael's mistress, the daughter of Inger, who is identified as the imperial concubine. He thus accepts an essentially humiliating role as the nominal husband of Eudokia Ingerine, so that the emperor can have both a wife and a mistress at his constant disposal. The delicacy of the situation is recognised when Michael insists on providing his friend Basil with a mistress, and 'gives' him his eldest sister Thekla, the *porphyrogennetos*.

By agreeing to these terms, Basil could see that Michael would be grateful to him as long as he loved Eudokia. And this seems to have been the case. When Eudokia gave birth to a son, Constantine, in about 859, Basil had to acknowledge the child as his own, although its paternity was in some doubt. Several years later, in 866, she had a second son, Leo, and on this occasion some sources record what must have been common knowledge: 'Leo the emperor was born to Michael and Eudokia Ingerine'.[88] Of course, Michael could never claim that Constantine and Leo were his sons, as that would have exposed the arrangement. So they were acclaimed as Basil's, except by those who doubted that this could be the case. How many courtiers were party to the understanding between the two men is not known. But it seems hardly possible that some did not observe the emperor's regular assignations with Eudokia, the wife of Basil.

In this famous *ménage à trois* of two male friends and the beautiful Eudokia Ingerine, Michael is the only one who benefits, and he does so illicitly. His wife, Eudokia Dekapolitissa, is empress but has no children because Michael is too busy with the other Eudokia. His friend Basil has to pretend that the two boys born to his wife Eudokia Ingerine, Constantine and Leo, are his own. Of course, they are Michael's illegitimate offspring. Meanwhile, the imperial couple remain childless and the dynasty's continuity is seriously endangered. After Michael's death, Eudokia has two more male children, Stephen and Alexander, who are more insistently described as Basil's own sons. In the *Funeral Oration* he later composed for his father, Leo's emphasis on his own paternity wishes to give the same impression. But doubts remained then as now. We can only be sure that Michael's domestic arrangements, while conforming outwardly to the marriage Theodora arranged for him, effectively undo the selection. Perhaps the lesson of Constantine VI's bride-show and unhappy first marriage still circulated around the court.

So, if by the display of beauties in 855 Theodora believed she could win her son away from what she considers an improper alliance, she is quite unsuccessful. The 'choice' of Eudokia Dekapolitissa is designed to provide Michael with a suitable and legitimate wife. But with the connivance of his friend Basil, her son subverts this aim and maintains only the form of a marriage, preferring to sleep with his mistress. As a consequence he produces no legitimate children; indeed, he has no offspring at all if Eudokia Ingerine's children are accepted as Basil's. A further result is that Basil assumes a critical position as Michael's best friend and Theodora has to witness his growing influence over her son, which she deplores. For all her mastery of the empire, she could not handle her son and his alliances. Both she and he would have been far better off if he had been allowed to marry his Viking love, whom Theodora viewed as a threat.

THEODORA'S FALL FROM POWER (856) AND
THE MURDER OF THEOKTISTOS

Although the chronicles, chiefly composed about a century after the events of the reign, disagree on details, most confirm that it was Michael's uncle, Bardas, who plotted to get rid of Theoktistos. As we have seen, he resented Theoktistos' hold on power in the Regency and felt sidelined by the experienced, older administrator. So some time in 855, probably after the imperial marriage which marked Michael's coming of age, he warned his nephew that Theodora was planning to elevate someone else to the throne, either through her own remarriage, or by marrying one of his sisters to a more suitable candidate. If that happened, Michael would be blinded and would never become emperor. Here Bardas is preying on the knowledge of what Irene had done to Constantine VI. He also taunts the young prince with the fact that he has no authority although he has gained his majority and could rule in his own name. Michael, therefore, is persuaded to collaborate in a plot to replace Theoktistos as the head of the administration.[89] Although the original intention was to force Theoktistos into exile, the plotters panicked and instead the eunuch was killed as he sought protection under a couch in the palace.[90]

Theodora was greatly distressed by the murder. In one of the most elaborate later chronicles she upbraids her son for murdering the figure who 'acted as a second father to him'.[91] While this is precisely the type of observation which should alert us to the real aims of the Continuators, it is both an interesting comment on Theoktistos' alleged attitude towards the young prince, and Theodora's view of her favourite. Her grief and anger is related to the fact that her position at court is greatly weakened by his death. Indeed, it escalates the process whereby Michael will claim his inheritance as an adult and then entrust it to his uncle, her own brother Bardas. So her worries are well founded. After taking his revenge on the official who had sent him into exile in 844 and prevented his efforts to influence the Regency, Bardas now gets Michael and the Senate to announce that the emperor has come of age and will govern on his own.[92] But what they mean is that his uncle Bardas has managed to convince Michael to leave the daily management of government to him. He will replace both Theoktistos and Empress Theodora.

While she is outmanoeuvred by the murder, Theodora clings to the remnant of power she has exercised as Regent. For two years she remains in possession of her quarters within the Great Palace. Here is an instance of that familiar problem of succession – the old empress-mother preventing the young one from taking up her rightful abode in the imperial *gynaikonitis*. In her obstinacy she effectively destroys any sentimental attachment between son and mother. Unlike Euphrosyne who decided to make a quick departure in 830, Theodora refuses to leave the palace. Worse still, when the emperor requests that Patriarch Ignatios should tonsure her, he refuses. In this he makes the perfectly correct case, according to the canons of the church, that no woman can be forced to take the veil; the adoption of monastic life must be a voluntary act. Ignatios undoubtedly recalls the schism which broke out after the forced tonsure of Maria of Amnia and her husband's second marriage. So he refuses to make Theodora and her daughters nuns against their will.[93] Both the church and the Great Palace combine to cause a stand-off. And this means that the deposition of Ignatios from the patriarchate in November 858 is likely to be linked to Theodora's expulsion from the palace, which probably occurred the previous summer, in August or September 858.

At first Michael makes a series of efforts to pacify his mother. He then tries to remove her; he expels three of his sisters to a monastery identified as Karianos, and the youngest Pulcheria, who is described as Theodora's favourite, is sent to the family monastery of Gastria.[94] Meanwhile he promotes Bardas to commander of the palace guards (*domestikos* of the *scholai*), thus setting him on a career which would lead to the very summit of the Byzantine bureaucracy. Eventually he is successful in forcing Theodora to leave the palace in which she had held sway for twenty-six years, and to join her daughter in the monastery of Gastria. According to the *Life of Theodora*, the murder of Theoktistos was the cause of her troubles. It records nothing specific about the eunuch's death, merely stating: 'Bardas hated him and killed him unjustly', but stresses Theodora's sadness at the murder of her favourite.[95] As a result, the empress was forced to leave the palace; her departure was involuntary. This is contrasted with Euphrosyne's decision, when she left freely and of her own will.[96]

THEODORA'S RETIREMENT FROM THE COURT (858)

However indignant she felt in this imposed exile from the court, Theodora could do nothing while Bardas was in charge. Some historians claim that she plotted to have him murdered, such was the strength of her feelings. The *Vita* suggests that certain senators wanted to restore to her the powers of Regent but she refused.[97] That she bore a grudge against her brother Bardas is certain, for he had usurped her place at the head of the government. The Regency was effectively set aside as Michael undertook his first military campaigns in the company of his other uncle Petronas, and to her chagrin Theodora witnessed their success. This period of her life is poorly documented for obvious reasons. Of her retirement, the *Vita* reports: 'So after that the holy and religious empress Theodora took pity on a number of men who came to her for protection and helped them out of her natural goodness and virtuous character and compassionate nature, a woman resplendent with virtue in many forms.'[98]

She may have benefited indirectly from the great victory celebrated in 863, when Petronas surrounded the forces of the Emir of Melitene and killed their leader. It appears that the imperial family's confined lives seem to be eased at this time and they return to the secular world. Theodora may have recovered her title of Augusta, if she is indeed included in the triumphal *acta* which document the existence of a plurality of empresses.[99] This is clear also from a letter Pope Nicholas I wrote to Theodora in November 866. In this case the pope is responding to Patriarch Ignatios' claim that he was ejected from office specifically because he refused to tonsure the empress and her daughters against their will.[100] This involvement of the Bishop of Rome in the internal history of the church of Constantinople was to lead to immense difficulties and quarrels, so it is interesting to observe the great weight laid by the legal patriarch on his relations with Theodora.

Did she then resume at least a part of her official role as empress-mother? This seems unlikely. In fact the main evidence for the rehabilitation of the imperial ladies is that Thekla, the eldest sister, is allegedly brought out of the monastery of Karianos in order to be given to Basil as his mistress.[101] She was dismissed by Basil in 867 and found another lover in John Neatokometes. But when Basil discovered this he had them both beaten and forced John to become a monk. Eventually Thekla founded a chapel dedicated to the first martyr Thekla in her house at Blachernai. It was said to be extremely beautiful and elegantly decorated. But she died bedridden. From this I think we may conclude that Thekla suffered very much from being a crowned *augouste* with no powers, a *porphyrogennetos* ambitious for imperial rule, who was deprived of all political influence.[102]

By this time Bardas has strengthened his grip on power and for the decade following Theodora's fall from power (856) he is the supreme ruler of Byzantium.[103] Michael obediently promotes his uncle to high office, by 862 to the position of caesar, implying that he would take over as emperor should anything untoward happen to Michael. Genesios records that Theodora expressed her anger at her brother by sending him a tunic/garment which was too short for him; it also had a golden partridge on it, which was interpreted as a sign of deceit.[104] This must have occurred quite close to 866 because it was understood as a prophetic image and poorly received.

Meanwhile, Basil's career also advanced in parallel with Bardas'. Michael used the dismissal of certain officials to promote his friend to higher positions, like that of *strator* (imperial groom), and later to one normally reserved to eunuchs (*parakoimomenos*). When Basil took on this post of chamberlain responsible for protecting the emperor's bed-chamber, he gained access to the very small circle of the ruler's intimate servants. The marital arrangements he had to endure brought him ever higher office and closer proximity to the emperor. By maintaining a deep friendship and assisting Michael in all his desires, the Macedonian managed to acquire a very strong position among those who had access to the emperor.

From this base he could suggest to his friend that Bardas' influence in government matters was unhealthy, that his uncle was plotting against him, and that he (Basil) could take care of these threats. Bardas had assumed control over every aspect of the administration, proving himself a brilliant organiser and a far-sighted patron of culture and learning. Higher education had been completely transformed by the appointment of men like Leo the Mathematician, who created new schools for the training of a younger generation in the classical seven liberal arts. Not only the business of government but new areas of missionary activity blossomed with Bardas' encouragement. At his insistence, Igantios had been deposed and a relative of the imperial family, Photios, appointed to the patriarchate. While this procedure had not failed to provoke opposition, notably from Pope Nicholas I in Rome, to whom Ignatios appealed, Photios had already made a great impact in his new role. By 866, his encouragement of Saints Cyril and Methodios was bearing fruit in the conversion of the Bulgars and the adoption of Christianity in its orthodox form in Moravia and other parts of the Slavonic world.

THE MURDER OF BARDAS (866)

Perhaps it was this very obvious success that irritated Basil. His antagonism to Michael's uncle deepened to the point at which he alerted his friend to an alleged plot: Bardas had imperial ambitions and would soon be taking over and getting rid of Michael, the real emperor. Whatever their substance, the rumours convinced not only Michael but also others who had probably suffered at the hands of the autocratic head of state. A group of conspirators formed and began to plot the overthrow of the caesar, as Bardas was called. The circumstances were provided by another planned invasion of Crete, in which Bardas and Michael both participated.

The plan takes shape around the enforced absence of the emperor and his uncle as the military expedition proceeds to Kepoi, a place known as the Gardens on the coast of the Thrakesion *thema*, where they would embark for Crete. At this point Symbatios, who is Bardas' son-in-law, gives the sign for the murderous attack.[105] It takes place on 21 April 866. Once Bardas is dead, and his body hacked to pieces, his genitals are stuck on a spear to make him suffer even in death, and paraded around the military encampment in the most humiliating fashion.[106] His murder and the treatment of his body cause divisions among the troops. Bardas had been appreciated in certain quarters. After his death, the campaign against Crete is immediately cancelled and Michael and Basil return to Constantinople. It is almost as if the campaign had been devised to facilitate the murder.

Although no evidence exists, someone must have assumed responsibility for the collection and burial of Bardas' dismembered body. It seems possible that Theodora now arranges for his remains to be interred at the monastery of Gastria, where his tomb is later recorded. If this is so, the idea of a family shrine must carry greater weight than Theodora's hatred of her own brother. Perhaps the achievements of his ten-year rule impressed her. After his death she did not want his memory to be forgotten and included him among her relatives in the shrine, which already contained the body of their mother Theoktiste. In this way she proceeded with the systematic creation of a site in which the family would be commemorated, and where she would eventually be laid to rest.

From 866 on, however, once Bardas is out of the way, Basil can see the way forward and it leads to his own assumption of power. He therefore persuades Michael III to associate him in imperial authority as co-emperor, playing on the claim that he, Basil, had saved Michael from death in Bardas' attack. Michael concedes and crowns him with the crown blessed by the Patriarch Photios and laid on the high altar of Hagia Sophia. The detailed account preserved in the chronicle attributed to Leo *grammatikos* seems entirely credible: on the Saturday of Whitsun 866, two thrones were put out, though there was only one emperor; and by the close of the following Sunday, there were two emperors, who sat on their thrones side by side.[107]

In this capacity Photios the patriarch addressed both of the Christ-loving emperors in two of his sermons: one on the unveiling of the mosaic image of the Virgin and Child in Hagia Sophia on 29 March 867, the other recapitulating the council held later that summer. 'Beloved pair of pious emperors, shining forth from the purple, connected with the dearest names of father and son ... whose preoccupation is Orthodoxy rather than pride in the imperial diadem ...'. And later, 'The Lord has looked upon His people and His inheritance with merciful eyes, in setting up and raising the truly imperial majesty of the state – His beloved son Basil. For it is clear that those things which the father has succeeded in achieving, and which words leap with joy to narrate, he is inheriting as his own portion and pride ...'.[108] Sitting on an imperial throne in the gallery, listening to Photios' words about the defeat of iconoclasts (Theophilos, Michael's father, is not named but ever so nearly) and all other heretics, Basil can see that all this power can be his if only he arranges things correctly.

Theodora's reaction to this development is not hard to imagine. Indeed, some later historians attribute to her, predictions that this Basil would prove to be the end of her family's dynasty.[109] Her hostility to the ambitious and deceptive horse-trainer must have been quite extreme. She saw how easily he persuaded Michael to follow his advice. But it is hard to know if Theodora herself was aware of the pact they had made back in 855 when Basil agreed to allow himself to be used in their marital arrangements. She may not have imagined the ties that bound her son and his great friend. She must have regretted that Eudokia Dekapolitissa failed to produce any children, since this seriously weakened the dynasty.

After her apparent release from Gastria in about 863, there is no information as to how Theodora spent her days. As an ex-empress and mother of the reigning emperor she had certain rights and would have attended certain ceremonies in the palace. There is no evidence that Michael awarded his own mother the title of *zoste patrikia*, given by Theophilos to his mother-in-law Theoktiste. But she was permitted a life of ease appropriate to a lady of her high station and spent her time in suitably Christian pursuits. In September 867 it appears that she was residing in a palace known as the house of Anthimios, founded by her son-in-law Alexios. He had been betrothed briefly to Maria, the imperial princess who died *c*.839, and had retired to his own monastery in the suburban quarter of Anthemios. Whatever her feelings about Michael's promotion of his friend Basil to the position of co-emperor, Theodora was now on better terms with her son. Indeed, she invited him to dinner on 25 September and he accepted the proposal and took measures to ensure that it would be an agreeable occasion. So son and mother had been reconciled to some extent. However, the planned dinner never took place.

THE DEATH OF MICHAEL III (867)

On the previous day, 24 September 867, Michael III had invited his co-emperor, Basil, and his mistress, Eudokia Ingerine, to dinner at St Mamas, the suburban palace where he liked to spend time, participate in chariot-racing, and enjoy the sea breezes of the Bosphoros. Anticipating the planned dinner with his mother which was due the following day, the emperor had sent his chamberlain, Rentakios the *protovestiarios*, out hunting. He wanted to have something good to bring to his mother's dinner table. This official who was in charge of the imperial wardrobe was therefore not around on 24 September. All this highly circumstantial detail is only recorded in the chronicles; it is completely ignored in the *Life of Theodora*, which has a different version of the empress's final years.

However, according to the tenth-century histories, at their dinner on 24 September Basil plied the emperor with wine and, when he was quite intoxicated, slipped away to the bedchamber and fixed the door bolt so that it would not lock. Further drinking occurred, Eudokia left the men, and once Michael was drunk Basil bid him a fond goodnight. The emperor retired, ordering another official to sleep in the position reserved for his chamberlain Rentakios who was still out hunting. But this substitute failed to perform the role of imperial protector adequately.[110] Incapacitated by drink and unaware of the lack of security, Michael fell into a deep sleep. So it was easy for Basil and his fellow conspirators to break into the unlocked bedchamber, and the friend of over ten years standing was the first to attack the sleeping figure. Basil used the same accomplices to murder Michael as those who had assassinated Bardas and all of them disappeared in mysterious circumstances afterwards. If these detailed accounts are taken at face value, Basil plotted the murder, succeeded in killing Michael, and then arranged to have himself acclaimed sole emperor. As he had already been crowned, no further ceremony was required. He merely had to be acclaimed by the army, the Senate and people, which was achieved without difficulty.[111]

In the chronicle tradition this brutal murder is later witnessed by Theodora who had expected her son to dine with her the following day. When she is informed of the acclamation of Basil as sole emperor, she rushes to the palace of St Mamas where she finds Michael's body wrapped in a carpet. According to Leo the Grammarian and the Continuator of George the Monk, Theodora and her daughters, who are immediately alerted to the murder, mourn Michael's death together. They assist in transferring his body to a monastery in Chrysopolis, on the Asian side of the Bosphoros opposite the St Mamas Palace, where the emperor is unceremoniously buried. There, mother and sisters perform the rites of commemoration of the emperor in his very unimperial tomb. If true, this must have been a particularly dreadful event for the elderly widow.[112]

THEODORA'S DEATH AND BURIAL

The *Vita* of Theodora preserves a quite different tradition of these years after 856, in which Michael III outlives his mother. It includes a lengthy description of Theodora's dying moments, at which she delivers a magnificent oration and blesses the family, and mentions a visit by Michael and his wife Eudokia Dekapolitissa. Even if it is entirely contrived, it none the less creates the desired effect of the saintly woman speaking her last words to her assembled offspring in harmony and peace. Had Theodora predeceased her son, he as the ruling emperor would then have buried her beside her husband, his father Theophilos, in the imperial mausoleum. But this did not happen for Theodora was buried at *ta Gastria*, the monastic foundation where her mother and possibly her brother were already installed. Instead, as we have seen, it was more likely Theodora who had to bury her son in an obscure monastery while Basil was being acclaimed as the sole emperor.

Like so many imperial widows, Theodora lived on too long, neglected and probably resented by Basil I. After the reference to her mourning over the body of her son, there is no further mention of her in the chronicles until she dies at an uncertain date. Then, they claim, the reigning emperor, Basil I, buries her body in her own monastery of Gastria. Of these two conflicting versions of Theodora's last days neither is at all informative. The saintly account leaves her to be buried where she in fact intended, in her own foundation. The chronicle version supposes that she dies elsewhere and her body has to be transferred to Gastria by the emperor. But after the murder of her son, Theodora must know that she will not be permitted an imperial burial beside her husband Theophilos, and probably makes it clear that she will join her mother at *ta Gastria*. Her wishes were respected by her daughters who were most likely at her deathbed and made sure that the funeral rites were correctly performed over her grave in her own foundation of Gastria.[113] They too would eventually find their tombs in the same monastery, apart from Anna who had elected to be buried with Euphrosyne in her monastery. There is thus no need to involve Basil I in this responsibility. We can assume that Basil had a bad conscience about the empress, given what insults he had inflicted on her family, but his courtiers are already busy reconstructing his rise to power and his beneficent rule as a miraculous delivery from the drunkard Michael III.

In the tenth century, the disposition of the family members at the Gastria monastery is recorded as follows:

On the right side looking towards the East, the blessed Theodora, wife of Theophilos, and her three daughters. Opposite in a stone larnax, Petronas who was *domestikos* of the *scholai* and brother of the blessed empress Theodora. And in the narthex of the same church, Theoktiste [her mother], and nearby Irene, daughter of caesar Bardas, and further on the *katomagoulon* [lower jaw] of Bardas himself.[114]

The arrangement seems to have been set in place by Theodora once she realised that the family she had done so much to support had been effectively replaced by Basil the Macedonian.

As we have seen, Theodora's eldest daughter Thekla is said to have died in her own house at Blachernai, which she had converted into a monastery dedicated to Thekla, the early Christian martyr. So in her case the body would have been brought to Gastria for burial in the family shrine. The other two, Anastasia and Pulcheria, joined her in due course, according to Theodora's plans. Whether or not she had intended for her brothers to be buried there, they too found a place in the family shrine. And the daughter of Bardas, who is otherwise unknown, but who may have been named after her aunt Irene of Chrysobalanton, also joined him there. At least at *ta Gastria* the family from Paphlagonia would be reunited in a shrine dedicated to their memory. And as a saint of the Orthodox Church Theodora's tomb would become the centre of a cult, which elevated the standing of all her relatives as well.

CONCLUSION: THEODORA'S IMAGE

In addition to her saintly role, so insistently drawn by the *enkomion* which forms her Life, Theodora is given a reputation as a fearless leader, equally overbearing to Arabs and Bulgars in some of the chronicles. The idea that she might have sent an embassy to Khan Boris, warning him that she would lead her own forces against him if he dared to invade the empire, seems very fanciful. But there may be something in her reported claim that a victory over a female head of state would not be such a great achievement. We may doubt that this frightened Khan Boris (called Bogoris) into renewing a peace treaty, because Theodora also suggested redrawing the frontier to the Bulgars' advantage. Under these terms he could agree.[115] But behind it we may sense that Theodora's presence, her experience of imperial power and her determination to head the Regency in the appropriate fashion, gave her a distinct authority.

She also stood up to the caliphs, according to the historian Bar Hebraeus, who reports that the Arabs thought they could take advantage of a widowed empress and her young son. 'Seeing that it was a woman who ruled the country, the Arabs regarded the Roman homage with contempt and broke the peace. Then Theodora the Queen sent an army against Cicilia in AD 861 and enslaved all the country of Anazarbos.' There follows an account of her negotiations with the Arab ambassador, a eunuch named Nashif, when the queen offered to make peace but demanded 20,000 Christian prisoners of war in exchange for the 20,000 captured Arabs. When Nashif tried to take them anyway, 'Theodora killed them. Others say Nikola her eunuch killed them without the Queen's command.'[116] This 'image' of the empress-mother as a ruler negotiating maximum advantage from a successful military campaign, is hardly that of a weak woman. The ambassador had certainly been impressed.

A similar character sketch is preserved in the *Acts of David, Symeon and George*, when Symeon refuses to accept the 'compensation' set aside by Theophilos for his iconophile victims. In this account, which does not need to elevate the empress's authority, Theodora's reaction to the holy man is firm. She grows angry at Symeon's outburst and dismisses him, saying: 'For as I received and learned from my spouse and husband, I will rule with a firm hand. You will see.'[117] While this is merely a threat, it is directed at one of the holiest advisers she had, an iconophile who will have to change his mind and accept her proposal for the absolution of Theophilos. The episode, therefore, constitutes rather a humiliating step for Symeon: his forthright condemnation will be withdrawn and he will have to bow before the empress's will. Given the highly apologetic nature of the text, which is designed above all to demonstrate the far-sighted wisdom of the saints, their fervent resistance to iconoclasm and responsibility for the return of icon veneration, Theodora's stand at this stage may well reflect a moment of opposition. And it is the empress who wins.

Another contemporary text draws on an older tradition to praise the empress, citing her 'manly nobility in feminine garb'.[118] While this is a typically sexist formulation, commonly used of women who appear to act as men, the text also stresses the empress's determination to end the schism caused by iconoclast persecution and 'to restore the firm and undisputed correctness of the faith'. This she does by restoring the images, so that the whole purpose of 'rendering her reign sound' is intimately connected to the restoration of icons. Despite the propagandistic nature of such writing, Theodora emerges as a formidable leader, later identified as 'the great orthodox empress'.[119]

Coupled with the favourable descriptions of Theodora's attention to the financial resources of the empire, and the undeniable pride she reveals in her good administration, these instances suggest a distinctly strong woman – not at all the type to be led by her eunuch advisers. In addition, her central role in the restoration of the holy images, and her success in achieving a pardon for her deceased husband, may well be documented in a ninth-century prototype of the icon of orthodoxy. This image fits with most of the sources, which are determined to turn Theodora into a saint. But since she was quite an ordinary member of a provincial family before her marriage to the emperor, their efforts require a great deal of manipulation, which distorts the written record of what she did.

The most glaring example of this occurs in the comforting deathbed scene of the *Vita*, where Theodora, surrounded by her surviving children, bids farewell to them in a saintly fashion. Instead, it is more likely that she died a bitterly disappointed ex-empress, totally marginalised from the court of Basil I, now ruled by Eudokia Ingerine. It must have been galling to witness the power of her son's mistress, whom she had tried to remove through the mechanism of a bride-show held in 855. Worse still, her son, for whom she had made such strenuous preparations to conserve his right to rule, had been murdered. His murderer had usurped the throne and now ruled in his place. And since Michael had no legitimate children by his legal wife Eudokia Dekapolitissa, his death brought to an end the Amorion dynasty. Not even Theodora's four daughters had offspring who might have laid claim to perpetuate the dynasty of Amorion founded by Michael II. Thus, the ruling family to which she had devoted her entire life had been set aside by a murderer and usurper. Basil I had disrupted all her hopes for the future. No wonder that predictions of his nefarious role were attributed to her, and were linked by her to Theophilos. According to these inventions, even before he died in 842, Theophilos had prophesied that Basil would be the end of the dynasty.[120]

But by one of those tantalising paradoxes of history, the Macedonian usurpation may not have destroyed the dynasty of Amorion. For if Leo was indeed the son of Michael rather than Basil, Theodora's blood flowed in his veins. The emperor who ruled as Leo VI (886–912), also nicknamed 'the Wise', would be the grandson of Theophilos and Theodora. After many difficulties, *his* son Constantine VII Porphyrogennetos in turn would eventually succeed in perpetuating the same line. Thus the family from Amorion to which Theodora had committed all her affection and political skills continued to reign until the mid-eleventh century. It finally came to an end only when her namesake, Empress Theodora, another *porphyrogennetos*, died in 1056.

Of course, Theodora was not to know that she had succeeded against all the odds. But Basil's ambivalent attitude towards his son, Leo, may reflect the truth. He had always favoured the eldest, Constantine, who had been crowned co-emperor but died prematurely at the age of about twenty, leaving Leo next in line for the succession. Despite a period of imprisonment, when Basil refused to recognise his claims, eventually Leo became emperor and is known as an author, not only of religious works (sermons, hymns) but also of a military treatise and an important collection of laws. It would be greatly to the credit of his paternal grandmother if he was indeed the son of Michael III, a descendant of the iconoclasts from Amorion.

Even if this can never be proven, Theodora's achievements remain significant. She overturned the religious policy of the family into which she had been married, and helped to make sure that iconoclasm would never again become the official policy of the state. She then 'held the helm of the state', as the Byzantines liked to describe their rulers, guiding the empire like a boat firmly to the safe and correct port. For fourteen years she prevented anyone from challenging the rights of her son, and he repaid her by failing to take his imperial responsibilities seriously. She also insisted on him choosing a wife of whom she approved, and this led to the complicated saga of Eudokia Ingerine's position at court. But perhaps, due to this error of judgement, the Amorion dynasty lived on under another name for centuries.

Her post-mortem triumph as a saint of the Byzantine church, still commemorated annually on 11 February, guarantees her a telling place in the history of the empire. On that date Theodora's Life is read in churches throughout the orthodox world and icons of her are displayed for veneration. Though the record may preserve some distortions of her real achievements, her role in the Triumph of Orthodoxy in 843 means that she is particularly praised every year on the first Sunday in Lent. Like Irene before her, she had undone the puritanical reforms of iconoclasm and reaffirmed the power of religious images as a central tenet of the church.

In order to achieve this dramatic change in ecclesiastical policy, she had asserted her right to rule as a woman, using the full power of an emperor to raise some individuals to positions of authority, condemn others to exile, deprivation of wealth and even death. Although she failed to consolidate her own rule and did not foresee her brothers' plot to remove her, she successfully preserved the imperial inheritance and passed it on to her son, Michael. That he proved so inadequate cannot be laid entirely at her door. True, she did not prepare him for ruling: first Bardas and then Basil managed to convince him that they could do so better. But he was the sole emperor until 866. She was, however, powerless to prevent Michael from devising a scheme to hold on to his mistress while marrying a suitable bride, a complex arrangement which deepened his relationship with Basil and led to his downfall.

The extent to which Theodora drew on the inherited knowledge of what Irene had achieved in 787 and after is not clear from contemporary sources. But the previous empress had established a vital precedent and the council which achieved its purpose at the second attempt provided a method by which iconoclasm could be reversed once and for all. Theodora was also guided in her early years by Irene's granddaughter, Euphrosyne, who had lived through the successful iconophile revival that followed the council of 787. Euphrosyne sustained Theodora's opposition to the intensified iconoclast persecution, of which they both disapproved, and provided her with a model of family commemoration expressed through personal monastic foundations. Since Theodora herself had apparently had so few imperial credentials, and so little preparation for the role of empress, this must have constituted a major support. Building on a strength that had grown through four generations of women, Theodora was able to consolidate the iconophile strands so deeply engrained in Byzantine society. It is a remarkable achievement.

CHAPTER 5

Conclusion

How did these three women who wore the purple manage to leave their exceptional influence upon Byzantium? Their achievement raises questions about the role of empresses in government. We need a more systematic understanding of female imperial power, its manipulation of high office and possible abuse of authority when women are 'behind' the throne. Once they have the chance to exercise power in their own name, as I hope I have shown, women are just as purposive and effective as men. The question, however, is under what circumstances could they seize imperial authority for themselves? In the terminology of Byzantium, how did females, identified as Eves, change themselves into Adams? Was any reversal of their subordinate role a consequence of their feminine charms and guile, their deceitful nature and their ability to persuade men who should have suspected their designs?

As I have frequently stressed in the preceding pages, gender identities are constructed and assigned to women and men in all societies. For women in Byzantium, their roles as daughters, wives, mothers and widows were recreated by each generation according to social norms and expectations. Of course, 'norms' and 'expectations' are laid down by male authorities who prescribe suitable behaviour for females in all of these stages of life. For centuries Church Fathers, theologians, monastic leaders and lay writers – all men – had been engaged in this process of definition, which set limits on what women were permitted to do. Similar processes may be observed in western medieval societies and in the early world of Islam. At root, this determination to control women springs from their fertility, which alone can ensure the survival of the social group, clan, tribe, state or nation. But from early Christian times, men also perceived the need to regulate the lives of women who dedicated themselves to the service of Christ and refused the normal role of sexual reproduction. So whether they chose to avoid marriage and motherhood or followed that expected path, Byzantine women were trained according to social norms imposed by their male kin. These were reinforced by legal regulations and consolidated by institutions such as the female monastery.

Given the weight and extent of gender roles, the influence exercised by Irene, Euphrosyne and Theodora is unusual. In eighth- and ninth-century Byzantium all women, even at the top of the social hierarchy, were constrained by the same definitions of what made their behaviour acceptable, good or worthy of praise. Blinding a son, to take an extreme example, is hardly acceptable. Yet Charles the Bald perpetrated the same action as Irene and survived theological (and possibly social) condemnation. So there are situations in which even the most 'unnatural' of acts may be accepted. And here lies a clue to the anomalous combination of social norms and exceptional issues which may help to explain how our three empresses achieved their ends and managed to break out of the spheres in which empresses were expected to operate.

In order to muster the skills, determination and means to play the role they did, there must have been resources in the interstices of Byzantine society, which they could draw upon: resources which helped to legitimise their exceptional behaviour and even inspired and encouraged their ambitions. Such resources – which I will term 'the imperial feminine' – are indeed found in a rich vein of traditions, myths, symbols, images and customs. These manifest a relationship of women with authority and power; in a subordinate and supporting role, to be sure, but one that was none the less imperial.[1]

Three dynamic strands of this imperial feminine may be singled out. The first lies in the Late Antique transition from a Roman to a Christian society, marked by significant visual changes, which witnesses the introduction of the Virgin as a novel symbol of maternal value into an environment dominated visually by pagan monuments. It develops in symbiosis with imperial and civic rites into a powerful new cult. The second strand springs from the process of adapting Roman imperial structures to accommodate the needs of dynasty and claims to rule by inheritance, necessarily transmitted by women. The third, and perhaps most crucial, element lies in the development of New Rome, Constantinople, where imperial and public space, court structures and rituals – not least, as we have seen, the existence of a third sex of eunuchs, whom they could command – allowed ruling women to elaborate new roles.

From the intersection of elements of these three strands, the feminine is frequently associated with imperial power. This is a discontinuous phenomenon rather than any systematic combination. But it seems to have legitimised female access to an autocratic use of authority, and it revealed and preserved spaces (political, geographical and imagined) which women could utilise. It neither encouraged nor forbade this access. Rather, in exceptional circumstances, precedents in image and story permitted women to adopt a 'male' exploitation of forces within the imperial court and outside in Byzantine society at large.

In addition, there were the histories of previous empresses whose influence had altered Byzantium. Access to accounts of their roles may have provided an inspiration – a method of interpreting the status of empress. For the experience of an early medieval empress cannot be separated from her Late Antique ancestors. The entire court procedure, from inauguration to funeral rites, was built on a long inheritance, kept alive and renewed by each generation of officials devoted to the maintenance of tradition. Precedents could permit the exercise of both legitimate authority and indirect power.[2]

THE IMPERIAL FEMININE

The Virgin Among the Pagans

Among the many legacies of Byzantium, one particular aspect of the imperial feminine would have struck the young Irene when she arrived in Constantinople for the first time: the existence of many statues of gods and goddesses, beside numerous imperial statues. Aphrodite and the Muses, Herakles and Athena recalled the traditions of Hellenic antiquity, while full-length three-dimensional statues of empresses – Pulcheria, Eudoxia, Ariadne, Verina or Theodora – drew attention to past female leaders. Sometimes with their husbands, they were also often shown alone, standing on raised plinths in public spaces with inscriptions to identify them and to remind onlookers of their achievements. The acceptance of both pre-Christian divinities, female as well as male, and the commemoration of Christian empresses gave a distinctive character to the ancient capital. Unlike other cities which still preserved their ancient statuary, imperial women added a striking dimension to the visual impact of Constantinople.

These statues of notable females documented their activity as patrons of the church and protectors of the poor as well as sisters, daughters, wives and mothers of emperors. The city was adorned by several large images of Constantine I with his mother, Helena, either side of the True Cross, which she was supposed to have discovered in Jerusalem. For this and for her role in the foundation of Christian monuments, she had been acclaimed as a saint. And at this period between the seventh and ninth centuries her son was acquiring the same elevated holy status. In this way famous women of the past were acclaimed in very public fashion, which drew upon classical practices intensified by the move to the Queen City.

As well as these secular images, Constantinople was full of representations of the Virgin Mary, the divine protector of the city. Her role had grown gradually from the mid-fifth century onwards, greatly encouraged by female imperial patrons like Pulcheria and Verina, who established churches dedicated to her cult and celebrated her feasts in public procession and all-night vigils. Her power to save had been tested and found effective during the sieges of 626 and 717–18, when her icons and relics had played a part in securing the city's survival. In the previous chapters, I have suggested that women appear to have felt a close affinity to the maternal and protective capacities of the Ever-Virgin Mother of God. They participated in both the public aspects of her cult, the Friday evening vigils at Blachernai for instance, as well as making private devotions before her images. Empress Irene clearly shared the popular faith in the shrine of the Virgin *tes Peges*, while Theodora seems to have made her own personal dedication at the Blachernai shrine. Both of these churches were decorated with ancient images of the Virgin and Child to which individual women regularly directed their prayers for her intercession.

Female Dynasts

This striking visual presence of holy and imperial mothers also drew attention to the essential role of empresses in the construction of imperial dynasties, a critical aspect of their fertility. As wives and mothers they secured the continuity of the ruling family and helped to legitimise newcomers who had seized the throne by force. For Euphrosyne in particular this was a highly significant part of her function in linking the Syrian dynasty of the eighth century with the upstart from Amorion, who had no imperial credentials. Similarly both Irene and Theodora

243

conserved the claims of the families into which they had married and ensured that their sons inherited the paternal imperial authority. They drew on the Marian cult of motherhood, whatever its unique character, as well as the fecundity of previous empresses, whose devotion to dynastic needs had contributed to the survival of the empire.

In classical Rome, dynasty had mattered less and power was open to competitors. In other empires the choice of wives was a prerogative of the earthly ruler, or polygamy was permitted, as in Islam. In western medieval Christendom, there was no significant, permanent court structure. But in Byzantium, a powerful centralised court, with all its orders of precedence and hierarchy, revolved around what was now a dynastic imperial power. This was also a disciplined Christian regime, which strictly limited divorce. The outcome made empresses uniquely important. Because every new emperor was anxious to consolidate his credentials and ensure the succession of his eldest son to imperial power, he might need to call on his consort to play an important role, as wife, mother and possibly Regent. Usurpers such as Nikephoros I, Leo V and Michael II, all made such efforts and Michael's singular success may well owe something to his strategic second marriage, which raised Euphrosyne to prominence.

When Byzantium was threatened by conquests mounted both by the Saracens from the East and by the Bulgars from the West, a firmly established ruling dynasty became particularly important. It helped to guarantee the unchallenged succession of the legitimate heir, as in the case of Leo IV, acclaimed after his father's fatal wound during the campaign of 775. Of course, even the existence of legally designated co-emperors could not prevent the attempts of ambitious generals. But each successful conspirator who gained the throne by a military coup tried in turn to ensure the continuity of his own family. In this, each was dependent on his wife's fertility and ability to sustain an heir if the son was too young to rule at his father's death. Imperial widows might therefore find that they had new roles, which could prove critical to the dynasty.

The Queen City

In addition, through ceremonies that had over centuries established a public role for imperial consorts, women of the purple had access to a vast urban space in which they could demonstrate their authority. Although court activities often remained within the walls of the Great Palace, many occasions required the empress to go out into the city visiting churches, tombs and shrines. At other times, she left the palace for personal reasons and made her prayers and devotions as any other Christian might, albeit accompanied by guards, courtiers and perhaps other family members. Irene's exploitation of this part of the Late Antique inheritance seems quite striking: her determination to display imperial finery and largesse, even as far afield as western Thrace, suggests a clear grasp of the impact which such public activities could have. Following in the tradition dating back to Helena and developed by Pulcheria and others, the empresses also founded new churches and monasteries.

Creating such new shrines within Constantinople to commemorate their families was an effective way of planting a record of imperial women. All three of our empresses devoted their energies to the establishment of foundations, although Irene's monastery did not serve quite the same purpose as the others. But the survival of religious houses associated with each empress, where she and her immediate relations found their resting place, established new traditions in the capital city, noted by later pilgrims and visitors. These also secured the history of women who had married into ruling dynasties, rather than being born into them: outsiders to imperial circles. Even though Euphrosyne was born a *porphyrogennetos*, she returned to an imperial role as one who had been excluded from all power, reduced to almost the same condition as the youthful Irene and Theodora. And the commemoration of her family at the monastery that bore her name served a most important additional purpose, in that it recalled the legitimate marriage of her parents, the unhappy Maria and Constantine VI. Thus the traditions of the Queen City were far more considerable than even the spaces of the Great Palace, which granted empresses their own quarters, resources and staff. Within the urban space, it was possible to create institutions from shrines to monasteries with peculiarly female interests. These in turn preserved and reproduced the record of women's influence and authority.

Irene, Euphrosyne and Theodora drew on and reinforced these three resources of 'the imperial feminine'. Of course their activities are often condemned; churchmen, courtiers and male relatives combine in their disapproval of women acting as independent agents. They say it is illegal; to invoke such direct authority is quite improper; it is incompatible with the actions expected of someone holding such exalted office. But they accept that women may on occasion have to hold high office and act like male rulers for the survival of the empire. While denying any theoretical possibility, male commentators were forced to acknowledge greater flexibility and adaptability in practice.

WOMEN AND POWER

In medieval Byzantium, power is clearly 'the ability to develop and pursue a strategy even if it does not succeed', as well as the more common definition of 'the ability to make something happen'.[3] For strategy was always needed in Byzantium. It was an empire constantly concerned with defending, renewing and expanding its reach, defining its orthodoxy and preserving its protocols and appearances. In this situation, empresses evidently exercised power of the former kind to great effect. Nor was this confined to the spheres of the household and family; it might extend to much wider ecclesiastical, theological and diplomatic arenas. In the lifetime of their husbands such power is typically undocumented – little is recorded, although there are hints that women may exercise influence within the imperial bedroom. Such private channels of influence are recognised – petitioners to the emperor regularly address themselves in the first place to his wife. But once these women stand alone, nothing private can long remain outside the public domain of the court. There is little difference between private and public aspects of their power.

To identify Byzantine uses of overt power by an empress more specifically, once she is established with supreme authority, it may be helpful to compare the situation with practices in the medieval West. Inauguration as empress constitutes the first stage in the establishment of a specific role in government. The ritual has to be conducted according to certain rules that go back to the period of Late Antiquity. It involves vesting in special clothes, crowning with a crown and acclamation with the official title by Senate, army and people. While there are few references to the orb and sceptre in coronation procedure, empresses are depicted holding these attributes of imperial office on coins and seals and in official portraits.[4] The emphasis on tradition in Byzantium and the horror of innovation meant that each incoming empress received a similar ritual of elevation to a position at the head of the empire beside her husband the emperor. She thus became leader of the feminine part of the court.

In contrast, traditions of crowning, sacring and blessing queens in the eighth- and ninth-century medieval West were not well established, and new liturgical rites (*ordines*) might be written whenever the wife of a king was to be so honoured. Gradually, ecclesiastical and ceremonial methods developed to ensure the queen as a partner in government, as a patron of the church and protector of the poor. But she only acquired these attributes over centuries, and kings, theologians and bishops involved in the rite could alter and demean her status as a powerful female ruler. Their role might be critical in the recognition of the queen as an authority. Representatives of the church always played a much more prominent role, for example in the case of Hincmar's highly symbolic and impressive rite for Judith in 856.[5]

Further differences between women who rule in the East and the West relate to the existence of a permanent court in Constantinople with its own calendar or rituals and seasonal routines. In the West, the Bishop of Rome was probably the only official with a similarly fixed place of residence and administration. With the construction of Aachen as a Second Rome in northern Europe, Charlemagne may have sought to remedy the situation, which meant that he lived between one palace and another favourite villa, depending on the time of year. Even if Paderborn was also intended to be the Karlsburg (*urbs Caroli*) of the West, he still enjoyed the use of a variety of residences each with its own features – better hunting here, the hot baths there.[6] The court administration, his advisers and wives and children had to accompany him on his travels. Such mobility made it much harder to build and consolidate interests devoted to the position of the empress and her role in court ceremonies.

In 754 Pope Stephen II's coronation of Pippin and his wife Bertrada and the blessing of his family made clear the intimate connections between sacral authority and the Bishop of Rome. Furthermore, the idea of an imperial coronation in the West was an innovation of Pope Leo III, who thereby hoped to retain control over the designation of a western emperor. This always remained a specifically male ceremony; a feminine element was sometimes added but was never considered essential to the position of a queen. In contrast, ancient, secular, Roman methods for the acclamation of emperors prevailed in Byzantium and were systematically extended to their wives, now the bearers of the dynastic succession. As we have seen, the essential core of inauguration remained a traditional non-religious ritual.

The extent of western indebtedness to eastern inauguration rites has long been debated. In terms of regalia it seems that Byzantine emperors and empresses inherited from imperial Rome the use of orb, sceptre, crown and heavily bejewelled costumes worn at their coronations. In terms of consecration, the West introduced anointing with holy chrism, a sacred element derived from Old Testament practice, which had never found a place in the inauguration rites of the East Roman Empire.[7] There the stronger pre-Christian inheritance limited the patriarch's role, although it would later become as indispensable as that of his western counterpart. But the exclusive right of the church to endow a sacred character on western rulers by the use of chrism, continued to be ignored in the East.

ADAPTABILITY OF THE BYZANTINE SYSTEM

Although entirely custom-bound, the Byzantine system was none the less adaptable. Both male and female rulers were expected to perform all public roles correctly and not provoke scandals through inappropriate private activity. But despite the prescribed ritual in the life of an empress, circumstances might dictate alterations and her own personal interests might infringe this public role. Even in its most conservative pro-scriptions, Byzantine tradition could not take account of all possible developments. Hence the elaboration of novel ceremonies which may have been devised under pressure, without much thought as to their lasting impact, or when things do not go according to plan, as for instance, in the case of the baptism of Constantine V, described by the chronicler Theophanes.[8]

The *Book of Ceremonies* contains an account of how this should have been performed, but in 718 Leo III and his wife Maria did not observe it correctly. Instead, the emperor arrived at the church of Hagia Sophia on his own, leaving his wife (and the baby) to process from the Great Palace in the prescribed style. After the rite, the parents should have gone back together, but again Maria was not accompanied by her husband. Instead, she walked back to the palace distributing coin to the crowds who had gathered to watch the young prince carried to his baptism. As her husband had just crowned her *augousta* that same day, in recognition of the birth of her son, the crowds may have come to cheer her as well as the baby. Regardless of the person who thought up the adaptation, the empress made a decent ceremony of it. And it may have become part of the baptismal celebration, for much later we hear that Basil I added the distribution of largesse to the population after the christening of one of his sons.

The gendered roles of emperor and empress, constructed according to definite preconceived notions, together create a partnership, com-

plementing each other in the direction of the court. Since many ceremonies involve the separation of men and women, empresses supervise
the female sector while the emperor attends to the male participants. Of
course, the former is but a reflection of the latter, since women hold titles
only by courtesy of their husbands. None the less, the process of acceding
to an office, whether the rank of *zoste patrikia* (created around 830, see
chapter 4) or a more lowly one such as *kentarchissa* (wife of a military
leader in charge of one hundred men), gives each woman a fixed place
in the court hierarchy, a place in the ranking order at banquets, receptions
and the more mundane meetings of the court. For most women whose
husbands serve in the provinces, their induction to this round of ceremonial events provides another mechanism for integrating the regions
with the centre. They observe how the empress presides over her household, handles her children, her eunuchs and other servants; how she
wears her hair and if she has adopted new fashions in dress and jewellery –
all part of the process of disseminating imperial ideas through society.

Within the constitutional framework of imperial rule, the male was
expected to lead armies, direct government, defend orthodoxy and exercise imperial philanthropy (among the most basic duties of an emperor).
On the female side, his wife should give birth to legitimate children,
preferably sons, and perform all other duties of the imperial spouse, as
well as displaying piety and Christian charity. Within the representation
of the court as a reflection of the heavenly tribunal, the empress might
be a very strong advocate for clemency. In this way, Theodosia, the wife
of Leo V, succeeded in preventing the death of Michael of Amorion on
the day commemorating Christ's nativity. And when her husband agreed
to her plea not to throw his rival into the furnaces of the Great Palace on
25 December 820, he signed his own death warrant. For he was murdered
within twenty-four hours by Michael's accomplices, who had no such
qualms. But no one doubted that the empress had the right and the
power to intervene with her husband in matters affecting the court and
the imperial government.

Given this identifiable channel of influence, the empress might well
come to dominate over her husband. It was said of Prokopia that she
ruled the empire during the short reign of Michael I (811–13), while he
devoted himself to Christian philanthropy. This notion of the 'power
behind the throne' is familiar. The phrase is used of many different types
of influence, not merely womanly. But it clearly takes on particular force
in the case of rulers who are not predisposed to rule. Whether it is this

characteristic that permits their wives to assume a more powerful role, or that men of this disposition chose to marry forceful women who could exploit it and thus compensate for their husbands' feebleness, is immaterial. To the structural element of partnership in imperial ceremonial and court etiquette, the specific circumstances of individual marriages brought a constantly changing balance between male and female roles. Both objectively, in the conditions of court life, and individually, in the character of each couple, an emperor was naturally liable to be open to the influence of his spouse. The chroniclers and later historians who criticise this, fail to recognise a fundamental aspect of human behaviour. And the same applies to occasional stories of the unauthorised power of eunuch advisers.

FROM TEENAGE BRIDE TO SOLE EMPRESS

When a teenage bride-to-be first arrived at the Great Palace, those responsible for teaching her about her public role were primarily concerned to make sure that she would conform to the needs of the court. The brief of her ladies-in-waiting, her eunuch servants and the officials attached to her quarters, was to ensure that she understood the cycle of ceremonies at which she would appear. Since this role was highly symbolic, yet had no speaking part and took up a lot of time, the public sphere of an empress's life may well have been very dull. But through it she became aware of the constant pressure of interest groups, who sought to gain approval of particular policies or the favour of certain individuals. And because the empress was often perceived as a route to the emperor, she may sometimes have been pestered with requests to use her 'influence' with her husband. Through a mastery of her formal duties, imperial women could assess the strengths of different interest groups and social divisions in the Empire; identify ways to exploit the resources at their disposal, and learn how to secure the support of particular monastic communities, holy men, or senatorial factions.

These methods of achieving her aims must have stood the empress in good stead if she became widowed. In the position of Regent, even if she is only one among other officials appointed to direct the empire during the minority of her son, particular authority is vested in the mother of a minor who will become emperor at his majority. This official position permits widowed empresses to exercise more influence than they otherwise might. It is also an accepted feature of successions, which depend on a period of rule by committee before the young emperor designate can take up his authority. As we have seen (in chapter 1), in 642 the Senate of Constantinople preferred this relatively unstable mechanism to the rule of Empress Martina and her own son, who were condemned for usurping the authority of Herakleios' first family. And neither Irene nor Theodora was opposed as regent when Leo IV and Theophilos died. The custom was ingrained in Byzantium. As Poulet has shown, it also became accepted in the West but much later and with remarkable hesitancy.[9]

THE TRANSITION OF THE EIGHTH AND NINTH CENTURIES

In the circumstances of the late eighth and ninth centuries, when Irene, Euphrosyne and Theodora attained their positions, their influence was related to the broader situation of Byzantium. In response to the challenge of Islam, which claimed to be a final revelation of Allah to his chosen people, the Arabs, the Syrian emperors had reformed the empire. They devoted conspicuous attention to military defence and the organisation of effective fighting forces, both regional armies of part-time soldiers (*themata*) and the professional *tagmata*. Within the relatively new administrative system of provincial government, they concentrated attention on fortifications, roads and bridges to facilitate rapid movement of garrison forces, and the provision of horse relays to assist communication of imperial orders. They issued reliable coinage, a revised legal code, and consolidated a sense of dynastic rule which brought increased stability. In the course of this overall reform of imperial government, now reduced to about one third of its former extent, they also insisted on adopting the Mosaic ban on religious images and sought to eliminate their use in what remained of the Empire, in a movement known to us as iconoclasm.

Iconoclasm in Byzantium was a reaction to the rapid and highly successful spread of Saracen power in the East Mediterranean. For Islam rigorously enforced the Old Testament prohibition of idols, and used this to demonstrate that it was the true faith. By adopting a religious policy based on the same ban of religious images, and then successfully repelling the further assaults of Islam, the Syrian rulers instilled a deep affiliation between military victory and Christian worship without icons. Regardless of the way in which this combination was experienced, they secured the survival of Constantinople. While those who clung to their holy images were persecuted as heretics, Byzantine forces under their hero and leader, Constantine V, began to defeat Arab-led forces in the field. This emperor was also a theologian of iconoclasm, who emphasised that the only true image of Christ was in the Eucharist. Under his victorious campaigning, a highly successful integration of religion and politics proved long-lasting.

But the underlying disquiet provoked by the triumphs of the new monotheistic revelation to the Arabs should not be overlooked. The Byzantine Empire was reduced geographically to a fraction of its former Roman dimensions, and by the end of the eighth century the Arabs had occupied Egypt, North Africa, Syria and Palestine. Cyprus became a shared condominium, and Saracen expansion took over Crete and Sicily in the ninth century, two major islands which had for centuries guarded access to the Aegean and the waters of the western basin of the Mediterranean respectively. Their loss meant substantially increased danger to the remaining islands and coastlands under Byzantine rule. From new bases in the West, such as Fraxinetum in Provence, the Arabs would regularly raid coastal and riverine settlements, even Rome. Chroniclers and theologians deplored this new scourge of Christians, which became a permanent feature of the entire Mediterranean landscape. As in the East, they questioned how God could favour heretical pirates.

In such changing conditions, authorities in all parts of the old Roman world had to adapt their rule to deal with a new force. The response of the now isolated West took the form of a more strongly unified power linking northern Europe with Italy through the conquests of Charles, King of the Franks. With the encouragement of successive bishops of Rome, this extended Frankish authority drew on traditions associated with the ancient capital of the caesars. Without Muhammad, Charlemagne is inconceivable, as Henri Pirenne said. And the shift from a Mediterranean focus in western Europe to a northern concentration permitted the development of new markets, new trading connections and a novel form of economic growth. This is the core of 'the Pirenne thesis'.

My study of the formation of Christendom, which surveys the history of the Mediterranean world from the sixth to the ninth century, tried among other things to show why the Pirenne thesis is much too simple.[10] For if Islam had conquered Byzantium, it would have become the successor to Rome. Enhanced by the enormous wealth and strategic power of Constantinople, and fuelled by the shift of popular allegiance to the new faith that would have followed (as it did elsewhere), the Arabs would have rapidly spread their authority through the Balkans, into Italy and across the Alps. So while Pirenne was right to see that the rise of Charlemagne in western Europe was inconceivable without Muhammad, he failed to recognise that it was also Byzantium's successful resistance to Islam in the East, which permitted the rise of western Christendom. The critical factor of the Christian emperors of Constantinople in blocking further westward Muslim expansion has been ignored by generations of medievalists. Without the continued competition between imperial sovereignties in the East, the parcellised sovereignty characteristic of the Latin West would not have developed, which provided the framework for first feudalism and then the Renaissance. Without Byzantium, the iconoclasts of Islam would have replaced the entire extent of the ancient empire of Rome and become its true successor.

In both spheres of the Christian world the rise of Islam naturally caused uncertainty about the future and self-doubt, as well as economic retrenchment. In the eastern Mediterranean this was expressed in a tension between those Christians who had previously venerated religious images and those who identified holy icons as a cause of idolatry, which had to be prevented. How many were seriously disaffected by the order to destroy or at least remove icons from shrines and churches, is impossible to guess. As many historians have argued, probably more people were prepared to go along with the new policy than those determined to defend their images. This had been the case in seventh-century theological definitions issued by emperors. But among the anonymous mass of those without official positions, it seems that women particularly resented iconoclasm. For them, icon veneration often created an opportunity for personal devotion which they could not find elsewhere. Among men, a major source of resistance to iconoclasm seems to have grown up within monastic communities, where monks were often icon painters and manuscript illuminators.

Initially, the change of religious policy in Byzantium was accepted – the survival of the empire was at stake and Syrian reforms had to be adopted. The success of these measures in curbing Muslim raiding and eventually in securing greater safety on the reduced imperial frontiers was recognised. The same military machine proved equally effective against a revived Bulgar threat, so that by the reign of Leo IV both Arabs and Bulgars were held at bay. When the Khans threatened Constantinople in the early ninth century, iconoclasm again fortified the military in further victories. This intimate connection between the achievements of icon smashers on the battlefield and within the church was not discredited until the Arabs captured and sacked Amorion, the birthplace of Theophilos' father Michael (discussed in chapter 4).

Both iconoclast and iconophile theology developed against the backdrop of these grave threats to the survival of Byzantium. At times of extreme challenge military rulers invoked the need to prevent idolatry, which would restore God's favour; and at less difficult moments the icons might be restored to their venerable position. It was the female rulers of Byzantium who took up the cause of icons. Whether they had believed in the power of religious images from birth, or had limited knowledge of icon veneration, they tapped the deep wells of iconophile tradition to justify the change of policy, which aimed to reunite the estranged factions of the church. There were structural, social and gendered aspects to their insistence on condemning iconoclasm. To succeed, they used every form of political authority and power invested in their personal positions as widowed empresses, serving as regents for their young sons.

We do not know for certain whether they reintroduced the cult of icons because they were women, or whether the restoration of the traditional – and patriarchal – worship of icons needed women to oversee and authenticate its return, so great was the breakdown in male authority with the collapse of the extended empire. Perhaps not enough evidence has survived for us to be able to answer such a question. But there is more than enough evidence for us to ask it. This alone makes the case that Irene, Euphrosyne and Theodora were quite exceptional.

They did not rely on the 'indirect power' or 'influence' often exercised by a widowed empress and mother. To survive and realise their aims, they exploited divisions within the church, the military and civilian administrations, and among the monastic community. Between 785 and 787 Irene manifested an ability to manipulate different factions of the court, and forces beyond the empire, to make sure that she would get her way. There is no doubt that she played a leading role in dealings first with Patriarch Paul, then with the Senate of Constantinople, the army and later with Pope Hadrian. And her example was to inspire later efforts, even the unsuccessful attempt of Theophano, wife of Emperor Staurakios, to retain imperial power after his death.

During the lengthy process of adaptation to the Islamic conquest of North Africa, Palestine and Persia, our three empresses exercised their own power. By the end of the period, Byzantium had been forced to become one medieval state among many. From its ancient inheritance, formed by a profound Hellenistic tradition and strengthened by Roman imperial practice, the imperial centre had succeeded in maintaining a realm reduced to Asia Minor, part of the Balkans, southern Italy and the Aegean islands. It was a painful transition. Thanks to the empresses, it was also one which consolidated a firm commitment to iconophile practices after 843. Medieval Byzantium was then empowered to transmit its own version of both church and empire to neighbouring regions. The conversion of the Bulgars owes something to contacts renewed under Theodora, which came to fruition through the genius of Constantine-Cyril and Methodios, apostles to the Slavs, and the directives of Patriarch Photios. By establishing a way of incorporating extensive areas north and east of Byzantium, this would lead at the end of the tenth century to the conversion of the Rus.

A measure of this achievement can be gained by posing the rhetorical question, 'What if . . .?' What if the three women in purple had not taken control of the imperial machine and thus arrested an unbroken succession of male rulers, all committed to a vigorous commitment to iconoclasm? First, there would have been an important shift in political and diplomatic relations within the whole Mediterranean world. Alliances with the still idolatrous West would have become harder to negotiate, if not impossible, Byzantine rulers would have reoriented the empire towards the East, cutting itself off from the iconophile centre of Rome. Such a stand-off would have reduced the potential for fruitful cross-fertilisation, based on a shared Christian identity. It would not have permitted the marriage of Theophano to Otto II and the rediscovery of Greek and Arabic culture in the West under their son Otto III and Pope Sylvester II. It might have precluded the Christian co-operation involved in the crusades and the reconquest of the Holy Places from the Arabs.

In artistic terms, the iconoclastic tendencies of Northern Europe, such as the *Libri Carolini* and the symbolic art of Germigny, would have been strengthened. Non-figural art and a limited, aniconic repertoire of Christian art would have had a pervasive influence. Greek Christian communities under Islamic rule – which iconoclasm never had time to reach – would have been engulfed and purged of their holy images. Byzantine visual traditions would have withdrawn to decorative, non-figurative practices, considerably reducing the inspiration and range of figurative art in the West. In these circumstances, could the Renaissance have developed in Italy, so long influenced by Byzantium? If, for five hundred years, the East and the Byzantine provinces in southern Italy, as well as parts of northern Europe had followed iconoclast principles, would Rome have been able to defend its figurative element?

Again, to pose the question is to highlight the extraordinary role and influence of Irene, Euphrosyne and Theodora. But they played their role not because they were women but because they mastered and deployed imperial power. Their careers have been a study of this aspect, of how they exercised their authority. They were less true to their sex than to the purple.

After the usurpation of Basil I in 867, empresses never again exercised the same degree of imperial power. Under his determined strengthening of the patriarchal order, Byzantium returned to the norm of rule by men. Even during the minority of Constantine VII, his mother Zoë was not able to revive the influence of these women in purple, despite their strengthening of the imperial feminine. She was opposed by Patriarch Nikolaos Mystikos, a severe critic of Zoë's status as the fourth wife of an emperor, and a powerful advocate of male domination. Since her husband Leo VI had banned the possibility of Christians ever concluding a fourth marriage, Zoë had a full range of authorities arrayed against her and her son. The lack of powerful empresses until the reigns of the eleventh-century *porphyrogennetoi*, Zoë and Theodora, suggests that Irene, Euphrosyne and Theodora owed their ability to exploit the potential offered to a female ruler partly to the critical situation of the empire during the transition, as it sought to survive the onslaught of Islam. Due to the crisis in the patriarchal order, they could take advantage of their positions as a widowed regent or a step-mother of the young prince. After Basil I, alongside the veneration of icons, the patriarchal order secured its own restoration as well.

But by then, the empire's survival could ensure the spread of Byzantine styles of art and architecture, monastic organisation, liturgical practice, collections of prayers and hymns, and non-religious literature. Kiev and places further north and west took over the spiritual heritage of the empire as well as many administrative habits. Secular Byzantine imperial traditions were adopted by the rules of medieval Bulgaria, Serbia and Hungary. They influenced the growth of the Holy Roman Empire in the West with its double-headed eagle symbol, and developed into their fullest expression in the lands of Holy Russia. But it is primarily in artistic forms, the use of mosaic, fresco and icon painting, that Byzantine influence can be seen. The West had never lost its ability to reproduce the human image, which was defended in narrative terms by Pope

Gregory. Many different schools of medieval art, however, developed under the impact of Byzantine skill and craftsmanship, not only in Russia but also in Venice, southern Italy, Sicily, Cyprus and Crete, long after these areas had been lost to imperial control. Finally, in the work of Domenikos Theotokopoulos, nicknamed El Greco, sixteenth-century traditions of icon painting from Crete and Venice passed into the Renaissance art of Spain.

These long-term influences may be traced in part to the second restoration of icon veneration in 843 effected by Empress Theodora. Thanks to her insistence, Byzantium in the late ninth century renewed and developed styles of icon painting which were to become the hallmark of its art, almost the defining characteristic of an imperial culture that endured for another half-millennium and more. It was this manifestation of Byzantine culture that was so warmly embraced by the Slavs and which is so visible today in many areas of the Balkans, south-eastern Europe and Russia. Icons undoubtedly play a vital role in the revival of orthodoxy today, where individual worshippers may often be seen stopping to offer signs of respect and affection to holy images displayed at wayside shrines, outside churches, and in public spaces. Whether considered as an element of ancient superstition or a valued tool of instruction, it is an integral part of the Byzantine inheritance. The tradition of icon painting captures something of the essence of the empire's civilisation. And more than any other three individuals, it was three women of the imperial purple, Irene, Euphrosyne and Theodora, who were responsible for its triumph.

Sources and Notes

ON THE SOURCES USED FOR THIS STUDY
Historians of the Middle Ages have considerable difficulty in reconstructing the lives of medieval women. This is largely due to the fact that medieval men, who kept most of the records, did not share our twenty-first-century interest in the female half of humanity. Even though some women have left their own written record, like Dhuoda, who wrote a *Manual* for her son, we still know little about their daily existence, their diet, health, what gave them pleasure or pain. Others are known from legal documents which established monasteries and charitable institutions, by making grants of land and income; some wrote wills, which divide property and bequeath possessions. But such records reveal little of the personal feelings of the donor; they have a formulaic quality which reinforces the Christian character of donations made for the good of one's soul.

When none of these personal records survive, the lives of medieval women have to be constructed from what male writers report of them. Their undisclosed assumptions about the female nature, its inherent weakness and tendency to immorality, have to be countered. Women rarely capture the entire attention of a male chronicler, and when they do it is often because of some alleged scandal. Sometimes the accusation of sexual, financial or religious impropriety is made simply because an individual woman attains undue prominence. Learning to read the signs of this prurient interest in medieval texts, and to compensate for it, requires practice. Even the most sympathetic male authors feel obliged to stress how saintly, devout and philanthropic their female subjects were – as if women could not be described in less loaded terms.

Rulers of both sexes, of course, had to live up to certain ideals. But when a historian wishes to condemn an emperor or king, there is the method of invective: a formal way of reducing a man's standing, which may include attacks on his morals, implying adultery, incest or sexual depravity. An interest in the occult, prophesy or magic indicates heresy, inappropriate in one selected by the hand of God to rule over a chosen people. But for women in public life it is much simpler for authors to fall back on the sin of Eve, the first woman, which condemned all the female sex to inferior positions. Only the 'saintly' could rise above this destiny, and they were very few.

In the case of the three Byzantine empresses who form the subject of this study, however, there is even less evidence. Nothing recorded by them in their own words has been preserved, other than official pronouncements, laws, or statements put into their mouths by male writers. We may assume that they supervised their own records and wrote letters; but if they did, such documents have not survived. So in contrast to most biographers, who rely on the writings of their subjects, we have to find other ways of reconstructing the lives of these empresses. Their characters have to be built up from what is recorded *about* them, yet all the available information is filtered through male eyes and preconceived ideas about women.

So while there are many Byzantine views of Irene, Euphrosyne and Theodora, we completely lack a record of their own perspectives and personal preferences. Guessing at what they might have written in their private diaries is the stuff of historical novels (of which there are many). Every history of Byzantium, however, presents a view of these women, generally accepting the biased opinions of the chief chroniclers of the time. Some are more overtly misogynistic than others but in general they reproduce medieval perceptions: that women should be confined to household and domestic activities with the addition of Christian duties. As wives, mothers and later widows, however, empresses were often able to take a more active role in government. This development is noted by contemporary male historians, who reveal their unease and discomfort at such unusual activities. Interpreting their partial accounts is a major challenge. In many cases it is hard to establish what women rulers actually achieved. Contemporaries often attribute all the credit for good decisions to male advisers, military and religious, while they blame the imperial women for bad results when a scapegoat is needed.

An additional problem arises from the purposive destruction of much contemporary evidence. Surviving sources for the history of Byzantium in the eighth and ninth centuries document only the views of the religious party which proved triumphant in the conflict over icons: the iconophiles (those who love icons). Their systematic obliteration of the opposing iconoclast theology (the views of the icon-breakers) means that they present a highly biased interpretation. Nothing good or positive can be ascribed to the icon-smashers, who persecuted the pious icon-lovers during two long periods of official iconoclasm. All excellence is the result of those who favoured the holy images and restored them to their place of honour in the church.

This imbalance in the surviving sources is also marked by a tendency to emphasise the sphere of religious practice at the expense of all others. The quarrel over icons thus dominates all the records and magnifies it to the most central issue in eighth- and ninth-century history. But there are grounds for understanding the period as one in which the survival of the empire was the most pressing issue. Without major reforms of military and fiscal administration, Byzantium might have been overrun by the Arabs or the Bulgars. Irene, Euphrosyne and Theodora all had to attend to such matters. But in the surviving sources they are identified primarily as iconophile leaders, so a good deal of special pleading can be discerned in what is recorded about them.

Fortunately, there are several indirect ways of overcoming this bias, which also leaves so many aspects of empresses' lives undocumented. First and foremost, they shared in the life-cycle of élite women of their time, which had an established pattern. Maternity was their primary role and they were expected to produce children, especially sons. The birth of a daughter is regularly ignored in the contemporary sources. Wealthy women were also expected to supervise their households, look after their poorer relatives, practise philanthropy on a broader scale, and to behave as models of Christian motherhood. The education of their children, at least until the age of seven or so, was their responsibility. Of course, they had servants to help and to make sure the children received appropriate lessons. Both girls and boys were educated, though the traditions of 'spindle and distaff' were considered essential for girls only.

This stress on education also implies that women from élite families in Byzantium were themselves educated and probably literate. They may have relied on scribes to write for them but it seems very unlikely that they did not read, for the level of understanding and culture required by members of the ruling élite was quite high. Since letters are addressed to them in the expectation that they would respond, their ability to carry on a correspondence may be assumed. If women were exiled to monasteries, which served as prisons, and received letters there, it seems reasonable to suppose that they wrote their own answers. But these have not been preserved. While male authors kept copies of their own writings, including letters, their female respondents are not represented in letter collections until a much later date.

After they had passed beyond the child-bearing years, the life-cycle of élite women presented different possibilities. Many found a greater freedom to pursue a wide range of philanthropic social activities, which took them out of their homes and brought them into contact with poorer and less advantaged people. Women were often widowed at a relatively young age and some realised a significant increase in control over their lives as a result. Whether they remarried or preferred to remain single, or decided to abandon the world and take monastic vows, at this stage in their life-cycle they could sometimes exercise choice, beyond the controlling hand of father, husband or male relatives. But it is clear from the sources that real choices were generally restricted and even the wealthiest and most independent women were regularly forced to comply with a future determined by others.

In the early Christian centuries, emperors had taken a particular interest in heiresses. They were often ordered to marry rather than disperse the fortunes they had inherited to the church or other philanthropic institutions. The same pressure continued to be exercised in Byzantium, as St Athanasia found in the ninth century, when an imperial edict was issued instructing unmarried women and widows to marry foreigners (*ethnikoi*), men from beyond the empire. Her flight into the church was respected but indicates how limited were her real alternatives. Finally, before their deaths many élite women arranged where they wished to be buried and constructed family shrines for themselves and their immediate relatives. Such information is often indirectly reported in the sources and it is necessary to work out from death notices how certain individuals came to be buried in special tombs.

Once established as the wife of an emperor, the empress's daily routine was determined by an elaborate cycle of court functions: the calendar of feasts, parades, church liturgies and secular ceremonies which had to be observed. These rituals must have monopolised many hours of every day passed not only by the all women of the court, but also of course by their husbands, from the emperor down to the humblest sergeant. Court activities are recorded in the *Book of Ceremonies*, which survives in a single but not complete copy of the tenth-century edition. It was probably put together on the orders of Constantine VII (emperor from 945 to 958) and includes a number of sixth-century records as well as later material. Most of them take the form of generic proscriptions, a guide as to how to perform certain ceremonies: for the marriage of an emperor, the celebration of Whitsun, the first day of the New Year and so on. Since a great many demand the participation of the empress, this source fixes certain aspects of her imperial life in a particular pattern.

Another fruitful way of illuminating the lives of these empresses lies in the investigation of the physical conditions in which they lived at different periods. For while they might be promoted very rapidly to high office, they must also have noticed how privileged circumstances could be altered overnight, usually because of decisions taken by their male relatives. In succession, we find Irene banished from the capital to a remote island, Euphrosyne and her mother sent into a monastic exile, and Theodora forced to retire from the court. These events, as well as the changes that took place more slowly over time, can be investigated more fully from sources which are not directly concerned with empresses. The Lives of saintly nuns and abbesses, ecclesiastical regulations and other records which document the organisation of female monasteries are particularly helpful.

Finally, non-literary sources provide some help in answering the question, what did empresses do? Did they ever take initiatives of their own? Irene and her son Constantine VI, for instance, are commemorated in the domed church of St Sophia in Thessaloniki, in monograms of their names set in the mosaic decoration of the apse arch. No chronicler of the time attributes to them responsibility for this. Yet the archaeological record is quite clear: they may be considered the patrons of a fine mosaic programme, which should therefore be linked with the period of their joint rule, during the years 780–97. Further evidence of the building activity of empresses is preserved in records devoted to the monuments of Constantinople (the *Patria*), and reveals that they practised imperial philanthropy on quite a large scale. Their initiatives are commemorated in un-speaking stones, paintings and mosaic decoration (most of which have not physically survived in today's Istanbul).

There is so little material however, much of it posing many difficulties, that in writing these biographies I have had to speculate and to make certain assumptions. In all cases I have interpreted what is recorded about Irene, Euphrosyne and Theodora in the context of the female life-cycle of medieval women. Thus I have given special weight to factors often ignored, such as the age at which they could perform particular functions; the pattern of behaviour of other élite women; the personnel available to such women in the form of household servants, eunuchs, scribes and escorts, and the resources they could employ in matters of personal choice. The lives of women who were contemporaries of our three female emperors may be only partially known, but from different aspects one can build up a composite picture. And from elements which include activities undertaken to satisfy their needs (visiting particular shrines, praying in front of icons, restoring or constructing churches to hold family tombs and so on), it is possible to imagine how the empresses passed their time.

On this basis I have sometimes stated a case more assertively than the sources may warrant. Where the conditional tense should repeatedly be used, I have often employed the present. While citing the sources and my interpretation of them, I have not stressed the element of guesswork involved in the historical reconstruction. I have used whatever bits of information seemed applicable to bridge the gaps. I am all too aware that my biographies are uneven and patchy, given that so much remains unknown. If this is considered a reason for abandoning the effort to write about Irene, Euphrosyne and Theodora, then I am guilty of finding them too interesting.

I am convinced that such imaginative reconstruction can produce valuable insights into the lives of all medieval women. Despite the difference in their status as empresses, which brought them access to resources restricted to a tiny circle of privileged women, Irene and Theodora in particular, came from provincial backgrounds common to many families. When they left their natal homes, they must have had an upbringing familiar to many girls not only in the Byzantine Empire but also in the medieval West. In a different way Euphrosyne's childhood also personifies a common experience: the dramatic changes of family fortune which afflicted those who fell foul of imperial and regal power in the Middle Ages. Her life of exile in monastic seclusion was shared by many others. All three women came from families in the shadow of wealthier, grander people, who inhabited the centres of power and participated in the government of the day.

They grew up in the same Christian culture, believing devoutly in the judgement that would determine their fate after death. They took steps to try and ensure their reputations as good Christians. Naturally, they aspired to promote their own families in similar ways and tried to take advantage of circumstances which might favour their relatives. From this common background, individuals in Byzantium might occasionally move from their poorly documented provincial homes to careers in the great metropolis of the capital city, Constantinople. Men were more likely to make such a transition, for the empire was open to talented soldiers, craftsmen, intellectuals and ascetic figures. But, in specific conditions, women too could take part in such a radical process. And through their ability to adapt to the demands of a new career as empress, we can trace their feminine skills in a fashion comparable to men.

ABBREVIATIONS

Primary sources

AASS   Acta Sanctorum, third edition (Paris/Rome, 1863–70)

Acts of David... J. van den Gheyn, 'Acta graeca ss. Davidis, Symeonis et Georgii Mitylenae in insula Lesbo', *Analecta Bollandiana* 18 (1899), 209–59; tr. D. Domingo-Foresté, in Talbot, ed., *Byzantine Defenders of Images*, 149–241

Annales Mosellani in *MGH, Scriptores in usum scolaruum*, vol. XVI, 494–9

Bar Hebraeus *Chronography of Gregory Abu'l Faraj*, 2 vols., ed. and tr. E. A. Wallis Budge (London, 1932)

Byzantine Defenders of Images Alice-Mary Talbot, ed., *Byzantine Defenders of Images. Eight Saints' Lives in English Translation* (Washington, DC, 1998)

Council *in Trullo* The Council in Trullo *Revisited*, eds. G. Nedungatt and Michael Featherstone (Rome, 1995) = *Kanonika*, vol. 6

DAI, I and II Constantine VII Porphyrogenitus, *De administrando imperio*, 2 vols., ed. and tr. G. Moravscik and R. Jenkins (Budapest, 1949 and London, 1962)

DC I and II Constantine VII Porphyrogenitus, *De cerimoniis aulae byzantinae*, books I and II in one volume, ed. I. I. Reiske (Bonn, 1829)

DOC P. Grierson, *Catalogue of the Byzantine Coins in the Dumbarton Oaks Collection* (Washington, DC, 1966–99)

Genesios *Iosephi Genesii regum libri quattuor*, eds. A. Lesmüller-Werner and I. Thurn (Berlin/New York, 1978); Genesios, *On the reigns of the Emperors*, tr. A. Kaldellis (Canberra, 1998)

George the Monk George the Monk, *Chronicon*, 2 vols., ed. C. de Boor (Leipzig 1904), revised edn P. Wirth (Stuttgart, 1978)

Holy Women of Byzantium Holy Women of Byzantium, ed. Alice-Mary Talbot, (Washington, DC, 1996)

Kedrenos George Cedrenus, *Synopsis historion*, ed. I. Bekker, 2 vols. (Bonn, 1838–9)

Leo grammatikos Leo grammatikos, *Chronographia*, ed. I. Bekker (Bonn, 1842)

Life of Theodora A. Markopoulos, 'Vios tes autokrateiras Theodoras', *Symmeikta* 5 (1983), 249–85; tr. M. Vinson, in *Byzantine Defenders of Images*

Mansi J. D. Mansi, *Sacrorum conciliorum nova et amplissima collectio*, 53 vols. (Paris/Leipzig, 1901–25), repr. Graz 1960

MGH *Monumenta Germaniae Historica, Scriptores, Epistulae, Concilia*

Michael the Syrian Michel le Syrien, *Chronique*, 3 vols., ed. and tr. J.-B. Chabot (Paris, 1924)

Nikephoros *Nikephoros Patriarch of Constantinople, Short History*, text, translation and commentary by C. Mango (Washington, DC, 1990)

Parastaseis syntomoi chronikai (in *Patria Konstantinouoleos*), repr. with Eng tr. Averil Cameron and Judith Herrin, *Constantinople in the Early Eighth Century: the* Parastaseis syntomoi chronikai (Brill, 1984)

Patria II, III Patria Konstantinoupoleos, sections II and III, ed. T. Preger, 2 vols. (Leipzig, 1901–7), repr. New York, 1975; German tr. A. Berger, *Untersuchungen zu den* Patria Konstantinoupoleos (Bonn, 1988)

Photius *Photius, Patriarch of Constantinople, Homilies*, tr. C. Mango (Cambridge, Ma., 1958)

PmbZ Prosopographie der mittelbyzantinischen Zeit, eds. F. Winkelmann, R.-J. Lilie et al., Part I (641–867), 4 vols. (Berlin/New York, 1998–2001)

RFA   *Royal Frankish Annals* (*Annales Laurissenses*, ed. F. Kurze) in MGH, Scriptores VI, 134–218

Scriptor incertus   *Syggraphe Chronographiou ta kata Leonta uion Barda tou Armeniou periechousa*, Historia de Leone Bardae Armenii filio, ed. I. Bekker (Bonn, 1842), bound with Leo grammatikos

Sym mag   Symeon magister et logothetes, *Chronicle*, ed. I. Bekker (Bonn, 1842), bound with Leo grammatikos

Theodore   *Theodori Studitae Epistulae*, ed. G. Fatouros, 2 vols. (Berlin/New York, 1991)

Theophanes   *Theophanis Chronographia*, ed. C. de Boor, 2 vols. (Leipzig 1883), repr. Hildesheim/New York, 1980; *The Chronicle of Theophanes Confessor*, tr. C. Mango and R. Scott (Oxford, 1997)

Th Syn   *Theophanes Continuatus*, ed. I. Bekker (Bonn, 1838)

Secondary material

Bury, *ERE*   J. B. Bury, *A History of the East Roman Empire from the Death of Irene to the Accession of Basil I* (London, 1912)

Speck, *Konstantin VI*   Paul Speck, *Kaiser Konstantin VI. Die Legitimation einer fremden und der Versuch einer eingenen Herrschaft*, 2 vols. (Munich, 1978)

Treadgold, *Byzantine Revival*   Warren Treadgold, *The Byzantine Revival 780–842* (Stanford, 1988)

Journals

BF   *Byzantinische Forschungen*

BZ   *Byzantinische Zeitschrift*

DOP   *Dumbarton Oaks Papers*

GRBS   *Greek, Roman, and Byzantine Studies*

JÖB   *Jahrbuch der Österreichischen Byzantinistik*

TM   *Travaux et Mémoires*

REB   *Revue des études byzantines*

SCH   *Studies in Church History*

ZRVI   *Zbornik Radova Vizantoloskoğ Instituta*

SOURCES CITED IN THE INTRODUCTION

Council of Nicaea: *Sacrorum conciliorum collectio nova et amplissima* ed. J. D. Mansi (Paris, 1902, repr. Graz, 1960), vol. XIII, cols. 415D–E (my translation)

The Life of Saint Theodora the Empress, para. 3, tr. Martha P. Vinson, *Byzantine Defenders of Images* ed. Alice-Mary Talbot (Washington, DC, 1998), 363–6

The Life of Sts. David, Symeon and George of Lesbos, para. 27, tr. Douglas Domingo-Forasté, in *Byzantine Defenders of Images* (as above), 215

Procopius of Caesarea: *History of the Wars*, book I, ch. xxiv, 36–7, ed. and tr. H. B. Dewing (London/New York, 1914), 230–2

The Life of Patriarch Nikephoros I of Constantinople, p. 48, tr. Elizabeth A. Fisher, in *Byzantine Defenders of Images* (as above)

SOURCES FOR CHAPTER 2: IRENE

The sole surviving history which provides a narrative of the lifetime of Irene, the first of our women in purple, is a *Chronicle* (*Chronographia*) attributed to Theophanes the Confessor, abbot of the Megas Agros monastery. It is part of a world history and covers the years AD 284 to 813. After the Triumph of Orthodoxy in 843, a *Life of Irene* was compiled to elevate the empress's sanctity as an iconophile. It is based on the record of Theophanes and adds little of significance. The other documents of her reign include her two laws and various official letters sent in her name. Whether she actually wrote them or merely signed what had been composed by her ministers is unknown. References to her rule occur in many theological writings of the period, but Theophanes remains the most important source for the entire period of her life.

Much of the *Chronographia* had been put together by George the *synkellos*, assistant to the Patriarch of Constantinople in the late eighth and early ninth centuries. George had compiled a history going back to the creation of the world, when he was a monk in an ancient monastery near Jerusalem, before he arrived in the Byzantine capital. Both he and Theophanes knew the empress, her son and her courtiers. From George's dossier it is evident that he had access to several eastern records in Syriac which had preserved the tradition of writing a World History, and one probably from Rome, so he was informed by many non-Constantinoplitan accounts of the period.

Later Byzantine writers maintained this interest in all history from the Creation forward, reflecting a serious attempt to account for the whole span of human time. In the tradition of a Christian World History, events are recorded according to the year of the world, *Anno Mundi*, dating from the Creation, with additional use of the indiction, a late Roman dating system related to tax returns. The year of the Lord, *Anno Domini*, is also sometimes employed but the Byzantines preferred the other methods of dating. Taken in conjunction with their firm belief in the passing significance of this world in comparison with the next, which carried the promise of eternal life, such authors set the contemporary events they witnessed in a longer overview.

It seems likely that Theophanes inherited the accounts prepared by George the *synkellos*, which he edited and extended up to the year 813. By AD 800, the world according to the *Anno Mundi* had reached the seventh millennium (year 6293). At that time Irene was in sole control of the empire, as Theophanes records. While he preserves a clear record of her reign, the difficulty of having so few additional records which concentrate specifically on the empress is evident. There are many occasions between 780 and 802 which are passed over in silence, when no other written or unwritten evidence helps to fill out the picture and no historical analysis is preserved.

Fortunately, the *Chronographia* was carefully edited by C. de Boor and has now been brilliantly translated into English by Cyril Mango and Roger Scott. Their version, with its helpful notes, has been frequently cited in this study. The Lives of Tarasios and Nikephoros, iconophile patriarchs, as well as other defenders of icons have also been recently translated. Other contemporary documentation such as the Acts of the second Council of Nicaea, the *Codex Carolinus* of Frankish and papal correspondence, and the *Libri Carolini* are not available in reliable English versions.

I have provided my own translations of these as well as of later Byzantine sources such as the much quoted *Book of Ceremonies*.

While many other records of the history of the ninth century survive, most were written long after the events they describe and often with a clear intent to represent the past in a particular light. A similar purpose lies behind the world histories composed in the eleventh and twelfth centuries, when Irene's actions were reinterpreted in order to stress her significance as a champion of the veneration of icons. Though it is tempting to accept the satisfying image they present, it is clear that writers such as Skylitzes and Kedrenos have to distort other elements of the historical record in order to construct a view of Irene as a devout iconophile from her birth onwards. References to Irene in contemporary western sources preserved in Latin constitute a much more valuable resource, however distorted their understanding of Byzantium. Some much later compilations in Syriac attributed to Michael the Syrian and Bar Hebraeus also preserve somewhat mythic traditions of the empress.

Thus, when discussing Irene, historians from the ninth century onwards tried to fill the gaps in the contemporary historical record, fleshing out the barest accounts of her actions with suppositions. In the process they inevitably presented her role to meet a particular purpose. Michael the Syrian, for instance, preserves an explanation of the rivalry between Irene and her son which is unknown to Theophanes. But it is one often used by male writers, for it turns on allegations that the empress maintained illegitimate sexual activities with her courtiers. Immoral and inappropriate behaviour is a charge levelled against both men and women but it carries a heightened charge when the person accused is a woman usurping imperial power.

In addition to these chroniclers, the *Patria Konstantinoupoleos* preserve many references to Irene, often of a quite legendary character. This collection of short stories about the monuments of the capital was compiled in the eleventh century from many earlier sources. While the process of trying to identify the founder of a building from inscriptions, statues, images and myths associated with it is hardly a reliable historical method, the source contains many valuable hints and plausible connections. To ignore such a text, simply because it often accepts evidence which can be proved inaccurate, would be to set aside one of the few collections of material which sustain a relatively neutral position on the rulers of the iconoclast periods. I have therefore cited the *Patria* wherever its brief notes document a credible account.

Nearly a century ago Charles Diehl devoted a book to Byzantine women, including Irene and Theodora among his *Figures byzantines* (Paris, 1906). While these essays draw attention to the importance of empresses and aristocratic women, it is hardly surprising that they now seem very dated. Their stories are, inevitably, dominated by the unusual features of their lives, though Diehl also compiled a composite picture of a typical well-to-do female inhabitant of the capital, who represented more normal Byzantine women. His interests have been carried on by many historians including Steven Runciman, whose excellent contribution to *The Byzantine Aristocracy* (Oxford, 1984) concluded by wondering if the skills of Byzantine women might have something to do with the survival of the empire for so many centuries, and Donald Nicol, in *The Byzantine Lady. Ten Portraits 1250–1500* (Cambridge, 1994), which explicitly takes Diehl's essays as a model.

Unlike the first Theodora, wife of Justinian I, who has attracted numerous biographies, the three women in purple studied here have not received much attention except as iconophiles. Dominique Barbe's *Irène de Byzance. La femme empereur* (Paris, 1990) went more deeply into the character of this ruler, but found it necessary to create a historical novel about her. Recently, Lynda Garland included Irene and Theodora in her study, *Byzantine Empresses: Women and Power in Byzantium, AD 527–1204* (London, 1999), but while covering such a long period, the individual chapters are rather brief sketches. Barbara Hill has adopted a more theoretical approach to female rulers of the eleventh and twelfth centuries (*Imperial Women in Byzantium, 1025–1204*, London, 1998), which is useful for earlier empresses as well. Michael Angold's recent general book, *Byzantium. The Bridge from Antiquity to the Middle Ages* (London, 2001), attributes certain initiatives to Irene and Theodora, reflecting an increasing awareness of Byzantine women. So there is every chance that the serious study of female rulers in Byzantium will continue.

NOTES TO CHAPTER 2: IRENE (PAGES 51–129)

[1] Nikephoros, ed. de Boor, para. 88; tr. Mango, 163.

[2] Theophanes, AM 6261, de Boor I, 444; tr. Mango/Scott, 613.

[3] By 787, new bishoprics on Aigina, Monemvasia and the western islands of Kerkyra (Corfu), Zakynthos and Kephalonia reveal the same determination to bring outlying areas back into the orbit of imperial government; see J. Darrouzès, 'Les listes épiscopales du Concile de Nicée (787)', *REB* 33 (1975), 5–76.

[4] *Ta Charagmata tou Parthenonos*, eds. A. K. Orlandos and L. Vranoussis (Athens, 1973), nos. 80, 83, 67, 82. Cf. more elegant inscriptions on marble fragments once attached to other ecclesiastical fittings, which indicate the existence of other churches.

[5] Theophanes, AM 6258, de Boor I, 440; Mango/Scott, 608.

[6] P. Magdalino, *Constantinople médiévale* (Paris, 1996), 18–19, 58, argues that the mid-eighth-century attack of the plague constitutes a low point in demographic terms and thereafter Constantinople begins to expand.

[7] The regions of Asia, Pontos and Thrace, which had been under thematic administration much longer, were able to provide masons, plasterers, brickmakers, and five thousand labourers to do the hard work.

[8] F. Winkelmann, *Quellen zur Herrschenden Klasse von Byzanz im 8. und 9. Jahrhundert* (Berlin, 1987), 215–18; E. Patlagean, 'Les débuts d'une aristocratie byzantine et le témoignage de l'historiographie: système de noms et liens de parenté aux IXe–Xe siècles,' in M. Angold, *The Byzantine Aristocracy: IX–XIII Centuries* (Oxford, 1984), 23–43, esp. 29.

[9] P. Schreiner, 'Reflexions sur la famille impériale à Byzance (VIIIe–Xe siècles)', *Byzantion* 61 (1991), 181–93, esp. 191; R.-J. Lilie, *Byzanz unter Eirene und Konstantin VI (780–802)* (Frankfurt am Main, 1996), 36.

[10] Winkelmann, *Quellenstudien*, 157, 193; Lilie, *Eirene und Konstantin VI*, 36–8, and see n. 121 below.

[11] Or might have dated back to an earlier connection, as Lilie proposes, *Eirene und Konstantin VI*, 40–41.

[12] J. Ebersolt, *Le grand palais de Constantinople* (Paris, 1910), 104–8.

[13] An honorific title coined from the masculine Augustus, employed for emperors. It was bestowed on Eudokia as an addition, since she was already empress (*basilissa*). On the official titles used for empresses, see S. Maslev, 'Die staatsrechtliche Stellung der byzantinischen Kaiserinnen', *Byzantinoslavica* 27 (1966), 308–43; G. Rösch, *ONOMA BAΣIΛEIAΣ* (Vienna, 1978), 110–11; D. Missiou, 'Über die institutionelle Rolle der byzantinischen Kaiserinnen', *JÖB* 30/2 (1982), 489–98; R. Hiestand, 'Eirene Basileus – die Frau als Herrscherin im Mittelalter', in H. Hecker, ed., *Der Herrscher. Leitbild und Abbild in Mittelalter und Renaissance* (Düsseldorf, 1990), 253–83.

[14] DC, I, ch. 41, 208–16. While the text was written down later, it clearly drew on earlier precedents and can serve as a guide to the first formal acts that Irene undertook. For the coronation and wedding of an empress, there are four distinct parts of unequal length: the first concerns the crowning of the new empress, which takes place in the Augousteos, a large reception hall inside the Daphne, the oldest palace within the Great Palace compound. It is followed by the presentation of the newly crowned empress to different sections of the court and her official acclamation by the factions. This is by far the longest written section and its details show that the ceremony included and defined each group within the court. The third part is the brief wedding ceremony, which is performed by the Patriarch of Constantinople in the palace chapel of St Stephen. Finally, there is the wedding feast held in the banqueting hall of the Nineteen Couches. On the imperial costumes and regalia, see K. Wessel, *Reallexikon der byzantinischen Kunst*, III, 369–498.

[15] The order is given in the previous chapter, DC, I, ch. 40, 203. 17–18, where the *zostai*, who hold a position created in the ninth century, occupy the first place; see chapter 3.

[16] DC, I, ch. 40, 205–6. The ceremony is based on the coronation ritual for an emperor.

[17] G. Vikan, 'Art and Marriage in Early Byzantium', *DOP*, 44 (1990), 145–66; cf. Ph. Koukoules, *Vyzantinon Vios kai Politeia*, 6 vols. (Athens, 1948–55), vol. 4, 134–41; I thank Professor Bariša Krekić for his observation that the crowns are probably more like ancient filets tied around the head.

[18] The ceremony is filled out by several sections of the previous chapter of the *De cerimoniis*, relating to the marriage of an imperial prince, DC, I, ch. 39 (on the marriage of an emperor, 196–202), including descriptions of the wedding chamber, 198–202.

[19] DC, I, ch. 41, 214–16.

[20] The symbolism of these objects is not entirely clear: if they are intended to represent pomegranates, an allusion to the properties of that fruit in relation to female fertility would be entirely appropriate. Koukoules, *Vyzantinon Vios kai Politeia*, 4, 145–6, believes the *rodiones* are golden apples, symbols of love.

[21] Theophanes, AM 6262, de Boor I, 445, for the date; AM 6289, de Boor I, 472, for the chamber. See also Judith Herrin, 'The Imperial Feminine in Byzantium,' *Past and Present* 169 (2000), 3–35, esp. 25–7.

[22] G. Dagron, 'Nés dans la pourpre,' *TM* 10 (1994), 105–42.

[23] DC, II, ch. 21, 615–19.

[24] The prescribed form for the baptism of the son of an emperor is given in DC, II, ch. 22, 619–20.

[25] Theophanes, AM 6262, de Boor I, 445; Mango/Scott, 614.

[26] In the course of these four years nothing is recorded about Irene and her young son. They probably resided in the Great Palace and attended all formal ceremonies.

[27] For instance, when Sophia, widow of Justin II, refused to move out and allow Tiberios and his wife to occupy them; see Averil Cameron, 'The Empress Sophia', *Byzantion* 45 (1975), 5–21.

[28] Theophanes, AM 6268, de Boor I, 450; Mango/Scott, 621.

[29] G. Dagron, *Empereur et prêtre. Etude sur le 'césaropapisme' byzantin* (Paris, 1996), 98–9.

[30] Theophanes, AM 6291, de Boor I, 473–4; the eldest, Nikephoros, had already been blinded in 792 (ibid., AM 6284, de Boor I, 468) when the other four lost their tongues. How any rebels could have thought that these mutilated figures would make the figureheads of a successful coup is unclear, but as sons of Constantine V they had special imperial credentials. Even under Michael I in 812 this still counted for something (see below).

[31] Theophanes, AM 6272, de Boor I, 453; cf. I. Rochow, in Lilie, *Eirene und Konstantin VI*, 12 and 332–3.

[32] Indeed, the *Chronicle* of Theophanes records nothing relating to Irene or her family between 776 and 780.

[33] Kedrenos, II, 19–20; cf. W. Treadgold, 'An Indirectly Preserved Source for the reign of Leo IV', *JÖB* 34 (1984), 69–76.

[34] The so-called *Life of Irene*, which is based on the *Chronicle* of Theophanes, stresses her deep iconophile convictions in the same way; see W. Treadgold, 'An Unpublished Saint's Life of the Empress Irene (BHG 2205)', *BF* 8 (1982), 236–51.

[35] Law against infanticide/abortion: Council *in Trullo*, canon 91, G. Ralles and M. Potles, eds., *Syntagma ton theion kai hieron kanonon* ... 6 vols. (Athens, 1852–9), II, 518–19; tr. in G. Nedungatt and M. Featherstone, eds. *The Council in Trullo Revisited = Kanonika* 6 (Rome, 1995), 171.

[36] Miracles of the Virgin *tes Peges*, *AASS*, November III, 880; C. Mango, *Art of the Byzantine Empire 312–1453* (Englewood Cliffs, New Jersey, 1972), 156–7.

[37] Theophanes, AM 6273, de Boor I, 454; Mango/Scott, 626.

[38] Cécile Morrisson, 'L'impératrice Irène (780–802)', *Bulletin* (Club français de la Médaille) 84 (1984), 118–20; *DOC*, III, pt 1, 337, plate XIII, type 1. A. Christophilopoulou, 'He antivasileia eis to Vyzantion', *Symmeikta* 2 (1970), 1–144, esp. 20–29.

[39] Theophanes, AM 6273, de Boor I, 455.

[40] Theophanes, AM 6274, de Boor I, 455; *Royal Frankish Annals*, anno 781; *Annales Mosellani*, anno 781.

[41] Michael McCormick, 'Textes, Images et Iconoclasme dans le cadre des relations entre Byzance et l'Occident Carolingien', in *Testo e Immagine nell'Alto Medioevo*, Settimane di Studio di Spoleto 41 (1994), 95–158, esp. 127–33.

[42] Theophanes, AM 6274, de Boor I, 456; Mango/Scott, 629.

[43] N. Oikonomides, 'A Note on the Campaign of Staurakios in the Peloponnesos (783/4),' *ZRVI* 38 (1999/2000), 61–6.

[44] Theophanes, AM 6276, de Boor I, 457; Mango/Scott, 631.

[45] J. Darrouzès, 'Les listes épiscopales . . .'; the suggestion that Constantine V had created about eight new bishoprics in this area is not borne out by later evidence, but see E. Kountoura-Galake, 'New Fortresses, Bishops in eighth-century Thrace,' *REB* 55 (1997), 279–89.

[46] Theophanes, AM 6276, de Boor I, 457–8; Mango/Scott, 631.

[47] Ibid., this is confirmed in *The Life of the Patriarch Tarasios by Ignatios the Deacon*, ed. and tr. S. Efthymiadis (Aldershot, 1998), para. 10, where Tarasios is designated by Paul to be his successor.

[48] Theophanes, AM 6277, de Boor I, 458–60; Efthymiadis, ed., *Life of Tarasios*, para. 14.

[49] *Sakra divalis*, Mansi, XII, 984E–986D (Latin translation); ibid., 1002D–1007C (the Greek).

[50] Mansi, XII, 986D–990B.

[51] Ibid., XII, 1077C–86B; cf. Pope Hadrian's letter to the emperors, ibid., 1055A–72; E. Lamberz, 'Studien zur Überlieferung der Akten des VII. Ökumenischen Konzils. Der Brief Hadrians I an Konstantin VI und Irene (JE 2448),' *Deutsches Archiv*, 53 (1997), 1–43.

[52] Theophanes, AM 6278, de Boor I, 461–2; Efthymiadis, ed., *Life of Tarasios*, para. 26.

[53] 'Nika!' had been the slogan of those who rioted against Justinian's rule in 532, which led to the destruction of large parts of the centre of Constantinople; see Introduction.

[54] Theophanes, AM 6279, de Boor I, 462.

[55] The title *ek prosopou* suggests that he was her personal representative at the proceedings in Nicaea, but his presence is not noted in the records of the sessions, and is preserved in later sources only, see Lilie, *Eirene und Konstantin VI*, 37.

[56] Mansi, XII, 991–1154, and XIII, 1–486, for the full records; the Sixth Session (Mansi, XIII, 204–364) is translated by D. J. Sahas, *Logos and Icon. Sources in Eighth-Century Iconoclasm* (Toronto, 1986); cf. Herrin, *The Formation of Christendom* (London, 1989), 417–23; *Nicée II, 787–1987. Douze siècles d'images religieuses*, eds. F. Boespflug and N. Lossky (Paris, 1987).

[57] M.-F. Auzépy, 'La place des moines à Nicée II (787)', *Byzantion* 58 (1988), 5–21.

[58] Theophanes, AM 6280, de Boor I, 463; Mansi, XIII, 416E.

[59] Auzépy, 'La place des moines'.

[60] A. Kartsonis, 'Protection against All Evil: Function, Use and Operation of Byzantine Historiated Phylacteries,' *BF* 20 (1994), 73–102, on *enkolpia* with the Crucifixion; cf. K. Corrigan, 'Text and Image on an Icon of the Crucifixion at Mount Sinai', in R. Ousterhout and L. Brubaker, eds., *The Sacred Image East and West* (Urbana/Chicago, 1995), 445–62 (a detailed analysis of a more complex image with an epigram but one that may have drawn on earlier examples).

[61] P. Speck, *Theodoros Studites. Jamben auf verschiedene Gegenstände* (Berlin, 1968).

[62] Theophanes on the marriage, AM 6281, de Boor I, 463; cf. Lilie, *Eirene und Konstantin VI*, 199–202; Speck, *Kaiser Konstantin VI*, 203–8.

[63] Theophanes, AM 6281, de Boor I, 464.

[64] Theophanes, AM 6282, de Boor I, 464.

[65] Theophanes, AM 6282, de Boor I, 464–5.

[66] Theophanes, AM 6282, de Boor I, 464.

[67] Theophanes, AM 6283, de Boor I, 465–6.

[68] Theophanes, AM 6283, de Boor I, 466; W. E. Kaegi, Jr., *Byzantine Military Unrest, 471–843. An Interpretation* (Amsterdam, 1981), 246, 250–1, 160–2, 266–7.

[69] Theophanes, AM 6283, de Boor I, 466.

[70] Speck, *Kaiser Konstantin VI*, 224–5, 226–8, 230–1.

[71] Theophanes, AM 6283, de Boor I, 466–7; cf. the accusation made only in late Syriac sources that Constantine was scandalised by Irene's affair with Elpidios, and used this as a pretext to order that his mother should no longer be called empress: Michael the Syrian, *Chronique*, book XII, iii (vol. 3, fasc. i, 9), and Bar Hebraeus, book X, 119. This account is hopelessly confused with the much earlier revolt of Elpidios, *strategos* of Sicily, who fled to the Arabs (see above), and draws on the familiar tropes of accusing a woman in authority of both weakness and adultery (e.g. she made peace with the Arabs, 'according to a woman's custom').

[72] The date of her birth is not recorded and might have occurred earlier, since Constantine and Maria were married in November 788. Even if she was born in the Porphyra, Irene is never permitted the epithet *porphyrogennetos*, which would certainly have been given to a son. Dagron, 'Nés dans la poupre', 129–30, on the inclusion of daughters in the imperial family. But only the eleventh-century *porphyrogennetoi*, Zoë and Theodora, are given this name, ibid., 118.

[73] Theophanes, AM 6284, de Boor I, 467.

[74] Theophanes, AM 6284–5, de Boor I, 467, 468–9.

[75] Theophanes, AM 6284, de Boor I, 467–8; cf. Theodoros Korres, 'He Byzantinoboulgarike Antiparathese stis arches tou 9ou ai. kai he sphage ton strateumaton tou Nikephorou A' ste Boulgaria (Ioulios 811),' *Byzantina* 18 (1995/6), 167–93.

[76] Theophanes, AM 6284, de Boor I, 468.

[77] Theophanes, AM 6285, de Boor I, 469.

[78] Theophanes, AM 6287, de Boor I, 469; Efthymiadis, ed., *Life of Tarasios*, paras. 39–44.

[79] Theophanes, AM 6287, de Boor I, 469 (on Maria's tonsure), and see below on the monastery of the Virgin on Prinkipo.

[80] Theophanes, AM 6287–8, de Boor I, 470; cf. Efthymiadis, ed., *Life of Tarasios*, paras. 45–46, where Ignatios likens the patriarch to John the Baptist confronted by Herod for his opposition to the second marriage.

[81] Theophanes, AM 6287, de Boor I, 469.

[82] Theophanes, AM 6288, de Boor I, 470–1.

[83] Theophanes, AM 6289, de Boor I, 471. His tomb is not recorded in the list of imperial burials in the *Book of Ceremonies*.

[84] The event is recorded in a description by Constantine, Bishop of Tios, see below.

[85] Theophanes, AM 6289, de Boor I, 472; Judith Herrin, 'Blinding in Byzantium', in *Polypleuros Nous. Festschrift Peter Schreiner*, eds. Georgios Makris and Cordula Scholz (Munich/Leipzig, 2000), 56–68.

[86] Theophanes, AM 6198, de Boor I, 375; cf. his subsequent blinding of the Archbishop of Ravenna, who was exiled to Pontos but returned to Ravenna after the death of Justinian; see *Le Liber pontificalis*, ed. L. Duchesne, 2 vols. (Rome, 1886–92), I, 389; tr. R. Davis, *The Book of the Pontiffs* (Liverpool, 1989), 90, 91.

[87] On Theodote, see Lilie, *Eirene und Konstantin VI*, 274–7.

[88] For the coins, see Morrisson, 'L'impératrice Irène'; *DOC*, III, pt 1, 337–9, plate XIV. For a full discussion of this use of the title *basileus*, see Lilie, ibid., 277–9; L. Burgmann, 'Die Novellen der Kaiserin Eirene', *Fontes minores* 4 (1981), 1–36.

[89] Burgmann, 'Die Novellen', 16, 26.

[90] See the recent study edited by A. Davids, *The Empress Theophano* (Cambridge, 1994), with important contributions by Karl Leyser, Odilo Engels and Kriniye Ciggaar. A similar tendency is evident in eleventh-century England, where the widowed Queen Emma ruled with her two sons, and far better than they could alone. Her authority had also been established over time and people had become used to her regal ways; see P. Stafford, 'Queen Emma, women and power in eleventh-century England', in Anne J. Duggan, ed., *Queens and Queenship in Medieval Europe* (Woodbridge, 1997), 3–29, and her book, *Queen Emma and Queen Edith* (Cambridge, 1997); cf. R. Hiestand, 'Eirene-Basileus, die Frau als Herrscherin im Mittelalter', in Hecker, ed., *Der Herrscher*, 253–83.

[91] This Nikephoros is going to lead the coup against her in 802, see Treadgold, *Byzantine Revival*, 119–22, 127–8.

[92] Patria, III, ch. 173; DC, I, ch. 32, 173 for the *xenon*; Magdalino, *Constantinople médiévale*, 23–25; A. Berger does not believe in the existence of a Late Antique hippodrome in the area, *Untersuchungen zu den Patria Konstantinoupoleos* (Bonn, 1988), 588–90. On the *Patria Konstantinoupoleos*, see Note on the Sources for Irene.

[93] Theophanes, AM 6285, de Boor I, 469. The *ergodosia* at Eleutherios may have been part of the original construction, but they were surely expanded after the fire, even if they did not completely replace the Chrysion.

[94] For a most complete catalogue of Byzantine silks, see A. Muthesius, *Byzantine Silk Weaving AD 400 to AD 1200* (Vienna, 1997).

[95] Efthymiadis, ed., *Life of Tarasios*, para. 37, 187; In c.815–17 Theophanes the Confessor was imprisoned in a cell at the Eleutherios, confirming that the palace continued in official use.

[96] Theophanes, AM 6283, de Boor I, 467.

[97] Theophanes, AM 6295, de Boor I, 476.

[98] This dedication implies that the monastery was also under the protection of the Theotokos, see Treadgold, 'Unpublished Life of Irene', 245.

[99] See chapter 3 below.

[100] Patria, III, ch. 85; Berger, *Untersuchungen*, 341, 634; Magdalino, *Constantinople médiévale*, 30.

[101] Theophanes, AM 6293, de Boor I, 475. In addition, she cancelled the *komerkia* (sic), customs dues levied at Abydos and Hieron, on all merchandise passing through the Bosphoros. These were later reimposed by Nikephoros I.

[102] DC, I, ch. 32, 173. The palace complex, *oikos ton Eleutheriou*, sustained its identity, eventually becoming linked with another similar estate, see Magdalino, *Constantinople médiévale*, 25 n.49.

[103] Patria, III, ch. 77.

[104] Patria, III, chs. 17 and 154.

[105] Patria, III, ch. 9; Berger, *Untersuchungen*, 558, points out that the charge against Constantine V is quite legendary. For the account of the Bishop of Tios, see F. Halkin, *Euphémie de Chalcédoine* (Brussels, 1965), 81–106.

[106] Patria, III, ch. 142; *AASS*, November III, 880B–C.

[107] M.-F. Auzépy, 'La destruction de l'icône du Christ de la Chalcé par Léon III; propagande ou réalité?', *Byzantion* 60 (1990), 445–92, for a survey of the myths accrued to this alleged destruction. Since the pre-history of the Christ image is greatly disputed by modern experts, Irene's particular role cannot be specified.

[108] Michael I (811–13) is reported to have been very generous in his support of ecclesiastical institutions but no major buildings are attributed to his brief reign.

[109] According to the *Patria*, he had also served as *koitonites* (a eunuch official) of Irene, Patria, III, ch. 156; Theophanes, AM 6282–3, de Boor I, 465, 466; cf. Winkelmann, *Quellenstudien*, 156.

[110] Efthymiadis, ed., *Life of Tarasios*, paras. 21–23, 180–1.

[111] E. Patlagean, 'L'histoire de la femme déguisée en moine et l'évolution de la sainteté feminine à Byzance', *Studi Medievali* 3rd series 17 (1976), 597–623, repr. in her *Structure Sociale, Famille, Chrétienté à Byzance* (London, 1981); N. Delierneux, 'Virilité physique et sainteté feminine dans l'hagiographie orientale du IVe au VIIe siècle', *Byzantion* 67 (1997), 179–243; Herrin, 'The imperial feminine', 29–31.

[112] Anna Wilson, 'Female Sanctity in the Greek calendar: the *Synaxarion* of Constantinople', in Richard Hawley and Barbara Lewick, eds., *Women in Antiquity. New Assessments* (London, 1995), 233–47.

[113] Efthymiadis, ed., *Life of Tarasios*, para. 66 (p. 161.16), 203–4.

[114] Theophanes, AM 6282, de Boor I, 464. 19–21; Mango/Scott, 639.

[115] Ibid., de Boor I, 464.16–17; Mango/Scott, 638–9.

[116] Ibid., de Boor I, 464–5; Mango/Scott, 639.

[117] Ibid., de Boor I, 464.25; Mango/Scott, 639.

[118] Theophanes, AM 6295, de Boor I, 478.2; Mango/Scott, 656.

[119] Theophanes, AM 6290–1, de Boor I, 473–5; Winkelmann, *Quellenstudien*, 157, 193. The precise relationship between the empress and Constantine is unclear, but he must be either her brother, brother-in-law or cousin.

[120] Theophanes, AM 6304, de Boor I, 496.

[121] The (Tes)Serantapechos family is, however, well represented in later centuries in the administration of central Greece and Peloponnesos, indicating that Irene's

descendants continued to hold public office often at a high level in the region of her birth; see Judith Herrin, 'Realities of Byzantine Provincial Government: Hellas and Peloponnesos 1180–1205', *DOP* 29 (1975), 253–84, esp. 270–71, 276.

[122] *Royal Frankish Annals*, a. 798; Lilie, *Eirene und Konstantin VI*, 205 (stressing that Irene's position as emperor was much weaker than her son's); Speck, *Kaiser Konstantin VI*, 323–6, with a firm analysis of Nikephoros' concern to promote this image, which justified his coup d'état.

[123] Theophanes, AM 6291, de Boor I, 474; cf. the full description in DC, I, ch. 10 (71–86), and ch. 5 (47–52) for the acclamations of the day, and the nine receptions held at different places on the way back from the Holy Apostles, where the Blues and the Greens perform additional acclamations.

[124] N. Oikonomidès, *Les listes de préséance byzantins des IXe et Xe siècles* (Paris, 1972), 349 (Macedonia), 352 (Kephalonia).

[125] J. Darrouzès, *Notitiae episcopatuum ecclesiae Constantinopolitanae* (Paris, 1981), no. 2 (dated to the period of Nikephoros I, 802–11).

[126] Theophanes, AM 6290, de Boor I, 473; Mango/Scott, 651.

[127] The hint is contained in four words ('ut traderent ei imperium'); see Speck, *Kaiser Konstantin VI*, 326–8, 739, note 29; Lilie, *Eirene und Konstantin VI*, 206.

[128] This is the theory of Paul Speck, *Kaiser Konstantin VI*, 328–33, 359–66, on which see below.

[129] Modern historians regularly view Irene's sole rule as a period which marked a reduction in the power of Byzantium in relation to the West: Charles's authority growing as Irene's declines, see Lilie, *Eirene und Konstantin VI*, 205; W. Ohnsorge, 'Das Kaisertum der Eirene und die Kaiserkrönung Karls des Grossen', *Saeculum* 14 (1964), 221–47 (repr. in his *Konstantinopel und der Okzident* (Darmstadt, 1966) and in H. Hunger, ed. *Das byzantinische Herrscherbild* (Darmstadt, 1975); Janet L. Nelson, 'Women at the court of Charlemagne: A Case of Monstrous Regiment?', in John Carmi Parsons, ed., *Medieval Queenship* (Stroud, 1994), 43–62. In contrast, Irene's proposal to Charlemagne has been seen as a political alliance inspired by the fifth-century example of Pulcheria; see Christine Angelidi, *Pulcheria. La Castità al Potere (c.399–c.455)* (Milan, 1996), 137–8. She notes that the two empresses are commemorated on the same day, 7 August, in the *Synaxarion* of Constantinople.

[130] *Opus Caroli Regis Contra Synodum (Libri Carolini)*, ed. Ann Freeman, MGH, Concilia, II, suppl. I (Hannover, 1998); Ann Freeman, 'Scripture and Image in the *Libri Carolini*', in *Testo e Immagine nell'Alto Medievo*, Settimane ... 41 (1994), 163–88; M.-F. Auzépy, 'Francfort et Nicée II', in *Das Frankfurter Konzil von 794. Kristallisationspunkt Karolingischer Kultur*, ed. R. Berndt, 2 vols. (Mainz, 1997), I, 279–300; Herrin, *The Formation of Christendom*, 434–44.

[131] *Vita Hadrianis*, para. 97, records the burial of Pope Hadrian on 26 December of the 4th indiction (795) and *Vita Leonis*, para 1, Leo III's election the following day; see *Liber pontificalis*, I, 514, II, 1; *The Lives of the Eighth-Century Popes*, tr. R. Davis (Liverpool, 1992), 172, 179.

[132] *Das Constitutum Constantini*, ed. H. Fuhrmann, MGH Fontes iuris Germaniae (Hannover, 1968). On the apocalyptic dimension to the coronation, see W. Brandes, ' "Tempora periculosa sunt." Eschatalogisches im Vorfeld der

Kaiserkrönung Karls des Grossen', in *Das Frankfurter Konzil*, I, 49–79.

[133] D. Bullough, 'Europae Pater', *English Historical Review* 85 (1970), 59–105; Herrin, *The Formation of Christendom*, 295, 446–53. For the possibility that Charles intended to construct his own city on the model of Constantine at Paderborn, renamed Karlsburg, see R. Collins, *Charlemagne* (London, 1998), 140.

[134] *799. Kunst und Kultur der Karolingerzeit*, 3 vols., ed. C. Stiegemann and M. Wemhoff (Mainz, 1999), esp. the articles by M. Becker, I, 22–36, and D. Bullough, III, 36–46; and *Liber pontificalis, Vita Leonis*, paras. 11–15, II, 4–5, on the plot and Leo's decision to visit Charles, tr. 184–7; and *RFA*, a. 799.

[135] *RFA*, a. 800, 801, for the details, which are entirely overlooked in the *Vita Leonis* (where all the ceremonial receptions are focused on Leo on his return from Charles in 799, paras. 19–20, II, 5, tr. 188–9); see also Collins, *Charlemagne*, 144–7.

[136] P. Classen, 'Karl der Grosse, das Papstum und Byzanz' in *Karl der Grosse: Lebenswerk und Nachleben*, ed. W. Braunfels, 5 vols. (Düsseldorf, 1965–8), I, 537–608; and 'Italien zwischen Byzanz und den Franken', *Settimane di Studio ... 27* (1981), 919–71. For recent bibliography, see Lilie, *Eirene und Konstantin VI*, 206–10.

[137] Speck, *Kaiser Konstantin VI*, 333–50, 359–66; cf. Lilie's critique, *Eirene und Konstantin VI*, 213–15.

[138] Herrin, *The Formation of Christendom*, 459–62.

[139] Since hair style might also denote loyalty to the eastern capital, a ceremonial comb and scissors might accompany the costume; see Herrin, *The Formation of Christendom*, 425. On the imperial insignia and official costumes, see K. Wessel, 'Insignien', *Real-lexikon der Byzantinischen Kunst* III, 369–498.

[140] On unction, see Janet L. Nelson, 'National Synods, Kingship as Office, and Royal Anointing: an Early Medieval Syndrome', *SCH*, 7 (1971), 41–59; 'Symbols in Context: Rulers' Inauguration Rituals in Byzantium and the West in the Early Middle Ages', *SCH* 13 (1976), 97–119 (both repr. in her *Politics and Ritual in Early Medieval Europe* (London, 1986).

[141] Theophanes, AM 6294, de Boor I, 475; *RFA*, a. 802, Lilie, *Eirene und Konstantin VI*, 210–12.

[142] Theophanes, AM 6295, de Boor I, 476–9.

[143] Theophanes, AM 6295, de Boor I, 480; Treadgold, Unpublished Life of Irene, 245; cf. Mango/Scott, 659 n.16.

SOURCES FOR CHAPTER 3: EUPHROSYNE

Of the three women featured in this study, Euphrosyne commands the least attention and is noted in fewest sources and most rarely. Indeed, this chapter represents an attempt to restore some sense of her biography, since it is completely lacking in contemporary accounts. The reasons for such neglect are obvious: Euphrosyne only attained a momentary instance of fame when she became the second wife of Emperor Michael II. Although the chroniclers note that she had to be brought out of a monastery for the marriage, and that she returned to the monastic life shortly after her husband's death, they barely trouble to consider her significance.

One source which may illuminate her life is therefore the monastic milieu in which she passed many years. While the monastery founded by the Empress Irene on the island of Prinkipo is not well documented, it functioned like most other female communities of the time, and so its routines may be established by comparison with other records. Sources for the monastic life of women are found in the Lives of female saints of the period, many of whom founded or directed such communities. Recently a collection of such Lives has been edited by Alice-Mary Talbot, thus making available translations of some of the most interesting texts. From this more general background, we can get closer to the specific details of Euphrosyne's life through the few letters addressed to her mother, Maria, by St Theodore of the Stoudios. This iconophile leader, who died in exile in 826, was a prolific letter-writer, and through his correspondence with other nuns and secular women a composite picture of their role in sustaining iconophile practices can be built up.

Once established as empress, Euphrosyne again moves into a well-documented position, although very few activities are directly associated with her. At least we can guess at the major tasks she is required to undertake as the wife of Michael II. Her role as stepmother to the young prince Theophilos is totally undocumented until she arranges his marriage (which is mentioned in two different versions: the *Life of Theodora* and tenth-century compilations of the writers who continued the *Chronographia* of Theophanes). Then, a chance account of the battle for Amorion in 838, preserved in much later Syriac sources based on Arabic accounts of the campaign, mentions an initiative taken by Euphrosyne. This is found in the *World History* attributed to Bar Hebraeus, and the *Chronicle* of Michael the Syrian, sources compiled very much later than the ninth century but which appear to derive from earlier ones. Their descriptions of the Arab campaign to capture Amorion, which proved entirely victorious and are therefore much more detailed than the Greek versions, present a surprising picture of the now widowed empress. Euphrosyne sensed an imminent danger to her stepson's power and alerted him to the threat of civil war.

In trying to reconstruct Euphrosyne's situation during the reign of Theophilos the obvious bias of the sources, nearly all iconophile and most compiled in the tenth century, creates many difficulties. While the emperor's achievements were certainly recorded by iconoclast authors sympathetic to his ideals, their accounts were systematically destroyed after his death. In their place, the compilations of Leo *grammatikos*, Theodosios Melissenos, the Continuator of George the Monk and pseudo-Symeon (Symeon the magister), all draw on the Chronicle of Symeon *logothetes*, of which there is no critical edition or translation. Another group of anonymous authors, called collectively the Continuators of Theophanes, were commissioned by Constantine VII (945–59) to compile a historical record from 813, the point at which the abbot of Megas Agros ended his *Chronographia*. Writing, as they did, over a century after the events of Theophilos' rule, they had a clear agenda: to glorify the founder of the Macedonian dynasty, which succeeded that of Michael III of Amorion in 867, and to vilify the heretical iconoclasts. Everything they learned about the first half of the ninth century is viewed through this lens of deeply prejudiced opinions.

Few of the Emperor Theophilos' activities are presented as a coherent policy; most are subjected to critical analysis from a religious perspective. When no relationship to theology can be ascertained, the record may be quite inoffensive. But as soon as ecclesiastical politics are involved, the condemnation is immediately noticeable. The persecution of icon venerators, which lessened under Michael II and strengthened again under Theophilos, naturally forms a key element. Martyrs such as Euthymios, who died after a severe whipping, and dedicated iconophiles like Methodios, the papal legate, Lazaros a painter and the brothers Theophanes and Theodoros, who were tattooed, are the heroes; Theophilos is the arch-villain. It is all very predictable. In addition, while the persecutor and heretic is shown in the worst possible light, losing his self-control, mad with fury at iconophile resistance, his wife, his stepmother and mother-in-law are all portrayed as good women, that is, iconophiles. The implication of these accounts is almost gender-specific: women are the guardians of orthodox iconophile practice, it is claimed, while male emperors who model themselves on the Syrian rulers of the eighth century are always wicked icon-smashers.

In none of these stray references is there any sense of Euphrosyne as an individual or as a representative of dynastic power. Yet she was clearly a person of a certain character, who was aware of both of these aspects of her life. Her ability to preserve a sense of imperial inheritance through the many years in which she and her mother were ostracised from the court indicates as much. But to establish a serious biography of her is still a hazardous business and this chapter has more conditional verbs than the others.

NOTES TO CHAPTER 3: EUPHROSYNE (PAGES 130–184)

[1] Theophanes, AM 6274, de Boor I, 455.

[2] Had she been crowned as empress, Maria's coronation would have been performed by her husband, the sole male emperor, Constantine. He was still only sixteen years old but much younger heirs were sometimes forced to crown older men as co-emperor. The fact that Irene did not wish to allow her son to exercise his imperial rights, let alone share the imperial status with Maria, reflects her desire to control the young couple.

[3] Theophanes, AM 6281, de Boor I, 463.

[4] M.-H. Fourmy and M. Leroy, 'La Vie de S. Philarète,' *Byzantion* 9 (1934), 85–170. A new edition and English translation is under preparation by Professor Lennart Rydén.

[5] Marie-France Auzépy, 'De Philarète, de sa famille, et de certains monastères de Constantinople', in C. Jolivet-Lévy, M. Kaplan and J.-P. Sodini, eds, *Les Saints et leur sanctuaire à Byzance* (Paris, 1993), 117–35; Claudia Ludwig, *Sonderformen byzantinischer Hagiographie und ihr literarisches Vorbild* (Frankfurt am Main, 1997).

[6] What this implies about his relationship with Euphrosyne and his possible knowledge of her future is not clear. Some have seen the composition as Niketas' way of using his strong family connections to get out of exile.

[7] Ludwig, as above, 76–7.

[8] Martha Vinson, 'The Life of Theodora and the Rhetoric of the Byzantine Bride Show', *JÖB*, 49 (1999), 31–60, esp. 47–52.

[9] Vinson, 'Rhetoric of the Bride Show', 42–6, on the methods of vilification.

[10] Theophanes, AM 6300, de Boor I, 483; Vinson, 'Rhetoric of the Bride Show', 41–6; Paul Speck, 'Ein Brautschau für Staurakios?', *JÖB* 49 (1999), 25–30.

[11] Other sources record that Nikephoros was unusually ascetic and quite unlikely to have behaved in the manner of which he is accused by Theophanes.

[12] *The Chronicle of John Malalas*, tr. Elizabeth Jeffreys, Michael Jeffreys and Roger Scott (Melbourne, 1986), book 14, 3–4, 191–3.

[13] *Parastaseis syntomoi chronikai*, ch. 141, Eng. tr. 141.

[14] P. Magdalino, 'Paphlagonians in Byzantine high society', in *He Byzantine Mikra Asia* (Athens, 1998), 141–50, claims that 'Irene is likely to have been influenced in her choice by her chief minister and adviser, the powerful eunuch Staurakios, who according to one version of the *Life of Philaretos* supervised the entire proceedings' (149). While this draws attention to the less important role of young Constantine VI in the selection of his bride, there is no evidence that Staurakios favoured a girl from Paphlagonia because it was his original homeland; he seems to have come from Cappadocia. Nor is it necessary to attribute the choice of Maria to his influence; Irene would certainly have had her own ideas on what sort of girl she wanted.

[15] Auzépy, 'De Philarète', 121.

[16] For a contemporary use of the name Hypatia with similar connotations, see J. van den Gheyn, 'Acta graeca ss. Davidis, Symeonis et Georgii Mitylenae in insula Lesbo,' *Analecta Bollandiana* 18 (1899), para. 19 (*Acts of David . . . in Byzantine Defenders of Images*, 193–6): St Symeon cures a young woman (Hypatia) by renaming her Febronia and allowing her to dedicate herself to the monastic life.

[17] R.-J. Lilie, *PmbZ*, 1705, 540–1.

[18] *The Life of the Patriarch Tarasios by Ignatios the Deacon*, ed. and tr. S. Efthymiadis (Aldershot, 1998), paras. 39, 41, 44, on the shameful and untrue accusation of poison.

[19] Theophanes, AM 6287, de Boor I, 469.

[20] Theophanes, AM 6288, de Boor I, 470.

[21] *Synopsis Chronike*, ed. K. N. Sathas, *Mesaionike Bibliotheke* 7 (Venice, 1894), 128; Treadgold, *Byzantine Revival*, 271, 310, for Gastria (but it is not clear whether the Gastria was already functioning); Theophanes, AM 6295, de Boor I, 478, for Prinkipo.

[22] W. Treadgold, 'An Unpublished Saint's Life of the Empress Irene,' *BF* 8 (1982), 237–51.

[23] John of Ephesos, *Ecclesiastical History* II, 12, cited in Judith Herrin, 'In search of Byzantine women: three avenues of approach,' in *Images of Women in Antiquity*, eds. Averil Cameron and Amélie Kuhrt (London, 1983), 167–89; *Life of Saint Anthousa, daughter of Constantine V*, Eng. tr. *Byzantine Defenders of Images*, 24.

[24] *Life of St Athanasia of Aegina*, paras. 4–5, on the lack of fruit and lying on stones, ed. L. Carras, in *Maistor. Essays for Robert Browning*, ed. Ann Moffatt (Canberra, 1984), Eng. tr. *Holy Women of Byzantium*, 145–6; *Life of St Irene of Chrysobalanton*, paras. 14 and 38, ed. and tr. J.-O. Rosenqvist (Uppsala, 1986), on the single robe. While this is a much later text and may be a fiction, the details of monastic life it preserves seem to fit closely with what is known about nuns in the late eighth century. See also Alice-Mary Talbot, 'Women's Space in Byzantine Monasteries', *DOP* 52 (1998), 113–28.

[25] *Life of St Theodora of Thessaloniki*, paras. 22, 37, in *Holy Women of Byzantium*, 183, 195–6.

[26] Such a form of detention was quite different from the disciplinary measures taken against monks who committed grievous sins that required correction; see the *Rule of the Monastery of St John Stoudios* established by St Theodore, para. 25 'places of confinement', in *Byzantine Monastic Foundation Documents*, eds. J. Thomas and G. Constable (Washington DC, 2001), 107–8.

[27] *St Athanasia of Aegina*, para. 15, Eng. tr. 148; *Life of St Irene of Chrysobalanton*, ch. 13, 52–64, on evil spirit possession.

[28] S. Efthymiadis, 'Le Panégyrique de S. Théophane le Confesseur par S. Théodore Studite (BHG 1792b),' *Analecta Bollandiana*, 111 (1993), 259–90. For a summary of Megalo's life, see Mango/Scott, introduction to the *Chronographia* of Theophanes, pp. xlv, xlvii–xlviii. She is said to have developed a highly ascetic life, which drew attention to her in unflattering ways, but nothing reliable about her monastic existence is recorded. For the ceremonial self-dedication liturgy, see J. Goar, ed., *Euchologion sive Rituale Graecorum* (Venice 1730, repr. Graz 1960), 382–8.

[29] *Theodori Studitae Epistulae*, no. 323, ed. G. Fatouros, 2 vols. (Berlin/New York, 1992), II, 465–6.

[30] Council *in Trullo*, canon 45; tr. G. Nedungatt and M. Featherstone, eds., *The Council in Trullo Revisited = Kanonika* 6 (Rome, 1995), 126–8; Judith Herrin, ' "Femina byzantina": The Council *in Trullo* on women', *DOP* 46 (1992), 95–105.

[31] A brief notice about her life (c.756/7–808/9) is preserved in the *Synaxarion* of Constantinople, see *Byzantine Defenders of Icons*, 23–4. The claim that Irene wanted her to share imperial power with her seems a little exaggerated.

[32] *Theodori Studitae Epistulae*, ed. Fatouros, no. 62 (I, 173–4), cf. the letters to their mother Maria, 227, 309, 514 (II, 360–1, 452–3, 765–6).

[33] J. Gouillard, 'La femme de qualité dans l'oeuvre de S. Théodore le Studite', *JÖB* 30 (1982), part III, 445–52.

[34] Treadgold, 'Unpublished Saint's Life', 244–5.

[35] E. Malamut, 'La moniale à Byzance aux 8e–12e siècles', in K. Nikolaou, ed., *Taxis tou Orthodoxou Monachismou, 9ou–13ou aionou* (Athens, 1996), 63–76; Alice-Mary Talbot, 'A Comparison of Male and Female Monasticism', *Greek Orthodox Theological Review* 30 (1985), 4–20.

[36] *Synaxarion* notice for St Anthousa of Mantineon, *Byzantine Defenders of Images*, 16–19, esp. 18.

[37] Theophanes, AM 6295–6, de Boor I, 479–81, records the rebellion but does not link it to the deposed empress; this is a later addition (not in Genesios or Th Syn).

[38] Theophanes, AM 6301, 6304, de Boor I, 484, 497.

[39] Theophanes, AM 6303, de Boor I, 490–1; John Haldon, *The Byzantine Wars* (Stroud, 2001), 71–5.

[40] Theophanes, AM 6298, de Boor I, 481; Nikephoros' learning is described by Ignatios in his *Life of Patriarch Nikephoros I*, see Eng. tr. *Byzantine Defenders of Images*, 52–6. On the debate over the method of his selection, see G. Dagron, *Empereur et prêtre. Etude sur le 'césaropapisme' byzantin* (Paris, 1996), 231–2.

[41] Theophanes, AM 6301, de Boor I, 484.

[42] Theophanes, AM 6303, de Boor I, 492–3; Mango/Scott 674–5.

[43] Scriptor incertus, 335–40; Theophanes, AM 6305, de Boor I, 500–02; A. P. Kazhdan, *A History of Byzantine Literature (A.D. 650–850)*, (Athens, 1999), 208–11, on the author identified as the unknown writer, Scriptor incertus; David Turner, 'The Origins and Accession of Leo V (813–20)', *JÖB* 40 (1990), 713–201.

[44] Th Syn, 8–10; although Genesios records the story, 1: 6–8, he does not stress its significance.

[45] See H.-G. Beck, 'Byzantinische Gefolgschaftswesen', *Bayerische Akademie der Wissenschaften, Phil-Hist. Kl. Sitzungsberichte* (1996), 1–32, repr. in *Ideen und Realitaeten in Byzanz* (London, 1972), esp. 18–22.

[46] Irene died on 9 August of the same year, so no revolt in her name could be taken seriously, Theophanes, AM 6295, de Boor I, 408.

[47] Theophanes is unaware of a dinner party given for the two soldiers who were then invited to marry their host's daughters; Genesios, 22–3, has a splendid version disconnected from Bardanes, and the fullest elaboration is found in the mid-tenth-century Continuators of Theophanes (Th Syn, 44–5), although even here Thekla is not named.

[48] Theophanes, AM 6295, 6296, de Boor I, 479–80.

[49] Th Syn, 10, 16.

[50] Treadgold, *Byzantine Revival*, 226, assumes this was c.813, just after Leo V's accession.

[51] Theophanes, AM 6305, de Boor I, 502; Scriptor incertus, 340, on Michael of Amorion.

[52] J. F. Haldon, *Byzantine Praetorians* (Bonn, 1984), *Poikila Vyzantina* 3, 233, 239–40, 293–5, 298. Irene had dissolved the leading guard troops of the capital after 786, when their iconoclast loyalty made them a force hostile to her plan to restore icon veneration.

[53] Scriptor incertus, 346.

[54] Theophanes, AM 6305, de Boor I, 501.

[55] Scriptor incertus, 346, 349.

[56] Scriptor incertus, 350–62; Paul Alexander, 'The Iconoclastic Council of Saint Sophia and its Definition', *DOP* 7 (1953), 58–66.

[57] Leo grammatikos, 210–11, Genesios, 17–18.

[58] Paul Lemerle, 'Thomas le Slav', *TM* 1 (1965), 255–97.

[59] Th Syn, 78–9; Dagron, *Empereur et Prêtre*, 42, 49.

[60] But there is no official record as none of his acts have survived. The victorious iconophiles very effectively destroyed most of the evidence of their iconoclast opponents.

[61] *Theodori Studitae Epistulae*, no. 514, ed. Fatouros, II, 765–6.

[62] Leo grammatikos, 211; *Life of Patriarch Nikephoros*, in *Byzantine Defenders of Icons*, 130–1, the emperor orders 'a profound silence as regards any mention of icons'. Dagron, *Empereur et Prêtre*, 306–7.

[63] Th Syn, 78–9; Genesios, II, 14 (35), sees this improper marriage as evidence

of the emperor's lack of reason; cf. Pseudo-Symeon = Sym mag, 620. The two later Syriac sources, Michael the Syrian, 72, and Bar Hebraeus, 129, have roughly the right date but lots of 'absurd rumours' about how Euphrosyne did indeed bear the emperor a son but had it killed because she realised that it would be Jewish (on account of his Jewish and Athinganoi sympathies). It would corrupt the Syrian dynasty and bring shame on the ruling house, therefore it had to be put to death! Some iconophile sources ignore the marriage, see Treadgold, *Byzantine Revival*, 426 n.339.

[64] Leo grammatikos, 210, George the Monk, 789–90; Sym mag, 620–1. For the invalid nature of the marriage, see Th Syn, 79–86.

[65] Patria, III, 77.

[66] Sym mag, 328.

[67] D. Papachryssanthou, 'La Vie du patrice Nicétas: un confesseur du second iconoclasme', *TM* 3 (1986), 309–51; see also chapter 2.

[68] DC, II, ch. 42, 647.11; cf. P. Grierson, 'The tombs and obits of the Byzantine Emperors', *DOP* 16 (1962), 3–60.

[69] Auzépy, 'De Philarète', 122; cf. Speck, *Kaiser Konstantin VI*, 385, calls it an act of piety.

[70] Theodote may have buried Constantine VI at their monastery, but it is also possible that his remains were sent back to Maria, his first wife, to be buried on Prinkipo; see Grierson, 'Tombs and Obits', 54; cf. Lilie, *Eirene und Konstantin VI*, 274–7.

[71] *Vita Philareti*, 155, cf. family tree in Auzépy, 118–19, 122. But if they were not all dead and buried by 820, this information is irrelevant. Philaretos and Theosebo must have been interred but not necessarily the others. The two monasteries where her uncles and aunts were buried are not known from other sources; see R. Janin, *Les monastères de l'empire byzantin*, 2nd ed. (Paris, 1969), 76, 218.

[72] P. Geary, *Phantoms of Remembrance* (Princeton, 1994), and E. Van Houts, *Memory and Gender in Medieval Europe 900–1200* (London, 1999), 65–92, esp. 69–77, stressing the significance of oral testimony and the fact that women are more likely to provide it.

[73] Treadgold, *Byzantine Revival*, 247, and n.63 above.

[74] This of course separated the young prince from his stepmother, who appears to have remained an iconophile. But during the reigns of her husband and stepson, Euphrosyne kept her religious convictions discreetly in the background. Her upbringing had taught her how unwise it was to resist the official line on icons too publicly.

[75] See, for example, seals of two eunuch officials, Niketas, in charge of the empress's dining room, and Nikolaos, her notary: W. Seibt, *Die Byzantinische Bleisiegel in Österreich*, vol. 1: Kaiserhof (Vienna, 1978), nos. 48 and 80.

[76] In the Uspensky *taktikon*, c.842–3, i.e. at the end of the reign of Theophilos; see N. Oikonomidès, *Les listes de préséance byzantines des IXe et Xe siècles* (Paris, 1972), 47–63.

[77] In addition to the famous letter, partly translated by C. Mango, *The Art of the Byzantine Empire 312–1453* (Englewood Cliffs, New Jersey, 1972), 157–8, see the

list of silks sent to Frankia in 824, J. Ebersolt, *Les arts somptuaires de Byzance* (Paris, 1923), 57.

[78] *RFA* a. 824, merely records 'letters and presents'.

[79] Often silks produced many years before were brought out of storage to be sent as such gifts; A. Muthesius, 'Silken Diplomacy', in J. Shepard and S. Franklin, eds., *Byzantine Diplomacy* (Cambridge, 1992), 237–48.

[80] They were cited by Pope Hadrian in his letter addressed to the council of 787, which was not translated into Greek in its entirety.

[81] Michael II's letter to Louis the Pious, *MGH Concilia* II, 2 (Hannover, 1908), 475–80, with partial translation in Mango, *Art of the Byzantine Empire*, 157–8.

[82] Turner, 'The Origins of Leo V', 173–201, esp. 185–6 on Theodore's punishment; he addresses many letters to this Irene. See also A. P. Kazhdan and A.-M. Talbot, 'Women and Iconoclasm', *BZ* 84/85 (1991/2), 392–408; P. Hatlie, 'Women of discipline during the Second Iconoclasm', *BZ* 89 (1996), 37–44.

[83] Judith Herrin, 'The domestic and private context of icon veneration in Byzantium', in A. Mulder-Bakker and J. Wogan-Browne, eds., *Household, Family and Christian Tradition* (Turnhout, 2002 forthcoming).

[84] I. Ševčenko, 'Hagiography of the Iconoclast Period', in *Iconoclasm*, eds. Anthony Bryer and Judith Herrin (Birmingham, 1977), 113–31.

[85] Leo grammatikos, 213, Genesios, III, 1 (36); George the Monk, II, 797; in fact, although he was only sixteen there was no obvious alternative candidate.

[86] Leo grammatikos, 213.

[87] Genesios, III, 1; Th Syn, 84; W. Treadgold, 'The Problem of the Marriage of the Emperor Theophilos', *GRBS* 16 (1975), 325–40; but cf. Lilie, *PmbZ* 8167 (which favours a date of birth between 800 and 805). This would be dependent on Michael and Thekla celebrating their marriage at roughly the same time, which is not clearly established. In addition, the earlier birth date does not fit well with the declaration by Theophilos in 842, when he realised that he was dying, that he was still so young: see chapter 4.

[88] Dagron, *Empereur et Prêtre*, 57–8.

[89] Sym mag, 624.

[90] A. Markopoulos, 'Vios tes autokrateiras Theodoras (*BHG* 1731)', *Symmeikta* 5 (1983), 249–85; *Life of Theodora*, tr. Martha P. Vinson, in *Byzantine Defenders of Images*, with her important commentary in *JÖB*, 49 (1999), see chapter 4.

[91] Theophilos sends couriers to bring Theodora to Constantinople along with many other beauties, *Life of Theodora*, para 3.

[92] K. Nikolaou, 'Oi gynaikes sto bio kai sta erga tou Theophilou', *Symmeikta* 9 (1994), 137–51.

[93] Henry Maguire, ed., *Byzantine Court Culture from 829 to 1204* (Washington, DC, 1997), esp. his own contribution, 'The Heavenly Court', and that of A. P. Kazhdan and M. McCormick, 'The Social World of the Byzantine Court'; Oikonomidès, *Listes de préséance byzantines*, 21–9.

[94] Edited by Oikonomidès, *Listes de préséance byzantines*, 47–63.

[95] As Liutprand of Cremona discovered to his dismay in the mid-tenth century. His protests at the higher ranking of Bulgarian ambassadors, who took priority

over those from Otto I, reveal ignorance of Byzantine seating plans, as well as his own discomfort at being treated less well by Nikephoros II than by Constantine VII; see F. A. Wright, *Liudprand of Cremona. The Embassy to Constantinople and Other Writings* (London, 1930, repr. 1993).

[96] *Life of Theodora*, para. 4; Leo grammatikos confirms this, 214; but cf. Th Syn, 86.

[97] It forms a sharp contrast to the involuntary, forced departure of Theodora in 856, see chapter 4.

[98] Th Syn, 90.

[99] E. Van Houts, *Memory and Gender*, 84–90.

[100] Michael the Syrian, vol. III, book 12, section xx, p. 95; and Bar Hebraeus, I, 136, preserve the account of a man sent by Theophilos' mother, which seems too circumstantial to be doubted; see A. A. Vasiliev, *Byzance et les Arabes* (Brussels, 1935), I, 158.

[101] As above. For obvious reasons the Byzantine accounts of the defeat are much less detailed and fail to mention this incident. But as it provides a crucial explanation as to why Theophilos abandoned the defence of Amorion, the Arab sources appear entirely credible.

[102] Bury's masterly analysis, *ERE*, 263–71 mentions the Syriac sources but does not use them, cf. Haldon, *Byzantine Wars*, 78–82.

[103] On the Forty-Two Martyrs of Amorion, see A. P. Kazhdan, 'Hagiographical Notes', *Byzantion* 56 (1986), esp. section 14, 151–60.

[104] Sym mag, 628–9 (with Euphrosyne, this is the original version); cf. Th Syn, 90–91 (with Theoktiste, who was probably long since dead).

[105] Treadgold, *Byzantine Revival*, 310, calculates that she is two when this incident occurs.

[106] This is how the earliest version of the story is related by Pseudo-Symeon, see Sym mag, 628–9.

[107] Ioannes Scylitzes, *Synopsis historiarum*, ed. I. Thurn (Berlin/New York, 1973), 52–3.

[108] Sym mag, 629–30; Th Syn, 91–2.

[109] See chapter 2.

[110] DC, II, ch. 42, 647.14.

SOURCES FOR CHAPTER 4: THEODORA

Theodora is the only one of our empresses for whom a real biography exists. At last, you might think, a Byzantine source devoted to one of our 'women in purple', even though it may have been written quite some time after her death, by an unknown author. Most medieval histories remain anonymous and were often written long after the death of their subjects. But this text should provide a more reliable basis for our investigation than existed for either Irene or Euphrosyne. Sadly, this is not so. The author has a particular aim, which does not include a serious historical account of Theodora's role in ninth-century Byzantium. He is concerned to show how she became a saint when she restored the icons to their honoured place in the Byzantine church. Only those parts of her life which help to build up this iconophile role are treated.

In addition, he follows the rules for an imperial *basilikos logos*, adapting a rhetorical genre used to praise emperors for an exceptional woman. According to this literary model, established in the fourth century AD by Menander, aptly known as the Rhetor, there are certain aspects of the subject's life which must be covered: country of origin, family, birth and upbringing, temperament, accomplishments, actions (normally war and peace), fortune, comparison with others, death and epilogue. Earlier in the ninth century Niketas displayed a similar knowledge of the form in devising his Life of his grandfather Philaretos (see chapter 3). Despite the formal restrictions, this account should provide information about Theodora.

This is not the case, largely because Theodora serves as a symbolic link between the bad dynasty of Amorion (founded by Michael II, dominated by the wicked heretic and iconoclast Theophilos, and justly brought to an end by the death of Michael III), and the new dynasty established by Basil I in 867. Writing under the latter or his son, Leo VI, the author is required to whitewash Basil's past, extol the achievements of his dynasty, and demonstrate the religious errors and poor administration of the previous regime. His account is part of the process of sanctification which will establish Theodora as a holy woman for her notable role in reversing iconoclasm. This certainly makes it easier to concentrate on those parts of the life which demonstrate her saintliness and to omit or skate over others.

Since the author clearly knew very little about Theodora's background, her birth and upbringing receive much less attention than her accomplishments. Under this heading he can demonstrate Theodora's moral character, her quintessentially imperial traits, and the excellent virtues she embodied, which made her the obvious choice for empress. Having established how she came to be such a holy, devout and strong-minded Christian, an account is given of her marriage to the Emperor Theophilos. Her moral superiority is assured by her dedication to iconophile practices, while he remains a heretic, unable to reject the iconoclast principles of his father and his teacher, John the Grammarian. It is then a straightforward progression to her saintly activity in reversing her husband's iconoclasm and restoring the icons to their revered place in the church. Where a male subject would need to be praised for military victories and philanthropic activities, Theodora accomplishes all this and more through her superior qualities, which are reflected in her decision to condemn and uproot heresy. So this biographical source turns out to be a complex construct designed to promote one particular view of the empress.

Several other accounts of Theodora's family and life are preserved in histories compiled later than this Life and suffer from similar trends of distortion. Many concentrate less on Theodora and more on Theophilos, presenting him in the most unflattering terms. So while authors known as the Continuator of George the monk, Leo the *grammatikos* and Symeon the magister, use the material in the Life, they have a novel purpose: to create a negative portrait of the iconoclast emperor. They tend towards invective while the Life is unashamedly encomiastic. By identifying these basic functions, which are often well disguised by the generic models being followed, it may be possible to balance the highly uncritical with the most critical and take account of some of the inbuilt prejudices. But it is difficult to learn anything reliable about Theodora from sources written with such specific purposes.

From non-Greek sources a rather different picture emerges, one in which the empress features as a devoted wife and later a determined imperial widow. An Arabic account of the court of Theophilos, written by a diplomatic from Muslim Spain, survives by chance in translation – the original document is now lost. More detailed descriptions of Muslim victories in the regular Byzantine–Arab warfare of the mid-ninth century are preserved in Arabic sources (often of a much later date) than the Greek. The Byzantines were clearly much less willing to record their defeats in detail. Diplomatic correspondence between Constantinople, Rome and the centres of Carolingian power in the West contains a certain amount of information in Latin sources, such as the letter of Pope Nicholas I to Theodora. But this is still a very minimal documentation on which to base a biography.

Fortunately, the empress's central role in the restoration of icons features in several contemporary writings by iconophile saints and heroes, like Patriarch Methodios, and Theophanes *graptos*. Although the *Synodikon of Orthodoxy* does not survive in its original form of 843, the liturgical commemoration of the overthrow of iconoclasm and the return of the holy images contains much information about the event. Like the Life of Theodora, most of this is slanted to demonstrate her iconophile principles. None the less, more is preserved than for either of our other female rulers.

Yet modern historians have generally interpreted this evidence in a highly specific and gendered fashion. A prime example is the tendency to ignore Theodora's contribution to the restoration of icons, found in the 1995 *Oxford Dictionary of Byzantium* (entry on the Triumph of Orthodoxy, vol. III, pp. 2122–3). Here the eunuch Theoktistos 'overcame the reluctance of the empress' to restore the icons by gaining a pardon for Theophilos; arranged for the iconoclast patriarch to be deposed and replaced him by Methodios; held all the preliminary meetings to discuss how to proceed, some in his own house (which is correct) and generally stage-managed the whole event. While Theoktistos *was* a key player in the Triumph, it seems to me excessive to attribute the whole plan to his intervention. The sources can also be read another way – to suggest that Theodora also had an interest in restoring the holy images.

So this chapter poses particular problems of interpretations. Between the Scylla of the tenth-century accounts, which transform Theodora into a saint, and the Charybdis of modern (male) historians, who refuse to accept any of these claims and instead elevate the role of her male relations and advisers, there is a dangerous chasm. Navigating the heavy currents and treacherous undertow, I have tried to document a view which allows her some role without setting her up as a paragon of virtue.

NOTES TO CHAPTER 4: THEODORA (PAGES 185–239)

[1] A. Markopoulos, 'Vios tes autokrateiras Theodoras (*BHG* 1731)', *Symmeikta* 5 (1983), 249–85, para. 2, 257; *Life of Theodora*, tr. Martha P. Vinson, in *Byzantine Defenders of Images*, 362.

[2] *Costantino Porfirogenito, De Thematibus*, ed. A. Pertusi (Vatican, 1952), 72, 136–7, says it had been part of the Boukellarion but the area around Gangra, from

which Philaretos and his family came, had previously fallen under the Armeniakon. K. Belke, *Paphlagonien und Honorias. Tabula Imperii Byzantini*, vol. 9 (Vienna, 1996), 73–4; Treadgold, *Byzantine Revival*, 222–3.

[3] The *katepano* of Paphlagonia later assisted an official sent from Constantinople to the Crimea and on up the River Don to a site where the castle of Sarkel was constructed; see Th Syn, 123.

[4] The Life of George of Amastris suggests that the Rus constituted a novel and extremely frightening enemy during an attack prior to 842; see S. Franklin and J. Shepard, *The Emergence of Rus 750–1200* (London, 1996), 27–31.

[5] Paul Magdalino, 'Paphlagonians in Byzantine high society', in *He Byzantine Mikra Asia* (Athens, 1998), 141–50, traces this association of the inhabitants of Paphlagonia back to the early tenth century when a series of well-placed eunuchs from the region began to establish a prominent profile in the capital.

[6] D. Papachryssanthou, 'La Vie du patrice Nicétas, un confesseur du deuxième iconoclasme,' *TM*, 3 (1986), 309–51. This includes the brief *Synaxarion* notice, read on his name-day, which can be interpreted to mean that the family was related to Empress Irene. On this problematic relationship, which turns on the phrase 'hos syggenes', see F. Winkelmann, *Quellenstudien zur Herrschenden Klasse von Byzanz im 8. und 9. Jahrhundert* (Berlin, 1987), 184.

[7] Of course, eunuchs were created in many other places, occasionally for medical reasons. A slightly later example is furnished by the story preserved in the *Acts of David* ... (probably written after 863): a local man on the island of Aphousia, to which David's brother Symeon was banished in about 838, brought his youngest son to the saint begging for him to be castrated. The boy suffered from a large hernia which hung down to his knees and as a result his father wanted the saint to bless the operation. Through Symeon's appeals to the Lord, 'the doctor of all', the tumour shrank and the swollen mass was restored to its natural health, para. 24, 205–6. See K. Ringrose, *Transcendent Lives, Eunuchs and the Construction of Gender in Byzantium* (Chicago, forthcoming).

[8] Winkelmann, *Quellenstudien*, 116, points out how difficult it is to separate the many officials of patrician rank named Niketas who were active under Irene. Ibid., 155, on the *strategos* of Sicily who built the church to St Euphemia: 'epiklen Monomachou'; see also F. Halkin, *Euphémie de Chalcédoine* (Brussels, 1965), 104. Whether this is the same as Niketas *strategos* of Sicily between 797–799, who was honoured with a fragment of the saint's relics in 797, is unclear.

[9] Theophanes, AM 6295, de Boor I, 477, gives the geographical origin but no indication of his eunuch status; Kedrenos, II, 29, claims his surname was Klokas, but see Winkelmann, *Quellenstudien*, 157. During his visit to St Ioannikios, accompanied by another eunuch official of Theophilos, they are identified as very distinguished visitors, and immediately get involved in a petition to the Empress Theodora, see *Life of Ioannikios*, in *Byzantine Defenders of Images*, 328–9.

[10] The *Vita* only mentions her adopted name, Theoktiste, while Florina is recorded in the chronicles.

[11] Magdalino, 'Paphlagonians', 142.

[12] On the standing of the family, Treadgold, *Byzantine Revival*, 268–7, claims

they were very well connected, but Vinson emphasises the fecundity of the family, see 'The Life of Theodora and the Rhetoric of the Byzantine Bride Show', *JÖB*, 49 (1999), 50–51, with a helpful comparison to the similar qualifications of Maria of Amnia: 'a fertile wench from sturdy, and safely obscure, provincial stock'. Cf. *PmbZ*, vol. 4, no. 4707 (on her uncle Manuel) and no. 7286.

[13] Their good deeds are identified as 'the very first of the famous stories about them', *Vios*, 258; *Life of Theodora*, 363.

[14] Vinson has identified her allusions to New Testament parables, which are inserted to indicate her knowledge of scripture, 'Rhetoric of the Bride Show', 36.

[15] See D. Afinogenov, 'The Bride-show of Theophilos: Some Notes on the Sources', *Eranos* 95 (1997), 10–18, esp. 11. Attributed to various fourth- or early fifth-century authors, Proclus, Pseudo-Chrysostomos and Gregory of Neocaesarea, the exchange occurs in a sermon on the Annunciation. It was included in the Imperial Menologion B which means that it could have been known to tenth-century historians. I am grateful to Dr Afinogenov for discussion of this point.

[16] It is difficult to be sure of the order of birth of the daughters, but Anastasia and Anna must be the two little girls on this particular coin issue, see P. Grierson, *DOC*, III, pt. 1, 428; plate XXII, 4.

[17] Sym mag, 328. This is not recorded in any of the earlier and more reliable sources for Theodora.

[18] Another indicator of sea trade at this time is recorded in the *Acts of David . . .*, para. 24, where secret iconophiles from the capital (*philochristoi*) send a cargo ship filled with the necessities of life to monks exiled on the island of Aphousia (206–7). While the story is associated with a miracle and probably has no basis in fact, the assumption that such cargoes could be sent to support banished iconophiles seems entirely likely. On many excavated sites, like Athens and Corinth in Greece, or Sardis and Ephesos in Asia Minor, a notable absence of coin finds spans most of the seventh and eighth centuries, and is ended by coins minted by Theophilos.

[19] Patria, III, 41; Th Syn, 174, and see below.

[20] Judith Herrin, 'The Imperial Feminine in Byzantium,' *Past and Present* 169 (2000), 3–35, esp. 26 on the *zone* as a sort of medieval epidural.

[21] On 26 December 831 (*Acts of David . . .*, para. 22, Eng. tr. 202, where his death is characterised as a most honourable birthday gift to Christ. On the scurrilous pamphlets, see N. C. Koutrakou, *La propagande impériale byzantine. Persuasion et réaction (VIIIe–Xe siècles)* (Athens, 1994), 132–3.

[22] No patriarchal acts survive from this period as the victorious iconophiles made sure that the records of their enemies were completely destroyed.

[23] C. Van de Vorst, 'La translation de S. Théodore Studite et de S. Joseph de Thessalonique', *Analecta Bollandiana* 32 (1913), 27–62, esp. 46 and 58; Papachryssanthou, 'La Vie du patrice Nicétas', 325, para. 2.

[24] Treadgold, *Byzantine Revival*, 297; this is a supposition based on the consequences of John's appointment, but quite a credible one.

[25] The verses are reproduced in the *Acts of David . . .*, para. 23 (Eng. tr. 204); George the Monk cont. 807 (*vitae imperatorum recentiorum*); cf. Margaret Mullett,

'Writing in early mediaeval Byzantium', in *The Uses of Literacy in Early Mediaeval Europe*, ed. Rosamund McKitterick (Cambridge, 1990), 156–85.

[26] *Patria*, III, 41; A. Berger, *Untersuchungen zu den Patria Konstantinoupoleos* (Bonn, 1988), 441: the Diegesteas was originally the bath of Dagistheiou, and the *embolos*, a portico.

[27] *Patria*, III, 155; though in another entry the church of St Pantaleimon is attributed to 'Theodora the wife of Justinian when she came from Paphlagonia' (ibid., III, 93). The tell-tale geographical association confirms that this is indeed our Theodora, not the sixth-century empress, despite P. Magdalino, *Constantinople médiévale* (Paris, 1996), 21 n.26; cf. Berger, *Untersuchungen*, 689.

[28] A. Ricci, 'The road from Baghdad to Byzantium and the case of the Bryas palace in Istanbul', in *Byzantium in the Ninth Century. Dead or Alive?*, ed. L. Brubaker (Aldershot, 1998), 131–49; P. Magdalino, 'The road to Baghdad in the thought-world of ninth-century Byzantium', in ibid., 195–213.

[29] *Patria*, III, 65; Magdalino, *Constantinople médiévale*, 46–7; C. Mango, *Le développement urbain de Constantinople (IVe–VII siècles)*, (Paris, 1990), 17–18.

[30] Treadgold, *Byzantine Revival*, 322–3.

[31] DC, I, p. 507; Constantine VII Porphyrogenitus, *Three Treatises on Imperial Military Expeditions*, ed. and tr. John F. Haldon (Vienna, 1990), text C, lines 808–84, pp. 146–51, and notes, 285–93, with the proposed date of 837. Cf. Michael McCormick, *Eternal Victory* (Cambridge, 1986), 146–50; Marie-France Auzépy, 'Les déplacements de l'empereur dans la ville et ses environs (VIIIe–Xe siècles)', in *Constantinople and its Hinterland*, eds. C. Mango and G. Dagron (Aldershot, 1995), 359–66.

[32] *Asyngkrite faktonarie*, see Alan Cameron, *Circus Factions. Blues and Greens at Byzantium* (Oxford, 1976), 11–13.

[33] V. Minorsky, 'Marvazi on the Byzantines', in his *Medieval Iran and its Neighbours* (London 1982), 455–69, preserves an account of the imperial couple attending Hippodrome events together. While this refers to a later period, the participation of the empress in such public events is well documented.

[34] Al-Maqqari, *The History of the Mohammedan Dynasties in Spain*, bk 4, 4, tr P. de Gayangos (London/New York, 1964); E. Manzano Moreno, 'Byzantium and al-Andalus in the ninth century', in Brubaker, ed., *Byzantium in the Ninth Century*, 215–27. In the 1930s the manuscript containing Yahya's report was partly published by E. Lévi-Provençal; subsequently it was lost, reflecting the fragmentary survival of medieval written documents.

[35] Despite the claims of Peter Schreiner, 'Réflexions sur la famille impériale à Byzance (VIIe–Xe siècles)', *Byzantion* 61 (1991), 181–93, esp. 189, 191. I am grateful to Professor M. Marín for her help on the topic of veiling among medieval Muslim women.

[36] Their names vary, depending on the sources. Most of them date from much later and all have a vested interest in documenting the death of the heretic Theophilos. The *Acts of David, Symeon and George*, martyrs on the island of Lesbos, was written closest in date, about twenty years later, and has a clear but unusual list, which includes Sergios Niketiates, a relative of the empress and apparently an

iconophile. He had therefore been left off the list of regents by Theophilos. This is one of the earliest mentions of the men who assisted the newly widowed Theodora, and Sergios is listed before all the others, while Manuel is omitted. Th Syn, 146, and Genesios record the name of Manuel, but he had probably died in battle in 838. See A. Christophilopoulou, 'He antivasileiu eis to Vyzantion', *Symmeikta* 2 (1970), esp. 29–43.

[37] His existence is confirmed in an episode from a 'spiritually beneficial tale', see D. Sternon, 'La vision d'Isaïe de Nicomédie', *REB* 35 (1977), 5–42; and it has been suggested that he may have kept in touch with Theodora, a sort of distant spiritual father.

[38] Jane Baun, *The Apocalypse of Anastasia*, unpublished Ph D thesis (Princeton, 1997).

[39] See, for example, the *Chronicle* of George the Monk, a ranting excoriation of the emperor, in comparison with which those saints' *Lives* which document the actual tortures of persecution seem almost mild.

[40] *The Absolution of Theophilos* is one of two texts recording these events, ed. W. Regel, *Analecta Byzantino-Russica* (St Petersburg, 1891), 25–6; cf. the discussion in A. Kartsonis, 'Protection against All Evil: Function, Use and Operation of Byzantine Historiated Phylacteries', *BF* 20 (1994), 73–102; D. Afinogenov is planning to re-edit the texts. There are two separate accounts, the Repentance and Absolution of Theophilos, and many MSS, which are supplemented by the *Life of Theodora*, ch. 8, and later versions, e.g. the *Life of Irene of Chrysobalanton*. The death-bed repentance gets its first developed treatment in the *Acts of David ...*, paras. 26–8 (210–18), i.e. about twenty years after the event; cf. the Synodical Letter to Theophilos, probably written soon after 843, *The Letter of the Three Patriarchs ...*, eds. J. A. Munitiz, J. Chrysostomides, E. Harvalia-Crook and Ch. Dendrinos (Camberley, 1997).

[41] See particularly, A. Markopoulos, 'The rehabilitation of the Emperor Theophilos', in Brubaker, ed., *Byzantium in the Ninth Century*, 37–50, esp. 41–5, 48–9.

[42] *Acts of David ...*, paras. 27–28; *Byzantine Defenders of Images*, 212–18.

[43] It is preserved in the *Synodikon vetus*, see C. Mango, 'The liquidation of Iconoclasm and the Patriarch Photios,' in *Iconoclasm*, eds. Anthony Bryer and Judith Herrin (Birmingham, 1977), 133–40.

[44] Vinson, 'Life of Theodora', 372 n.68 sees the meeting in his house as a preliminary to the meeting of 843 which took place in Hagia Sophia; Mango supposes that Theoktistos is key, see 'The Liquidation of Iconoclasm'.

[45] Mango, 'The Liquidation of Iconoclasm'; this later version is also preserved in the *History* of Genesios, 4.2–3.

[46] *Life of Theodora*, ch. 10 (Eng. tr. 375, 376).

[47] See also the brief account by Theophanes, a priest responsible for recording the return of the relics of Patriarch Nikephoros, ed. T. Joannou, *Mnemeia hagiologica* (Venice, 1884, reprinted Leipzig, 1973), 115–28, esp. 122–4, with Latin tr. in PG 100, 164A–B.

[48] An official description of the commemoration of the Feast of Orthodoxy, as it

was celebrated in the court calendar on the first Sunday in Lent is preserved in DC, I, ch. 28, 156–60, with a mention of Patriarch Theophylaktos (933–56), the son of Romanos I Lekapenos.

[49] J. Gouillard, 'Le *Synodikon de l'Orthodoxie*', *TM* 2 (1967), 1–316; there is one reference to 'the Isaurian heretics', i.e. Leo III and Constantine V, and a marginal note adds a special anathema to Constantine Kopronymos, the Isaurian, see lines 171–2, pp. 56–7. Emperors are never condemned by the church in official documents because, even if heretical, they are chosen by the hand of God.

[50] Dmitry Afinogenov, 'The Great Purge of 843; A Re-Examination', in *Leimon. Studies presented to Lennart Rydén on his sixty-fifth birthday*, ed. Jan Olaf Rosenqvist (Uppsala, 1996), 79–91; for the estimate of 'two to three thousand', see Gouillard, *Synodikon*, 127–8.

[51] *The Annales of St-Bertin*, tr. Janet L. Nelson (Manchester, 1991), and of *Fulda*, tr. Timothy Reuter (Manchester, 1992), preserve no record of any contacts with Byzantium in the 840s. In 843 the three sons of Louis the Pious met to agree a territorial division (the Treaty of Verdun), which provided only temporary respite from their regular fratricidal warfare. In the West this decade was marked by severe natural disasters – extreme cold, earthquake, famine – and by attacks of Norsemen in the north and west, and by Saracens along the coasts of Italy and Provence.

[52] *The Homilies of Photius, Patriarch of Constantinople*, ed. and tr. C. Mango (Cambridge, Mass, 1958), 286–96; cf. R. Cormack, *Writing in Gold* (London, 1985), 141–78; cf. his more recent, *Painting the Soul. Icons, Death Masks and Shrouds* (London, 1997), 46–7.

[53] L. James and R. Webb, 'To Understand Ultimate Things and Enter Secret Places: Ekphrasis and Art in Byzantium', *Art History*, 14 (1991), 1–17.

[54] The icon is discussed in the British Museum catalogue, *Byzantium*, ed. D. Buckton (London, 1994), no. 140; and in the Catalogue, *The Mother of God. Representations of the Virgin in Byzantine Art*, ed. M. Vassilaki (Athens, 2000), no. 32, 340–1 On the *Hodegetria*, see C. Angelidi, 'Un texte patriographique et édifiant: le "discours narratif" sur les Hodègoi', *REB* 52 (1994), 113–49; an English version of this fundamental investigation is published in the Athens Catalogue, 373–421; Cormack, *Painting the Soul*, 41–6.

[55] R. Cormack, 'Women and Icons and Women in Icons', in Liz James, ed., *Women, Men and Eunuchs. Gender in Byzantium* (London, 1997), 24–51; idem, *Painting the Soul*, 41–6, 62–3, 89–94, and figs 11–13; on St Theodosia, see the brief notice of the *Synaxarion*, in *Byzantine Defenders of Images*, 5–7.

[56] I. Hutter, 'Scriptoria in Bithynia', in *Constantinople and its Hinterland*, 379–96; K. Corrigan, *Visual Polemics in Ninth-century Psalters* (Cambridge, 1992).

[57] Theodora's death date (11 February) and the first Sunday of Lent provide occasions when her *Life* is read.

[58] DC, II, ch. 42, 645.5–9, where Michael and Theodora are held responsible; cf. P. Grierson, 'The tombs and obits of the Byzantine emperors', *DOP* 16, (1962), 34. Leo *grammatikos* records the destruction of Constantine's tomb

later, under Michael III's sole rule, but as his chronology is unreliable this cannot constitute a firm reason for not associating the event with the Triumph of 843.

[59] DC, II, ch. 42, 645.16–17, and see chapter 2.

[60] DC, II, ch. 42, 645.14–16, immediately preceding the reference to Irene's sarcophagus.

[61] Ioannou, *Mnemeia hagiologica*, 122–4.

[62] Van de Vorst, 'La translation de S. Théodore'.

[63] Gouillard, 'Synodikon', 57.

[64] See the letter of Pope Nicholas I to Michael III, *MGH, Epistulae merowingici et karolingi aevi*, vol. VI, ed. E. Perels, no. 82, 433–9.

[65] Charles only gained a secure control over the territories he claimed in 869 and enjoyed supreme power for 8 years, see Janet L. Nelson, *Charles the Bald* (London, 1992).

[66] In addition to Theoktistos, Theodora's advisers include Nikolaos, the eunuch named in later Syriac sources, and probably others known only from seals, e.g. Ioannes or Baanes, *PmbZ*, nos. 3253, 3303, 3336, 722. Photios probably gained his first public post under Theoktistos and was appointed an ambassador in 855.

[67] The prominence of Theoktistos, who has won the empress's confidence and is not going to tolerate any rivals, is betrayed in a highly confused account of the eunuch forcing her uncle Manuel out of the palace, Genesios, 4.8; Bury, *ERE*, 155; Patricia Karlin-Hayter, 'Etudes sur les deux histoires du règne de Michel III', *Byzantion* 41 (1971), 452–96, analyses this legend.

[68] E.g. in 845, Bury, *ERE*, 275–6.

[69] Sym in George Interpolated, 814; V. Christides, *The Conquest of Crete by the Arabs (c. 824)* (Athens, 1984), 85–8. Since this is the sole source and may be invented, it only serves to indicate how insecure Theoktistos felt and her other courtiers thought Theodora was.

[70] The Continuators of Theophanes note that he was signally unskilled in military matters, Th Syn, 202–3.

[71] By 867 only Syracuse remained in Greek hands and it would soon fall to the Arabs.

[72] A. A. Vasiliev, *Byzance et les Arabes*, 1 (Brussels 1935), 214–18. On the identity of the commander, possibly Sergios Niketiates, see *PmbZ*, vol. 4, no. 6664, but then he could not have been killed in the attack on Crete in 843. By land there were few clashes until 851 when annual raiding across the frontier began again. The Byzantines responded forcefully to Arab attacks and secured some victories, though these are not fully reported, see Christides, *The Conquest of Crete*, 164–5.

[73] DAI, I, 232–3; II, 186.

[74] Th Syn, 162–3; S. Runciman, *The History of the First Bulgarian Empire* (London, 1930), 102. As Bury points out, *ERE*, 385 n.5, it seems highly unlikely that a Bulgarian princess had been captured and then returned, but the legendary story associates Theodora with the process.

[75] Th Syn, 164; in the *Annales of St-Bertin*, 136–7, Hincmar notes the process of

conversion and provides a secure date (866) but ignores the role of the Byzantine missionaries.

[76] Bury, *ERE*, 276–9; P. Lemerle, 'L'histoire des Pauliciens d'Asie Mineure d'après les sources grecques', *TM* 5 (1973), 1–144; C. Ludwig, 'The Paulicians and Ninth Century Byzantine Thought', in Brubaker, ed., *Byzantium in the Ninth Century*, 23–35.

[77] Th Syn, 172.

[78] And this does not need to be a saintly characteristic as many saints of the church have a wilful desire to dispose of material wealth; their philanthropy reaches new proportions by depriving their families of all basic support, as in the case of Philaretos.

[79] *Acts of David . . .*, para. 29, 219–20.

[80] Patricia Karlin-Hayter, 'L'enjeu d'une rumeur', *JÖB* 41 (1991), 85–111, esp. 88.

[81] After the death of Maria, Theodora's only son-in-law Alexios Mousele withdrew from court life and gave up his title of caesar.

[82] See C. Angelidi, *Pulcheria. La castità nel potere (c.399–c.455)* (Milan, 1996), 138.

[83] Vinson, 'Rhetoric of the Bride Show', 55–7; J.-O. Rosenqvist, *The Life of Irene of Chrysobalanton* (Uppsala, 1986), xxiv–xxix, on sources used by Irene's author.

[84] The idea that all potential brides might have been sent off to the capital to participate confirms my view that the bride-show is essentially a mechanism for binding the provincial elites more closely to the centre of government (see chapter 3). But there is no evidence that hundreds of hopeful candidates descended on the Great Palace demanding to be allowed to participate. Whatever the reality, officials in charge made sure that only a select and suitable number were recruited by this means.

[85] *Oraison funèbre de Basile I par son fils Léon VI le Sage*, eds. I. Hausherr and A. Vogt, *Orientalia Christiana*, 26, no. 77 (Rome, 1932), 42–4, 52–4.

[86] Shaun Tougher, 'Michael III and Basil the Macedonian: just good friends?' in Liz James, ed., *Desire and Denial in Byzantium* (Aldershot, 1999), 149–58.

[87] Patricia Karlin-Hayter has untangled this amazing development in a famous article appropriately entitled, 'L'enjeu d'une rumeur'.

[88] Leo grammatikos, 249.3, cf. C. Mango, 'Eudocia Ingerina, the Normans and the Macedonian Dynasty', *ZRVI* 14/15 (1973), 17–27.

[89] Patricia Karlin-Hayter, 'Etudes sur les deux histoires du règne de Michael III', *Byzantion* 41 (1971), 452–96; Genesios and Th Syn also report the involvement of certain military officers of middling rank, who had been removed from their positions and were therefore dissatisfied. In a somewhat fantastical plot they say Theodora's sister Kalomaria, who had been married to Arsaber, was involved as a lookout. Several versions are preserved.

[90] Bury, *ERE*, 469, calculates the precise date: 15 March 856, counting Michael and Theodora's joint reign of fourteen years, with the date in George the Monk Cont., 823, and an addition to the chronology of Nikephoros.

[91] Genesios, 4.9, records her anxiety; Th Syn, 171.9, her anger.

[92] Meeting on 15 March 856, George the Monk Cont., 823: *monos autokratorei*.

[93] This is known from an important source: the *Libellus* of Ignatios addressed to Pope Nicholas I, written by Theognostes, Mansi, XVI, 293–301, esp. 296C–D.

[94] The question of whether Karianos is another monastery somewhere in Constantinople or the palace built by Theophilos is confused – some of the sisters remain in *ta Karianou*, probably their private residence now used as a secure place where they can be confined. Pulcheria, the youngest, and Theodora appear to have ended up at Gastria.

[95] *Life of Theodora*, para. 11, Eng. tr. 377.

[96] Cf. chapter 3, n.96 and 97, and the key word *hekousios*.

[97] *Life of Theodora*, para. 12, Eng. tr. 378.

[98] Ibid. para. 10, Eng. tr. 377.

[99] Bury, *ERE*, 177, n.3; see DC, I, ch. 69, 332, cf. J. B. Bury, 'The Ceremonial Book of Constantine Porphyrogennetos', *English Historical Review*, 22, (1907), 209–27, 417–39, esp. 434.

[100] Letter of Pope Nicholas, *MGH Epistulae*, vol. VI, no. 95, 547–8, dated 13 November 866. This is one of nine sent from Rome to the East in the pope's effort to remove Photios from the patriarchate and restore Ignatios.

[101] The chronology of Basil's liaison with Thekla is rather unclear. If Michael III offered his friend Basil his sister as some form of compensation for the fake 'marriages' of 855, there is quite a long and unexplained delay between her exile from the palace in c.858 and her return from *ta Karianou* in c.863.

[102] Th Syn, 147–8. Again the information is given only by the Continuators, but it is curious that they record Thekla's death there, and the term 'bedridden' may have some basis in fact. If Thekla had ever entertained any imperial ambitions, the birth of her younger brother Michael thwarted them, as Patricia Karlin-Hayter noticed, 'L'enjeu d'une rumeur', 107–9. In this respect she is a forerunner of the much more famous Anna Komnene. A. P. Kazhdan, 'Constantin imaginaire'. Byzantine legends of the Ninth Century about Constantine the Great', *Byzantion* 57 (1987), 196–250, esp. 248, suggests that Thekla may here be standing in for her mother Theodora, in the same way that St Helena was taken as a forerunner of Irene, when male authors wished to attack the medieval empresses indirectly. There is no evidence for the treatment of the other daughters, but they appear to have survived the period of exile with their mother and in 867 they accompany her on her last recorded appearance, see below.

[103] As noted by Bury, *ERE*, 161–2, 434–7, and in a memorable passage by Romilly Jenkins, *Byzantium. The Imperial Centuries, AD 610–1071* (London, 1969), 160–1, the period 856–67 was one of the most glorious in Byzantine history. Bardas made a substantial contribution to the development of higher education and the patronage of culture, as well as handling all the necessary military and administrative matters.

[104] Th Syn, 207: a most beautiful garment woven with golden partridges, cf. Genesios, 4.22, where the short tunic is interpreted as a prediction of Bardas' death.

[105] Th Syn, 204–6.

[106] According to Genesios, 4.24.

[107] Leo grammatikos, 245–6.

[108] Photios, Homily XVII and XVIII, tr. Mango, 290–1, 311.

[109] The prediction occurs in Th Syn, 233, where Theodora attributes it to Theophilos; cf. George the Monk Cont., 821.

[110] Th Syn, 209–10, has the story of the bolt, which is critical.

[111] Genesios, 4.28; Bury, *ERE*, 447.

[112] Leo grammatikos, 251–2; cf. the different version in Th Syn, 210, where the body is struck by *prokeiton andron* of the emperor in the palace at St Mamas (i.e. Michael III's men now working for Basil), and the precise date and hour is given. Much later, at the accession of Leo VI in 886, Michael's body was transferred to the Mausoleum of Constantine at the Holy Apostles. Leo did not personally participate in the ceremonial transfer of relics, but the deed could be interpreted as an act of filial piety. In this way Michael III joined Basil I in death, as the *Book of Ceremonies* records, DC, II, ch. 42, 642.17–18.

[113] DC, II, ch. 42, 647.19–20.

[114] DC, II, ch. 42, 647.16–648.8.

[115] Th Syn, 162. This is typical of the stories preserved by the Continuators which are unknown to any earlier writers.

[116] Bar Hebraeus, 140–42.

[117] *Acts of David . . .*, para. 27 (Greek text, 245; Eng. tr. 215).

[118] *The Life of Michael the Synkellos*, ed. and tr. Mary Cunningham (Belfast, 1991), para. 25 (100–1).

[119] Ibid., para. 36 (122–3).

[120] Genesios, 4.26 (though earlier John was responsible, 3.15). This is the Theodora of legend noted by Karlin-Hayter, 'Deux histoires', 495–6.

CHAPTER 5: CONCLUSION (PAGES 240–257)

[1] See 'The imperial feminine in Byzantium', *Past and Present* 169 (2000), 3–35.

[2] Christine Angelidi, *Pulcheria. La Castità al Potere (c.399–c.455)* (Milan, 1996), 137–8, suggests that Pulcheria created a particularly significant model for Irene and Theodora.

[3] See the helpful analysis by Pauline Stafford, 'Emma: the Powers of the Queen in the Eleventh Century', in Anne J. Duggan, ed., *Queens and Queenship in Medieval Europe* (Woodbridge, 1997), 3–29, esp. 10–12.

[4] Klaus Wessel, 'Insignien', *Reallexikon der byzantinischen Kunst*, III, 369–498.

[5] Janet L. Nelson, 'Early Medieval Rites of Queen-Making and the Shaping of Medieval Queenship', in Duggan, *Queens and Queenship*, esp. 306–10.

[6] My discussion in *The Formation of Christendom* (London, 1989), 446–8, presupposes the advantage of a fixed administrative centre, but cf. Roger Collins, *Charlemagne* (London, 1998), 136–40.

[7] Janet L. Nelson, 'Inauguration rituals', in her collected essays, *Politics and Ritual in Early Medieval Europe* (London, 1986), 282–307.

[8] Theophanes, AM 6211, de Boor, I, 400.

[9] A. Christophilopoulou, 'He antivasileia eis to Vyzantion', *Symmeikta* 2 (1970),

1–144, esp. 15–20; André Poulet, 'Capetian Women and the Regency: the Genesis of a Vocation', in John Carmi Parsons, ed, *Medieval Queenship* (Stroud, 1993), 93–116, esp. 104–16.

[10] *The Formation of Christendom* (revised paperback edn, London, 2001).

Index